D1526501

Jane Austen's Beginnings
The Juvenilia and *Lady Susan*

Jane Austen's Beginnings
The Juvenilia and *Lady Susan*

Edited by
J. David Grey

Foreword by Margaret Drabble

U·M·I Research Press

Ann Arbor / London

Produced and distributed by
UMI Research Press
an imprint of
University Microfilms Inc.
Ann Arbor, Michigan 48106

Library of Congress Cataloging in Publication Data

Jane Austen's beginnings : the juvenilia and Lady Susan / edited
by J. David Grey.
    p. cm—(Nineteenth-century studies)
    Bibliography: p.
    Includes index.
    ISBN 0-8357-1916-2 (alk. paper)
    1. Austen, Jane, 1775-1817—Criticism and interpretation.
2. Austen, Jane, 1775-1817. Lady Susan.   I. Grey, J. David.
II. Series: Nineteenth-century studies (Ann Arbor, Mich.)
PR4037.J35   1989
823'.7—dc19   88-39518
                                                               CIP

British Library CIP data is available.

For my second mother,
Edna Chase Grey,
with love and gratitude

Letter 31.

Lady Susan to M.ʳˢ Johnson

Upper Seymour S.ᵗ

My dear Friend,

That tormenting Creature, Reginald is here. My Letter which was intended to keep him longer in the Country, has hastened him to Town. Much as I wish him away however, I cannot help being pleased with such a proof of attachment. He is devoted to me, heart & soul. — He will carry this note himself, which is to serve as an Intro: :duction to you, with whom he longs to be ac: :quainted. Allow him to spend the Evening with you, that I may be in no danger of his return: :ing here. — I have told him that I am not quite well, & must be alone — & should he call again there might be confusion, for it is impossible to be sure of Servants. — Keep him therefore

"Letter 31: Lady Susan to Mrs. Johnson"
(Lady Susan *MS; Courtesy Pierpont Morgan Library*)

Contents

Figures

Foreword

Margaret Drabble

Jane Austen's juvenilia have long delighted her innumerable "common readers," for whom the discovery of a new Austen manuscript would represent the highest felicity. We seize eagerly upon these early fragments, and would have done so even had they been less entertaining in their own right. But the fact is that Austen's burlesques, her *History* and her tales and sketches and proto-novels constitute one of the most remarkable collections ever discovered from so young a pen. Only the intense childhood fantasies of the Brontës can rival them in interest and achievement, and in promise of later triumphs. It is well that they were not consigned to a wastepaper basket, or left "in a drawer, for study by scholars" (as her collateral descendant, Joan Austen-Leigh, here provocatively suggests might have been advisable). I rejoice to concur with the contributors who find them accessible, amusing, and remarkably self-sufficient. One does not need a degree in English literature to appreciate their wit and their extraordinary narrative confidence.

Nevertheless, they also repay study. A good case is made here for both studying and teaching some of the juvenilia. They create a context and a sense of a tradition for the student; they illuminate, for the scholar, the development of an extraordinary individual talent. They mark (and mark consciously, moreover) a peculiarly important moment in the shift of sensibility, from the formal, balanced, rational values of an Augustan and Johnsonian world, to a world of sentiment, extravagance, Gothic horror, picturesque enthusiasm and romanticism. We see here, in such works as "Jack & Alice," "Love and Freindship," "Lesley Castle," and "Evelyn," the mixture of materials and attitudes that create the delicate, perplexing. balanced oppositions of the mature novels, and the complex yet lucid and confident moral judgments of the mature novelist. As many of the contributors to this volume are concerned to establish, we see burlesqued and exaggerated in the early works the excesses and limitations that are more seriously pursued in the fuller portraits of Catherine Morland, Marianne Dashwood, Mary Crawford and Emma Woodhouse. The connections are clear, at times striking.

Yet so, also, are the dislocations and differences. There is little in the later work to echo or develop the astonishing anti-heroine, Lady Susan, who has now, predictably, been adopted by some feminist critics as an example of a "free woman," unhindered by the usual concepts of female and more particularly maternal duty. She remains an isolated, an alarming creation, from another fictional universe. And in some of the shorter fragments there are also hints of another Jane Austen, a fiercer, wilder, more outspoken, more ruthless writer, with a dark vision of human motivation (how brilliantly those three sisters battle, in unredeemed sibling rivalry!) and a breathless, almost manic energy. Many critics less extreme than John Halperin have been disturbed by what he calls their "startling . . . hostility and cold detachment." Her cynicism, her alarming portraits of obsessional behavior, her summary dismissal to sudden death of only momentarily lamented figures reveal a less humane, less polite talent than that with which she is usually credited. True, one should not take too seriously the violent deaths of poor Edward and Augustus, the abrupt hanging of the perfidious and murderous Sukey, or the trials of poor Elizabeth Johnson, who ran on foot after her galloping mounted mother through Wales on a picturesque tour, in a fine perspiration, and wearing out many a pair of shoes. But the relish in the discomfiture of some of these not-quite-flat, not-quite-stereotypical characters is, indeed, startling, invigorating, shocking all at once. These sketches provide an excellent antidote to the conventional view of Jane Austen as a calm, well-mannered novelist, confined to a narrow social world of subtle nuance and at times crippling decorum. Here she forgets or has not yet learned to be constrained by her manners, and reveals that she knows more than a girl of her age should. She is thought to have been only twelve or thirteen when she wrote, in "Jack & Alice," the extremely funny dialogues between Lady Williams and the claret-addicted, love-lorn Alice Johnson. How brilliantly offensive is Lady Williams's "forgiveness" of the indiscreet and suffering Alice: "My dear Girl dont vex yourself about the matter; I assure you I have entirely forgiven you every thing respecting it; indeed I was not angry at the time, because as I saw all along, you were nearly dead drunk" (19).

The assurance, the insouciance, are by any standards remarkable, and there are equally remarkable moments scattered richly through the juvenilia and the unpublished works. It is good to see this varied collection of essays, which takes its subject seriously but without undue solemnity, and which will surely add to the enjoyment and enlightenment of many readers, both professional and amateur.

Preface

J. David Grey

This editor went on record, facetiously and foolishly, in October 1979, when, at the inaugural meeting of the Jane Austen Society of North America, he claimed "Love and Freindship" was his favorite Jane Austen novel. Needless to say, that was the only vote this novel got in the poll. He should have explained it was important to him, personally, for bringing him back into the fold. A rereading, twelve years earlier, took place on the First Avenue bus, uptown, and all but rerouted the driver back downtown, Bellevuewards. Unrestrained hilarity has its limits in public.

To continue the parable, this editor found others who had similar subversive tendencies with the result that, in 1987, a five-day marathon affair with an adolescent genius took place at the Waldorf-Astoria. They flocked to it in droves, many unaware what was in store for them—had Jane Austen actually written more than six novels?! Had they any value? It was discovered that she had and they did and that they were called by various names by sundry aficionados: "Love and Freindship," *Volumes the First, Second* and *Third*, the Juvenilia, "Catharine," "Evelyn"; and, of course, they encountered the infamous Lady Susan.

Two champions were there, Walt Litz and Juliet McMaster. Happily they had just become involved as advising editors to UMI Research Press; fortuitously they suggested the possibility of this volume to that press. And so ends the tale of the genesis of the book in hand.

The contributors were uniformly enthusiastic in their eagerness to have a say. Common themes run throughout: Jane Austen's precocious use of language; the sources of, and reasons for, her sardonic wit; parallels with the later novels; evidence of the revolutionary transition in novel-making that she is about to launch; influences of her upbringing, the backgrounds against which she wrote, and her masterful reflection of both; *Lady Susan* and the road not taken. Most agree on the indication that a major talent looms. There are a *few* dissenters; they also have the floor. And what have they to say?

Of all contemporary critics, Professor **A. Walton Litz** has been the most consistent champion of Jane Austen's juvenilia. In the introductory paper in this volume, he remarks on the progress of her stylistic devices, from the sheer burlesquerie of the beginnings to the threshold of her discovery of free indirect speech in *Volume the Third*. He gives more conclusive evidence than we have had before that Jane Austen's attachment to these early pieces lasted into the period of her residence at Chawton. Litz challenges her audience to forget the pejorative term "juvenilia" and to make a more diligent investigation of these not-so-minor works.

John McAleer proves in his biography of Jane Austen (to be published in 1992) that he has "learned" a good deal from her early pieces, is able to draw significant conclusions from them and, thereby, shed new light on a period of her life (before her correspondence begins) that other biographers have glossed over. Her family influences—they were all avid readers and many of them writers; their partiality to theatricals—their wide-flung connections, prior to and right up to the end of the eighteenth century, all are drawn upon to depict a canvas against which Jane Austen matured both intellectually and creatively. Influences from her reading and the intervening critical response to them are extensively discussed. In conclusion, Professor McAleer agrees with Brigid Brophy that Jane Austen's juvenilia *were* her education.

For **John Halperin**, a recent controversial biographer, these works are divided, half-way chronologically, between literary satire and social comedy. They are "by no means brilliant" and only "intermittently entertaining." His 1982 essay is included in this collection because it provides an honest and well-documented argument from another viewpoint. His contention is that these early works honed her wit to a degree that offered detachment sufficient for her ironic genius. With explicit reference to most of the individual pieces Halperin warns against too stringent a division, "both by chronology and subject matter," between the adolescent and mature Jane Austen.

Claudia Johnson writes from a conviction that Jane Austen's juvenile writings not only supersede contemporary fictional creations but also are instrumental in the enterprise of demystifying them. The incipient novelist intends to expose custom by underscoring its vapid conventions. Virginia Woolf's deference to the author's youthful audacity is emphasized and renders the apolitical, nonhistorical reputation frequently attributed to Jane Austen as empty as the manners she is satirizing. Given the revolutionary time frame of the juvenilia's production (1787–94), her treatment of the female experience can be considered highly controversial and reformist as opposed to conservative. Through a close reading of select passages and a comparison with other authors (Opie and More, for instance), Jane Austen's preeminence is established even at this early stage of her literary career.

Jane Austen's extrahistoricity is almost as legendary as the lady herself, yet one of her first works was "The History of England." **Christopher Kent** investigates the eighteenth-century attitude towards the study of history—a "subject for girls (to aid in and improve their conversation!), not boys, who were supposed, rather, to be *in* history." As might be expected, Jane Austen rejected such typecasting. Professor Kent discusses her early involvement with this anti-Whiggish venture whose extraordinarily witty presentation has given it the widest exposure among all the pieces in the juvenilia. He concludes with substantial proof that history continued to claim Jane Austen's attention into her adult years.

To quote **Laurie Kaplan** quoting Dr. Johnson, her intention here is to provide "a code of critical and intellectual criteria against which the [common] reader [can] compare and contrast" literary conventions: Jane Austen's adherence to, and flaunting of, them. Professor Kaplan invites the reader of two centuries later to transcend the role "progress" has cast him in as an "uncommon" reader. The Augustan society of Jane Austen's youth was in transition and we can learn much about that revolution from this young lady by becoming active rather than passive in our reading attitudes. The creative reader is the good reader. These initial offerings of Jane Austen furnish the reference points necessary to assume that important role. A fuller appreciation of the mature novels will be the reward.

Ellen Martin's explication of Jane Austen's use of language provides an irresistible argument in favor of the value of the early writings. Martin unties (and ties again) the knots of Jane Austen's metaphors and, more intriguing, her metonyms. "[Her] bare bones nonsense narrative embodies the perfect undecidability of meaning that characterizes rich, true literature." Professor Martin employs Jane Austen's use of symbols to obliterate the threadbare proposition that the scope of her themes is limited. By eschewing the romanticism of historical implications she frees her characters, in her own metonym, to fill their empty pockets. The figurative language draws the reader, "the decipherer," into the active involvement suggested by Dr. Kaplan.

Deborah Knuth contends that Austen's early writings remind the modern reader how important were the friendly relationships between women. Professor Knuth proves that, as precursors of the tone surrounding sisterly connections in the major novels, the relationships between friends in the minor works are scarcely secondary to those involving courtship and marriage that are so commonly accepted as Jane Austen's too often repeated themes. Indeed, she claims greater endurance in the friendships between the female characters than in their marriages: friendships serve needs that would otherwise remain unfulfilled. Coincidentally, this was Jane Austen's experience in her adult life.

Behind a great deal of careful research, **Mary Gaither Marshall** presents an authoritative account of four of the five surviving literary manuscripts of Jane Austen: those of the juvenilia and *Lady Susan*. After discussing the environment in which Jane Austen's earliest jottings blossomed, she gives a definitive, comprehensive description of the manuscripts themselves, their provenance up to the auction sales of the 1980s, and the publishing history of the definitive editions.

Patricia Meyer Spacks considers the nonhappenings and apparent motivelessness of many pieces in the juvenilia (which she refers to—and not derogatorily—as "small fictions" with "tiny plots") Jane Austen's conscious, intelligent, and legitimate reaction to both the mores and literature of the eighteenth century. Although she was patently enjoying herself, reveling in the absolute sway held over her characters, she was simultaneously developing her perfection in that essential ingredient of the novel-characterization. In her vastly important role as innovator she was increasingly aware of the "necessary intertwinings of plot and character." Jane Austen's initial obsession with narcissism, with what happens when self-interests conflict, reached a transitional stage in "Catharine, or the Bower." Catharine awakens to her capabilities to interpret and, in that awakening, "promises a plot."

Juliet McMaster is confident that, given the opportunity, "Love and Freindship" can serve in the classroom either on its own or as an introduction to the major works. She offers three possible levels of treatment. First, as a burlesque this work parodies contemporary literary taste in a hilarious and subtle, an informed and instructive way. Second, the text itself deserves scrutinizing for the intricacies of its syntax and would be beneficial in composition courses, she suggests. Third, Professor McMaster points to the many instances where "Love and Freindship" foreshadows the development of characterization in the later works, most especially in the heroines' perplexities with the interaction between life and literature. With all deference due to Elizabeth Bennet's opinion, Juliet McMaster proves her instruction *is* worth knowing.

Edward Copeland has no doubt that Jane Austen's formative years, as were those of any late eighteenth-century female in a middle-class household, were spent in the companionship of the *Lady's Magazine*. His research has unearthed sources there that bear striking similarities with her plots, themes, the structure and general trend of early compositions—Austen's fiction about fiction. Rapid advance in consumerism and the consequent economic crises for women (actually amounting to a "plight") translate from the pages of this journal to those of the juvenilia and from there to the major novels. In her inimitable fashion, Jane Austen confronts this pernicious "enemy" by using it to supply the jokes of her youthful effusions. "The paradoxical affinity of sentimental literature and consumerism," "the disparity between formal realism and sentimental convention" provided the bases for her ironic outlook.

Joan Austen-Leigh and the editor of this volume are two of the three cofounders of the Jane Austen Society of North America (Henry Burke, Baltimore, being the third). Curiosity about "the family's" current attitude towards works it secreted for such a long time prompted an invitation to contribute to this collection. *Lady Susan* was coaxed into publication in the second edition of the *Memoir,* fortuitously written by Ms. Austen-Leigh's great-grandfather. Aside from a few scattered pieces, another half century intervened before the first volume of the three juvenile notebooks appeared. The present scion upholds her forebears and argues that prevention of publication of the manuscripts might only have been achieved through their unimaginable destruction. Read them, then, at your peril and if you must. The *imprimatur* is still grudgingly relinquished.

Against a panorama of theory on eighteenth-century female education and conduct, **Barbara Horwitz** paints as sympathetic a picture of Lady Susan as that lady's behavior will allow. We find her "compelling"; her contemporaries would probably have considered her villainous but only insofar as her education (as she herself readily admits) had been neglected. This, coupled with having been spoiled as a child, makes her attempts at conscious self-vindication and unconscious self-deception less culpable, more understandable. "Artless" and "artful" are the key words in this discussion. Jane Austen's reflection on the prevailing attitudes toward rearing and education produced this portrait of a consummate, for her time, "antiheroine."

Jane Austen's attention to detail is mythic. According to medical experts in the 1960s she so clearly described, in correspondence, the symptoms of her own final ailment that, almost 150 years later, a diagnosis was possible. **Beatrice Anderson** similarly "diagnoses" Lady Susan's personality flaws in modern clinical parlance juxtaposed with Jane Austen's depiction of the lady's character traits. If there were any doubt concerning Jane Austen's profound, intuitive, and revealing knowledge of humanity, allay it herewith. Lady Susan emerges, semitriumphantly, as a compassionate creation of her time and an early monument to her creator's unfailing genius.

Hugh McKellar is another strong advocate of accepting *Lady Susan* for what it is rather than condemning it for what it is not. He defends both Jane Austen and her antiheroine against unfair expectations or an attempt to pigeonhole either or both of them. His witnesses in this "trial" range from St. Paul to Muhammad Ali, Queen Victoria to Agatha Christie. His verdict: *caveat lector.* Be prepared for the surprise and/or displeasure involved in making Lady Susan's acquaintance.

Susan Pepper Robbins makes an excellent case for Frederica Vernon's sole letter being the turning point in Jane Austen's decision to abandon epistolary for narrative fiction. At this juncture in the novel the mirror needs the lamp; the letter as effective document becomes affective gesture and requires the presence of a narrative voice. Parents and children undergo a role-reversal—the direction in which Jane Austen was moving between *Lady Susan* and "Elinor and Marianne." The narrator is forced to step in as "lost parent," the first instance in Jane Austen's career being the "Conclusion" to *Lady Susan*.

There is nothing quite so exciting as performing before a live audience. How much less frequent is it for literary experts to appear as a panel, live, in front of a lay audience of Jane Austen buffs with the discussion so delimited. That happened in New York and the Basildon Room at the Waldorf-Astoria was charged with electricity by **Gina Barreca**, **Rachel Brownstein**, **Jan Fergus**, **Donald Stone** and their moderator, **Juliet McMaster**. Insightful comments led to another (expected) phenomenon—instant feedback. Their acquiescence to allow this hair-down presentation to be included here is a credit to their indulgence and, it might be added, their sense of commitment. The transcription, edited by **Susan Schwartz,** reproduces that same electrified atmosphere and is tangible proof that, 200 years later, the juvenile writings of Jane Austen invite serious consideration and, even more to the point, the fun and liveliness they must have engendered at Steventon Parsonage.

A glance at the extent of the bibliography that **David Gilson** and the **editor** have prepared will make it obvious that these works have not gone totally unnoticed since they began appearing in 1871. But the fitfulness of the recognition has been allowed to yawn for too long. This is the first critical booklength treatment of any portion of the *Minor Works*. There have been a few doctoral dissertations, enlightened for the most part, plus sporadic treatment in literary journals—but the subject matter has been overly subject to editing and anthologizing, i.e., peripherizing and sublimating. It is hard to absorb that near oblivion, veritable interment by comparison with what has been produced on the major novels, so quickly followed the raves from lofty quarters that the 1920s, 1930s, and 1950s evoked. Even the "new" Jane Austen lost her bloom with undeserved rapidity.

There is only one other genius that performed so exquisitely so soon, in my opinion, and that was Mozart. (Erna Schwerin, founder of the Friends of Mozart, agrees and has no hesitance devoting "serious" time to the juvenile Mozart at the Society's productions.) Well, there is perhaps Mendelssohn; but he was "older," sixteen. And the Brontës. An approach to their juvenilia, however, is tantamount to subduing Angria itself.

There will be those who will mutter something about this being a pretentious, presumptuous, even unnecessary venture. I sincerely hope they will leave their prejudices and sensibilities behind and take the plunge.

For better or for worse, then, let it be proclaimed that, yes, there are more than "the six" and they warrant warmer acceptance and closer inspection. Maybe the twenty-first century will find "Elinor and Marianne" and "First Impressions"; the remainder of those juvenilia Brian Southam conjectures missing; or, all those missing letters that Cassandra had no access to, both from and *to* Jane. It would be grand to be around for any one of those eventualities—and the criticism it generates.

Acknowledgments

Without the support of Juliet McMaster and A. Walton Litz this book would not exist. Personal contacts at two institutions require thanks: Julia Blanchard at the Pierpont Morgan Library and Kathy Firkin at the Bodleian. Elaine Goodman's equanimity rendered the formidable (thanks to JA's distinct orthography and the vagaries of two dozen contributors) typing assignments manageable.

Then, several friends have been subject to my own especial temperament— and helped anyway: my boss, Isidore Bernstein, who turned a blind eye when I needed extra time (thanks, Harriet); Kate Greenfield, who assisted in the proofreading in between classes at school; Laura Nardelli, also at school, who translated a long treatise on the *J* and *LS* only to discover there wasn't the germ of a new idea in it; and Kevin Agard, a calming agent who guided me through the intricacies of two word processors brought in for this assignment. Recognition is due two adult counterparts of Mrs. Dashwood's offspring, Helen Dickerman and Joan Drexler, and my own sister, Dorothy Thompson, for just about anything I asked of them. I would like to thank Jo Modert and Harriet Avery for their support. I would also like to thank Molly Thomas and Francesco Real for their assistance.

It was the enthusiastic response of the attendees at the New York AGM that enabled me to convince UMI Research Press of the urgency attending the dearth of information about the subject, and that the "beginnings" of Jane Austen's pen are, in fact, the beginnings of nineteenth-century literature. Thanks, then, to JASNA and its leadership, headed by Lorraine Hanaway, President. Thanks also to Joan Austen-Leigh, Susan Schwartz, and David Gilson—but they're here on their own. As are the other contributors whose understanding has been enlightened and cooperation unimpeachable.

Textual Note

Parenthesized numbers within the text are references to *Volume VI: Minor Works* of the Oxford edition of *The Works of Jane Austen,* first published by R.W. Chapman in 1954 and revised by Brian Southam in 1969. References to the major novels use the standard abbreviations, e.g., *SS = Sense and Sensibility.*

　　Jane Austen's "unique" spelling and punctuation have been strictly adhered to throughout. The use of "*sic*" has been avoided for ease of reading. Titles of the three notebooks have been italicized as published works (e.g., *Volume the First*), as has *Lady Susan.* Individual pieces appear within quotation marks (e.g., "Love and Freindship").

Jane Austen: The Juvenilia

A. Walton Litz

To begin with, "juvenilia" is probably the wrong term, but I shall follow custom and use it. In Latin *juvenilis* refers to a young man or woman between age of 21 and 35 or 40, and this sense still held in seventeenth-century England. Donne's *Juvenilia,* for instance, contains works of his early manhood. In Jane Austen's own writings, juveniles are young adults of fifteen and over. In *Sense and Sensibility* (vii) Sir John Middleton is referred to as "a blessing to all the juvenile part of the neighbourhood," which seems to include those already out in society. But later in the nineteenth century the term became more and more restricted as the privileged world of childhood was carefully segregated from the fallen world of adult experience. In his fascinating book *The Image of Childhood* Peter Coveney shows that the Romantic poets of Jane Austen's time stressed (as she did) the continuity between childhood and maturity; both were part of the organic growth of human consciousness. Later, the Victorian cult of the child set up a barrier of nostalgia and regret between early adolescence and the grown-up world. "Juvenilia" became associated with blessed immaturity.

To my knowledge Jane Austen's early fictions, written between 1787 and 1794–95 (if one accepts that date for *Lady Susan*), were not commonly called juvenilia until the 1930s, and even then a classically trained scholar such as Mary Lascelles was probably using the term in an older sense. But the pejorative implications of the term juvenilia—the attitude that seeks to separate the early fictions from the major novels—was part of the Victorian world in which Jane Austen's earliest works were first published. The story of how her earliest writings reached print has cultural as well as literary implications.

In the first edition of the *Memoir* (1870) James Edward Austen-Leigh mentioned "an old copy-book containing several tales, some of which seem to have been composed while she was quite a girl," but went on to say that "the family have, rightly, I think, declined to let these early works be published."

The interest aroused by the *Memoir* led to a reconsideration of this ban, and in the second (1871) edition of the *Memoir* Austen-Leigh included the brief skit "The Mystery" (from *Volume the First*) as "a short specimen of [Jane Austen's] childish stories." He also provided a somewhat fuller description of the earliest writings.

> There are copy books extant containing tales some of which must have been composed while she was a young girl. . . . Her earliest stories are of a slight and flimsy texture, and are generally intended to be nonsensical, but the nonsense has much spirit in it. . . . [H]owever puerile the matter, they are always composed in pure simple English. . . . One of her juvenile effusions is given, as a specimen of the kind of transitory amusement which Jane was continually supplying to the family party.

"Flimsy . . . puerile . . . transitory." The language of the *Memoir* reflects the family's uneasy response to the early writings (some members were said to oppose their publication as "unfair" to Jane Austen's memory).* Like Henry James's super-subtle children, a young lady under fifteen years old who could write knowingly of theft, deformity, drunkenness, and bastardy was subversive to the Victorian cult of the child. Presumably *Lady Susan* (also included in the second edition of the *Memoir*) was more acceptable because of its sophisticated point of view, although Austen-Leigh's half-sister Anna (Mrs. Benjamin Lefroy) "was not disinclined to the juvenilia, but deprecated any disclosure of what she called the *Betweenities*"—an attitude which seems more consonant with Romantic and modern ideas about personal growth and development.

The same ambiguity toward the juvenilia is found in William and Richard Austen-Leigh's *Life and Letters* (1913), although they describe more early items and print a brief extract from "Catharine" (*Volume the Third*). But soon this reticence had to give way to changing ideas about apprentice work and the demand for a fuller "portrait of the artist." *Volume the Second* was published in 1922 under the title *Love and Freindship,* with a preface by G.K. Chesterton. *Volume the First* followed in 1933, edited by R.W. Chapman, and with the appearance of *Volume the Third* in 1951 (also edited by Chapman) the record of the years 1787–ca.1795 was complete. All the scattered publications could then be brought together in the Oxford volume of *Minor Works* (first published by Chapman in 1954 and revised by Brian Southam in 1969).

Before turning to the works themselves, I would like to make one observation about the attitude toward childhood and adolescence that seems to have governed the Austen household and fostered the remarkable early writings of Jane Austen. The household must have been totally free of the extreme views, represented by Rousseau and Augustine, that over the centuries formed and

---

* See Joan Austen-Leigh's article in this volume.

reformed the image of childhood. Rousseau's claim, in *Emile* (1762), that "there is no original sin in the human heart" would have been rejected as nonsense, but the Calvinistic or evangelical view would have seemed equally absurd. It's hard to imagine Mr. Austen following the advice given in James Janeway's *A Token for Children* (1671–72): "take some time daily to speak a little to your children one by one about their miserable condition by nature. . . . They are not too little to die, not too little to go to hell." The environment in which Jane Austen began to write appears to have been marked by a realistic and tolerant understanding of what young people can and cannot accomplish, and by a keen interest in growth and education. It was an atmosphere in which the standards and manners of adult life were always visible, but not harshly enforced. It was, in short, a world idealized by Jane Austen when she fashioned the successful marriages in her mature novels.

How could these writings, produced between the ages of 11 and 20 and never intended for publication, have the power to appeal to us after the passage of nearly 200 years? I would like to think that part of the attraction is their intrinsic wit and energy, and the sharp insights they give us into English life near the end of the eighteenth century. If Jane Austen had never written anything more, and the juvenilia had been recently discovered in a croquet box in Twickenham, I do think they would have been published and read with great interest. But it is too difficult an act of the imagination to go on with this scenario. These are the first works of the artist who was later to write the great novels, and it is as preliminaries to those novels that her juvenilia claim our greatest attention. Without indulging in the procrustean formulas of Queenie Leavis or Marvin Mudrick, who see the later works as programmatic rewritings of the juvenilia, we can find the major themes of her mature art—and even some of her distinctive techniques, even her "voice"—taking shape in the early writings. The juvenilia might be subtitled after Fanny Burney "The History of a Young Lady's Entrance into the World"—and into the world of fiction.

Although they were written for the immediate amusement of herself and her family, there is good evidence that Jane Austen kept the juvenilia in mind while writing her later works. In a letter to Cassandra of August 1814 Jane Austen says of a carriage trip that "it put me in mind of my own Coach between Edinburgh & Sterling"—an allusion to "Love and Freindship" that Cassandra was sure to catch. More telling are the changes made in the juvenilia around 1809, when Jane Austen resumed writing after the depressing years in Bath and Southampton. It was at that time that she made inquiries about "Susan" (later *Northanger Abbey*), which had been sold in 1803 but never published, and started to revise the originals of *Sense and Sensibility* and *Pride and Prejudice*. As part of this new interest in writing she returned to her earlier writings. An addition to "Evelyn" contains a letter dated "Augst 19th 1809," and although

Brian Southam believes the hand is not Jane Austen's the style rings true to me. The letter contains the news that "Our Maria, our beloved Maria is no more, she breathed her last on Saturday the 12th of Augst," a fact that Mr. Gower has forgotten to convey to Maria's parents over the past week. Well, in 1809 the 12th of August *was* a Saturday; it was also the day when Parliament rises and the grouse season opens, and the excitement of all that presumably distracted Mr. Gower from attention to lesser matters. This strikes me as a quintessential Jane Austen touch.

Other changes, this time in "Catharine," show Jane Austen's continuing involvement with the juvenilia. Writing to Cassandra on 24 January 1809, shortly after the publication of Hannah More's *Coelebs in Search of a Wife,* she said: "You have by no means raised my curiosity after Caleb;—My disinclination for it before was affected, but now it is real; I do not like the Evangelicals.—Of course I shall be delighted, when I read it, like other people, but till I do I dislike it." Soon afterwards *Coelebs* entered "Catharine" as an up-to-date substitute for "Seccar's [*sic*] explanation of the Catechism" (published in 1769), one of the books Mrs. Percival bought for Catharine in order to "breed [her] up virtuously." This change has often been discussed. What I think has not been noticed is the fact that the substitution of Mrs. Percival for Mrs. Peterson throughout the manuscript also resulted from a recent experience. On 7 October 1808 Jane Austen wrote to Cassandra that "We have got a new Physician, a Dr. Percival, the son of a famous Dr. Percival of Manchester, who wrote moral tales for Edward to give to me." (Thomas Percival was the author of *A Father's Instructions; consisting of Moral Tales, Fables, and Reflections, designed to promote the Love of Virtue.*)

Looking at the juvenilia as we must through the lens of the mature novels, what strikes one most is Jane Austen's swift and sure progress toward the threshold of her distinctive way of feeling and telling. "Catharine" and *Lady Susan* represent major advances when we compare them with some of the knockabout pieces in *Volume the First.* The stages in the composition of the juvenilia—the movement from burlesque to what the authors of the *Life* called rather condescendingly "immature story-telling"—have often been charted, and I won't rehearse them here. I would like to point out, however, that this movement is encapsulated in *The Loiterer,* the weekly periodical that James and Henry Austen edited (and largely wrote) while they were at St. John's College, Oxford, in 1789–90.

The Loiterer is virtually an index to Jane Austen's early interests, both literary and social, and provides the best contemporary introduction to the world of the juvenilia. Almost every essay uses techniques of irony, parody, and mock-serious narrative, showing how common this form of criticism was in the Austen household. The early issues are rather crude burlesques (such as James's "Diary of a Modern Oxford Man," No. 4), but in the later issues, especially those written by Henry, there is a movement away from simple burlesque and parody toward a more complex merging of narrative structure with ironic methods, a tendency which foreshadows Jane Austen's own development after "Love and Freindship." *The Loiterer* appeared at a crucial time in Jane Austen's early life, when she was—as Virginia Woolf vividly imagined—a young girl of fifteen "laughing, in her corner, at the world"; and whether or not she helped in the writing (I believe she did), *The Loiterer* played a major role in her artistic education.

To me the most interesting of the juvenilia are "A Collection of Letters" (especially the third letter), "Evelyn," and "Catharine, or The Bower," since in these pieces we can glimpse the writing to come. The dialogue exposes individual personalities, not stock characters, and the narration—in Marilyn Butler's words—"so closely tracks the heroine's consciousness that it often approximates to 'free indirect speech.'" To me this subtle blending of the author's voice with the voices of her characters was Jane Austen's greatest achievement, and her major legacy to the nineteenth-century novel. In some ways *Lady Susan* (whatever date we assign to its composition) represents a cautious retreat from what Jane Austen was attempting in "Catharine." It almost seems as if Jane Austen were frightened by what she discovered in writing "Catharine," or at least felt that she did not yet have the skills needed for sustained "free indirect speech." In its manners and characters *Lady Susan* is a move back into the more familiar world of eighteenth-century satire and comedy; as has often been noted, *Lady Susan* was formed out of Jane Austen's literary experience, not the actual world of the 1790s that she knew so well. And its epistolary structure (which we know was also the form of "Elinor and Marianne," written at about the same time) likewise marks a retreat to safer and more familiar ground. It is not until *The Watsons* that we hear again the distinctive voice that occasionally controls the narrative in *Volume the Third*.

In his searching review of the 1870–71 *Memoir,* Richard Simpson made a judgment that has become the motto for almost all serious study of the juvenilia. "It is clear that she began, as Shakespeare began, with being an ironical censurer of her contemporaries. After forming her apprentice hand by writing nonsense, she began her artistic self-education by writing burlesques. . . . That the critical faculty was in her the ground and support of the artistic faculty there are several reasons for believing." This is brilliant and telling commentary, all the more so because Simpson wrote it without much evidence before him. But taken too literally it can lead to a purely "literary" view of the juvenilia which implies that Jane Austen lived only through books, and that her early artistic education was solely a matter of exploring and then discarding, by means of irony and satire, the conventions of the late-eighteenth-century novel. This is all true, but early on she is also exploring the manners of her time; engaging with current ideas (some of them political); and even in an indirect way learning how a woman could express her deepest feelings through fiction. I hope this furthers discussion about issues such as these, as well as the more familiar topics. When that happens we shall discover that Jane Austen's own artistic life calls into question one piece of advice she gave to her niece Anna: "till the heroine grows up, the fun must be imperfect."

What a Biographer Can Learn about Jane Austen from Her Juvenilia

John McAleer

Jane Austen's juvenilia consists of 27 individual pieces, totaling about 90,000 words, which she wrote between the ages of 11 and 17—a period of seven years (1787–93)—and later copied into three, slim, quarto notebooks—*Volume the First, Volume the Second,* and *Volume the Third.*

"Eight years . . . what might not eight years do?" asks Anne Elliot in *Persuasion.*[1] Jane Austen herself answered that question. The span of time allotted her at Chawton was eight years. Consider what she wrought in that interval. Yet what of the seven years that encompassed the juvenilia? On 8 April 1805, Jane Austen wrote to Cassandra, "Seven years I suppose are enough to change every pore of one's skin & every feeling of one's mind."[2] She was alluding, of course, not to Scripture's measure of seven years as a term of completion but to the folk belief that the human body renews itself every septennium. We suggest that a great deal can happen in seven years, especially when that interval embraces the years of adolescence.

At 17 some people feel grown up. At 17 Marianne Dashwood observes: "At my time of life opinions are tolerably fixed. It is not likely that I should now see or hear anything to change them" (*SS,* 93). Maybe, at that age, Jane Austen felt the same. Certainly, as the juvenilia attest, she had taken a seven-league step in the septennium then closing. In fairness to her, however, we must point out that she knew, a few years later, that to attain 17 was not to arrive at the pinnacle of enlightenment. In *Northanger Abbey,* she says of Catherine Morland: "Her mind [was] about as ignorant and uninformed as the female mind at seventeen usually is" (*NA,* 18). "One does not care for girls," she said later, "till they are grown up."[3] Maturity, she knew, was not attained at 17.

Cassandra Austen once characterized her sister's juvenilia as "trifles."[4] Her nephew, James, described them as "childish stories," the matter "puerile," the texture "slight and flimsy."[5] By characterizing them as "juvenile effusions,"[6] and, again, as "immature or fragmentary fictions [that] call for hardly any comment," R.W. Chapman left those earlier assessments unchallenged (v). So did John Bailey. "Love and Freindship," he said, was "of no particular importance," since it "tells us nothing about her that we did not know before or could not guess." He found most of the rest of the juvenilia "not very good anything at all." "One of the worst of the literary habits of our day," he lamented, "is that of fishing out of drawers and cupboards the crudities and juvenilities of authors who have subsequently written famous books."[7] David Rhydderch's estimate of the nonage scripts concurs. To him they were the "inconsequent scaffoldings that help in the fruition of any work of art." Had the great novels never been written, he said, "no doubt these copybook tales and fantasies would have lain in darkness. . . . "[8]

Chapman found the juvenilia of no more interest to the biographer than the critic, believing they "added little to the [Austen-Leigh's] picture of Jane Austen,"[9] and B.C. Southam is in basic agreement with him, characterizing them as a "mixture of fantasy and family history" (460), yet insisting that "for the most part the references are sunk too deeply for us to identify biographical details."[10] Others allow the biographer a glimmer of hope. "They are not," writes Christopher Gillie, "discernibly biographical, but . . . they tell us something about how the mind of Jane Austen, the novelist, grew up."[11] Douglas Bush agrees: "The satirical objectivity of these early writings does not make them a portrait of the artist as a young girl and young woman, but they reveal her nonetheless, and the process and evidence of her development are of compelling interest."[12] "Jane is always *commenting*," Frank O'Connor said. "You're always aware of her as a person in the story. . . . She just nudges you very, very gently and says, 'Listen to this. Watch the tone in which this is said.'"[13] We have no light stick we can apply to the juvenilia to alert us to those moments when Jane Austen is speaking to us in her own person, nonetheless a perservering scrutiny of the juvenilia can tell us much that we can learn nowhere else.

The juvenilia provide us a context within which to identify and scrutinize environmental factors crucial to Jane Austen's formation. They tell us what she read and what that reading contributed to her critical standards. They tell us what interested her during a pivotal stage of her existence. Finally, they give us a glimpse of a writer emerging from her seven-year apprenticeship carrying with her resources acquired during that interlude, sturdy materials and well-forged tools that will serve her ably in the years to follow. Certainly the picture we get does not resemble Mrs. Mitford's recollections of her as "the prettiest, silliest, most affected, husband-hunting butterfly" she could ever recall.[14]

In his "Biographical Notice" of his sister, Henry Austen says: "It is difficult to say at what age she was not acquainted with the merits and defects of the best essays and novels in the English language" (*NA & P,* 7). That was not puffery. As our awareness of the books she had access to increases, our respect for her pursuit of letters grows. Internal evidence enables us to identify more than 50 works familiar to the author of the juvenilia, including works by Shakespeare, Rowe, Addison, Pope, Johnson, Richardson, Fielding, Sterne, Walpole, Goldsmith, Sheridan, Boswell, Goethe, Lennox, Burney, Edgeworth, Charlotte Smith, and Gilpin. Not only did she know them, she knew them well enough to take liberties with them. For example, Gilpin, in conjunction with some prints in his *Observations on the Mountains and Lakes of Cumberland and Westmoreland,* promulgates what he calls his "doctrine of grouping larger cattle": "There is . . . no way of forming *two* in a group, but by uniting them . . . with *three,* you are almost sure of a good group. . . . *Four* introduces a new difficulty in grouping. . . . The only way in which they will group well, is to *unite three . . .* and to *remove the fourth."*[15] In "Evelyn," however, the youthful Jane Austen contrived a solution that never occurred to Gilpin. As Frederic Gower approaches the Webbs' house he finds it is "in the exact centre of a small circular paddock." (The analogy to a spider's *web* is inescapable). A paling and a border of trees encloses the paddock. The remainder is "unincumbered, the surface of it perfectly even & smooth, and grazed by four white Cows which were disposed at equal distances from each other," resulting in a scene which Frederic found "uncommonly striking" (181). So much for Gilpin.

Willoughby admires Pope "no more than is proper" (47). Jane Austen may have agreed. In "A Fragment" she spoofs the poet's celebrated line, "The proper study of mankind is man," when her flippant moralist says of the poor, "To study their wants, & to leave them unsupplied is the duty, and ought to be the Business of Man" (71). Though severe on Goldsmith's *History of England,* Jane Austen apparently thought better of him as a novelist. The Vicar of Wakefield's pride in his wife's gooseberry wine is recalled in "The Visit," when Miss Fitzgerald boasts that her grandmother "excelled in Gooseberry Wine."[16] Mrs. Marlowe, one of the few amiable women in the juvenilia—in the Scottish tale, "Lesley Castle"—finds her counterpart in the amiable Mrs. Marlow in Sophia Lee's *The Recess,* likewise a Scottish tale.[17] Arabella, Jane Austen's "Female Philosopher," surely owes both name and avocation to her creator's interest in *The Female Quixote,* the heroine of which is Lady Arabella.[18] Jane Austen liked to romp with names, as when she gave Fanny Price's mother the name of Fanny Ward thus coupling the names of two of her favorite novelists, Fanny Burney and Ann Radcliffe, *née* Ward. And she loved a pun quite as much as she relished games with names. "Ask for me tomorrow," says Shakespeare's mortally wounded Mercutio, "and you shall find me a grave man."[19] In "Love and Freindship," Edward, mortally injured when his coach overturns, echoes Mercutio when he says, as he expires, "Laura I fear I have been overturned" (99).

We find overwhelming evidence that Jane Austen was early an omnivorous reader in her deflationary burlesques of contemporary novelists. While seldom, as Mary Lascelles notes, do her jibes aim "merely at this or that wretched novel or novelist," she lays heavy siege to false conventions and stock attitudes then well entrenched.[20] Mary Russell Mitford boasted that, as a teenager, she once read 50 novels in a month. Belonging to a household that relished novels and steadily patronized the circulating libraries, Jane Austen might well have been able to make the same claim. In 1814, she wrote of having "torn through the third vol. of the 'Heroine,'" in an evening.[21]

Throughout the juvenilia Jane Austen raises parodic havoc with facile emotionalism, the cant of sentiment, the flawless hero, matchless heroine, foundling child, the exalted pedigree, the shackles of parental authority, youthful defiance, spontaneous attachment, love-at-first-sight, tears, fainting, running mad, fantastic recognition scenes, fortuitous encounters, unmotivated narrative digressions, confidantes, self-revelation, friendship easily given, reckless benevolence, excessiveness, calculated irrelevancy, forced difficulties, inept imitations of Richardson, sudden reversals, conduct books, absurd closures, inflated rhetoric, cliché diction, gothicism, epistolary absurdity, trivialized history-writing, and neglect of time scale. Nothing escaped her scalding wit. Such thoroughness bespeaks a tremendous amount of reading. Letting neglect of time scale stand surety for the remainder, we cite three instances. In "Frederic & Elfrida," Charlotte, on arriving home, takes a nine-hour walk in a grove of poplars adjacent to her father's parsonage (5). In "Jack & Alice," Lucy's betrothed mourns her death "with unshaken constancy for the next fortnight" at the end of which time he marries somebody else (28–29). In "A Tale," two brothers travel "for three days & six Nights without Stopping" (177).

As she reproved the follies of bad novelists so did Jane Austen condemn social evils. Of paramount importance to her was the mercantile interest determining many marriages. Marriage, in fact, had become an important means of gaining property, the mere consideration of interest or gain outweighing all other factors. Dowerless herself, Jane Austen could expect to be disadvantaged by this system, yet, apart from that, its inherent unfairness outraged her and provided her with a theme to which she returned repeatedly, pitying the women whom circumstances compelled to connive for gain and scorning the men who did so. Of Lady Williams, in "Jack & Alice," we are told: "In Lady Williams every virtue met. She was a widow with a handsome Jointure & the remains of a very handsome face" (13). Her jointure, not her face, procures her a prize catch for a husband. In "Amelia Webster," George Hervey, pressing a friend to marry his sister, says, "She will have two thousand Pounds & as much more as you can get" (48). Of her sister, Eloisa, Charlotte Lutterell says, in "Lesley Castle," "I should like to see the girl married & Cleveland has a very good estate" (121). In "The three Sisters," Mary Stanhope, one of three daughters living with a widowed mother of narrow means, is forced into marriage with an older man, ugly, unaffable, yet affluent. "What's the use of a great Jointure," she laments, "if Men live forever?" (64). The plight of a girl who had no family at all was especially deplorable. Southam notes, "The dilemma of the impoverished orphan is a recurrent topic in Jane Austen, a poignant example of the economic and social vulnerability of women in the eighteenth century."[22] For Jane Austen, the problem was close to home. In "Catharine," Cecilia Wynne is shipped to Bengal as a veritable mail-order bride: "It was . . . so opposite to all her ideas of Propriety, so contrary to her Wishes, so repugnant to her feelings, that she would almost have preferred Servitude to it" (194). What Jane Austen was describing here was the lot of her father's orphaned sister, Philadelphia Austen. Catharine's comment on the situation surely is Jane Austen's own: "To a Girl of any Delicacy, the voyage in itself, since the object of it is so universally known, is a punishment that needs no other to make it very severe" (205). This observation Catharine addresses to the uncomprehending Camilla Stanley which leads us to a second social evil, in Jane Austen's eyes something fully as grave as mercenary marriage, the superficial education provided to women in the eighteenth century.

Then, basically, a woman's education was limited to what Jane Austen called "accomplishments," mere ornamental acquisitions which E.N. Williams identifies as "English, a little French, book-keeping, drawing, needle-work, dancing, with perhaps a little music, or Italian."[23] This was the type of education the rich Welsh tailor gave his daughter in "Jack & Alice." It was, of course, of no use to her in procuring her the husband of her choice (20). In "Catharine," discussing the vacuous Camilla herself, Jane Austen reflects further: "She was . . . naturally not deficient in Abilities, but those Years which ought to have been spent in the attainment of useful knowledge and Mental Improvement, had all been bestowed on learning Drawing, Italian, and Music . . . and she now united to these Accomplishments, an understanding unimproved by reading and a Mind totally devoid of either Taste or Judgement" (198). Frank W. Bradbrook argues that Jane Austen believed the exaggerated idealism many women espoused was a consequence of such an education and that conviction lies behind much of her "criticism of female triviality."[24]

Jane Austen's social awareness in the juvenilia extends to other matters also. Lady Greville's condescending treatment of Maria, in "From a Young Lady in distress'd Circumstances," points, notes A. Walton Litz, to her awareness of "the alliance between economic and social power."[25] For the poor she shows a concern both in "A Fragment" and in her Goldsmith marginalia. In the latter place she says, "How much are the poor to be pitied, and the Rich to be Blamed."[26] The later juvenilia, Southam points out, especially reveal the "ignorance, pride, folly, malice, calculation, or self-interest that so often underlie the parade of manners."[27] Yet Jane Austen's sympathies were not Jacobin. Alistair Duckworth rightly observes that her "deepest impulse was not to subvert but to maintain and properly improve a social heritage,"[28] while Litz concludes that her ultimate subject matter is the "basic conflicts between socio-economic necessities and the need for spiritual freedom."[29]

From his study of the mature works, Duckworth educes that Jane Austen believed "there is a natural moral order stemming from God" and "that the role of education is to call the individual to an awareness of his duty to God and to his social trust."[30] Southam insists further: "Jane Austen believed that rank, intellect, brilliance, education or breeding are nothing without principles and moral sense."[31] From every quarter critical opinion converges on the belief that the assumptions that underlie her art are Johnsonian and that Johnson's ideas about "the moral discipline of the mind" greatly assisted Jane Austen in arriving at and maintaining a consistent moral viewpoint. In her elegy on Mrs. Lefroy, Jane Austen says that what was true of Johnson was true of Anne Lefroy—she was irreplaceable. In her letters she several times refers to "my dear Dr. Johnson."[32] The virtuous Fanny Price keeps a copy of Johnson's *Idler* on her bedside table (156). While the very nature of burlesque limits Johnson's influence on the juvenilia, such details add credibility to Henry Austen's declaration that Johnson was her favorite prose moralist (*NA & P,* 7). Nonetheless, commenting on "Love and Freindship," Bush remarks "a precocious display of moral criteria which do not lose their force in a farcical setting."[33] In "Letter the fourth," Miss Grenville's counsel is typically Johnsonian: "Perfect Felicity is not the property of Mortals, & no one has a right to expect uninterrupted Happiness" (161). In "The Female Philosopher" Johnson's views are endorsed when Julia Miller discourses on the "instability of human pleasures and the uncertainty of their duration" and observes that "all earthly Joys must be imperfect."[34] Claudia Johnson notes further that Jane Austen, in one of the earliest of the juvenilia, "Jack & Alice," felt secure enough in her allegiance to Johnson's moral teachings to lampoon him with an "hilarious parody of his characteristic antithetical, tripartite sentence structure"—"Tho' Benevolent & Candid, she was Generous & sincere; Tho' Pious & Good, she was Religious & amiable, & Tho' Elegant and Agreable, she was Polished & Entertaining."[35] Notable is the debt in "Lesley Castle," to *Rambler #*17, where Charlotte Lutterell, obsessed with food to the virtual exclusion of all else, amusingly illustrates the danger Johnson alluded to when he warned against concentrating upon a single object "till it has wholly ingrossed the imagination."[36]

"Johnson," says Peter De Rose, is "one of the few writers to whom Jane Austen explicitly and favorably alludes in her Juvenilia and in her major novels."[37] This predilection is central to her achievement, for, as Litz has affirmed, by showing that the "novelist can combine absolute fidelity to the details of life . . . with the maintenance of a consistent moral viewpoint, Jane Austen salvaged fiction from slavish subservience to its audience and re-established it as an independent form."[38]

Marvin Mudrick says that romantically minded critics complain that Jane

Austen is "intolerably sensible." And well they might, for she believed that experience, observation, and reflection offer a more trustworthy basis for action than the delusions of sentimentalism. She was of one mind with Johnson, as Bush points out, that "excessive sensibility brings self-indulgent evasion of moral standards ... invulnerable egotism, self-righteousness, and hypocrisy that knows nothing of genuine benevolence or love, that sustain contempt for ordinary decency, and that warrant injuring and robbing the 'unworthy.'"[39] "She loved and revered Dr. Johnson the best," Ernest Baker says, "her moral philosophy was identical with his."[40] Litz clarifies further: "Jane Austen ... was committed both to a Johnsonian system of morality and a 'pre-romantic' feeling for life."[41] In the juvenilia the debt to Johnson is sometimes illustrated by mothers who are swayed by their emotions and fathers who are ruled by reason. Thus in "The three Sisters," Georgiana Stanhope says: "We neither attempted to alter my Mother's resolution, which I am sorry to say is generally more strictly kept than rationally formed" (61). While in "Love and Freindship," Sir Edward Lindsay says of his son's romantic folly: "Where Edward in the name of wonder ... did you pick up this unmeaning Gibberish? You have been studying Novels I suspect" (81). In "Evelyn," his Lordship dismisses Frederic Gower's naive proposal with cold, inexorable logic: "To suppose them alive is destroying at once the Motive for a change in my sentiments concerning the affair" (188).

Southam observes that the "impact of great writing upon an undeveloped mind is not to be measured by obvious affinities, borrowings, or allusions. It is a force which works subtly upon the moral temper, touches the imagination, coloring the vision and interpretation of reality. One would judge that the external influences most generally at work in the mature novels are Johnson's moral rationalism, Richardson's intense observation of human conduct, and the judgement of Cowper."[42] Applying the same tests to the works of Jane Austen's nonage, Johnson's influence is seen to be pervasive. Disregarding, for the moment, those observations meant to indict specific false conventions and stock attitudes, to consider those which reflect Jane Austen's true moral temper, we see that she aligns herself with Johnson in her disapproval of hypocrisy, equivocation, self-indulgence, inconsiderateness, vanity, conceit, selfishness, insincerity, ingratitude, superficiality, obstinacy, presumption, impulsiveness, heedlessness, arrogance, and condescension. No less firmly does she ally herself to him in her endorsement of reasonableness, order, unity, prudence, discretion, politeness, generosity, patience, restraint, self-control, self-discipline, elegance, breeding, and principle.

Jane Austen's juvenilia, Joan Rees says, attest to "the unusually early emergence of her critical faculty."[43] They attest further to her early allegiance to moral, social, and ideological assumptions central to her mature work. Several factors seem to have contributed to her precociousness. Preeminent among them was *The Loiterer,* an Oxford journal edited, 1789–90, by her brother James. Of the 60 issues published, 37 were written either by James or his brother Henry. These essays, Litz points out, "exhibit the same pervasive debt to Johnson that we find throughout Jane Austen's novels and letters."[44] They also burlesque the excesses of sentimentalism. In essay 59, Henry Austen, to use Litz's phrase, supplies "A catalogue of stock devices and shopworn phrases burlesqued in the Juvenilia."[45] The *Loiterer*'s narratives are cast in epistolary form except for the later ones which favor a narrative framework. The juvenilia follow the same pattern. Half a dozen *Loiterer* essays condemn mercenary marriage; others advocate improved education for women and condemn the affectations of the fashionable world. Certainly these matters were discussed in the Austen household. Perhaps, though, it is mere chance that the phrase "first impressions" appears in James's first essay, and the phrase "love and friendship" in Henry's essay, number 27, though it should be noted, Jane Austen's "Love and Freindship" was begun just two months after *The Loiterer* ceased publication.

Of particular interest to us is the ninth *Loiterer*. It contains a letter written by "Sophia Sentiment." Some critics detect here the hand of the 12-year-old Jane Austen because, in "Love & Freindship," the chief victim of sentiment is Sophia. Yet, if female authorship is insisted upon, it might just as well have been written by her whom Jane Austen, at 21, hailed as "the finest comic writer of the present age," her sister Cassandra.[46]

Enough parallels exist between *The Loiterer* and the juvenilia to make it apparent that the tastes and assumptions of the latter reflect the tastes and assumptions of Jane Austen's brothers, and, therefore, of the Austen household during the years when Jane Austen began writing. The likelihood is that some *Loiterer* essays were written when the brothers were home on holiday from Oxford and that their sister sat in on the discussions that attended their formulation or heard them read aloud at family hearthside gatherings. Assuredly they not only supplied her with ideas, they stimulated her to write.

Another family-oriented activity that, for a time, coincided with the juvenilia years was the staging of amateur theatricals. These the Austens presented between 1782 and 1790, at Steventon, eventually in their barn, but, for five years, in the parsonage itself, in the common sitting room. We know of nine plays they produced. There must have been others. Clara Thomson surmises that reading plays in this period gave Jane Austen her first impulse to authorship.[47] Three of these early pieces, "A Mystery," "The Visit," and "The First Act of a Comedy," are plays. Even without these, however, the lively dialogue found throughout the juvenilia, as well as references to Shakespeare, Sheridan, Rowe, and Townley, bespeak a growing familiarity with drama. The well-entrenched family practice of reading aloud in the evening also must have sharpened Jane Austen's ear. At this activity, she herself excelled. The juvenilia themselves evidently were read to a family audience and often reread.

The barn presentations began when the dynamic Eliza Hancock, by then the Comtesse de Feuillide, Jane Austen's first cousin, stayed with the Austens, in 1787. Since the 1770s in England, private theatricals had been the rage in fashionable circles. From childhood Eliza had performed in them, both in England and in France. It may not be a coincidence that Jane Austen began composing the juvenilia in 1787, the same year the amateur theatricals at Steventon moved into high gear and she heard prologues written by James being declaimed from the stage. We know of three plays staged there that year, as well as of two others given early in 1788. About this time, too, Jane Austen returned to Steventon after ending her formal schooling. These enhanced home theatricals must have seemed to her then a new phase of her education.

In 1787, Egerton Brydges, novelist, poet, and putative cousin of Mrs. Austen, also gave a helping hand with the Steventon dramas. Brydges' status as a writer, however tentative, must have made him a celebrity in this rural hamlet. He did not pass unnoticed by Jane Austen. Not only did he furnish hints utilized later for her characterization of Sir Walter Elliot, and perhaps Mr. Collins, his deficiencies as a writer were a source of fresh insight.

At least two of the playwrights whose works were performed at Steventon were women, Susannah Centlivre and Hannah Cowley. Jane Austen could, as well, have taken encouragement from that fact.

Richard Sheridan's impact on the juvenilia was especially marked. Jane Austen knew *The Rivals, The Critic,* and *The School for Scandal. The Critic* was the inspiration for the two whispering scenes in "The Mystery," the recognition scene in "Love and Freindship," and, in the same piece, the line "We fainted alternately on the sofa." "Love and Freindship" may be indebted as well to *The Rivals* which furnishes an instance of a young woman who rejects an eligible suitor because a heroine in a novel would never accept a suitor, however eligible, who has been chosen for her by a father or guardian. Southam surmises that Lady Williams, in "Jack & Alice," is modeled on Lady Candour, in *The School for Scandal.* A lost work which Jane Austen refers to, "The School for Jealousy," possibly written by her, may owe something to Sheridan's play (170–72).

In "The three Sisters" Mary Stanhope anticipates the ambitions of the Mansfield Park household, by demanding from her husband-to-be "a theatre to act plays in" (65). As at Mansfield, the amateur theatricals of the Austens had to manage with small casts. Jane Austen may be alluding to that fact when, in "Jack & Alice," a masquerade is attended by "an entire neighborhood" consisting of *seven* people (12). In "Love and Freindship," when an acting company of four members staged *Macbeth,* Gustavus single-handedly played the three witches and Philander acted *"all the rest,"* save Lady Macbeth and Banquo (108). Similar exigencies must have plagued the repertory company made up of Austens.[48] Such challenges must have stimulated Jane Austen's resourcefulness and maybe even encouraged her to make do with a compact society.

The *coups de theatre* with which Jane Austen ends her novels in lieu of replicating the drawn-out closures of other novelists, conceivably originated in a preference implanted by the Steventon theatricals. So, too, "the sudden descents of language and action," which Southam says recall the comic melodrama to which popular playwrights had recourse "to ridicule the idealization of impulsive love and elopement."[49]

In *Pride and Prejudice,* Darcy tells Elizabeth that he was, in childhood, "almost taught . . . to care for none beyond my own family circle" (*PP,* 369). Austen family intimacy may well have taken that direction. James Edward Austen-Leigh acknowledges that the Austens formed a close family circle and "were inclined to live somewhat too exclusively within it."[50] He spoke from personal insight since his own mother's strained relations with her in-laws stemmed from her jealousy of Austen family intimacy. Jane Austen entered readily into that intimacy or, as Southam characterizes it, "intense clannishness." She was, says Mary Augusta Austen-Leigh, "gifted with strong family instincts."[51] E.M. Forster inclined to the same view: "The family was the unit within which her heart had liberty of choice; friends, neighbors, plays and fame were all objects to be picked up in the course of a flight outside and brought back to the nest for examination. They often laughed over the alien trophies, for they were a hard humorous family."[52]

If the reading interests, writing activities, and theatrical ventures of her family engrossed the youthful mind of Jane Austen, family closeness surely made such receptivity possible. Several factors account for that closeness. While Steventon (lying in a folding of the Hampshire chalk downs and cut off from the outside world by poor roads, as local communities invariably were in that era) had had—by these circumstances—social and cultural self-sufficiency thrust upon it, the Austens, even so, were no ordinary, little, countrified household presided over by a naive Vicar Primrose. George Austen had been a scholar at Oxford and was a bookish man fully qualified to prepare for Oxford his own sons as well as other young gentlemen of his locale. Moreover, in the absence of his cousin, Thomas Knight, chief landholder at Steventon, George was, in effect, Steventon's squire. Nor is that all. In "Catharine," that jewel of the juvenilia, Jane Austen introduces the Dudleys, "a very noble Family . . . more famed for their Pride than their opulence, tenacious of . . . Dignity," and looking to their daughter "as the future restorer, by a Splendid Marriage, of the dignity which their reduced Situation . . . had so lessened" (195–96). The situation of the Austens themselves invites comparison. George Austen had rich relatives but counted no aristocrats among his forebears. The heritage of his wife was another matter. She was the great-granddaughter of the eighth Lord Chandos, and grandniece of Handel's patron, the first Duke of Chandos, and descended from Sir Thomas White, founder of St. John's College, Oxford, and the Merchant-Taylors School. She was, as well, descended from the Lord Mayor of London, Sir Thomas Leigh, who escorted Elizabeth to her coronation. Through him she was related to the Duke of Ancaster, the Duke of Marlborough, and William Pitt, prime minister of England through much of Jane Austen's lifetime. Ensuing generations of this family would produce Lord Melbourne and Winston Churchill. Her father was a Fellow of All Soul's, Oxford; his brother, the witty Theophilus Leigh, was, for 50 years, master of Balliol. Her rich cousin Thomas was heir to Stoneleigh Abbey; her brother James, heir to the riches of the Perrots. Her cousin and name sake, Cassandra Leigh, Mrs. Samuel Cooke, was the author of the novel, *Battleridge* (1799), published as written "by a Lady of Quality."[53] We may add that, in Jane Austen's girlhood her brother James married, in turn, a granddaughter of the Duke of Ancaster and a grandniece of the second Lord Craven, himself a cousin through the Leigh family. Her sister became engaged to another Craven cousin and her first cousin Eliza married a French count. Her brother Edward, adopted by his cousin, Thomas Knight, became the heir to the Knight fortune, and married the daughter of Sir Brook Bridges. Need we wonder why Jane Austen professed to "like first Cousins to be first Cousins and interested about each other"?[54]

Was Jane Austen impressed with her maternal heritage? Shake her mother's family tree and out fall forebears whose names were Wentworth, Woodhouse, Churchill, Willoughby, deBourgh, D'Arcy, Fitzwilliam, Gardiner, Watson, Middleton, Tilney, Brandon, Gre[n]ville, Bertram, Ferrars, Dashwood, Elliot, Musgrave, Bingley, Bennet, and Dudley. The names Dashwood, Willoughby, Musgrove, Elliot, Gre[n]ville, Dudley, and Wentworth actually turned up in the juvenilia, and Fitzwilliam, too, if we include a fictional entry Jane Austen made in her father's marriage register. For further confirmation of Jane Austen's pride of ancestry, we point to a remark made to Cassandra in a letter written, in 1808, from Godmersham: "it is pleasant to be among people who know one's connections & care about them."[55] With such a heritage, D.J. Greene points out, "it cannot have been so pleasant to be snubbed by those closer to the charmed center of the aristocratic circle. . . . Jane Austen must have been subjected to a wealth of such condescension before the picture of Lady Catherine took final shape."[56] In the juvenilia Lady Catherine is prefigured in Lady Harcourt, Mrs. Dudley, and Lady Greville. Q.D. Leavis conjectures, indeed, that the incident that called Lady Greville into existence was the void from which Miss Bingley, Lady Catherine, Mrs. Norris, and Elizabeth Elliot all emerged.

Political and theological convictions also encouraged the Austens in their intense clannishness. Both the Knights and the Leighs had Stuart ties, and, apparently, the Austens too, since, in her "History of England," Jane Austen avers that the inhabitants of her father's alma mater, Oxford, were "always loyal to their King & faithful to his interests" (148). The Leighs were kin to Charles I's favorite, the ill-fated Earl of Strafford, and, at heavy cost to themselves, sheltered Charles at Stoneleigh when adversity overtook him. Jane Austen's "History," and the marginalia she introduced into her copy of Goldsmith's *History,* affirm her Stuart allegiance. Consistent with that loyalty is her statement in the "History," "I am myself partial to the roman catholic religion" (147). That should not surprise us. The first Lord Chandos was a creation of Queen Mary. The first Lord Leigh was a creation of Charles I, and Stuart blood flowed in the veins of some of his grandchildren. Accordingly we must ask ourselves if the Austens did not harbor feelings that socially isolated them from such staunch Whigs as their sometimes neighbors, the Mitfords.

Jane Austen's contentment within the family circle was assured by her cordial relations with her sister, Cassandra. Annette Hopkins, taking into account Cassandra's witty illustrations done for the "History of England," asks "whether Jane's own talent may not have received quickening through association with Cassandra."[57] In her dedication to "The beautifull Cassandra," Jane ascribes to her noble sentiments, innumerable virtues, rational conversation, polished manners, and refined tastes (44). Her letters show us that she always valued Cassandra's view of things above her own.

The earlier pieces of the juvenilia, mostly concerned as they were with books rather than life, made only a limited call on Jane Austen's potential. For her that was not enough. She wanted, she said, "to create, not to reproduce."[58] The actual world around her interested her, not the make believe world of others. After visiting the Liverpool Museum and British Gallery, she wrote to Cassandra: "I had some amusement at each, though my preference for Men & Women, always inclines me to attend more to the company than the sight."[59]

In her later juvenilia, Jane Austen redirected her considerable powers of ridicule into experiments in social criticism, exploring the absurdities of the world around her. The pieces that best record this shift of emphasis are "Lesley Castle," "The three Sisters," and "Catharine." Mary Lascelles notes: "In 'Lesley Castle' burlesque is not the sole aim; in 'The three Sisters' it is not even prominent." She sees "no very arduous transition from these two pieces to 'Elinor and Marianne.' "[60] Southam concurs: "In place of burlesque melodrama, she takes the problems of conduct and judgement that could face a girl in her day-to-day relationships, especially in the testing situations of love and marriage."[61] A "hard, critical comedy that searches affectation and display," he said, had routed what Chesterton called her "nursery jests."[62]

Julia L. Epstein records the changes in blunter terms: "From simple burlesque to acrid social criticism, a movement that develops across the juvenilia, becoming more and more biting as Austen's ironic powers evolve."[63]

Catharine Percival, Bush says, is a "clearly recognizable Austen heroine."[64] With "Catharine" we see Jane Austen awakening to her full potential. Joan Rees describes its significance in these terms: "Among the juvenilia, 'Catharine' offers the clearest prophecy of what is to come. Less rooted in literary criticism than the rest, 'Catharine' indicates the development of Jane Austen's narrative style; the characterization is growing out of the caricature, becoming more careful and consistent. . . . "[65]

Alan McKillop thought of *Northanger Abbey* as "the comprehensive result of Jane Austen's early reactions to and exercises in prose fiction."[66] While that is true, *Northanger Abbey* is, by no means, the sole result of those reactions and exercises. Litz says: "Where a serious concern for manners is dominant we are [in the juvenilia] entering a world alive with suggestions of the later fiction."[67] Hopkins is yet more inclusive: "If the *Watsons* fragment is included in these youthful studies, there is not a single one of the six mature novels whose beginnings, if only minutely, cannot be detected here, in a genre, a situation, a character, or a mere name."[68]

A brief, volume by volume, survey of the juvenilia is instructive. In "Frederic & Elfrida," after a long delay for which the heroine is responsible, Frederic—after showing an interest in another woman—marries Elfrida. Thus is Frederick Wentworth's situation anticipated. Lady Harcourt, in "Henry and Eliza," seems a tentative sketch both of Mrs. Allen and Lady Bertram. Mary Stanhope's concern about Mr. Watt's age (he is 32), in "The three Sisters," anticipates Marianne Dashwood's concern about Colonel Brandon's age (he is 35). This same piece, in several ways, anticipates *Pride and Prejudice.* Mary Stanhope's delight at being able, as a married woman, to chaperone her sisters and her friends to all the winter balls will be echoed later by Lydia Bennet. Mr. Watt's adaptability in choosing a wife heralds the wooings of Mr. Collins. Mrs. Stanhope seems an early sketch of Mrs. Bennet; and her concern that Watts choose a wife from among her daughters, and not among the Duttons, finds a parallel in Mrs. Bennet's dismay that Mr. Collins went to the Lucases for a bride (60).

Rhydderch says that Jane Austen, like Gibbon, "dearly loved the sound of three."[69] Never was this more apparent than in her fascination with sisterly trios. There are three Thorpe sisters in *Northanger Abbey,* and three marriageable young ladies, Catherine, Isabella, and Eleanor. The three Dashwood sisters appear in *Sense and Sensibility.* In *Pride and Prejudice,* three of the Bennet sisters figure prominently and three women are prominent in the opposing camp: the Bingley sisters and Lady Catherine's daughter. *Mansfield Park* gives us three Ward sisters in one generation, and three of their daughters growing up together in the next. *Emma* is concerned with three marriageable young ladies— Emma, Harriet, and Jane. There are three Elliot sisters in *Persuasion.* The juvenilia prepares us for the appearance of this pattern. In addition to the Stanhope sisters in "The three Sisters," there are the three Miss Cliftons with whom Mountague falls in love in "Sir William Mountague." Three sisters appear in "A Fragment" and three in "A Tale, Scraps." In "Jack & Alice" we meet the three Simpson sisters. In "Edgar & Emma" Mr. and Mrs. Wilmot enter accompanied by their eldest daughters. In "Catharine" Catharine passes a happy childhood companioned by the two Wynne sisters. In this same work Lady Halifax has three daughters.

Jane Austen's own family of intimates included the three Bigg sisters and the three Lloyd sisters. Martha Lloyd eventually became a member of the Austen household, creating a triumvirate there. Eventually Jane Austen came to look on her niece, Fanny, as "another sister." Why this obsession with three? Surely there is more to it than Gilpin's assertion that three "groups well."

In "Lesley Castle" we find not only a first outline of Sir Walter Elliot in Sir George, but Lady Susan Vernon's prototype in Lady Susan Lesley. Lady Scudamore in the "Collection of Letters" (Letter number five), likewise prefigures Lady Susan, as does the cruel mother in "A Tour through Wales." In "Love & Freindship" Edward and Laura see their expectation vanish when Marianne's mother marries and moves to Ireland. A like misfortune is to befall Emma Watson. Here, also, Macdonald's expulsion of Sophia and Laura anticipates General Tilney's expulsion of Catherine Morland. Frank Bradbrook finds a first hint of Mary Bennet in Julia Miller of "The Female Philosopher." Lady Greville, in "A young Lady in distress'd Circumstances," keeps Maria out in the cold even as Mrs. Norris consigns Fanny to an unheated room at Mansfield Park, and Lady Catherine keeps Mrs. Collins standing out of doors.

In *Volume the Third,* anticipations are conspicuous in "Catharine." There is the scene at the ball, a fixed piece in the mature novels; the aunt who, in her hypochondriac obsessions, is a precursor of Mr. Woodhouse and Mary Musgrove; and Edward Stanley, ancestor of Tom Musgrave, Frank Churchill, and Henry Crawford. Mudrick sees Elizabeth Bennet prefigured in Catharine's "forthrightness of opinion,"[70] while Halperin sees her in Catharine's "natural Unreserve and Vivacity."[71] Camilla Stanley is a first outline of Isabella Thorpe. Southam sees Catharine herself as "a sketch for Catherine Morland."[72]

Mudrick describes "Catharine" as "a kind of grab-bag of attractive bits and pieces . . . which Jane Austen will have the time and skill to sort and organize later."[73] In a sense this claim applies, with equal validity, to all of the juvenilia. The fact is, Jane Austen consistently employed great economy of means. In the juvenilia we observe her choosing those incidents, characters, plots, and themes which would constitute the basic stock of materials from which she would construct much that is found in the mature novels. Jane Austen relished the challenge that rules, disciplines, and restricted sources offered, just as she elected to live her life within the confines of an intimate family-centered world. Even her recreations, from what we know of them, were of the kind that invited her to pit her wits and reflexes against difficulties that admitted only of logical solutions dependent on astuteness, adroitness, and common sense—word games, card games, spillikins, country dances, the pianoforte, needlework. To everything she did she brought superior competence. Her copperplate hand was beyond reproach. Her letters, according to her niece Caroline, always were folded and sealed with a surer touch than others could manage.[74] Her skill as seamstress especially commands our notice. Frowling she wrote to Cassandra, "We are very busy making Edward's shirts, and I am proud to say that I am the neatest worker of the party."[75] Like her mother, she was adept at remaking garments for further use. Although she fails to come to grips with the implications of her remark, Q.D. Leavis was certainly on to something when she used the idiom of needlework in commenting on the new uses Jane Austen found for the original materials of the juvenilia: "Much of her novels consists of manipulation and differentiation of characters and group-relations made long before in cruder and more general or merely burlesque pieces of writing; rarely is anything abandoned, however slight, Jane Austen's practice being rather thriftily to 'make over.'"[76]

We know that Jane Austen was aware of her aristocratic heritage. (Was it that heritage Henry was referring to when he paraphrased Donne's phrase, "Her pure and eloquent blood/Spake in her cheeks," to pay tribute to her? [*NA & P,* 5].) It is likely that she was, as Greene asserts, "acutely conscious" of "her intellectual superiority to many of those who patronized" her.[77] Her intellect, of itself, was guaranteed to make her a formidable presence in any encounter. Joan Rees concedes that fact in these terms: "Jane Austen must have been a disconcerting young girl. . . . [Her juvenilia] demonstrates her acute sensitivity to the fine differences of human relationships, her wit and humor, and her exceptional intelligence. It is not surprising that Philadelphia Walter [her cousin] was nonplussed."[78] Was there a time when Jane Austen saw herself as "almost taught . . . to think meanly of all the rest of the world, to *wish,* at least, to think meanly of their sense and worth compared with my own" (*PP,* 369)? We must allow for that possibility. Commenting on Lady Greville's rude treatment of Maria, Yasmine Gooneratne suggests that Jane Austen had "translated into fictional form—perhaps as a vent for irritated exasperation," some comparable episode she herself had experienced.[79] Mrs. Leavis suggests that the incident that called Lady Greville into existence was the void from which Miss Bingley, Lady Catherine, Mrs. Norris, and Elizabeth Elliot all emerged. "These later inventions," she states, "were intended to get on the reader's nerves because they were aspects of social intercourse that had got on Miss Austen's."[80]

In view of Jane Austen's penchant for often harkening back to the carriage as status symbol, we must allow for the possibility that Mary Stanhope's determination to upstage her neighbors with a high hung carriage, "blue spotted with silver," reflected some youthful yearning had by Jane Austen herself. In those early years it would have been natural for her to have wanted, like the heroines in the books that she read, to have succeeded to the eminence to which her heritage seemed to entitle her. Certainly she fantasized about this. In the entry she introduced into her father's register, she announced her impending marriage to a man whose four names were assigned, presently, to four men of affluence who, by marrying them, raised four of her deserving heroines from obscurity—Henry Frederick Howard Fitzwilliam (assuming, of course, that Mr. Howard did marry Emma Watson). And when she dedicated "Catharine" to Cassandra she asserted that, owing to Cassandra's patronage of "The beautifull Cassandra" and "The History of England," these works had "obtained a place in every library in the Kingdom, and run through threescore Editions" (192). By then she had begun to realize that if she was to attain a status commensurate with her heritage, she must get it through her own initiative.

Jane Austen's determination in those years, and her resentment that economic circumstances had reduced the social consequence of the Austens to a state much beneath that to which their Leigh ancestry entitled them, may well account for the acerbity of her assessments of others, in the juvenilia. "So young and so untender," commented Augustine Birrell as he contemplated the juvenilia in 1922.[81] Later critics agreed. Mudrick has characterized the juvenilia as "close observation without sympathy, common sense with tenderness," and remarks their "hard compelled detachment."[82] John Halperin says these earliest works are startling in their "hostility" and "cold-blooded" in their detachment.[83] To have carried such bitterness into her adult years could have been destructive to Jane Austen's art. As early as "Catharine," however, tolerance and tenderness overwhelmed bitterness. Of Catharine Percival at 16, we are told, "She had too much good Sense to be proud of her family, and too much good Nature to live at variance with any one" (226). Coupled with common sense and amiability was Jane Austen's genuine capacity for compassion. The difficult circumstances which poverty had visited on Cecilia Wynne had stirred Catharine's deep concern and she deplored Lady Halifax's condescending behavior toward both Cecilia and her sister, Mary, quite as much as Jane Austen's readers, skillfully manipulated by her, would disdain Mrs. Norris's condescending treatment of Fanny Price.

Experience and a reflective mind, conditioned by the prudent counsels of a wise father and the wisdom of Dr. Johnson, may have been the only influences needed to persuade pride and resentment to capitulate to tolerance and humility. Yet we should not discount the influence of Anne Lefroy. Jane Austen wrote no elegy marking the death of her father. She did write one commemorating the death of Anne Lefroy. And there she stresses Mrs. Lefroy's "tenderness of soul," and "warmth of heart without pretence" (441). And there we are told that Mrs. Lefroy raised her voice only in the cause of virtue. And here, for once, Jane Austen asked to be allowed to put reason aside to indulge the mystical notion that her own birthday and the anniversary of Mrs. Lefroy's death fell on

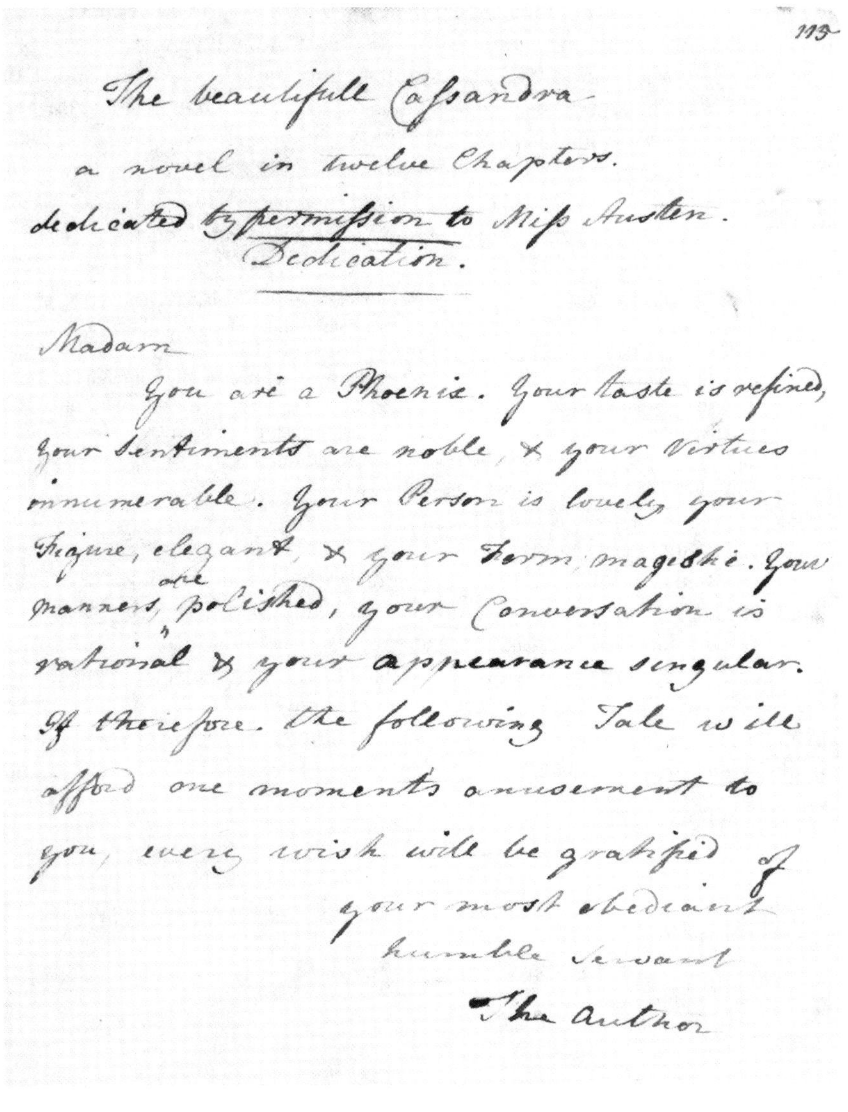

113

The beautifull Cassandra

a novel in twelve Chapters.

dedicated by permission to Miss Austen.

Dedication.

Madam

You are a Phoenix. Your taste is refined, your Sentiments are noble, & your Virtues innumerable. Your Person is lovely, your Figure, elegant, & your Form, magestic. Your Manners, are polished, your Conversation is rational & your appearance singular. If therefore the following Tale will afford one moments amusement to you, every wish will be gratified of

your most obedient
humble servant
The Author

Figure 1. Dedication to "The beautifull Cassandra"
(Volume the First *MS; Courtesy The Bodleian Library, MS Don.e.7*)

the same date because heaven wanted to entwine their destinies. Presumably she wanted to be a conductor of those attributes that Anne Lefroy exemplified—virtues antipodal to coldness, bitterness, want of compassion. And, surely, in the mature works, she resembles the generous-hearted Anne Lefroy much more than she does the unsparing satirist who wrote most of the juvenilia.

In her introduction to "The beautifull Cassandra," Jane Austen spoke of Cassandra as a "phoenix" (44). In what sense Cassandra, phoenix-fashion, had renewed herself, we cannot guess. That Jane Austen herself did emerge renewed from her seven-year journey through the wonderland of her juvenilia, however, is clear. She, indeed, merits the title of phoenix.

Of Jane Austen, Virginia Woolf wrote in *The Common Reader:*

> Nothing is more obvious than that this girl of fifteen, sitting in her private corner of the common parlor, was writing not to draw a laugh from brother and sisters [*sic*], and not for home consumption. She was writing for everybody, for nobody, for our age, for her own. . . . One of those faeries who perch upon cradles must have taken her on a flight through the world directly she was born. When she was laid in the cradle again she knew not only what the world looked like, but she had already chosen her kingdom. . . . At fifteen she had had few illusions about other people and none about herself. Whatever she writes is finished and turned and set in its relation, not to the parsonage, but to the universe.[84]

On 10 August 1814, Jane Austen wrote to her niece, Anna: "Your Aunt C. does not like desultory novels. . . . I allow much more Latitude than she does—& think Nature and Spirit cover many sins of a wandering story."[85] Encompassing Jane Austen's nature and spirit is something that criticism, after two centuries of struggle, has not yet satisfactorily accomplished. One thing, however, is certain—whoever takes up that challenge must be grateful that the juvenilia are there to point the way to go. "The juvenilia were her own education," Brigid Brophy insists.[86] And what an education they were, for her and for us.

Notes

1. R.W. Chapman, ed., *The Oxford Illustrated Jane Austen,* New York and Oxford, 1983, V, 82. Hereafter references will be cited in text.

2. *Jane Austen's Letters to Her Sister Cassandra and Others,* ed. R.W. Chapman, second edition, London, 1952, p. 148.

3. *Letters,* p. 402.

4. Brian Southam, *Jane Austen's Literary Manuscripts,* London, 1964, p. 6.

5. James Edward Austen-Leigh, *A Memoir of Jane Austen,* London, 1906, pp. v, 42.

6. R.W. Chapman, *Jane Austen: Facts and Problems,* Oxford, 1948, p. 144.

7. John Cann Bailey, *Introductions to Jane Austen,* London, 1931, p. 113.

8. David Rhydderch, *Jane Austen: Her Life and Art,* London, 1932, p. 29.

9. Chapman, *Jane Austen: Facts and Problems,* p. 146.

10. Southam, *Jane Austen's Literary Manuscripts,* p. 6.

11. Christopher Gillie, *A Preface to Jane Austen,* London, 1974, p. 23.

12. Douglas Bush, *Jane Austen,* New York, 1975, p. 42.

13. Frank O'Connor, "Jane Austen: *Pride and Prejudice*" [radio broadcast 8 May 1955], in *The Invitation to Learning Reader,* ed. Lyman Bryson, New York, 1955, p. 148.

14. *Life of Mary Russell Mitford,* ed. A.G.K. L'Estrange, New York, 1870, I, 305–60.

15. William Gilpin, *Observations on the Mountains and Lakes of Cumberland and Westmoreland,* London, 1786, II, 259.

16. Oliver Goldsmith, *The Vicar of Wakefield,* Boston, n.d., pp. 2, 35.

17. Sophia Lee, *The Recess,* New York, 1972, pp. 13 ff.

18. VI, 172; Charlotte Lennox, *The Female Quixote,* New York, 1986, pp. 6 ff.

19. *Romeo and Juliet,* Act III, sc. ii.

20. Mary Lascelles, "Miss Austen and Some Books," *London Mercury* 29 (1933–34), 530.

21. *Letters,* p. 377.

22. Southam, *Jane Austen's Literary Manuscripts,* p. 40.

23. E.N. Williams, *Life in Georgian England,* London, 1967, p. 51.

24. Frank W. Bradbrook, *Jane Austen and Her Predecessors,* Cambridge, England, 1966, p. 90.

25. A. Walton Litz, *Jane Austen: A Study in Her Artistic Development,* Oxford, 1965, p. 29.

26. Mary-Augusta Austen-Leigh, *Personal Aspects of Jane Austen,* London, 1920, p. 33.

27. Southam, *Jane Austen's Literary Manuscripts,* pp. 30–31.

28. Alistair Duckworth, *The Improvement of the Estate: A Study of Jane Austen's Novels,* Baltimore, 1971, p. 80.

29. Litz, p. 24.

30. Duckworth, p. 80.

31. Southam, *Jane Austen's Literary Manuscripts,* p. 52.

32. *Letters,* 181. I am indebted to Gaye King for the suggestion that Jane Austen's use of the phrase "my dear Dr. Johnson" may have sometimes been facetious, since Mrs. Thrale used it often and Jane Austen was familiar with Mrs. Thrale's *Letters.*

33. Bush, p. 49.

34. Claudia L. Johnson, "The 'Operations of Time, and the Changes of the Human Mind': Jane Austen and Dr. Johnson Again," *Modern Language Quarterly* 44:1 (1983), 25; VI, 172.

35. Johnson, p. 25; VI, 13.

36. Johnson, p. 28.

37. Peter L. De Rose, *Jane Austen and Samuel Johnson,* Washington, D.C., 1980, p. 6.

38. Litz, p. 57.

39. Bush, pp. 48–49.

40. Ernest Baker, *The History of the English Novel,* London, 1935, VI, 64.

41. Litz, p. 13.

42. Southam, *Jane Austen's Literary Manuscripts,* p. 9.

43. Joan Rees, *Jane Austen: Woman and Writer,* New York, 1976, p. 33.

44. A. Walton Litz, *"The Loiterer:* A Reflection on Jane Austen's Early Environment," *Review of English Studies,* New Series 12:47 (1961), 253.

45. Ibid., p. 260.

46. *Letters,* p. 8.

47. Clara Linklater Thomson, *Jane Austen: A Survey,* London, 1929, p. 231.

48. Thomson, pp. 25, 231.

49. Southam, *Jane Austen's Literary Manuscripts,* p. 23.

50. James Edward Austen-Leigh, p. 16.

51. Mary Augusta Austen-Leigh, p. 13.

52. E.M. Forster, *Abinger Harvest,* New York, 1936, p. 164.

53. Judith Tomlin, "Cousins of Jane Austen: Some New References," *The British Journal for Eighteenth Century Studies* 8 (1985), 195.

54. *Letters,* p. 415.

55. *Letters,* p. 207.

56. Donald J. Greene, "Jane Austen and the Peerage," *PMLA* 68 (1953), 1028.

57. Annette Hopkins, "Jane Austen's 'Love & Freindship,'" *The South Atlantic Quarterly* 24 (1925), 37.

58. Mary Augusta Austen-Leigh, p. 104.

59. *Letters,* p. 267.

60. Mary Lascelles, *Jane Austen and Her Art,* Oxford, 1939, p. 10.

61. Brian Southam, "Juvenilia," in *The Jane Austen Companion,* ed. J. David Grey, New York, 1986, p. 251.

62. Ibid., p. 30.

63. Julia L. Epstein, "Jane Austen's Juvenilia and the Female Epistolary Tradition," *Papers on Literature & Language* 21 (1985), 407.

64. Bush, p. 53.

65. Rees, p. 41.

66. Alan Dugald McKillop, "Critical Realism in *Northanger Abbey*," in *Jane Austen: A Collection of Critical Essays,* ed. Ian Watt, Englewood Cliffs, N.J., 1963, p. 52.

67. Litz, p. 24.

68. Hopkins, p. 48.

69. Rhydderch, p. 131.

70. Marvin Mudrick, *Jane Austen: Irony as Defense and Discovery,* Princeton, N.J., 1952, p. 27.

71. John Halperin, *The Life of Jane Austen,* Baltimore, 1984, p. 46.

72. Southam, *Jane Austen's Literary Manuscripts,* p. 44.

73. Mudrick, p. 27.

74. Caroline Austen, *My Aunt, Jane Austen,* London, 1952, p. 7.

75. *Letters,* p. 10.

76. Q.D. Leavis, "A Critical Theory of Jane Austen's Writings," *Scrutiny* 10 (1941), 66.

77. Greene, p. 1029.

78. Rees, p. 45.

79. Yasmine Gooneratne, *Jane Austen,* Cambridge, 1970, p. 39.

80. Leavis, p. 66.

81. Augustine Birrell, *More Obiter Dicta,* New York, 1924, p. 40.

82. Mudrick, p. 36.

83. John Halperin, "Unengaged Laughter: Jane Austen's Juvenilia," *The South Atlantic Quarterly* 81:3 (Summer 1982), 287.

84. Sheila-Kaye Smith and G.B. Stern, *More about Jane Austen,* New York, 1949, p. 12.

85. *Letters,* pp. 395–96.

86. Brigid Brophy, "Jane Austen and the Stuarts," in *Critical Essays on Jane Austen,* ed. B.C. Southam, London, 1968, p. 36.

Unengaged Laughter: Jane Austen's Juvenilia

John Halperin

The juvenilia—short tales, sketches, fictional letters, scraps of epistolary novels, bits of plays, some highly imaginative English history—show among other things that as a girl Jane Austen (1775–1817) was already well-read. By the time she was in her teens her literary taste was set. Above all, she was addicted to novels—novels of all kinds. Richardson was her favorite novelist and she knew his works intimately, but she read all the fiction she could get her hands on. She was less tolerant of contemporary novels. As an adolescent she already viewed popular and sentimental fiction with the critical eye of the satirist; her early works ridicule the sentimental excesses and sensational unrealities of current popular fiction—mostly the novel of "sensibility" and the Gothic novel of "terror."[1] If it is unusual to find an 11- or 12-year-old girl spending much of her time writing so determinedly, it is even more unusual to find her, at so tender an age, already a confirmed parodist and cynic. She read nothing without passing judgment upon it. The ironic, satirical vein was one Jane Austen was of course to mine so skillfully in later years and works. The well-known "Love and Freindship" and "The History of England," and especially the later juvenilia, particularly "Catharine," show unmistakable signs of comic talent; by the time of the last-named work the writer was 17 years old. Much of the contents of the three volumes probably was composed by Jane Austen between the ages of 14 and 18. Since we have no letters written by her before 1796, the juvenilia are the purest guide to the things she thought about and interested herself in during her adolescence.

The earliest of the juvenilia (1787–90 or thereabouts; few of the pieces are actually dated) is largely literary satire, the later juvenilia (roughly 1791–93) largely social comedy. Between the two lies a fine line. What distinguishes

Reprinted with permission from *The South Atlantic Quarterly,* 81:3, Summer 1982. Copyright 1982 by Duke University Press.

both, perhaps, is an element of ridicule, or mockery, of contempt even, which emphasizes the faults and vices of others. There is a lot of hostility in satire. To write in the satirical vein demands a certain detachment, a moral distancing from the object of criticism. It demands a cold-blooded assessment of aesthetic and moral values. To this challenge Jane Austen, even as an adolescent, was equal. She seems by this time already to have acquired that detachment, that moral distance—that coldness. At the very least, by the time she was a teenager she knew a great deal about what, as a writer, she ought to avoid. As one critic has said, she "began by defining herself through what she rejected."[2]

What sort of teenager was this? It may seem appropriate to inquire what this early penchant for mockery and ridicule may tell us about Jane Austen's adolescent personality. Parody begins in antagonism; and for Jane Austen, says one critic, parody was always "the simplest reaction to feeling." Donald Greene has written: "One needs to remember that [Jane Austen] grew up in the great age of caricature, when Hogarth's engravings were on every wall, and Gillray, Rowlandson and the Cruikshanks were producing their twisted, grotesque distortions of the human frame." It is indicative that her only known attempt at sustained playwriting (*Sir Charles Grandison*) should be a burlesque. But Marvin Mudrick has argued persuasively in his famous study of Jane Austen that the parodic, the ironic mode was especially favored by her for reasons more purely personal—largely because such forms enabled her as a writer to remain "detached, from oneself as from others," and from "personal commitment." From the beginning, Mudrick says, Jane Austen was a spectator; she is always subject in her work to her own "hard compelled detachment," a "conscious shying from emotion" which took the form of ironic writing—parody and burlesque of others as a smoke screen to hide her own feelings. "Her temperament chose irony at once," Mudrick declares. "She maintained her distance by diverting herself and her audience with unengaged laughter."[3]

Certainly these earliest works are startling in their hostility and cold detachment; they betray many of the traits Mudrick insists are present in all of the fiction, and one could do worse than to examine them at least partially in this light. The juvenilia in many ways are precursors of what was to follow.

The juvenilia are precocious and sometimes amusing but they are by no means brilliant, as those who view them with passionate hindsight like to make out—nor are they more than intermittently entertaining. They are chiefly interesting in illuminating for us Jane Austen's first struggles to find a literary voice of her own. When she found it, it did indeed turn out to be the voice of irony—which she never abandoned. Irony, as we have seen, suggests detachment. It makes, as Mark Schorer has written, "no absolute commitments and can thus enjoy the advantage of many ambiguities of meaning and endless ambiguities of situation." It is, he concludes, "at the same time an evaluative mood, and, in a master, a sharp one." Schorer was speaking of Ford Madox

Ford here, but what he says about irony is apt enough for our purposes. For Jane Austen was already on her way to being a master—or rather a mistress—of the ironic mode. The conditions of her childhood must have favored the cultivation of an aesthetic objectivity, without which her later development in the creation of comic art would not have been possible.[4]

What conditions? Chiefly the vogue for literature of a peculiarly burlesqueable type; and the Austen family's passionate interest in literature of all kinds, and in responses to it. They encouraged the budding parodist to perform; she found plenty of material at hand. In the 1780s romances and sentimental novels, written largely by would-be inept imitators of Richardson, would have provided the most spacious targets for literary satire. Certainly, *The Loiterer,* in whose publication at Oxford James and Henry Austen, two of Jane's elder brothers, played the conspicuous roles, frequently warns against the excesses of sensibility in sentimental literature. It is the vein of *The Loiterer* in which the juvenilia commence.

Probably Brecht was right to say that tragedy deals with the suffering of mankind in a less serious way than comedy does. And let us remember, along with Christopher Fry, that so frequently comedy is an escape not from truth but from despair. Like comedy, satire is often deadly serious; equally often it is written out of despair (one thinks of Dickens). The satirist must be both serious and angry if he is to succeed in his chosen role of literary demolition expert. Such, certainly, is the role chosen by the young Jane Austen. Her wit is shrewdly applied in exposing the false values and absurd conventions of sentimental fiction and the general flaws of bad writing.[5]

One of the first tales in the initial quarto notebook of the juvenilia, *Volume the First,* is "Frederic & Elfrida." Though largely burlesque, it contains some revealing passages. Frederic and Elfrida, says the author, "loved with mutual sincerity but were ... determined not to transgress the rules of Propriety by owning their attachment." Very early (this piece probably was completed either in 1787 or 1788, when the writer was 12) Jane Austen seems to have been impressed by the advantages of holding back from the world's view one's feelings—of revealing as little as possible to others. Surely she accepted the idea current in the eighteenth century that excessive indulgence of emotion was bad—in literature, as in life. Of her heroine, the youthful author writes: "Elfrida ... had found her former acquaintances were growing too old & too ugly to be any longer agreable" (4, 11). Such heartlessness on Elfrida's part is of course condemned and laughed at; but the young writer's perception and understanding of heartlessness are impressive.

One of the most striking characters in *Volume the First* is the strong-minded part-time surgeon Lady Williams in "Jack & Alice," who "was too sensible, to fall in love with one so much her Junior" (which she does) and who in a memorable moment describes herself as "a sad example of the Miseries, in

general attendant on first Love" "Preserve yourself from first Love," she tells
the heroine, whose addiction to claret prevents her from paying much attention
to her mentor, "& you need not fear a second." Also noteworthy here is Charles
Adams, whom Jane Austen describes as "polite to all but partial to none . . .
lovely . . . lively but insensible." Pursued by an unwanted suitor, he lays a steel
bear trap for the lady, into which she obligingly steps. Later, considering a
proposal of marriage from an elderly duke, this same lady, her leg healed, is
tempted to accept it, on the ground "that one should receive obligations only
from those we despise." Instead, she is poisoned; the duke "mourned her loss
with unshaken constancy for the next fortnight" (15–16, 27–28). The "high-
spirited child" whom Brian Southam describes as the author of the juvenilia[6] is
also capable, it seems, of biting sarcasm.

In the next piece, "Edgar & Emma," the hero never appears, while the
heroine does little but cry—indeed, at the end she retires to her room in a fit of
weeping and, we are told, "continued in tears the remainder of her Life" (33).
"Henry and Eliza" traces the fortunes of its amoral, Moll Flanders-like heroine,
who, during an escape from prison, throws her two young sons out of the
window before her in order to allow herself to descend unencumbered.

In "The three Sisters," probably written in 1792 (when Jane Austen was
16: one must remember that she was born in *December* 1775), Mary Stanhope
is uncertain whether to go ahead with her marriage to Mr. Watts because, though
"He is extremely disagreable & I hate him more than any body else in the
world," and though "If I accept him I know I shall be miserable all the rest of
my Life," there is the equally important fact that "He has a large fortune & will
make great Settlements on me." Nor can she bear that he may offer himself to
one of her sisters should she refuse him, thus robbing her of her "triumph" over
them; she prefers "everlasting Misery" to such a humiliation. While Mr. Watts
cannot make Mary happy, reasons one of her sisters, "his Fortune, his Name,
his House, his Carriage will." Ultimately Mary decides that "if he will promise
to have the Carriage ordered as I like, I will have him." One of the sisters
concludes: she "is resolved to do *that* to prevent our supposed happiness which
she would not have done to ensure it in reality." For his part, Mr. Watts (like
Mr. Collins in *Pride and Prejudice*) doesn't especially care whom he marries,
so long as his wife is young and pretty. Mary finally accepts him with a reminder
of "the pinmoney" he has promised her, mumbling under her breath: "What's
the use of a great Jointure if Men live forever?" She goes on to make such
egregious material demands upon Mr. Watts as to make him demur. When he
tries one of the other sisters and is told she expects him to be good-tempered,
cheerful, considerate, and loving, he is equally shocked. After much protracted
negotiation Mary and Mr. Watts agree on settlements, and he leaves. "How I
do hate him!" says Mary, adding that she wishes never to see him again. There
are a number of ironic touches here characteristic of Jane Austen's later work—

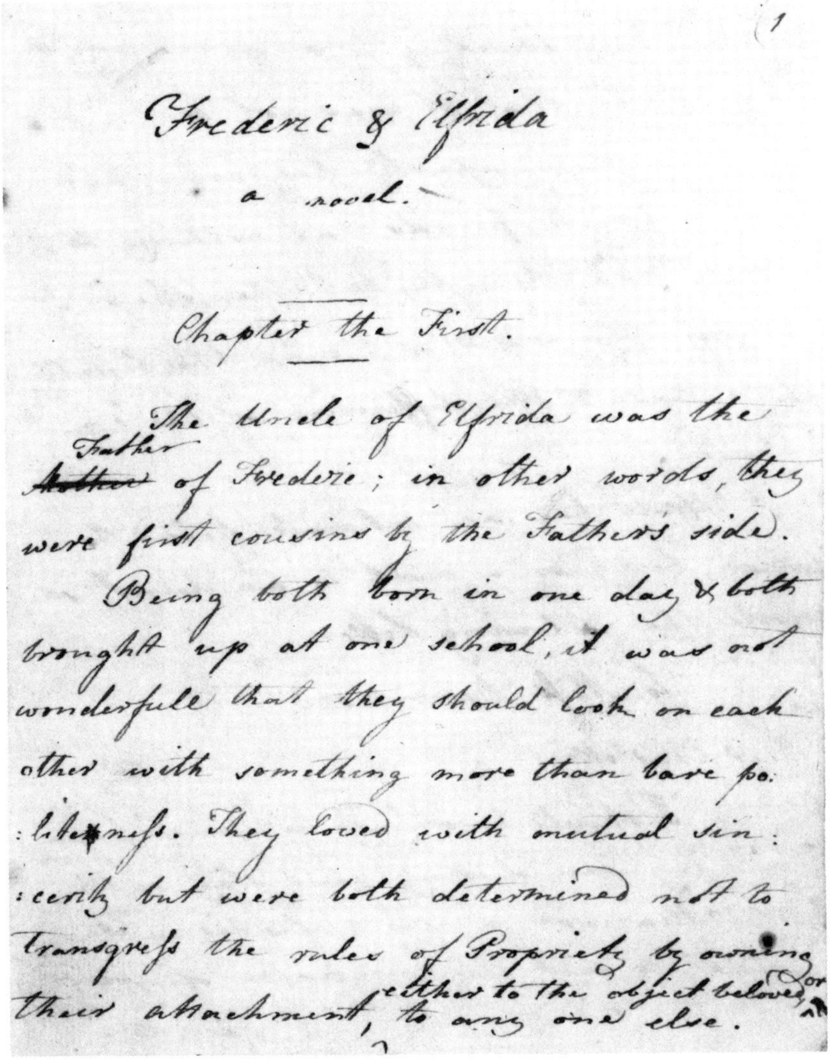

Frederic & Elfrida

a novel.

Chapter the First.

The Uncle of Elfrida was the ~~Mother~~ Father of Frederic; in other words, they were first cousins by the Fathers side.

Being both born in one day & both brought up at one school, it was not wonderfull that they should look on each other with something more than bare po:liteness. They loved with mutual sin:cerity but were both determined not to transgress the rules of Propriety by owning their attachment, either to the object beloved, or to any one else.

Figure 2. First Manuscript Page of "Chapter the First," in "Frederic & Elfrida: a novel"
(Volume the First *MS; Courtesy The Bodleian Library, MS Don.e.7*)

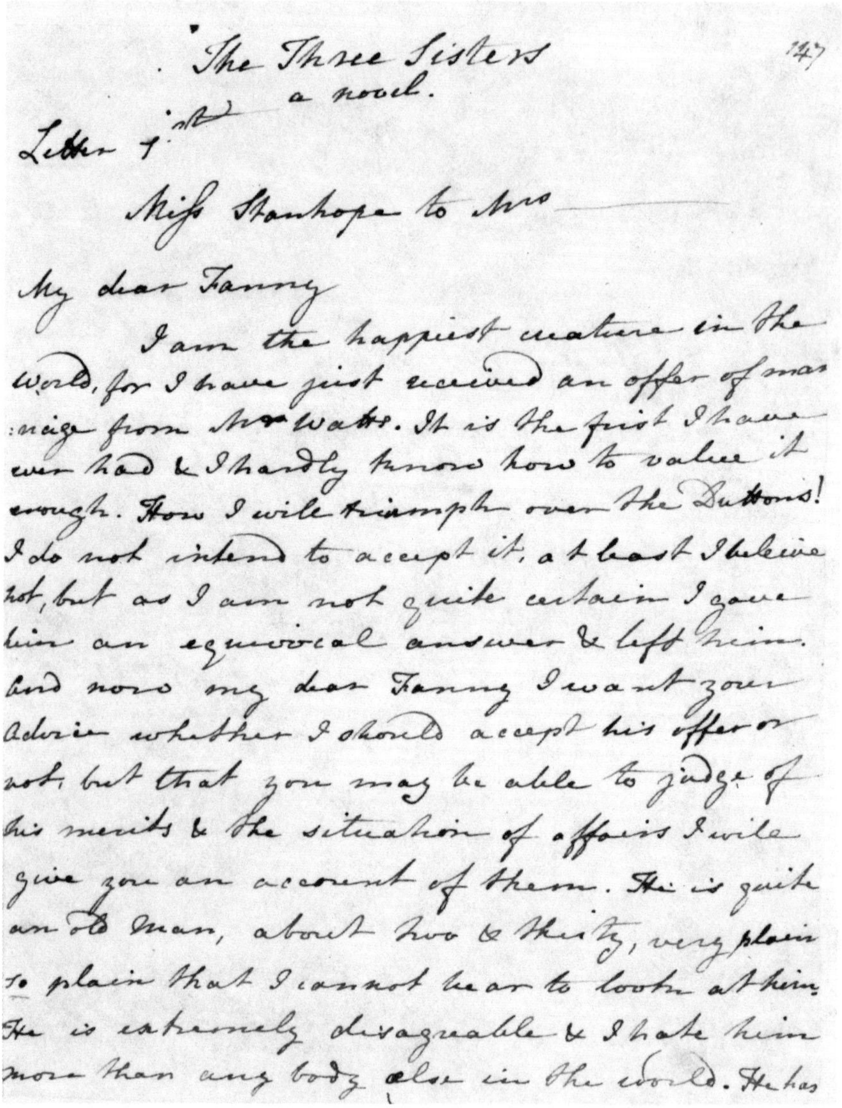

The Three Sisters
a novel.

Letter 1st

Miss Stanhope to Mrs. _____

My dear Fanny

I am the happiest creature in the World, for I have just received an offer of marriage from Mr Watts. It is the first I have ever had & I hardly know how to value it enough. How I will triumph over the Duttons! I do not intend to accept it, at least I believe not, but as I am not quite certain I gave him an equivocal answer & left him. And now my dear Fanny I want your advice whether I should accept his offer or not, but that you may be able to judge of his merits & the situation of affairs I will give you an account of them. He is quite an old Man, about two & thirty, very plain so plain that I cannot bear to look at him. He is extremely disagreable & I hate him more than any body else in the world. He has

Figure 3.   First Manuscript Page of "Letter 1st: Miss Stanhope to Mrs. . . . ," in "The three Sisters: a novel" (Volume the First *MS; Courtesy The Bodleian Library, MS Don.e.7*)

perhaps chief among them Mary's remark, upon being asked by a neighbor if she likes Mr. Watts, that "when there is so much Love on one side there is no occasion for it on the other" (58–59, 61, 63, 67, 69). "The three Sisters" is clever—and very cynical. The youthful author was aware early of the mercenary nature of many marriages, though she heartily makes fun of them here, and of the roles vanity, desire for position, fear of being an old maid, and the wish to shine at others' expense may all play when decisions of this sort are taken.[7] The tale also shows her very much aware of sibling rivalry. It is after all virtually impossible for siblings not to compete in some way; it is more than likely that this played a part in the formation of Jane Austen's personality. In *Pride and Prejudice, Northanger Abbey,* and *Mansfield Park* there are overt references to sibling rivalry in romantic matters; in *Sense and Sensibility* sibling rivalry is not actually mentioned—but there is plenty of it, especially between the Steele sisters. Jane Austen's sister Cassandra was two years older than she.

Volume the Second, the second quarto notebook of juvenilia, opens with "Love and Freindship" (dated June 1790), an epistolary "novel" of just under 10,000 words. This is one of the most important items among Jane Austen's earliest writings. Primarily it is a spoof of the novel of sensibility and its characteristically improbable romantic elements. The word "sensibility" is repeated again and again throughout the tale. Most of the characters are obsessed by their own sensibilities; being so self-absorbed, they do little but exhibit their sensibilities to others.

"Love and Freindship" is about emotional self-indulgence. At its center are two heroines who behave in such a way as to leave us in little doubt about the focus of Jane Austen's satire: "She was all Sensibility and Feeling. We flew into each others arms and after having exchanged vows of mutual Freindship for the rest of our Lives, instantly unfolded to each other the most inward secrets of our Hearts—." At a crisis the two ladies faint alternately upon a sofa—and they continue to faint whenever an "expected . . . blow to our Gentle Sensibility" is sustained. One of the heroines faints once too often, however, and dies as a result of a chill caught while lying on damp ground. She admonishes the other with her last breath(s) to "beware of fainting-fits. . . . Though at the time they may be refreshing and Agreable yet beleive me they will in the end, if too often repeated & at improper seasons, prove destructive to your Constitution. . . . One fatal swoon has cost me my Life. . . . Beware of swoons Dear Laura." Perhaps the single funniest moment occurs when the hero, covered with blood and dirt and speaking from the remains of a carriage that has been wrecked in the course of an arduous journey, remarks languidly to the hysterical heroine: "I fear I have been overturned" (85, 89, 102, 99). Everything that happens in the tale happens because someone possesses either too much or too little "Sensibility." Jane Austen is laughing here at sentimental behavior that, taken to an excess of self-indulgence, has become a form of affectation. She is also, incidentally, showing what happens when the epistolary novel falls into the wrong hands—those of the sentimental romancers, who have learned nothing from her favorite Richardson.[8] "Love and Freindship" is an amusing, though not very subtle, burlesque of the sentimental novel—written, astonishingly, when Jane Austen was just 14.

"Lesley Castle," the next item in *Volume the Second*, at 12,000 words is slightly longer than "Love and Freindship." It was written when Jane Austen was 16. Like "Love and Freindship," it is an epistolary "novel." "Lesley Castle" is interesting chiefly in demonstrating the advancing sophistication of Jane Austen's prose style—and her steady progress toward the form of the novel. It is in the old vein of burlesque: the target is again excessive sensibility. But one sees here the beginnings of the future novelist's dissatisfaction with mere parody as a personal style.

"The History of England from the reign of Henry the 4th to the death of Charles the 1st," written in 1791 (between "Love and Freindship" and "Lesley Castle") "by a partial, prejudiced, & ignorant Historian," so the author confesses, is genuinely witty. It attacks partisan, romanticized, trivialized, popularized history writing, seeing it as false to reality as the sentimental novel. A comic adaptation of Goldsmith's *History of England* (1764) and subsequent *Abridgement* (1774), it eschews dates and leaves out almost all the facts (as Goldsmith did); gives an enlightened (i.e., Yorkist) account of the fifteenth century; quite rightly identifies Henry VII as a "Monster of Iniquity and Avarice" and "as great a Villain as ever lived"; attacks Elizabeth I with venom; and lavishly praises the Stuarts, especially Mary Queen of Scots (Goldsmith was anti-Stuart). The account of the civil wars is of course a Royalist one ("Never certainly," says the author of this "History," "were there before so many detestable Characters at one time in England as in this period. . . . Never were amiable Men so scarce"). We must not forget that the Leighs, Jane Austen's mother's family, gave shelter to Charles I at Stoneleigh Abbey; loyalty to the Stuarts ran in the family. Among other things, the "History" shows us that at 15 many of Jane Austen's historical and political loyalties, like her attitudes toward fiction, were firmly set (140, 141, 148).[9]

Next in *Volume the Second* comes "A Collection of Letters" (1791). The second of these is remarkable chiefly for anticipating some of the names used later in *Sense and Sensibility:* there is a family named Dashwood, a hero named Edward, a jilt named Willoughby—and a colonel. In the third letter appears Lady Greville, a brutal snob who, in a memorable scene, rudely abuses a younger woman of humbler status while leaning out of a carriage—readers of *Pride and Prejudice* will inevitably be reminded of Lady Catherine de Bourgh. The fifth letter may suggest *Persuasion* in having at its center a family named Musgrove, but it is memorable primarily for its loutish hero and heroine, both of whom constantly pray for the death of her relations so they may have an income to marry on.

In the group of fragments called "Scraps," written mostly in 1793, there appear two sisters two years apart in age—roughly the distance in age, remember, between Jane Austen and her sister Cassandra. The younger of the two is described, in a piece called "The Female Philosopher," in a way that may encourage us to see her as a laughingly complacent self-portrait.

> Charlotte who is just Sixteen is shorter than her Sister, and though her figure cannot boast the easy dignity of Julia's, yet it has a pleasing plumpness which is in a different way as estimable. She is fair & her face is expressive sometimes of softness the most bewitching, and at others of Vivacity the most striking. She appears to have infinite wit and a good humour unalterable; her conversation . . . was replete with humorous Sallies, Bonmots and repartees. (171)

Three or four additional scraps bring "Scraps" to a conclusion—among them a playlet called "The First Act of a Comedy," which contains these deathless lines:

> I am going to have my dinner
> After which I shan't be thinner. (174).

Of "Evelyn" comparatively little need be said. It continues the attack on sentimental fiction; almost all of the characters are motivated exclusively by an oversupply or undersupply, as the case may be, of sensibility. Example: the owner of a gloomy Gothic fortress who refused to give his consent to the marriage of his recently dead son is harangued by the tale's hysterical hero, who wishes to know if the father isn't sorry now that he withheld that consent. The father isn't; the situation is made ludicrous by the confrontation between excessive and nonexistent "sensibility." As several critics have pointed out, a chief thrust of "Evelyn" is its attack on misplaced or distorted benevolence, benevolence uncontrolled by judgment[10]—a sort of subgenre under the heading of excessive sensibility. It is indicative that already, at 16, Jane Austen preferred hardness to softness, sense to sensibility.

The story is also significant in that it contains some of her earliest and most exact landscape description—though part of this undoubtedly is a burlesque of methods of describing landscape in fiction then current—and in suggesting the young writer's amusement with some early Gothic fashions. Gothic fiction had not yet, in the early 1790s, reached its full flower; in the next few years, in the works of Horace Walpole, Clara Reeve, Sophia Lee, Ann Radcliffe, and others, it was to do so.[11]

"Catharine," undoubtedly written both under and against the influence of such novels by Fanny Burney as *Evelina* (1778) and *Cecilia* (1782), is the first of Jane Austen's longer tales to eschew the epistolary form. A little more than 15,000 words of third-person narrative uninterrupted by chapter divisions, "Catharine," though at times written awkwardly, shows the youthful novelist coming closest, among all the pieces of the juvenilia, to the form she ultimately found in her major works. It is, at last, less literary criticism than genuine fiction. "Catharine" bids a temporary farewell to epistolary fiction (Jane Austen was to use the form again a few years later in *Lady Susan*); indeed, Mrs. Percival, Catharine's aunt and guardian, responds to Mrs. Stanley's pronouncement that "nothing forms the taste more than sensible & Elegant Letters" by replying that "a correspondence between Girls [is] productive of no good, and [is] the frequent origin of imprudence & Error by the effect of pernicious advice and bad Example. She . . . had lived fifty Years in the world without having ever had a correspondent, and did not find herself at all the less respectable for it—." That Jane Austen takes Mrs. Percival's side in this argument is made clear when the brainless Camilla Stanley remarks that correspondence "is the greatest delight of my life, and you cannot think how much . . . Letters have formed my taste," which is nonexistent.

But "Catharine" is interesting chiefly for the autobiographical echoes one hears in it, and for the ways in which it anticipates some future works by Jane Austen. Catharine's bosom companions, the Wynne sisters, bear some resemblance to the Lloyd and Lefroy girls, neighbors of the Austens at Steventon. The eldest of them goes off to Bengal to marry under circumstances which obviously point to the story of Jane Austen's aunt, her father's half-sister Philadelphia Hancock. And Catharine shares some characteristics of the young authoress herself. She is described as "a great reader"; "She had always [a book] about her." And: "The expectation of a Ball was indeed very agreable intelligence to [her], who [was] fond of Dancing and seldom able to enjoy it. . . . The very few Times that [she] had ever enjoyed the Amusement of Dancing was an excuse for *her* impatience, and an apology for the Idleness it occasioned to a Mind naturally very Active." Thus the 16-year-old country girl defends her passion for one of the pleasures of life to which she always looked forward.

Other things in Catharine's makeup may suggest Jane Austen at 16. Catharine is said to have "too much good Sense to be proud of her family, and too much good Nature to live at variance with anyone"; and to know that "Youth and Beauty . . . is but a poor substitute for real worth & Merit . . . there is certainly nothing like Virtue for making us what we ought to be, and as to a young Man's being young & handsome . . . is nothing at all . . . for he had much better be respectable." Catharine is nonetheless "in love with every handsome Man I see." By the end of the story she has learned "not to think Every Body is in love with me" and to absorb such truths as this one: "a young Man would [not] be seriously attached in the course of four & twenty hours, to a Girl who has nothing to recommend her but a good pair of eyes!" Jane Austen, remember, was 16. Of course some self-scrutiny is going on here. Among other things the young writer is looking at her own sentimental excesses and laughing at them. She may also be recalling, more ruefully, her dowerlessness.

There is also a bitter personal statement in "Catharine" about the quality of education many women of the time were likely to have. Camilla Stanley's "education" is described in some detail, the author concluding that the last 12 years of Camilla's life "had been dedicated to the acquirement of Accomplishments which were now to be displayed and in a few Years entirely neglected. . . . [T]hose Years which ought to have been spent in the attainment of useful knowledge and Mental Improvement, had been all bestowed in learning Drawing, Italian, and Music . . . and she now united to these Accomplishments, an Understanding unimproved by reading and a Mind totally devoid of Taste or Judgement." Jane Austen's novels often attack this method of "educating" women and heap scorn upon the "accomplishments" women were forced to substitute for genuine learning.

Some other themes of the later works are anticipated here, albeit vaguely. Like Elizabeth Bennet, Catharine tends to store up prejudices about people based on their personal appearance. Edward Stanley's arrogance and vanity—he is described as having "a vivacity of temper seldom subdued, & a contempt of censure not to be overcome, [and] possessed an opinion of his own Consequence, & a perserverance in his own schemes which were not to be damped by the conduct of others"—remind one of Darcy's. Catharine "[addressing] him with so much familiarity on so short an acquaintance, could not forbear indulging the natural Unreserve & Vivacity of her own Disposition, in speaking to him, as he spoke to her." This sounds like a warm-up for some of the exchanges between the hero and heroine of *Pride and Prejudice*. There are echoes too of *Sense and Sensibility* in the predicament of the Wynnes, who through a series of calamitous deaths "had been reduced to a state of absolute dependence on some relations, who though very opulent and very nearly connected with them, had with difficulty been prevailed on to contribute anything towards their Support"; and of Frank Churchill (in *Emma*) in Edward Stanley's peculiar combination of gallantry toward women and egregious self-absorption (210–11, 198, 207–8, 226, 227–28, 222, 236, 198, 221, 216, and 194).

Catharine herself is a significant departure from the usual type of heroine found in the juvenilia—a woman of spirit and intelligence, with a touch of irreverence, very much in Jane Austen's distinctive tradition, to be continued in the heroines of *Pride and Prejudice* and *Sense and Sensibility*. Lascelles has suggested that the heroine of "Catharine" more nearly resembles her namesake in *Northanger Abbey*.[12] In any case, it is clear that in "Catharine" Jane Austen was edging towards the major works she would begin to write during the latter half of the 1790s.

While the date of the composition of *Lady Susan* is disputed, it most likely belongs to the years 1793–94 and should thus be considered as belonging to the period of the late juvenilia, though not nominally a part of them.[13] *Lady Susan* is an epistolary "novel" of a little under 25,000 words. Jane Austen was about 18 when she wrote it.

The heroine of *Lady Susan* is one of Jane Austen's most disagreeable, unpleasant creations. Vain, greedy, heartless, cynical, and dishonest, she dominates this dark story. Perhaps the most striking thing about the tale is the 18-year-old Jane Austen's insight into the lower depths of the human character. Here is a mother who hates her own daughter; who declares that stubborn people must be "tricked" into doing what they don't want to do; whose considered opinion it is that "where there is a disposition to dislike a motive will never be wanting"; who feels drawn only to those "easily imposed on"; who looks "with a degree of contempt on the inquisitive & doubting Fancies of that Heart which seems always debating on the reasonableness of it's Emotions"; who believes that "Jealousy" is the best "support of Love" and indeed that "There is something agreable in feelings so easily worked on"; whose chief efforts throughout the story are devoted to "making a whole family miserable"; and yet who complacently remarks that she "never was more at ease, or better satisfied with myself & everything about me, than at the present hour." Somehow, for all her bad-tempered guile, Lady Susan remains a convincing character—a tremendous accomplishment for a young author.

Where did Jane Austen acquire the sort of insight and understanding requisite to draw such a character and make us believe in her? We know from her letters that she and her mother were not always congenial together—that the mother may have preferred the novelist's elder sister to Jane herself and that the younger daughter was often critical of the mother—but this alone would not explain the character of Lady Susan, whose vulgarity and cruelty Mrs. Austen, from all contemporary accounts, certainly could not match. It has also been suggested that there is something of Jane's cousin Eliza de Feuillide in Lady Susan (as in Mary Crawford in *Mansfield Park*), but the novelist knows so much about the sort of personality described here that one must conclude that some of that knowledge was instinctive rather than merely contextual—intrinsic rather than extrinsic. One notes that almost all of the characters are very catty. Every letter in the series brims with nasty cracks about others—cracks of the sort that may remind us of Jane Austen's own letters, especially the early ones. In *Lady Susan* almost everyone seems to be wishing inconvenience, pain, torment, and death upon everyone else; and within the confiding parameters of letters, at least, there is little dissembling about true feelings. "Facts are such horrid things!" Lady Susan's only friend reports to her, "& there is no defying Destiny."

The other characters in *Lady Susan*, though some of them are likeable, concern themselves generally, like most of the cast of *Sense and Sensibility* (the first draft of which was written in 1795, soon after *Lady Susan*), with questions of money, settlements, inheritances, entailments, and speculations on the length of life of fathers, uncles, and guardians, as if the world revolved around the issues of possession and ownership of land and houses. This world does so revolve; clearly it is a reflection of how the adolescent novelist saw her own world. As Lady Susan herself so candidly puts it, "where possessions are so extensive . . . the wish of increasing them . . . is too common to excite surprise or resentment." *Lady Susan* also provides some lessons in behavior. "Where Pride & Stupidity unite, there can be no dissimulation worthy notice," declares the story's hero. "Consideration & Esteem as surely follow command of Language, as Admiration waits on Beauty," declares the antiheroine—quite clearly, for once, in the novelist's (hopeful) voice. And: "Artlessness will never do in Love matters." At the end of the tale Jane Austen steps in in her own voice, as she would do so often in her novels, to resolve all things unresolved, tie up loose threads, and provide a catalogue of last things. "This Correspondence," she remarks, obviously having grown tired of the novel in letters, "could not, to the great detriment of the Post office Revenue, be continued longer," and so it abruptly terminates with a third-person account of the ultimate fate of everyone. There is some humor in the last few pages—and a good deal of coldhearted summary, in the mode of the endings of most of the novels. Lady Susan, we are told, finally forgets altogether the existence of her own daughter; in her next marriage "She had nothing against her, but her Husband, & her Conscience" (249, 250, 248, 269, 274, 293, 300, 303, 307, 248, 268, 274, 311, 313). It is an astonishing, frightening performance for an 18-year-old country girl—who somehow, within the confines of the Rectory at Steventon, acquired vision into the heart of darkness within man (or, more properly, woman) and learned to articulate her vision of that darkness with unerring conviction. Clearly the Rectory at Steventon was no Garden of Eden: indeed, the monsters may have seemed, to the young writer, always on the verge of taking it over. Reginald Farrer regarded *Lady Susan* very much as of a piece with the major writings—as indeed simply the first of them: "the cold unpleasantness of *Lady Susan* is but the youthful exaggeration of that irreconcilable judgment which, harshly evident in the first book, is the essential strength of all the later ones."[14]

Lady Susan represents an advance in some ways. We see the protagonist not through her own letters only but also through the eyes (and letters) of others, which gives us what amounts to the fullest human portrait Jane Austen had yet attempted. In Lady Susan there is no progress toward self-knowledge, as there would be in some of the later heroines. Brilliance without sense, breeding without principle, were for Jane Austen not enough: in this there is a foreshadowing of the mature author's perspective. Indeed, the psychological richness of *Lady Susan* anticipates much of what was to follow.

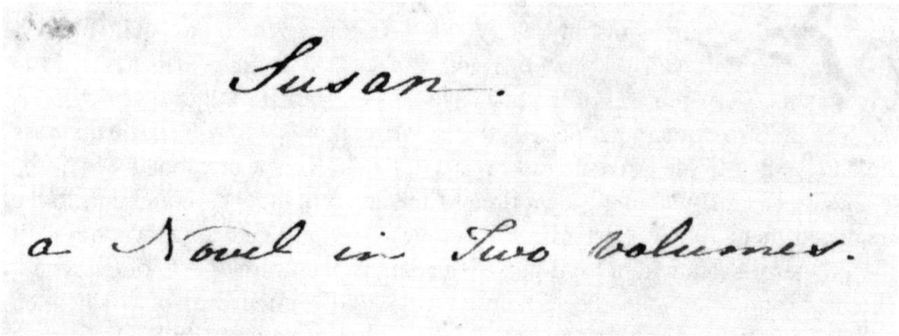

Susan.

a Novel in Two volumes.

Figure 4. The Sole Remains of the Original Manuscript of _Northanger Abbey_

This fragment is also, apart from the manuscript pages of the cancelled chapter from _Persuasion,_ the only surviving portion from the six major novels. The manuscript of "Susan" was sold to Crosby, a publisher, in 1803. Austen tried to repurchase it, unsuccessfully, in 1809. A few years later she referred to it as "Catherine," another "Susan" having appeared in the interim. It was renamed _Northanger Abbey_ by either Henry or Cassandra, and published posthumously in 1818.

("Susan, A Novel in Two volumes"; Courtesy Pierpont Morgan Library)

This brings us to the end of the juvenilia. (In all likelihood Jane Austen began to write her play *Sir Charles Grandison* in 1791 or 1792, but she worked on it only desultorily for a number of years and did not complete it until 1800.)[15] Despite failures of other sorts, one can say of the juvenilia as a whole that they are lucidly written: virtually everything Jane Austen wrote is dazzlingly lucid. The juvenilia are of course by no means uniform in quality or success. And most of them are of a mixed nature—lighthearted and somber, full of laughter and serious satire both. Inevitably this was a reflection of the writer, who must have been a disconcerting teenager.

Jane Austen learned early to laugh at her fellow men and women—a sign of detachment as well as humor. Indeed, the darker hues of this early work, its inherent cynicism, are often glossed over; the vision is sharp, sometimes unforgiving, often mocking. Clearly it is a mistake to regard the juvenilia as being separated, both by chronology and subject matter, from the maturer productions. We know that the first versions of what were to become *Pride and Prejudice, Sense and Sensibility,* and *Northanger Abbey* were written, all of them, in the middle and late 1790s. The juvenilia and the later work may equally be seen as sharing a community of theme and vision.

Catharine muses: "Sorrows are lightened by Communication." Jane Austen's youthful communications make it plain that she had other things on her mind besides comedy. As Virginia Woolf surmises, Jane Austen at 15 "had few illusions about other people and none about herself." The second-rate writings of first-rate writers, Mrs. Woolf concludes, are often most revealing (212).[16]

Notes

1. Douglas Bush, *Jane Austen,* New York, 1975, p. 18; and F.B. Pinion, *A Jane Austen Companion,* London, 1973, p. 9. For a good general discussion of the juvenilia, see Brian Southam, *Jane Austen's Literary Manuscripts: A Study of the Novelist's Development through the Surviving Papers,* Oxford, 1964, chapter 1 (hereafter cited as Southam).

2. Julia Prewitt Brown, *Jane Austen's Novels: Social Change and Literary Form,* Cambridge, Mass., 1979, p. 50.

3. On Jane Austen's adolescecent personality, the following are quoted in the text: George Levine, "Translating the Monstrous: *Northanger Abbey,*" *Nineteenth-Century Fiction* 30 (Dec. 1975), 337; Donald Greene, "Jane Austen's Monsters," *Jane Austen: Bicentenary Essays,* ed. John Halperin, Cambridge, England, 1975, p. 276; and Robert M. Polhemus, *Comic Faith: The Great Tradition from Austen to Joyce,* Chicago, 1980, p. 27. The several quotations from Mudrick are taken from Marvin Mudrick, *Jane Austen: Irony as Defense and Discovery,* Princeton, 1952, pp. 57, 62, 91, 36, 1, and 3, respectively. Jane Austen's *Sir Charles Grandison* is discussed by David Cecil in his foreword (p. x) to *Jane Austen's 'Sir Charles Grandison,'* ed. Brian Southam, Oxford, 1980.

4. Mark Schorer, "An Interpretation" of *The Good Soldier,* originally published in the *Princeton University Library Chronicle* in April 1948 and reprinted since in *Horizon* in August 1949 and

again as an introduction to the Vintage paperback edition of Ford's novel, New York, p. xiii. On Jane Austen's childhood, see Southam, p. 30.

5. Southam, p. 21.

6. Ibid.

7. Joan Rees, *Jane Austen: Woman and Writer,* New York, 1976, p. 36.

8. Southam, p. 26.

9. See also Southam's commentary, p. 29.

10. A. Walton Litz, *Jane Austen: A Study of Her Artistic Development,* New York, 1965, pp. 31–36, *passim,* but especially p. 34; and Rees, p. 40.

11. Southam, pp. 36–38.

12. Southam, p. 41; and Mary Lascelles's article on the subject in the *Review of English Studies* 3 (1952), 184.

13. Southam, chapter 3.

14. Reginald Farrer, "Jane Austen," *Quarterly Review* 228 (July 1917), 15.

15. The chronology I give for Jane Austen's *Sir Charles Grandison* is that suggested to me privately by Brian Southam. See also Southam's introduction to *Jane Austen's Sir Charles Grandison.*

16. Virginia Woolf is quoted from "Jane Austen at Sixty" (a review of Chapman's edition of the works), originally published in *Nation* (15 Dec. 1923), 433, and reprinted as "Jane Austen" in *The Common Reader,* New York, 1925.

"The Kingdom at Sixes and Sevens": Politics and the Juvenilia

Claudia L. Johnson

It is time to redress a long-standing wrong: to grant Jane Austen's early sketches more attention than they typically receive. In most studies, the juvenilia are passed over very quickly, and this despite the outstanding counterexamples set by critics such as B.C. Southam, Gilbert and Gubar, and A.W. Litz.[1] It is not mere attention that Austen's earliest writings have lacked, but rather a fundamental respect. Even granting how hard it is to treat the productions of children seriously, Austen's juvenilia are treated with striking condescension: their talent is marked, enjoyed, and finally disparaged. A tendency to damn the juvenilia with faint praise has been around ever since their existence was first divulged to the public in the *Memoir* of 1870, when they were noted for their "slight and flimsy texture" and their "clever nonsense." This deprecatory tradition continues to this day. Brooking no opposition, one recent critic has flatly stated, "The Juvenilia are precocious and sometimes amusing but they are by no means brilliant, as those who view them with passionate hindsight like to make out— nor are they more than intermittently entertaining."[2]

Austenians will recognize the familiar epithet "precocious," a term which merits some scrutiny. In the new *Jane Austen Companion*, B.C. Southam expresses discomfort with the word. Austen, he writes, was not a "precocious genius" but a "genius" working with the encouragement and culture of a literate and fun-loving family.[3] Although Southam never explains his distinction, it would appear that the term diminishes Austen in a way he does not approve. And nor do I, for it is freighted with implications of glibness. Tributes to "precocity" and "cleverness" conceal insults that touch Austen's stature as an artist. Replicating so much *apparently* admiring Austenian commentary, they take away with one hand what they offer with the other, and dwell as much on what Austen does not do as on what she does: praising her style, but stressing her "limitations"; commending her elegance, but insisting upon her lack of profundity.

Austenian scholars agree that Austen initiated her career by exploring and undermining the conventions governing fiction popular during her youth. One reason we have regarded Austen's juvenile productions superficial is, I think, that we ourselves have sometimes had rather superficial notions about conventions in the first place, tending to understand them as the staple ingredients of plot, character, or narration with which bad novelists concoct implausible stories with little or no bearing on "real life." But Austen herself never assails the silliness of conventions she unmasks, much less their staleness. She aims instead at their sway. My argument thus opposes one made most recently by George Steiner in *After Babel:* "The world of an Austen novel," he writes, "is radically linguistic: all reality is 'encoded' in a distinctive idiom." But that idiom, as Steiner goes on to insist, has no relation to anything beyond the "grammar" and "vocabulary" contained within her fiction: "Entire spheres of human existence—political, social, erotic, subconscious—are absent. At the height of political and industrial revolution in a decade of formidable philosophic activity, Miss Austen composes novels almost extraterritorial to history."[4]

Steiner's is perhaps the most authoritative version to date of a very old argument about Austen's essentially apolitical character. Thanks to recent scholarship, few readers today are so receptive as formerly to such contentions.[5] But because the "radically linguistic" character of juvenilia in particular is so conspicuous, many still tend to see them as "extraterritorial" to history and politics. But, as I shall argue, it is precisely through the "radically linguistic" qualities of the juvenilia that we can trace their social and political character. The genius of the juvenilia consists in their dazzling formal self-consciousness, a self-consciousness at once playful and deep. Sensitive to far-reaching and often very subtle implications, the juvenilia are devoted almost exclusively to exploring and exposing the agendas of fictional conventions, some of which are manifestly and some implicitly political. In Austen's hands, various aspects of literary discourse—genres, narrative styles and devices, plot structure, stock figures and phrases, and the like—are shown at their least innocent. By such techniques as reversal, literalization, protraction, condensation, and exaggeration, Austen disrupts the sway of conventions and wrests them from their natural-seeming status, precisely so that we can see them anew as *un*inevitable and artificial. Take "Jack & Alice," for example, where the temporal instability of the opening sentence calls attention to what George Eliot more soberly called "the make believe of a beginning": "Mr. Johnson was once upon a time about 53; in a twelvemonth afterwards he was 54, which so much delighted him that he was determined to celebrate his next Birthday by giving a Masquerade to his children & Freinds" (12). Like all parody, Austen's sentence is hyperconventional and anticonventional at one and the same time, unfolding codes which first seem unitary and uncomplicated only then to swerve blithely into baffling incoherence. Austen begins with the obtrusively predictable "once upon a time," the purpose of which is to situate us in the narrative present. Much to our bewilderment, however, by mid-sentence we are transported with no discernible purpose not one but two years after—or is it before?—the "beginning." Only after reading the sentence several times will we be able to orient ourselves temporally, and even then the process of reexamination will turn up doubts generated by the initial phrase *"about* 53" which we did not notice when reading the passage through for the first time, doubts which threaten the import of the entire sentence. What could this "about 53" possibly mean? Fifty-three, give or take a few years? If so, Mr. Johnson may well still be "about 53" two years later, when he decides to have a party. By concluding her sentence with an allusion to masquerade, among the most hackneyed motifs in eighteenth-century fiction, Austen resumes the placid conventionality with which she began, only now that conventionality has been undermined.

I dwell on this passage, even though it lacks direct political import, because it exemplifies an important feature of Austen's writing in general. Her practice here, and throughout the juvenilia, prohibits us from reading unthinkingly—as Catherine Morland later will—for her style persistently makes itself subject to doubt and invites skeptical reexamination. When such a style opens onto more evidently political material, the results can be quite subversive, for Austen's method enables and invites us to assess the interests which fictional conventions serve. Take, for instance, the following deceptively breezy opener to "Henry and Eliza: a novel," probably written between 1787 and 1790: "As Sir George and Lady Harcourt were superintending the Labours of their Haymakers, rewarding the industry of some by smiles of approbation, & punishing the idleness of others, by a cudgel, they perceived lying closely concealed beneath the thick foliage of a Haycock, a beautifull Girl not more than 3 months old" (33). Who are Sir George and Lady Harcourt? As their archetypical names attest, they are England's gentry Everyman-and-wife—not just any stock characters, but venerable figures in a national mythology, figures who had already been idealized in novels by Fielding and Richardson well before the very young Austen took up her pen. Only a few years later, during the 1790s, these same figures would be celebrated by Burke and his followers as the linchpins of moral and political stability: personally presiding over home and neighborhood, the dutiful holders of country estates (so the argument runs) develop those precious moral affections of gratitude towards superiors and solicitude for inferiors on which the well-being, indeed the survival, of England depends.

Sir George Harcourt and his lady are, then, motifs which emerge from a specific political context, and to use them straight is to perpetuate that context. But Austen does not use them straight, neither here, nor much later in *Mansfield*

Park, where the country estate ethos is so often discussed. To be sure, if we stopped with the first clause, everything appears to be running along as usual: "As Sir George and Lady Harcourt were superintending the Labours of their Haymakers. . . . " Such "superintendence" is precisely what gentlemen farmers should engage in, and Sir George and his lady appear even more exemplary when, in the next phrase, we learn that they "reward" the most industrious with "smiles of approbation." In coming years, such smiles would be commended for nurturing *personal* loyalties that ensured the continued cohesion of a hierarchical social structure in England. Conversely, the adherence to *abstract,* purely *rational* principles of justice and equality, in the minds of conservative English onlookers, promoted the downfall of France.

But by mid-sentence, the next phrase, inconspicuously tucked between commas, will take us by surprise: Sir George and his lady "punish the idleness of others," neither by stern glances, nor even by firm and authoritative admonishment, but rather "by a cudgel." Conventionally speaking, of course, this is not supposed to happen, and therein lies the brilliance of Austen's joke. Who would dare imagine Knightley, Darcy, or Mr. Bennet beating their negligent farmers? The shock here derives not from simple incongruity—i.e., a belief that such people do not do such things. It derives rather from an unexpected disclosure—i.e., a discovery that such people may indeed beat their farmers, but that certain novelistic forms do not permit us to imagine, much less to represent, realities of this sort. Austen's practice throughout the juvenilia is to seek out and bring to light the agendas that inherited forms conceal by violating those forms. In "Jack & Alice" Austen shows what pastoral conventions exclude when she mentions "her Ladyship's pigstye" and "Charles Adams' horsepond" (18) in conjunction with "a walk through a Citron Grove" (18). In "Love and Freindship," she unmasks crimes the rhetoric of sentimental fiction would cover up when she describes how a dashing hero "gracefully purloined" a "considerable sum of money" from his "Unworthy father's Escritoire" (88). And, returning once again to "Henry and Eliza," she forces upon our notice certain bodily realities which take etherealized characters in sentimental fiction completely by surprise: Eliza "began to find herself rather hungry, & had reason to think, by their biting off two of her fingers, that her Children were much in the same situation" (37).

The central enterprise of the juvenilia as I have presented it, then, is demystification: making customary forms subject to doubt by flaunting their conventionality. "Henry and Eliza" of course, like most of the juvenilia, was written before any actual unrest in England as a result of the events in France. I make no claims just yet about direct political commentary by Austen, who was after all as young as 11 when the earliest of these sketches were drafted. What I do claim is, first, an awareness of what we may call the ideological dimension of conventional figures, figures which would soon become more

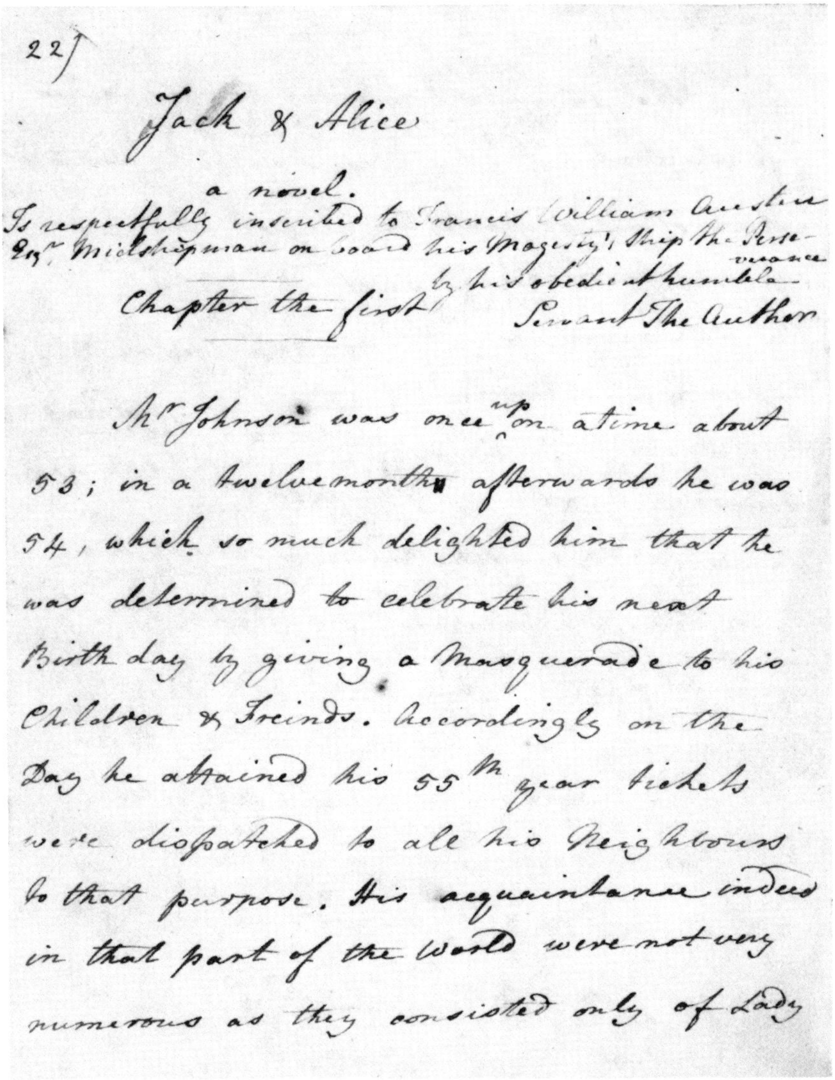

22

Jack & Alice

a novel.

Is respectfully inscribed to Francis William Austen
Esq.r Midshipman on board his Majesty's ship the Perse-
verance
by his obedient humble
Chapter the first
Servant The Author

Mr Johnson was once up on a time about
53; in a twelvemonth afterwards he was
54, which so much delighted him that he
was determined to celebrate his next
Birth day by giving a Masquerade to his
Children & Freinds. Accordingly on the
Day he attained his 55.th year tickets
were dispatched to all his Neighbours
to that purpose. His acquaintance indeed
in that part of the World were not very
numerous as they consisted only of Lady

Figure 5. First Manuscript Page of "Chapter the first," Including the
Dedication to Francis William Austen, from "Jack & Alice: a
novel"
(Volume the First *MS; Courtesy The Bodleian Library, MS Don.e.7*)

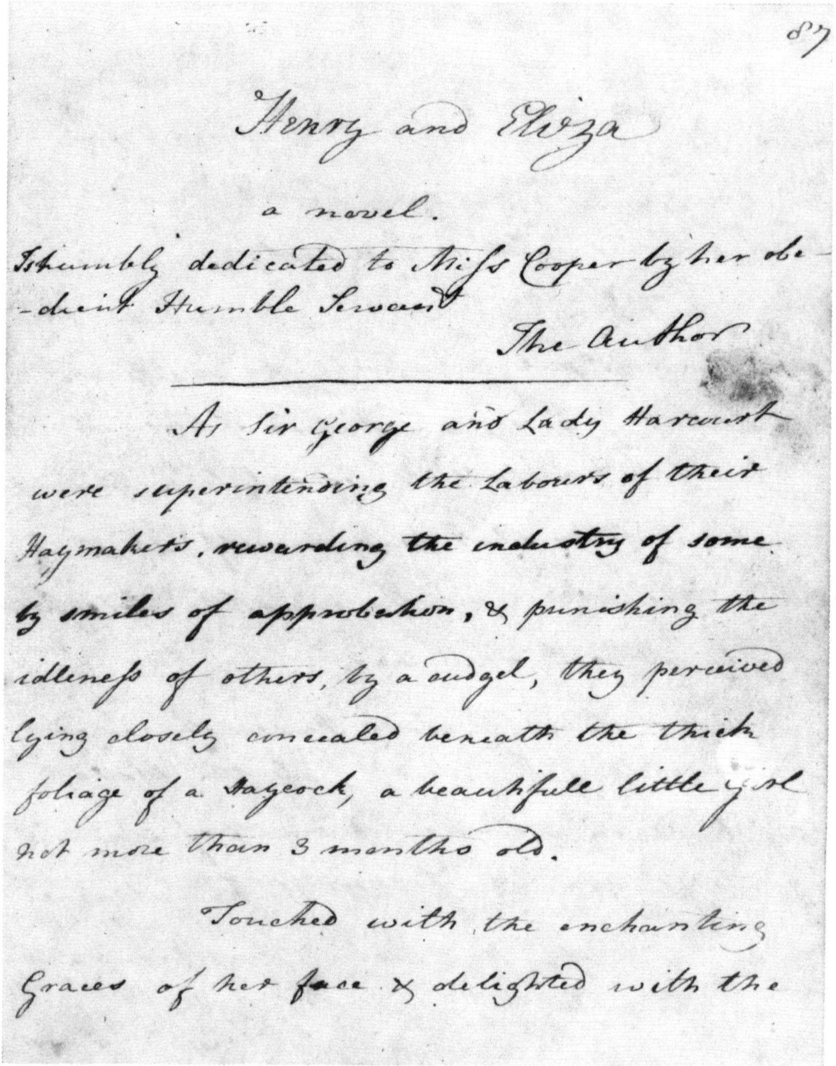

87

Henry and Eliza

a novel.

I humbly dedicated to Miss Cooper by her obe-
-dient Humble Servant
The Author

As Sir George and Lady Harcourt
were superintending the Labours of their
Haymakers, rewarding the industry of some
by smiles of approbation, & punishing the
idleness of others, by a cudgel, they perceived
lying closely concealed beneath the thick
foliage of a Haycock, a beautifull little girl
not more than 3 months old.

Touched with the enchanting
Graces of her face & delighted with the

Figure 6. First Manuscript Page of "Henry and Eliza: a novel," Including
the Dedication to Miss Cooper
(Volume the First *MS; Courtesy The Bodleian Library, MS Don.e.7*)

urgently politicized than they had in the past; and, second, a penchant for treating these figures skeptically, and thus undermining their authority, their claims on our credence. Later in her career, the stakes would be higher, and Austen's irreverence more daring and more deadpan. Austen manipulates the conventional valences of a figure like Sir Thomas Bertram, for example, with an irony just as sure-handedly, if not as comically, as those of Sir George Harcourt. Another caricature of gentry mythology, Sir Thomas also speaks the rhetoric of the venerable patriarch exacting gratitude, and his discourse is radically compromised—by his self-contradiction, his bluster, his ignorance, and not least of all, the dependence of his stateliness on the labor of slaves.

But in order to appreciate the politics of the juvenilia we must do more than credit the potency of Austen's irony. We must also excavate subtexts now obscure to us. Although most readers readily allow that Sir Thomas and his ilk are *national* figures, the political import of much of Austen's juvenile as well as mature fiction still remains unacknowledged because it focuses on subjects we define as essentially private and apolitical. I am referring, of course, to female experience, and the conventions structuring it. As the works of Burke, Wollstonecraft, More, Godwin, Edgeworth, Rousseau, and Burney (to name only a very few) attest, throughout the 1790s, the formative years of Austen's career, there were few subjects *more* anxiously debated as central to national well-being than female manners. Thus, portions of the juvenilia likely to appear to us variously as the most cute, slight, and precocious are often, in fact, the most laden with controversy. Consider the unfortunate Charlotte in "Frederic & Elfrida." The reigning quality of Charlotte's "character," we are informed on the first page, "was a willingness to oblige every one" (4). She is both "lovely" (4) as well as "good-temper'd & obliging" (7); she treats servants with "the greatest Condescension & Goodhumour" (7); and perhaps most impressive of all, she gladly proffers the compliments her hideous friend extorts from her. Could anything be wrong? Yes. Precisely because this young lady is so sweet, she is unable "to resolve to make any one miserable," and consequently she cannot say "no" to either of the two offers of marriage which come, in rapid succession, from gentlemen she has never met before. Like so many characters in the juvenilia, Charlotte has odd bouts of amnesia. "[I]t was not till that next morning that [she] recollected the double engagement she had entered into" (8)—whereupon she is so overcome with guilt that she throws herself into a deep stream and dies, shortly thereafter to become, as all good dead heroines become, the subject of an epitaph.

What exactly is the object of satire here? Silly girls who cannot seem to remember what they said from one minute to another? Silly novels that would have us believe that extravagantly ingenuous heroines manage to entangle themselves in innumerable romantic webs? Austen's parody comprehends such objects, to be sure, but it comprehends more as well. Austen treats conventions not as sterile devices, but as structures of human possibilities which evolve from specific social and political situations, and her irony here, as in the mature fiction, twists not once, but twice. What at first glance seems comic upon a second and closer examination seems all-too-serious, and all the funnier, finally, for being so. Charlotte's behavior, alas, has not been idiosyncratic: it has only slightly exaggerated what passes for standard behavior every day. So little are proper young ladies ever trained or expected to disoblige others, particularly suitors, by saying "no," that heroines as unlike as Elizabeth Bennet and Fanny Price both find it impossible to refuse marriage proposals and be believed.

Being sweet and agreeable is every good girl's object in life. Hannah More, among the most distinguished of reactionary authors, makes this abundantly clear in *Coelebs in Search of a Wife,* the volume Austen's Mrs. Percival uses to form her ward's errant mind in "Catharine, or the Bower." With a century of conduct literature behind her, there she urges upon woman the "positive duty of being agreeable at home," and the "absolute *morality* of being agreeable at home." Indeed, all other infractions—such as sacrifices of "veracity, religion, modesty, candour, or the decorum of [a woman's] sex"—are not conceived of as failures of morality *per se* but rather as lapses of "agreeableness."[6] Of course, as More well knew and as recent research into women's conduct literature has shown, "agreeableness" is not a politically neutral female grace, but as one thing needful to guarantee paternal authority without unseemly confrontations.[7] Remember, Sir Thomas Bertram is shocked when Fanny fails to exhibit that good-tempered, feminine agreeableness which makes daughters and wives so governable. Instead, he decries the shocking "wilfulness of temper, self-conceit" and "independence of spirit" which Fanny displays when she has the audacity *not* to defer to Sir Thomas's will, when she says "no" rather than the ductile "yes" grateful good girls owe their guides. In "modern days," Sir Thomas sputters, such independence is "in young women . . . offensive and disgusting beyond all common offense" (*MP,* 318)—and at the height of the Reaction, when the countryside was seen as swarming with Jacobin riff-raff out to ruin the nation's best families by debauching its daughters, Sir Thomas's position was not unusual. With so much riding on the code of good temper and agreeableness, can it be any wonder that Charlotte finds herself in a bind? Considered in this light, Charlotte's suicide appears not as a reversal but actually as a comically condensed fulfillment of conventional codes. Having failed to be agreeable in the proscribed way, Charlotte has no further *raison d'être,* much as Fanny Price believes that the comparably offensive crime of Maria Rushworth could be mitigated only by her "instant annihilation" (*MP,* 442). Once again, then, Austen's parodic manipulation of conventional material alienates us from such material precisely so as to oblige us to perceive and to challenge interests that would otherwise have gone unnoticed.

We have good reason to believe that Austen was well aware of the way in which her presentation of female characters in the juvenilia was politically coded: her own revisions to "Catharine, or The Bower" prove it beyond a doubt. In this sketch, probably drafted in 1792, the heroine's irritable aunt, Mrs. Percival, is presented as a redoubtable, highly opinionated political lady. As it so happens, she is a sour and overbearing reactionary. It is Mrs. Percival's oft repeated belief that the kingdom is "at sixes & sevens," "the whole race of Mankind were degenerating," "all order" has been "destroyed over the face of the World," and the "whole Nation [will] speedily be ruined" (200, 212). An arch-authoritarian, she pines not merely for the reign of Queen Elizabeth, but also for a restoration of what is termed the "manners" that marked her time, when behavior was regulated, and as a result, presumably, when political order itself was more respected. In 1809, after history had made the thrust of Mrs. Percival's arguments more clear, Austen took up her pen to make the following, highly suggestive emendation: she changes Mrs. Percival's recommendation of Archbishop Secker's *Lectures on the Catechism of the Church of England,* published in 1769, to Hannah More's *Coelebs in Search of a Wife,* which had just been published in 1809.

Austen's revision is so telling because it demonstrably links Mrs. Percival with that other political lady, Hannah More. Mrs. Percival's characterization certainly shows how little faith Austen had in the ideology of Tory conservatism to which many Austenian scholars believe she subscribed. By examining how that ideology bears on female manners in particular, the juvenilia begins a project that would occupy Austen for the rest of her career. In the case in point, Mrs. Percival has spied on her astonished ward, whose hand has just been seized and kissed by a coxcomb:

> "*Profligate* as I *knew* you to be, I was not prepared for such as sight. . . . All I wished for was to breed you up virtuously; I never wanted you to play upon the Harpsichord, or draw better than any one else; but I had hoped to see you respectable and good; to see you able & willing to give an example of Modesty and Virtue to the Young people here abouts. I bought you Blair's Sermons, and Coelebs in Search of a Wife. . . . But I might have spared myself the trouble—Oh! Catherine, you are an abandoned Creature. . . . I plainly see that every thing is going to sixes & sevens and all order will soon be at an end throughout the Kingdom."
>
> ". . . upon my honour [Catharine replies] I have done nothing this evening that can contribute to overthrow the establishment of the kingdom"
>
> "You are Mistaken Child, replied she; the welfare of every Nation depends upon the virtue of it's individuals, and any one who offends in so gross a manner against decorum & propriety is certainly hastening it's ruin." (232–33)

Catharine is surprised to find herself not only accused of immodesty, but also blamed for the downfall of the kingdom. But as I have shown elsewhere, the linkage of political survival with the private and domestic virtue of English subjects was an essential feature of reactionary apologetics during the 1790s,

and women, accordingly, found themselves and every aspect of their behavior—
their learning, their chastity, their exercise, their housewifery—at the center of
arguments about national security itself.[8] Many of the most uproariously funny
parts of the juvenilia will be lost on us unless we register the growing importance
granted to female manners during the time Austen wrote. Between the two of
them, the sisters of Lesley Castle, for example, exaggerate the two roles that
conventionally circumscribe female destiny: the delicately etherealized romantic
heroine who cares only about music, sensibility, love and friendship, on the one
hand; and, on the other, the bustling, robust housewife, who cares only about
her pantry, and who can scarcely utter a sentence that does not recur to linens,
sirloins, or syllabubs.

If not exactly amusing, Eloisa is nevertheless a strikingly stereotypical
creation. Unfortunate in love—her dashing sweetheart breaks his skull in a
riding accident—her main activities consist of fainting, singing, pining, and
wincing at the unfeeling vulgarity of her sister. Eloisa's irritable delicacy and
self-consuming ardor place her in the same league with Marianne Dashwood.
As sentimental heroines exemplifying certain ideals of feminine excellence, they
were vigorously criticized by moralists on both sides of the political spectrum
for their insufficient fortitude in face of the trials and duties of life, and for their
foolish indulgence of passions they ought rather strive to overcome. The
Rousseauvian provenance of her name alone marks Eloisa as the kind of woman
scolded by Wollstonecraft for being a "slave to love," and by Jane West for
failing "to expect with diffidence, enjoy with gratitude, and resign with submission."[9] Like Marianne, Eloisa grows so listless once her love is tragically
thwarted that her very life seems to slip away. Like many a delicately decaying
heroine, then, Eloisa could stand to pay attention to the really quite sensible
advice another dying, but loquacious sentimental heroine proffered earlier in
"Love and Freindship": "Beware of swoons Dear Laura. . . . A frenzy fit is not
one quarter so pernicious; it is an exercise to the Body & if not too violent, is I
dare say conducive to Health in its consequences—Run mad as often as you
chuse; but do not faint—" (102).

Alongside the romantic heroine, who does not care about food, stands the
ever-industrious housewife whose only object is to prepare it: "I never," Charlotte Lutterell avers, "wish to act a more principal part at a Wedding than the
superintending and directing the Dinner" (121). So little inclined is she to
sentiment, that when she learns that her sister's bridegroom is on the verge of
death, she can worry only about the wedding feast she has labored so hard to
cook: "Good God! (said I) you dont say so? Why what in the name of Heaven
will become of all the Victuals" (113). With the industry characteristic of her,
she immediately forms a "Devouring Plan" (114) so that the food will not go
bad. Tradition has it that Austen identifies with Charlotte, for both share a
respect for menu-planning as well as an ability to look upon the dramas unfold-

ing before them with a detachment "as cool as a Cream-cheese" (129). But it detracts nothing from this special relationship to observe that Charlotte's character is as conventionalized as her sister's. She too is doing—but doing with a vengeance—exactly what the keepers of order in her culture would have her do.

Soon enough, in fact, cooking such as Charlotte's would serve as a clear political cue. Just when reformists, such as Wollstonecraft, suggested that female occupations were confining, and opened more to women in the way of education and moral agency, conservatives for their part urged the primacy of women's domestic responsibilities. Domestic occupations, as Hannah More argued in *Coelebs,* are the only safe and proper arena for female intellect. Women only make themselves ridiculous and unpleasant, after all, when they aspire to emulate masculine erudition. But household activities bring the understanding of women into action proper to themselves. Domestic economy is "a field in which women of the best sense may honourably exercise her powers." Although England's most eligible bachelor, the exemplary Coelebs, professes himself "no epicure," he cannot forbear noticing that a young lady he meets serves dishes that were "out of season, ill chosen, and ill dressed," and not the least of what he admires in Lucilla Stanley is her utter devotion to domestic economy—examining provisions, planning menus, and feeding guests and siblings.[10] In Elizabeth Hamilton's anti-Jacobin novel, *Memoirs of Modern Philosophers,* the ludicrous Bridgetina Botherim proves herself to be a ninny of the progressive persuasion when she is stung by the innocent suggestion that she might know how to make a pudding: "'A pudding,' repeated Bridgetina, reddening with anger, 'I do assure sir, you are very much mistaken, if you think I employ my time in such a manner.'" We have it on Bridgetina's word that "novels and metaphysics" make up her studies, and as her well-meaning but entirely benighted mother tells us, she is "far too learned to trouble herself about doing any thing useful."[11] In a more serious vein, Adeline Mowbray, the unfortunate heroine of Amelia Opie's 1804 novel of the same name, much to her own misfortune, becomes intoxicated with progressive ideas. Her novel, however, is no burlesque. Though her views are discredited, Adeline herself is presented with ample sympathy, and this is at least in part because she fulfills every feminine duty. Despite her progressive political opinions, her heterodox ideas about marriage, and her extensive reading, she has gentle manners and is remarkably good in the kitchen, so much so that even spiteful neighbors who triumph in her shame regret that they can find nothing to reproach in her cuisine.

Adeline Mowbray's problems can help us identify another strand of political significance in Austen's juvenilia: eating itself. As we have seen already in Eloisa's case, as surely as in Marianne's, sentimental heroines worth their salt never express much interest in food. In "Love and Freindship," when the reprehensibly "insensible" Augusta asks her brother how he plans to provide his new bride with "Victuals and Drink," he angrily defends his wife's character: "Victuals and Drink! . . . dost thou then imagine that there is no other support for an exalted Mind (such as is my Laura's) than the mean and indelicate employment of Eating and Drinking?" (83). Proper women can like to cook, but must not under any circumstances like to eat. Perhaps the most shocking episode of *Adeline Mowbray* occurs when Adeline's husband, a big eater himself, resents it when she recovers her appetite after a bout of illness: "being no advocate for the equality of the sexes, he thought it only a matter of course that he should fare better than his wife."[12] Like the conventionally dutiful woman she is, despite her politics, she caters to his ravenous appetites without complaint, and for her own part dines privately on scraps.

Ladylike inanition has no honorable place in the antisentimental world of Austen's fiction, where the exigencies of life take priority over sentimental conventions which are not merely high-fallutin, but deadly. Catherine Morland proves herself *not* to be a conventional heroine when, after the mysterious Tilney fails to appear at a ball, she returns home not to weep or rave, but instead to "appease" her "extraordinary hunger." Fortunately, Catherine is untutored in the standards by which her unheroically healthy appetite may be judged. But Laura in "Love and Freindship" is another case. It takes the Regency's equivalent of a nervous breakdown before her hunger can be acknowledged. Heroism fails her when her beloved dies in a riding accident, and in her love madness she hallucinates every meal she has foregone: "Beware ye gentle Nymphs of Cupid's Thunderbolts, avoid the piercing Shafts of Jupiter—Look at that Grove of Firs—I see a Leg of Mutton—They told me Edward was not Dead; but they deceived me—they took him for a Cucumber—" (100). The joke here, of course, consists of seeing the earthy world sentimental fiction represses returning at last. But in different moods Austen treats "the mean and indelicate employment of Eating and Drinking" in females as no laughing matter. In works like "Lesley Castle" and "Love and Freindship," conventions are exaggerated in order to call attention to women's options: food or romance, survival or sentiment. But by the end of "Lesley Castle" the joke is dropped, for a moment at least, and the behavior of the villainous Louisa, whose adulterous crimes open this sketch, is given the following explanation in which this reader, at least, detects no irony, no playful sally, no dizzying display of formal virtuosity:

[S]he had been taught to disguise her real Disposition, under the appearance of insinuating Sweetness by a father who but too well knew, that to be married, would be the only chance she would have of not being starved, and who flattered himself that with such an extraordinary share of personal beauty, joined to a gentleness of Manners, and an engaging address, she might stand a good chance of pleasing some young Man who might afford to marry a Girl without a Shilling. (117)

Austen's heroines, in the juvenilia as in the mature fiction, cannot live on love. "Not being starved" is a good, if not the best, motive for marriage. Elizabeth Bennet disapproves of Charlotte Lucas's "disinterested" desire for an "establishment," but the narrator remains silent.

It is not high spirits and exuberance alone that typify the juvenilia, but an exceptional daring. The most stunning feature of Austen's early writing is the superb confidence of its voice, the authority it unhesitatingly arrogates unto itself as it dismantles the reigning conventions of contemporary fictions, as it exposes the moral and political assumptions those fictions reflect and reproduce. Virginia Woolf found such audacity unsettling: "the girl of fifteen," she wrote with appreciative dismay, "is laughing at the world."[13] But of course, youth made that laughter possible. Juvenile status, coupled with the assumed privacy of one's productions, confer the liberty of irreverence and irresponsibility upon any writer. And as Austen matured, the Reaction gained in strength, so that social criticism carried greater risks: Sir Thomas and Sir Walter are harder to assail than Sir George Harcourt, or even General Tilney; the political efficacy of the neighborhood, as represented by Mansfield, Kellynch and their environs, would prove less accessible to criticism than the impossibly utopian Evelyn. But Austen always remained a novelist of manners. To be such at her time was inevitably to be a political novelist, and to treat the conventions that govern life and fiction not as sacred dicta but as interested structures that both reveal and conceal, enable and repress is, I believe, to be a progressive novelist. Austen would dampen the satire that marks her early writing, but she never ceased interrogating the ideological underpinning of fiction itself.

Notes

1. Brian Southam, *Jane Austen's Literary Manuscripts*, London, 1964, pp. 1–44; Sandra M. Gilbert and Susan Gubar, *The Madwoman in the Attic*, New Haven, 1979, pp. 107–27; A.W. Litz, *Jane Austen: A Study of Her Artistic Development*, New York, 1965, pp. 3–39.

2. John Halperin, *Jane Austen*, Sussex, England, 1984, p. 38.

3. J. David Grey, A. Walton Litz, and Brian Southam, eds., *Jane Austen Companion*, New York, 1986, p. 248.

4. George Steiner, *After Babel*, New York, 1975, pp. 8–9.

5. See Marilyn Butler, *Jane Austen and the War of Ideas*, Oxford, 1975; Warren Roberts, *Jane Austen and the French Revolution*, New York, 1979; Ronald Paulson, *Representations of Revolution (1789–1820)*, New Haven, 1983; Mary Evans, *Jane Austen and the State*, London and New York, 1987.

6. Hannah More, *Coelebs in Search of a Wife*, 2 volumes, London, 1808, I, 347; II, 141.

7. See Mary Poovey, *The Proper Lady and the Woman Writer*, Chicago, 1984.

8. See my *Jane Austen: Women, Politics, and the Novel*, Chicago, 1988.

9. Mary Wollstonecraft, *A Vindication of the Rights of Woman,* ed. Miriam Kramnick, Harmonds-worth, England, 1975, p. 190; Jane West, *Gossip's Story,* 2 volumes, London, 1796, II, 51.

10. More, II, 218; II, 32.

11. Elizabeth Hamilton, *Memoirs of Modern Philosophers,* 3 volumes, Bath, 1800, I, 23.

12. Amelia Opie, *Adeline Mowbray,* 3 volumes, London, 1804, III, 49.

13. Virginia Woolf, *The Common Reader,* New York, 1953, p. 139.

Learning History with, and from, Jane Austen

Christopher Kent

On the eve of World War I Frederic Harrison described Jane Austen to Thomas Hardy as "a rather heartless little cynic . . . penning satires about her neighbours whilst the Dynasts were tearing the world to pieces and consigning millions to their graves." While she was writing, "not a breath from the whirlwind around her ever touched her Chippendale chiffonier or escritoire."[1] Within a year of Harrison's writing these words, the Dynasts were at it again, on an even greater scale. An Oxford tutor, H.F. Brett-Smith, served during World War I as an advisor to hospitals on reading matter for wounded soldiers. "For the severely shell-shocked," a former student recalled, "he selected Jane Austen."[2] Here we have a notable demonstration of the power of the myth of Jane Austen's extrahistoricity, though perhaps subhistoricity better captures the spirit of Harrison's dismissive comment.[3] While the French Revolution raged, Jane Austen barely looked up from her literary petit point. Who better to soothe minds unhinged at Passchendaele or the Somme? In the therapeutic calm of her pages history's victims could escape from their nemesis. Rudyard Kipling was apparently aware of this "Austen therapy": Brother Humberstall, the shell-shocked hero of "The Janeites," evidently underwent it. The resulting fantasy shows that Austen's fellow novelist had a much richer sense of the complex ways in which fiction and history interact than did either Frederic Harrison or the Oxford don.

The French Revolution ushered in the age of historicism. Jane Austen lived and wrote at the threshold of this new era of and for history. It is instructive and salutary for literary critics and historians alike to place her in her correct context, to see her dealing with history in the terms within which she and her contemporaries understood it, rather than our considerably different terms. This is to learn history with, and from, Jane Austen.

One of her earliest works is history—"The History of England." It bears a portentous date of completion: November 26, 1791. The author was nearly 16 years old. Across the Channel, the French Revolution which she would so often be accused of ignoring was nearly two and a half years old. Jane Austen had an unusual perspective of that event. A cousin to whom she was very close was the wife of an émigré noble. Eliza de Feuillide and her young son had been sent to England for safety by her husband the Comte de Feuillide, who had been an officer of dragoons in the Queen's Guard. He was an ardent royalist and an early participant in the aristocratic emigration, but was torn between opposing the Revolution and keeping his property. He would visit his wife in England during the winter of 1791 before returning to France to protect his land from forfeit. It was a risky business. He was to be snared during the Reign of Terror, and the guillotine that beheaded Louis XVI would take his head as well.

The dashing French countess was a seasoned campaigner in the *fêtes galantes* of Marie Antoinette's Versailles. She had brought a spicy whiff of Fragonard to the amateur dramatics and dances at Steventon. She may also have exposed her young cousin to that scandalous best-seller among the French beau monde, *Liaisons Dangereuses,* a book that could have helped inspire the precocious libertinage of *Lady Susan*.[4] In any case it seems reasonable to suppose that Eliza gave Jane Austen a privileged, if partial and prejudiced, view of events in France, one that was less favorable to the Revolution, one heavier with a sense of foreboding, than was usual in England in 1791—closer perhaps to the fears of Edmund Burke than to the hopes of William Wordsworth. In any case Jane Austen certainly had decapitation on the brain in 1791 as she wrote "The History of England," a distillation of the most violent episodes occurring in English history between the Wars of the Roses and the execution of Charles I (a period which saw the advent and [usually bloody] demise of four royal dynasties).[5]

This was not escape from History: in the context of 1791, Austen's work is big with capitalized History. It was rather revenge on history—on schoolroom history, a species of history-as-subject, still very much with us, that was largely a creation of the eighteenth century. We do not know much about Jane Austen's education. We do know that she was sent to two girls' boarding schools between the ages of seven and ten. The second of these, Abbey School near Reading, was one of the best in the country. There she was no doubt taught history. Although there is a certain tendency to regard history as essentially a boy's or man's subject, a tendency which professional historians have been inclined (at least until recently) to foster, such was not the case in the eighteenth century. Boys and men of any social or intellectual pretensions or ambitions studied the classics almost exclusively. History was not regarded as a serious intellectual discipline. It was too lightweight, too much a matter of memory, of rote learning. This view of history as a subject was to hold in England until well into the next century. It did not regain a serious position in the all-male universities of England until the late nineteenth century. History's weakness as a discipline was bound up in its weakness as a profession. A man might *make* history as a soldier or statesman. He might also *write* history as a participant, like Thucydides, Machiavelli, or Lord Clarendon. But to *study* history in our sense of doing historical research, that was pedantry. Such researchers did not even deserve the name of historian: they were antiquarians, a name redolent to this day of dusty, obscure trivia. To write history was essentially a literary activity aimed at capturing the interest of the general reader.

History was regarded as a particularly appropriate subject for girls. It has been suggested that the deep interest of Queen Mary II (wife of William II) in history made it fashionable in women's education.[6] To what end? Mrs. Hester Chapone was an influential writer on women's education. In her *Letters on the Improvement of the Mind. Addressed to a Lady* (1774) she declared, "the principal study, I would recommend, is *history*. I know of nothing equally proper to entertain and improve at the same time."[7] The entertainment lay in the excitement, the danger, the glamour of court, battlefield, and bedroom—all the staples of traditional "high" history. The improvement lay in the fact that it all happened, that it was true, not invented. Also in that it provided substitute experience, a knowledge of the world "at the expense of others" as another writer on women's education put it.[8] History fell into the category of "polite knowledge"—that is, it was public knowledge to which all who wished could have access. Not being recondite or exclusive, and hence affected, it was therefore peculiarly fitted to provide "materials for conversation."[9] With some knowledge of history a young woman might hope to avoid the condition of so many of her sex, "trifling insipid companions—so ill qualified for the friendship and conversation of a sensible man."[10]

Where did such knowledge begin? In the schoolroom, with a textbook, and a teacher. History paid the price of its popularity as a subject by being rendered teachable, even to the very young. The eighteenth-century history textbook shows this being done. History was reduced for childhood consumption into facts and dates, a process which is both infinitely compressible and expansible.[11] By sticking close to the text the teacher or governess might hope to keep his or her authority intact, an important consideration where the teacher's knowledge was limited.

Various history textbooks appeared on the market from the early eighteenth century onwards as astute publishers became aware of the profitable market developing. An example is *A New History of England from the Invasion of Julius Caesar to the End of George II's Reign* by "the Rev. Mr. Cooper," published by John Newbery, a pioneering entrepreneur in the field of children's books.[12] This 182-page volume, with 31 plates, is a monarch-by-monarch account which compresses the main facts and events of each reign into from two to four duodecimo pages. These main facts, chiefly military or political—battles, statutes and threats to royal authority—are sandwiched between the circumstances of each monarch's accession and demise, and rounded off by a pat judgment. Thus, for Charles I: "this monarch had many private virtues and would probably have been a worthy prince had it not been for the principles imbibed in his education, and the ill advice of his ministers," a judgment neatly combining evasion with a plug for the importance of education.[13] Accompanying each monarch is a portrait based on the fancy of an unknown engraver and accompanied by edifying doggerel. For James I, we have this:

> England's first Stuart, from Scotian clime
> Learned but pedantic, peaceful to a crime
> His weak yet arbitrary acts prepare
> A scene of ills for his succeeding heir.[14]

Yet another excuse for Charles I. But as an epitome of the view of James's reign in two couplets, not bad. Occasionally the dignity of facts military and political would be relieved by random fragments of what might today be called social history. During the reign of Richard II, we learn, his queen took to wearing long gowns, hence the introduction of the side saddle.[15]

A more interesting children's history, of slightly earlier date, is *The Chronicle of the Kings of England from the Norman Conquest until the Present Time* by the poet, publisher, and friend of Dr. Johnson, Robert Dodsley. Its purported author was one "Nathan Ben Saddi," who wrote in a mock-biblical style full of "Now it came to pass . . . " and "Wherefore the Lord smote him with sickness. . . . " Behind the heavy moralism and providentialism implicit in this vein, however, lay a distinct irreverence laced with salaciousness which one would think was not beyond the powers of detection of an alert child. Of Henry VIII Dodsley offers this Swiftian image: "His legs were as the postern of a gate, or as an arch stretched over the door of public offices of the land, and whosoever went out and whosoever came in passed beneath it and with idolatrous reverence lifted up their eyes and kissed the cheeks of the postern."[16] Dodsley was equally vivid and censorious in denouncing the "heaving softness" of the "snowy breasts" of Charles II's mistresses.[17] No wonder Mrs. Trimmer warned teachers and parents against the "impiety and disloyalty" of this "obscene" publication, which was made even more attractive in later Newbery editions by head and shoulders woodcuts of the monarchs by Bewick.[18]

No one was more alive than Mrs. Trimmer to the power of pictures to capture the interest of children. In 1792 she brought out *A Series of Prints of English History Designed as Ornaments for Those Apartments in Which Children Receive the First Rudiments of Their Education*. In dealing with Mary Queen of Scots Mrs. Trimmer dwelt on her "beauty . . . the affability of her address, the politeness of her manners and the elegance of her genius." Though Mary had "almost certainly" planned the murder of her husband, this "unfortunate queen" faced her own death with "a cheerful and smiling countenance."[19]

Written at almost exactly the same time as Jane Austen's "The History of England," Mrs. Trimmer's words suggest that, "Mr. Whitaker, Mrs. Lefroy, Mrs. Knight and myself" were not alone in their partiality for beheaded Stuarts.[20]

We have not yet mentioned Goldsmith, whose work is usually taken as the sole external point of reference for Austen's youthful history. She may have known of the other works in the textbook trade, indeed it seems reasonable to assume that she was exposed to some of them as a child. She certainly knew of Goldsmith's work, for she vigorously annotated a copy of one of them. Goldsmith wrote three different histories of England. The first was *An History of England in a Series of Letters from a Nobleman to His Son,* published by Newbery in 1764. Purporting to be a series of letters by a nobleman to his son at Oxford, it is interesting in that the letter format offers Goldsmith an opportunity to break away from the traditional monarch-to-monarch trudge. He proposes to divide English history into three epochs: to the Norman Conquest, to the execution of Charles I, and to the present. "Forget those of the vulgar ignorant herd of kings who seemed only to slumber on a seat they were accidently called to fill," he urges his reader. "History in general is precious or significant not from the brilliance of the events, the singularity of the adventures or the greatness of the personages concerned, but from the skill, penetration and judgement of the observer."[21]

The book apparently succeeded however, perhaps in the public schools and better grammar schools at which it was aimed. A group of publishers then offered Goldsmith 500 pounds for a four-volume history of England which he duly cranked out while writing *The Deserted Village* and *She Stoops to Conquer.* Both size and content suggest that it was aimed at a general readership, the octavo size was more dignified than the duodecimo typical of the juvenile, but less intimidating than the snobbish quarto. (One recalls Jane Austen praising an octavo at the expense of "those enormous great stupid thick quarto volumes" favored by the ladies at Manydown.)[22] In the preface to this work Goldsmith adopts a different and more authentic persona, that of the man of letters as historian. He frankly avows that the work is an abridgement, "his aim being not to add to our present stock of history but to contract it," to replace the existing abridgement with a work of greater literary merit, and save his readers the trouble of consulting the standard authorities: Rapin, Carte, Smollett and Hume.

The success of *The History* encouraged the publishers to launch an abridged edition. Goldsmith abridged himself and the result became the most successful of his histories, appearing in over 50 editions during the next century. The abridgement of an abridgement, in one volume duodecimo, with illustrations, was aimed directly at the schoolroom, and spawned such teaching aids as a *Study Guide* and *500 Questions.*[23] Jane Austen probably annotated her copy of Goldsmith, the four-volume version, at about the time she wrote her history.

Her marginal interjections are devoted mainly to the Stuarts (whom she cheers on from the sidelines, as it were, in their losing cause). In "The History of England," the Stuarts are introduced at the earliest possible moment and take over the story before they take over the throne. This identification with the Stuarts has been analyzed well by Brigid Brophy in terms of the circumstances of Austen's adolescence and family situation. She had extensive family associations with the Stuarts, significantly on the female side. Her mother's ancestors, the Leighs, had sheltered Charles I at Stoneleigh Abbey and were connected by marriage to Thomas Wentworth, beheaded as a loyal minister of Charles I. There was also a remote connection with the romantic Earl of Craven, brave soldier and devoted servant of the Stuarts. Donald J. Greene has made it plain how conscious Jane Austen must have been of her grand if distant aristocratic connections whose names would soon appear in the characters of her novels.[24] Not long out of the Abbey school (where the pupils, as ever, no doubt engaged in the competitive embellishment of family trees), approaching the brink of marriageability when her own social (and financial) claims would be put to severe proof, Jane Austen took control of History. The Stuarts were her people, her claim to a place in History, and as a historian she was quite as entitled as any other perpetrator of schoolroom history to have her way and give the Stuarts—and through them herself—the attention they deserved.

The main feature of "The History of England" is of course its exuberant wit. Yet the wit turns on a considerable degree of historiographical sophistication. Current notions of child development and learning theory locate the threshold of historical understanding quite late in adolescence. A "sense of the past," after all, requires a sense of one's own past. The difficulty of this problem for authors of school history texts is demonstrated by the persistence of the eighteenth-century solution—facts and dates. Jane Austen was a very precocious historian. She brashly inverts the Whig view of history, the convention within which most history is presented. By this convention the present determines what past developments deserve emphasis. Those which are deemed to contribute most to the present are played up, those which contributed least, the "dead ends," played down or eliminated. Although this makes for "relevant" history which enables the reader to relate to the past in present terms, it continually veers towards anachronism. Thus British history, in the eponymous version of Whiggism, is presented as the glorious unfolding of Liberty as if the spirit of modern Westminster-style parliamentary government were somehow present even in the tribal conclaves of the early Saxons. In this triumphal progress the Stuarts were not just out of step, but headed in the opposite direction. The supreme advantage of Whig history is that it provides a clear rationale for deciding what to put in, and more importantly, especially for the textbook author, what to leave out. It also gives the reader a certain sense of superiority, enabling him to recognize the importance of seemingly insignificant events, with the assistance of the author's nudging "little did she know that. . . . " This preoccupation with anticipations and forerunners can easily stray into absurdity, as Jane Austen realized, while she subverted Whiggish conventions to the cause of Tory history. Thus Margaret Tudor, daughter of Henry VII, "had the happiness of being grandmother to one of the first characters of the world"—Mary Queen of Scots (133). And the Duke of Somerset "was beheaded, of which he might with reason have been proud had he known that such was the death of Mary Queen of Scotland" (137).

Jane Austen's full-blooded Stuart partisanship is a dissenting comment on the new tone of political moderation that marked British historiography from the mid-eighteenth century. Hume in particular redressed the reigning Whig triumphalism by dealing sympathetically with the Stuarts, particularly James I, without slipping into Jacobite apologetics à la Carte (Thomas Carte, that is, the leading Tory historian). There was, however, a lively historiographical controversy centering on Mary Queen of Scots, whose guilt was decisively established by Britain's two ablest modern historians, Hume and William Robertson (both of whom were Scots), though not to the satisfaction of historians like William Tytler and John Whitaker (Austen's "Mr. Whitaker") who energetically argued the innocence of their injured heroine. On the other hand, Hume was attacked by anti-Stuart historians like the unjustly forgotten Mrs. Catherine Macaulay, whose political views tended to republicanism.[25] Hume found some satisfaction in being attacked from all sides, seeing it as evidence that he had indeed achieved a degree of balance hitherto unreached in national historiography.

It was at this time, too, that historians were seeking to establish a new narrative voice, an unobtrusive yet authoritative voice that would give the reader confidence in his competence and impartiality, a voice appropriate to the "dignity of history" (a phrase made famous by Robertson). Here again Hume provided a model. His calm, philosophic presence pervades his history, intervening usually through impersonal constructions such as "it is reasonable to infer. . . ." He rarely introduces himself directly, and when he does it is as "we"—the voice of gentlemen of good sense and understanding. Thus did the great philosopher of skepticism write a history which challenged the widespread doubts that "The History" of any country could be written, doubts that Voltaire, though himself a historian, captured in his corrosive dictum that history was "a pack of tricks we play on the dead."[26]

Goldsmith's history did not achieve Hume's dignity or tone of authority. Unlike Hume, who would not plead with his reader, Goldsmith in his preface openly appeals to his reader to accept his own professions of impartiality. Having admitted his great debt to Hume, he carefully distances himself from him politically, with a somewhat uncomfortable display of fence sitting.[27] But Goldsmith was aware of the arts of narrative authority and restrained his interventions, though occasionally introducing himself in the first person singular.

While more overtly sentententious and moralizing than Hume, he does manage to achieve a reasonably persuasive nonpartisan stance. His calculated ironicism permits him some generous comments on Mary Queen of Scots and Charles I ("all his faults seem to have arisen from the error of his education"),[28] and the characteristic observation that all the aggression and bloodshed unleashed by the Civil War was "in the end productive of domestic happiness . . . as if a previous fermentation in the constitution was necessary to its refinement."[29] Providence thus appears in the language of chemistry.

The young Jane Austen was plainly not persuaded by the novel notion of nonpartisan history. Nor was she taken in by the disappearing historian dodge. In her history she claimed the Voltairean prerogative of the historian as trickster. She is outrageously obtrusive, introducing her friends and relations, puffing her brothers and putting in a good word for her own "amiable Self" (143). No shams of concealment here. Just as history is about the exercise of power, so history writing *is* the exercise of power. If you do not support the house of York in the Wars of the Roses, "you had better read some other History, for I shall not be very diffuse in this, meaning by it only to vent my Spleen" (130). It is arbitrary: What are the "principle Events" of Henry VIII's reign (134)? The first is an utterly insignificant quote attributed to Cardinal Wolsey. Why have these words come down to us? That very fact proves history's arbitrary nature. It is also illogical: "The Crimes and Cruelties of this Prince [Henry VIII], were too numerous to be mentioned (as this history I trust has fully shown)" (135). And as for providence: Henry VIII's reformation was "of infinite use to the landscape of England in general" endowing it with a wealth of picturesque ruined monasteries, "which probably was a principal motive for his doing it" (135–36).

Apart from the problems of history's learnability and teachability as a subject for children, as testified to by the history texts on which "The History of England" was a commentary, there was also the problem of its suitability. "History, when divested of the graces of eloquence, and of that veil which the imagination is taught to throw over antiquity, presents a disgusting, terrible list of crimes and calamities; murders, assassinations, battles, revolutions, are the memorable events of history."[30] Maria Edgeworth was just one of many writers on child education who worried about this: "The simple morality of childhood is continually puzzled and shocked by the representation of the crimes and the virtues of historic heroes."[31] Not Jane Austen, however, who remarked of Edward IV that he was "famous only for his Beauty and his Courage, of which the Picture we have here given of him, & his undaunted Behaviour in marrying one Woman while he was engaged to another, are sufficient proof" (131). Perhaps the violence of history is one of its strengths in drawing children's interest. At any rate, a third of the people Austen chose to mention in her history met violent deaths—mostly beheadings. Of particular concern to teachers was the highly unedifying spectacle of regicide. It was bad even when committed by another monarch. Even Queen Elizabeth, when faced with the treasonous actions of Mary, "had no just pretensions to inflict punishment on her equal," according to Goldsmith.[32] And the execution of Charles was not the will of the people, but an act of "low bred malice"[33] committed by "a medley of the most obscure citizens." Jane Austen, interestingly, differed from Goldsmith even on this point, holding "the generality of the English" guilty of the deed (147). The execution of Charles I moved Hume to some sober reflections on the popular right to resist tyranny, and the possibility that in such deep a matter it was "perhaps laudable to conceal truth from the populace."[34] And from children, teachers might chorus. Especially children like Jane Austen who while "sound" on regicide was so for the wrong reasons.

In view of all this it was all the more surprising that history should have been judged a particularly appropriate subject for girls, as writers on female education were uneasily aware. The irony of extracting "polite knowledge" and "materials for conversation" from what Mrs. Chapone defined as, "little else than a shocking account of the wickedness and folly of the ambitious" clearly appealed to Jane Austen.[35] She makes great sport of introducing into "The History of England" numerous touches of gentility to make her characters fit for the tea table. She has particular fun with the word "amiable," a favorite eighteenth-century anodyne, which she uses repeatedly to describe figures as various as Henry V (129), Lady Jane Grey (133)—Hume also found her "amiable"—and the Protector Somerset (137). As if to demonstrate how violent and controversial historical episodes might be introduced into genteel conversation, she offers us this on the Civil War: "Never certainly was there before so many detestable Characters at one time in England as in this period of its History. Never were amiable Men so scarce" (146). Or this on Gunpowder Plot: "Truth being I think very excusable in an Historian I am necessitated to say that in this reign the roman catholics did not behave like Gentlemen to the protestants their Behaviour indeed to the Royal Family & both Houses of Parliament might justly be considered by them as very uncivil and even Sir Henry Percy tho' certainly the best bred Man of the party had none of that general politeness which is so universally pleasing, as his Attentions were entirely confined to Lord Mounteagle" (144–45). On the other hand she cannot resist going farther than either Goldsmith or Hume in discussing James I's partiality for handsome young men: "His Majesty was of that amiable disposition which inclines to Freindships, & in such points was possessed of a keener penetration in Discovering Merit than many other people" (145). The ironic tone approaches that of Gibbon here, and the word "penetration" seems carefully chosen.[36] A Mary Crawford, or an Eliza de Feuillide, might find "materials for conversation" in such history.

"And hardly any women at all" (*NA*, 108). Catherine Morland could not have complained of "The History of England." Nearly half its characters are women, and half its space is devoted to their exploits. Jane Austen's tract of English history is perhaps not so arbitrarily chosen as Brigid Brophy claims, for it is a period not only rich in royal bloodshed, but one in which women had considerable prominence in high politics. Henry VII's claim to the throne lay in the female Lancaster line, but he ensured it by marrying Elizabeth of York. The Stuart claim to the English throne also lay in the female line. The importance of Henry VIII's wives to the English Reformation is so well known that Austen forbore to make much of it, except to acquit Anne Boleyn and Catherine Howard of adultery. The last half of the sixteenth century of course saw women on the English throne, the Scots throne, and as the power behind the French throne. Such unnatural circumstances led John Knox to publish his famous pamphlet, *First Blast of the Trumpet against the Monstrous Regiment of Women* (1558). One wonders that Jane Austen identified more closely with Mary Queen of Scots than Queen Elizabeth, who after all never married. But then one must not chide her for not foreseeing spinsterhood, as she reproved the people of England for not foreseeing that her half-sister Mary would die childless and therefore "be succeeded by that disgrace to humanity, that pest of society, Elizabeth" (139). She may have been attracted by the Scots queen's masterful way with her husband, though we need no further reason for the attraction, as Austen makes clear, than that she was a Stuart.

Jane Austen returned to the matter of history in the education of women on two subsequent occasions. The best known is where Catherine Morland describes her dislike of history. Catherine is another victim of history, and through her the author is again addressing the issue of how history was used, and abused, in the schoolroom. Catherine seems not so much a victim of the juvenile textbooks parodied by "The History of England," as of too early exposure to "real solemn history" in octavo, or perhaps even quarto—the inappropriate use of adult history books as children's readers. As Henry Tilney sensibly observes, it is rather hard on historians to assume that the sole purpose of their labor was "the torment of little boys and girls," and to hold them "accountable for the difficulty of learning to read" (*NA*, 110). Fanny Price faced a similar problem, though characteristically without complaint: "Miss Lee taught her French and heard her read the daily portion of history; but he [Edmund] recommended the books which charmed her leisure hours" (*MP*, 23). Rather a pity, since Catherine and Fanny are the two characters in Austen's novels who seem to have the greatest instinctive enthusiasm for history—who show a sense of the past. However Fanny survives her experience of schoolroom history, for we later find her instructing her sister Susan: "What Fanny told her of former times, dwelt more on her mind than the pages of Goldsmith" (*MP*, 419).

There is every reason to believe that Eleanor Tilney, who was "fond of history" (*NA*, 108), better represented Jane Austen's own mature views than did Catherine Morland. Miss Tilney read the works of Hume and Robertson "with pleasure." Jane Austen's brother said that "her reading was very extensive in history and belles lettres."[37] One would like to know more about her reading. She owned a set of Hume's *History of England*.[38] She must have read Robertson, and it is impossible to believe that she was not familiar with Gibbon, in whose *Decline and Fall* the phrase "pride and prejudice" appears twice.[39] From her surviving letters we do know that she was particularly interested in contemporary history. John Bigland's *Letters on the Modern History and Political Aspect of Europe* (1804)—if Chapman's suggested identification of the reference is correct—is hardly a classic, but she and her niece Fanny read it together at Godmersham, probably aloud.[40] "The first and greatest article in a young Lady's education" was to read aloud well, according to one authority in such matters.[41] History books were a popular and proper choice for the exercise of such talent, which Jane Austen (according to her brother) possessed in abundance.[42] Austen declared herself "in love" with Captain Charles Pasley. This passion was based on *The Military Policy and Institution of the British Empire* (1810), a skilled analysis and critique of British military strategy against Napoleon which drew learnedly on historical precedents, particularly Roman, and was highly praised by Southey, Wordsworth, and Wellington.[43] She was an equally warm admirer of the great antislavery campaigner Thomas Clarkson, whose *History of the Rise, Progress and Abolition of the African Slave Trade by the British Parliament* (1808) was participant history with a vengeance.[44] And of Claudius Buchanan, missionary chaplain of the East India Company whose *Christian Researches in Asia* (1811) colorfully described the progress of Christianity against native "superstition" in India.[45] Such reading was quite in keeping with the keen interest in imperial affairs one would expect in one who belonged to a family with West Indian plantation connections and close ties with Warren Hastings, the brilliant, controversial Governor General of India. This is to say nothing of the naval and military activities of her brothers. Park Honan's recent biography makes even more untenable the amazingly durable myth that Jane Austen was somehow detached from the great events of her time. She certainly knew that she was living "in history," and she followed events with well-informed interest.

Yet Sandra Gilbert and Susan Gubar have recently attempted to "dehistoricize" Austen in the name of feminist literary criticism. They choose to identify her with Catherine Morland and maintain that she "refused to take historical 'reality' seriously."[46] They put forward the following remarkable reading: "Ignoring the political and economic activity of men throughout history, Austen implies that history may very well be a uniform drama of masculine posturing that is no less a fiction (and a potentially pernicious one) than Gothic romance."[47] This feminist version of history is the mirror image of the conventional chauvinistic view of history as a men's club. Happily, this gender stereotyping of history as a subject (one which, if it existed in Jane Austen's time, was if anything reversed) is currently dissolving, at least in this author's experience as a university teacher. Women, like Jane Austen, study history, because, like Jane Austen, they live in it.

Figure 7. "The History of England"
(Volume the Second MS; Courtesy The British Library)

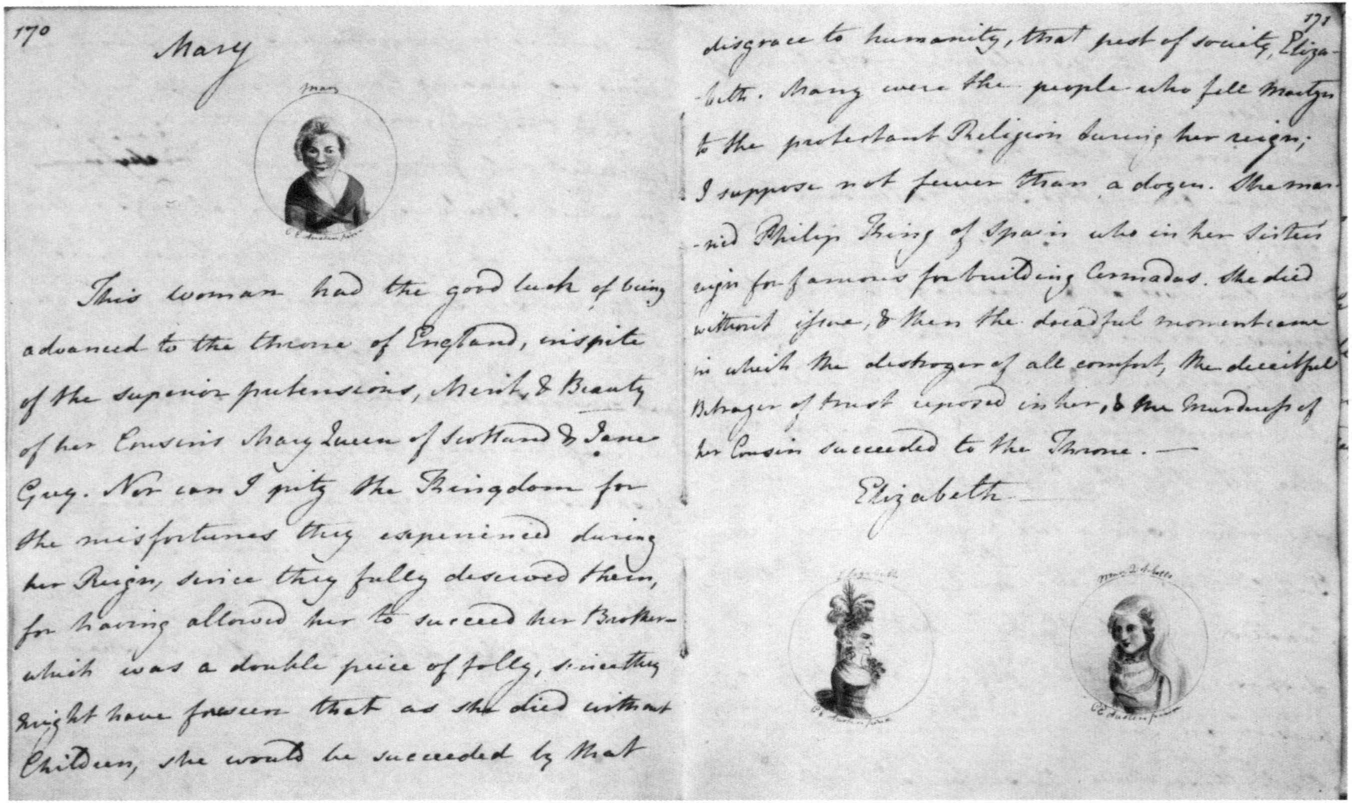

170

Mary

This woman had the good luck of being
advanced to the throne of England, inspite
of the superior pretensions, merit & Beauty
of her Cousins Mary Queen of Scotland & Jane
Grey. Nor can I pity the Kingdom for
the misfortunes they experienced during
her Reign, since they fully deserved them,
for having allowed her to succeed her Brother—
which was a double piece of folly, since they
might have foreseen that as she died without
Children, she would be succeeded by that

disgrace to humanity, that pest of society, Eliz:
:th. Many were the people who fell Martyrs
to the protestant Religion during her reign;
I suppose not fewer than a dozen. She mar-
:ed Philip, King of Spain who in her sister
Eliz:ths reign was famous for building
Armadas. She died without Issue, & then the
:without Issue, & then the dreadful moment came
in which the destroyer of all comfort, the deceitful
Betrayer of trust reposed in her, & the Murderess
of her Cousin succeeded to the Throne. —

Elizabeth

Notes

1. Frederic Harrison to Thomas Hardy, 10 Nov. 1913, Dorset Country Museum, 1779. I owe this transcription to Martha and Albert Vogeler.

2. Martin Jarrett-Kerr, "The Mission of Eng. Lit.," letter in *Times Literary Supplement,* 3 Feb. 1984, p. iii.

3. This topic has been touched in my "'Real Solemn History' and Social History," in David Monaghan, ed., *Jane Austen in a Social Context,* London, 1981, pp. 91–93.

4. The suggestion is offered in Warren Roberts, *Jane Austen and the French Revolution,* London, 1979, pp. 128–29.

5. Mrs. Austen, remarking on the closeness of her two daughters, is reported as remarking "if Cassandra were going to have her head cut off, Jane would insist on sharing her fate." James Edward Austen-Leigh, *A Memoir of Jane Austen* (1870), ed. R.W. Chapman, London, 1926, p. 16.

6. Dorothy Gardiner, *English Girlhood at School: A Study of Women's Education through Twelve Centuries,* London, 1929, p. 429.

7. Hester Chapone, *Letters on the Improvement of the Mind Addressed to a Lady* (1774), London, 1822, p. 140.

8. Wetenhall Wilkes, *A Letter of Genteel and Moral Advice to a Young Lady,* Dublin, 1740, p. 152, cited in Gardiner, p. 431.

9. Chapone, p. 140.

10. Ibid., p. 182.

11. The problem of history for children is discussed in Maria Edgeworth and Richard Lovell Edgeworth, *Practical Education,* London, 1798, pp. 352–66.

12. Seen in an edition of London 1772 in the Osborne Collection, Toronto Public Library. I am very grateful to the staff for their assistance in examining a number of eighteenth-century history texts, and to *The Osborne Collection of Early Children's Books 1476–1910: A Catalogue,* 2 volumes, Toronto, 1958–1975, for valuable bibliographical information.

13. Cooper, p. 142.

14. Ibid., p. 136

15. Ibid., p. 103.

16. London, n.d., pp. 66–67. This edition is dated around 1795 in the *Osborne Catalogue,* II, 781. The original edition appeared in 1740.

17. Dodsley, p. 113.

18. Quoted in *Osborne Catalogue,* II, 781.

19. Sarah Trimmer, *A Description of a Set of Prints of English History Contained in a Set of Easy Lessons,* London [1792], I, 29.

20. "The History of England from the reign of Henry the 4th to the death of Charles the 1st," in *Volume the Second,* ed. Brian Southam, Oxford, 1963, pp. 140–41. All internal notes refer either to this volume or to *The Novels of Jane Austen,* ed. R.W. Chapman, third edition, London, 1933, by volume and page.

21. William Goldsmith, *An History of England in a Series of Letters from a Nobleman to His Son,* London, 1764, I, 4–5.

22. *Jane Austen's Letters,* ed. R.W. Chapman, Oxford, 1952, p. 304.

23. Florian Jolly, *Guide to the Study of the History of England in a Series of Questions upon Goldsmith's Abridgement,* London, 1814; James Adair (pseud.), *500 Questions Deduced from Goldsmith's History,* London, 1811.

24. Donald J. Greene, "Jane Austen and the Peerage," *PMLA* 68 (1953), 1017–31.

25. Victor G. Wexler, *David Hume and the History of England,* Philadelphia, 1979, pp. 34–35, 64.

26. Cited in Judith N. Shklar, "Learning without Knowing," *Daedalus* (Spring 1980), 62. Yet Voltaire praised Hume's history as "perhaps the best written in any language" (Wexler, p. 90).

27. Goldsmith, I, vi-viii.

28. Ibid., III, 315.

29. Ibid., III, 316.

30. Edgeworth and Edgeworth, 351.

31. Ibid.

32. Goldsmith, III, 129.

33. Ibid., III, 305, 310.

34. David Hume, *The History of England from the Invasion of Julius Caesar to the Revolution in 1688* (1778), Indianapolis, 1983, V, 544.

35. Chapone, p. 171.

36. Hume judged that the passion of James seems not to have contained in it "anything criminal or flagitious," V, 533. Goldsmith discreetly drops the word "criminal," III, 178.

37. Mary Augusta Austen-Leigh, *Personal Aspects of Jane Austen,* New York, 1920, p. 38.

38. R.W. Chapman, *Jane Austen: Facts and Problems,* Oxford, 1948, p. 37.

39. Anthony W. Shipps, "Pride and Prejudice," *Notes and Queries,* New Series 23 (1976), 510.

40. *Jane Austen's Letters,* p. 333.

41. Wilkes, p. 149.

42. Mary Augusta Austen-Leigh, p. 61.

43. *Jane Austen's Letters,* p. 292; C.W. Pasley, *The Military Policy and Institutions of the British Empire,* London, 1914, pp. 9, 54–61.

44. *Jane Austen's Letters,* p. 292.

45. Ibid.

46. Sandra M. Gilbert and Susan Gubar, *The Madwoman in the Attic: The Woman Writer and the Nineteenth Century Literary Imagination,* New Haven, 1984, 133.

47. Ibid., p. 134.

Jane Austen and the Uncommon Reader

Laurie Kaplan

In essay #4 of *The Rambler* (Saturday, March 31, 1750),[1] Doctor Samuel Johnson asserts the amorphous but very real presence of the "Common Reader," defined variously by the critics as the educated, reasonable man, the representative of Augustan taste and common sense, who has formulated rational assumptions about his world. Johnson's Common Reader "is surely not the average man nor the common man in any sense of low social status, but the universal man in the neoclassical sense."[2] He is not "the critic and the scholar," Virginia Woolf tells us in her volume of essays entitled *The Common Reader,* for "he is worse educated. . . . He reads for his own pleasure rather than to impart knowledge or correct the opinions of others."[3] The Common Reader, in fact, often is identified as the "Publick," but for Johnson, the "Publick" meant an extremely narrow segment of the eighteenth-century population.

The foremost spokesman for the Augustan Age, known for his moral vision, intellectual power, elegant prose, and subtle wit, Johnson assumed that the Common Reader shared his own taste and moral judgment, his concern with Truth and Human Nature. Johnson wrote for a Publick he deemed fully capable of judging and "responding to literature and being changed by it."[4] In his essays and *Lives,* Johnson neither lowers his standards for nor patronizes his Common Reader; rather, he credits the Publick with his own fine sense of social responsibility and rationality. In the last paragraph of his "Life" of Thomas Gray, Johnson says that he "rejoice[s] to concur with the common reader,"[5] with a reading public whose taste, judgment, and literary habits he has certainly helped to shape. When he stresses the literary merits of the *dulce et utile,* the delightful as well as the useful, or the value of the "accurate observation of the living world" (Rambler #4), he assumes his readers' concurrence and approval.

This paper formed the basis of a group discussion at the 1987 meeting of the Jane Austen Society of North America. A short version was published in *Persuasions* 9 (December 16, 1987).

About what his readers read, and why they read, Johnson, in *The Adventurer* #137 (Tuesday, February 26, 1754), writes that the fickle Publick chooses books more or less at random out of "spite, vanity, and curiosity, hope and fear, love and hatred":

> Some are fond to take a celebrated volume into their hands, because they hope to distinguish their penetration, by finding faults which have escaped the public; others eagerly buy it in the first bloom of reputation, that they may join the chorus of praise, and not lag, as Falstaff terms it, in "the rearward of the fashion."
> Some read for style and some for argument: one has little care about the sentiment . . . ; another regards not the conclusion . . . [;] they read for other purposes than the attainment of practical knowledge. . . .
> Some read that they may embellish their conversation, or shine in dispute; some that they may not be detected in ignorance, or want the reputation of literary accomplishments: but the most general and prevalent reason of study is the impossibility of finding another amusement equally cheap or constant, equally independent on the hour or the weather. He that wants money to follow the chase of pleasure through her yearly circuit, and is left at home when the gay world rolls to Bath or Tunbridge; he whose gout compels him to hear from his chamber the rattle of chariots transporting happier beings to plays and assemblies, will be forced to seek in books a refuge from himself.

Jane Austen knew and wrote for this fickle Common Reader, for a well-read Publick seeking amusement along with a "little learning." The readers of *Pride and Prejudice* and *Emma,* like the readers of *Rasselas,* judged manners, morals, and literature according to standards of elegance and propriety delineated in such neoclassical periodicals as Addison's *Tatler,* Addison and Steele's *Spectator, The Adventurer,* Mackenzie's *The Mirror,* and, of course, *The Idler* and Johnson's *Rambler.* The essayists provided, in essence, a code of critical and intellectual criteria against which the reader could compare and contrast not only a new work but the whole of society.

The essayists were not alone in providing codes for the Common Reader, for during the eighteenth century the novel was reaching a new reading public. Changing social and economic conditions gave rise to a readership who appreciated exotic tales, sentimental novels, and romances. By the middle of the eighteenth century, booksellers, not patrons, dictated topics and forms, and circulating libraries made novels, which were considered "typical example[s] of the debased kind of writing by which booksellers pandered to the reading public,"[6] more readily available to readers. Thus, the public taste was being shaped by many authors who wrote only to entertain, and therefore to sell; who wrote, that is, simply to fulfill the literary expectations of a broader population group than the Common Readers acknowledged by Johnson.

Jane Austen's juvenilia shows that from her youth she knew and could use effectively the conventions of both the essayists and the novelists, but that she strove to transcend the confining tendencies of such conventions as the epistolary or picaresque structure, Gothic trappings, and the "participating narrator."[7] Her particular target in the juvenilia was the sentimental novel, one of the most popular forms of literature in the late eighteenth century, and obviously a source of universal pleasure in the Austen household, if only for the inherent comedy in the plots and characterizations. Familiarity with the extravagant conventions of this form, especially the focus on the characters' ability or inability to exhibit emotion, or "sensibility," allowed Jane Austen the latitude simultaneously to tease her readers, to challenge their literary expectations, and to criticize the "fictitious morality" of the novels of sensibility.[8]

As early as 1787–90, Jane Austen established a particular relationship with her audience, and, like Dr. Johnson, she assumed that her readers shared her taste and standards for morality. In the very early composition from *Volume the First* entitled "Jack & Alice," the young author shows that she is well aware of her readers' theories and assumptions about fiction. "Before I proceed to give an account of the Evening," the narrator announces in Chapter the First, "it will be proper to describe to my reader, the persons and Characters of the party introduced to his acquaintance" (12).[9] Jane Austen's acknowledgment of "my reader" in *Volume the First* is facetious, for her dedications show that she composed for an identified audience—a social group with "common," that is, shared, values and assumptions: her own family, "who are great Novel-readers & not ashamed of being so," as Jane Austen herself reveals in a letter to Cassandra.[10] What is important here, however, is the control over the text gained by the young writer, for she uses standard conventions, with which her readers would have been perfectly familiar, to explore multiple voices, various points of view, new plot complexities, and absurd juxtapositions in order to thwart her audience's demands and expectations.

In Chapter the Second of "Jack & Alice," the narrator cajoles the audience: "Alice Johnson was the unhappy sixth whose heart had not been able to withstand the power of [Charles Adams's] Charms. But as it may appear strange to my Readers, that so much worth & Excellence as [Charles Adams] possessed should have conquered only [Alice Johnson's heart], it will be necessary to inform them that the Miss Simpsons were defended from his Power by Ambition, Envy, & Selfadmiration" (15). As the narrator challenges the reader's assumptions about fiction, about the relationship of the characters to plot, about the relationship of the characters' expression of emotion to the situation, passive reading is impossible, for Jane Austen constantly manipulates the action and characterization. In fact, by Chapter the Fourth, the narrator of "Jack & Alice" begins to tease the reader not only about how the characters react to episodes in the plot but also how the audience expects plot to resolve:

My Readers may perhaps imagine that after such a fracas [as had taken place between Lady Williams and Alice], no intimacy could longer subsist between the Johnsons and Lady Williams, but in that they are mistaken for her ladyship was too sensible to be angry at a conduct which she could not help perceiving to be the natural consequence of inebriety & Alice had too sincere a respect for Lady Williams & too great a relish for her Claret, not to make every concession in her power. (18)

This same technique is used in *Persuasion,* when the narrator reports: "[Lady Russell] and Sir Walter, did *not* marry, whatever might have been anticipated on that head by their acquaintance" (*P,* 5) (or by Jane Austen's readers), and at the very end of *Persuasion,* the narrator questions her audience: "Who can be in doubt of what followed? When any two young people take it into their heads to marry, they are pretty sure by perseverance to carry their point, be they ever so poor, or ever so imprudent, or ever so little likely to be necessary to each other's ultimate comfort. This may be bad morality to conclude with, but I believe it to be truth" (*P,* 248).

In all these cases, Jane Austen creates a narrator who is detached from the action, who borrows the voice of the neoclassical essayists to comment on some of the very silly novelistic conventions so in demand by the public. The author criticizes popular literature by creating burlesques; she imposes on some quite fantastic episodes her own realistic view of how literature should mirror life, and her narrators offer solutions and explanations that provide ironic contrasts to contemporary novels. Jane Austen seems to flaunt her ability to play with traditions. When the narrator of *Northanger Abbey* tells the reader that she is well "aware that the rules of composition forbid the introduction of a character not connected with [her] fable" (*NA,* 251), there is the sound of laughter echoing behind the serious language of the text. The ironically phrased "bad morality" quoted above and the reference to the strict Augustan "rules of composition" show that Jane Austen is amused by what she can do with the literary and stylistic conventions of contemporary writing.

Perhaps the most ironical relationship of author to readers is established in *Volume the Second* by the "partial, prejudiced and ignorant Historian" (138) who, in relating "The History of England from the reign of Henry the 4th to the death of Charles the 1st," reminds them *nota bene* that "there will be very few Dates in this History." The dates her readers will need to know she "shall of course make choice of" (142). What date does she choose for "Henry the 8th"?—"the 6th of May," for she maintains that: "It would be an affront to my Readers were I to suppose that they were not as well acquainted with the particulars of this King's reign as I am myself. It will therefore be saving *them* the task of reading again what they have read before, & *myself* the trouble of writing what I do not perfectly recollect, by giving only a slight sketch of the principal Events which marked his reign" (142). The hilarious "History" was obviously intended for pure amusement, to be shared when the Readers at Steventon spent an evening reading aloud. Southam notes that "Jane Austen's pieces, with their fragile, often allusive humour, were designed for such an intimate hearing. She could depend on the full understanding of her listeners."[11]

The juvenilia depend on general as well as specific allusions for a successful humorous effect. The most amusing pieces are, of course, the longer, for Jane Austen's subtle method of character development profits from the character's repeated interaction with the elements of the plot. Stock allusions to governesses who elope with butlers ("Jack & Alice"), to lost [or misplaced] children ("Henry and Eliza"), and to deathbed revelations generate their own appreciative chuckles. In "Love and Freindship," for example, Jane Austen subverts the sentimentality of the standard deathbed scene. After Sophia has swooned for the last time and, as a result, lies on her deathbed, she offers very particular advice to Laura: "Run mad as often as you chuse; but do not faint—" (102). Laura herself tells the reader that she has "most faithfully adhered to" those words of wisdom.

Jane Austen, however, is never content with using the conventions superficially. Instead, she probes the essence of generalized predicaments (revealing secret identities, for example, or discovering lost cousins, parents, grandfathers) and focuses on the absurdity of the situations the characters have gotten themselves into. The marriage plot is another device that Jane Austen considered inherently comical, a point of view reflected in piece after piece in the juvenilia. Her special forte for these plots develops all sorts of episodic, unrelated, unbelievable adventures for perfectly believable characters—ladies of fashion, fortune hunters, gamesters, drunks, and perceptive young women. When she burlesques the marriage plots, Jane Austen demonstrates a precocious talent, for she parodies such novelists as Fanny Burney, Henry Fielding, Samuel Richardson, and Mrs. Radcliffe, all of whom the Austens would have read.[12] Confident of her family's ability to connect the general and the specific and to trace her allusions, the young author concocts her comedies by exaggerating the kinds of extravagant relationships and improbable coincidences that were the stock-in-trade of the popular novelists of the period. It is as though she cannot wait to lead her audience into traps resulting from their own reading experiences.

More than a hundred years after Jane Austen wrote her juvenilia, Virginia Woolf conjured up a vision of Jane Austen's brothers' and sisters' amusement "when Jane read out loud ["Love and Freindship,"] her last hit at the vices which they all abhorred. . . . [N]othing is more obvious than that this girl of fifteen, sitting in her private corner of the common parlour, was writing not to draw a laugh from her brothers and sisters, and not for home consumption. She was writing for everybody, for nobody, for our age, for her own."[13] What is tricky here is that fluctuations of taste often dictate comedic form and content; the reader's amusement, then, is subject to the changes of taste, so that what Jane Austen's audience found funny may baffle the reader today. The general as well as the specific references and allusions have been lost as the novel has changed and the reading public has grown. It is imperative, therefore, for Jane Austen's readers today to familiarize themselves with the kinds of literature Johnson's Common Readers read and the circulating libraries disseminated.

Samuel Johnson's and Jane Austen's Readers commended the social experience of reading aloud, of talking about the ideas, the elegance of language and phrasing, the form, and the moral values of a literary work. The process of reading aloud, which necessarily shares ideas, values, and myths, also establishes a common vocabulary of images, symbols, and tastes. For the modern world, however, reading aloud, with the wider implications of seeking a more perfect understanding of the work and gaining insight into the self, is more or less passé. It is questionable whether readers today are involved in what Virginia Woolf called creating "out of whatever odds and ends [they] can come by, some kind of whole—a portrait of a man, a sketch of an age, a theory of writing."[14] Are we, in effect, Uncommon Readers, distanced from each other by time and place, holding widely divergent opinions about religion and politics, about the qualities of elegance and style? We seem unused to "creating" portraits of the characters and landscapes of the time, and we do not often comment on the style and grace of a writer's prose. Yet in reading Jane Austen's books over and over again, we begin to delight in the balance and the symmetry of the sentences and the form, the elegance of phrasing. We note how perfect it is for Lady Susan, in letters from her own hand, to turn elegance of expression into an evil, and for Jane Austen to parody her own poised style. We begin to see how the young author turned "Amelia Webster" into a commentary on contemporary letter writing, "The beautifull Cassandra" into a lampoon on picaresque romantic quests, and "Henry and Eliza" into a critique of the fairy-tale motif.

Jane Austen's early work endorses many of the Augustan Publick's literary expectations: the epistolary form, the balanced structure; subtle irony, satire, and wit; elegance of the story's setting, nobility of at least one character's rank; moral value, rational judgment, and truth to nature. Delighting her readers and refusing to use the novel as a purely didactic tool, Jane Austen incorporates all the iconic metaphors and symbols recognizable to her "Readers," whom she often addresses directly, in full expectation of their collusion with her against the rogues and villains who populate her fiction. Contemporary readers would have easily identified common allusions—to Humphrey Repton or Capability Brown, to Richardson or Mrs. Radcliffe, or to Shakespeare and Sheridan. They would have quickly recognized the general sources of her burlesques of contemporary dramas, memoirs, or Gothic and adventure fiction, and her parodies of bad writing would have had them fainting alternately on sofas in fits of laughter.

Naturally, we read differently from those readers, which means that to be good readers and to interpret accurately we have to study the texts attentively. Like Jane Austen's contemporary readers, we, too, are saddened when, for example, Charlotte does her duty by her family and pragmatically marries the odious Mr. Collins. Yet, those contemporary readers perhaps felt rather relieved as well, for they understood the financial implications of spinsterhood in Georgian England and the position of single women in society. Those readers would have interpreted correctly the subtle snubs intended by Lady Greville in "From A young Lady in distress'd Circumstances to her freind" (*Volume the Second*) and by Lady Catherine De Bourgh in *Pride and Prejudice,* for neither lady will leave her coach, forcing both Maria and Charlotte to stand outside exposed to the wind.[15] Jane Austen's contemporaries would also have seen the social symbolism in Eliza's rebuttal to Lady Catherine's rudeness about the impossibility of her marrying Mr. Darcy. When Eliza says, "He [Mr. Darcy] is a gentleman; I am a gentleman's daughter; so far we are equal" (*PP,* 356), the modern reader must remember that, although Longbourn is not Pemberley, equality was becoming a relative ideal.

When we read that Sir Walter Elliot takes up "a very good house" in Camden-place as his residence, we are likely to misinterpret Jane Austen's intent. Camden-place, the narrator tells us, is a fitting abode for Sir Walter and Miss Elliot, for it provides "a lofty, dignified situation, such as becomes a man of consequence" (*P,* 137), a position close to the center of action; Jane Austen's acute Common Reader, however, would have known that Camden-place was actually a new, probably unfinished, poorly constructed group of buildings, all outward appearance and show.[16] All in all, modern readers must "work" to read Jane Austen's novels well, but by "creating" when we read fiction, as Virginia Woolf suggested, and by becoming actively involved in the context as well as the text, we can discover the assumptions the Austens shared about art and life, assumptions that the Readers of Jane Austen's novels would have held, too.

The juvenilia are perhaps even more challenging for today's readers, for the abbreviated, parodic forms, full of literary caricatures and stock situations, demand extra attention. Jane Austen's audience would have been perfectly familiar with and therefore would have had certain expectations of the epistolary form—the form of many of the pieces included in the juvenilia: "The three Sisters" (*Volume the First*), "Love and Freindship," "Lesley Castle," and the intriguing "A Collection of Letters" (*Volume the Second*), and, of course, *Lady Susan.* Doctor Johnson in *The Idler* #84 promotes the value of reading autobiographies, letters, and memoirs; he explains that "the writer of his own life has at least the first qualification of an historian, the knowledge of the truth." Those works "in which the writer tells his own story" become, perhaps, the most representative pieces of Augustan literature, yet Jane Austen asks implicitly that we also "know" the limitations of the epistolary novel so that we can detect what she is doing that is new. In "A Collection of Letters," the individual letters develop as vignettes, for Jane Austen captures all the tones and shades of each writer. Each voice is individual and interesting. In fact, Maria Williams does such a good job conveying her "distress'd circumstances" that we want to know more about her verbal fencing with Lady Greville. In *Lady Susan,* although Jane Austen works within the neoclassical form (letters), she constantly experiments with content (the evil heroine who tells her own story). As Johnson points out, there is no better way to discover the truth of the situation than to hear it from the historian—in this case, Lady Susan herself.

Jane Austen's Readers would have quickly recognized in her work the great Johnsonian abstractions—Truth, for example, and Vanity, Pride, and Self-Delusion. She shares the Augustan's concern with ideals, vices, and virtues, but she transforms pure concept by individualizing or characterizing, by making the general more specific. Through ironic distancing, Darcy's and Elizabeth's pride and prejudice, and Elinor's and Marianne's sense and sensibility evolve naturally from the text, from their interaction with the plot and other characters. In the juvenilia those abstractions are painted with a much broader brush, to the extent that the characterizations often dissolve into caricatures. Laura and Sophia, the charming cousins in "Love and Freindship," become the epitome of female silliness; "Youth, Beauty, Birth, Wit, Merit, & Money" (21) supplant the Johnsonian ideals in "Jack & Alice," and the frailties of all the characters are exposed by their quests for these abstractions. Lady Susan discloses her own self-importance and vanity, her lack of responsibility and duty, her heartlessness and selfishness. Meanwhile, Jane Austen detaches herself from the action, satisfied to watch her characters with a satiric eye, and only occasionally does she step in to reveal explicitly the vice or the virtue attached to the individual.

The reader today is struck by the playful spirit and ironic control in the juvenilia. Jane Austen paid close attention to advanced and elaborate literary principles, and to her readers' growing sophistication in terms of literary technique. The early works reveal the unpolished facets of Jane Austen's developing art, and, because she wrote these pieces for the amusement of a very specific audience, reading them may be laborious for those who have not read her major novels first. "Unfortunately," as Southam points out, "we, as readers outside the family circle, a century and a half later, cannot hope to enjoy [the] knowledge of books and people familiar to the household, and for the most part the references are sunk too deeply for us to identify biographical details or parody of specific works."[17] The youthful writer makes demands on the modern reader, demands that the Readers she was writing for—her family and friends—would have met equally, demands that we, the Uncommon Readers, find difficult.

What *do* we need to know to read Jane Austen's novels well? What is our relation to the text? Are we active or passive readers? Can we generate a social or literary context for each novel or a background against which the story is set?

To read Jane Austen well, to relate effectively to the text, to be able to "create" a "sketch of an age," today's Uncommon Readers must become Johnsonian Common Readers; that is, we must all be actively involved in a process of exchange and interpretation. We, too, must heed the eighteenth-century abstractions so favored by the Augustans, the vices and virtues that are human nature: melancholy, selfishness, snobbery, indolence, vanity, diligence, dignity, rationality, and so on. To appreciate and interpret the satire and social commentary, we have to delve into the text and discover Jane Austen's own ideas about Gothic romances and sentimental writing, about the country house ethos and Duty, and about the improvement of the estate. To recreate the social context, we have to note how Jane Austen places the individual in the society, and how the character conforms to or ignores society's rules.

Because Jane Austen's fiction reflects issues of concern not only to the Country Families but also to the more middle class Common Reader, who craved the sentimental novel and loved extravagances of heightened sensibility, we must ascertain the social and moral values of an age in flux. We have to reinterpret what some critics call the author's minimalist approach, which dissects the tenets of eighteenth-century "realism." By focusing on the activities of daily living and on the realistic details of "average" life, Jane Austen transforms the Augustan's preoccupation with rank and status into stories about the rise of another class.

The Uncommon Reader today must necessarily excavate the gardens and explore the estates of Jane Austen's landscapes to decode certain enigmas related to the literary conventions, the social context, the formalities of style of the compositions. The Uncommon Reader's attention should focus both on what Jane Austen includes in her text and on what she leaves out. If her novels are subject to the standards of the time, the Uncommon Reader must identify those standards; if her novels penetrate private as well as societal mores, the Uncommon Reader must differentiate between the two.

The good reader's role is to engage the text in active inquiry. Our own sense of isolation as well as our lack of shared context makes the reading and rereading of Jane Austen's novels all the more pleasurable and instructive, especially when we recognize the parts of the whole. People who would *not* rather be reading Jane Austen allow her words to remain passively flat on the page; the new Common Reader, entering into a conspiracy with the author and the narrator, "creates," as Virginia Woolf says, by making those words come to life.

Notes

1. Samuel Johnson, *The Works of Samuel Johnson,* vol. 1, New York, 1834. All further quotations from Johnson's essays are taken from this edition.

2. Rene Wellek, "The Later Eighteenth Century," *A History of Modern Criticism: 1750–1950,* New Haven, 1955, p. 55.

3. Virginia Woolf, *The Common Reader: First Series,* New York, 1925; 1953, p. 1.

4. Leopold Damrosch, *The Uses of Johnson's Criticism,* Charlottesville, Va., 1976, p. 1.

5. Johnson, vol. 2, p. 302.

6. Ian Watt, *The Rise of the Novel,* Berkeley, 1957, p. 54.

7. Ibid., p. 296.

8. A. Walton Litz, *Jane Austen: A Study of Her Artistic Development,* New York, 1965, p. 10.

9. Jane Austen, *The Works of Jane Austen,* ed. R.W. Chapman, rev. Brian Southam, third edition, five volumes, London, 1954, rev. 1969. All internal notes referring to the works of Jane Austen are taken from Chapman's edition.

10. *Jane Austen's Letters,* ed. R.W. Chapman, Oxford, 1932, I, p. 38.

11. Brian Southam, *Jane Austen's Literary Manuscripts,* London, 1964, p. 6.

12. See Mary Lascelles, *Jane Austen and Her Art,* London, 1939, pp. 41–83. (Cited by A. Walton Litz as the best survey of Jane Austen's reading.)

13. Woolf, pp. 138–39.

14. Ibid., p. 1.

15. Frances Beer, ed., *The Juvenilia of Jane Austen and Charlotte Brontë,* New York, 1986, p. 373.

16. Patricia Bruckmann, "Sir Walter Elliot's Bath Address," *Modern Philology* 80 (1982), 56–60.

17. Southam, p. 6.

The Madness of Jane Austen: Metonymic Style and Literature's Resistance to Interpretation

Ellen E. Martin

"Run mad as often as you chuse; but do not faint—" (102).[1] Thus the expiring Sophia to Laura, the heroine of "Love and Freindship." If running mad is so distinctively preferable to fainting, we should consider just what running mad means. As late as *Emma,* Austen shows us how Harriet, besieged by gypsies, almost faints herself into a real predicament, while her animated companion rushes nimbly away cross-country. Here Laura has advanced from the end of Letter 8, when the reunion of Edward and Augustus proves "too pathetic for the feelings of Sophia and myself—We fainted Alternately on a Sofa" (86). They take turns fainting much as they would at playing cards, spelling each other to keep up their sentiment's current. Generic fainting episodes occur in Letters 10, 11, and 12, but in Letter 13 a difference in styles of reaction appears: "Yes dearest Marianne they were our Husbands. Sophia shreiked & fainted on the Ground—I screamed and instantly ran mad—. We remained thus mutually deprived of our Senses some minutes, & on regaining them were deprived of them again—. For an Hour & a Quarter did we continue in this unfortunate Situation—Sophia fainting every moment & I running Mad as often" (99). Now each heroine acts out individually the rapid exchange of sentience and depriva-tion (virtually blurring the distinction between the two) they had earlier divided between them.

Laura theorizes that, while Sophia grew susceptible to a chill through fainting in the evening dew, she herself through "repeated fits of frenzy, had so effectually circulated and warmed my Blood as to make me proof against the chilling Damps of Night" (101). There seems to be a connection between main-taining health and consciousness, and running mad. Perhaps morality is the individual's resolute attempt to sustain consciousness of one's true situation: to draw back from this mental confrontation is to faint; to persevere in it entails running mad.

What language is used in this state? When she runs mad, Laura says: "Talk not to me of Phaetons. . . . Give me a violin—. I'll play to him & sooth him in his melancholy Hours—Beware ye gentle Nymphs of Cupid's Thunderbolts, avoid the piercing Shafts of Jupiter—Look at that Grove of Firs—I see a Leg of Mutton—They told me Edward was not Dead; but they deceived me—they took him for a Cucumber—" (100). Such a wild succession of images can only convey nonlogical, almost unrecognizable ideas. From the violin, comprehensible as an icon of solitary melancholy, and the latent, unpursued allusion to Phaeton; through the misattribution of Jupiter's thunderbolts to Cupid and Cupid's arrows to Jupiter—a mix-up that compromises Jupiter's power with passion, and taints Cupid's passion with mastery—Laura proceeds to the indigestible leg of mutton, obtrusively substituting for the leg of the wrecked hero, and interpretable only by a desperate appeal to the heroine's conflation of culinary and sexual appetites; and the cucumber, the climax of deception and nonrecognition, an object which the earlier reader must associate with sandwiches, and which the modern reader is doomed to glimpse fleetingly as a bad phallic image. The mutton and the cucumber get us into trouble as soon as we try to understand them. Interpretation leads to either triviality or impropriety. Yet we feel we ought to try to comprehend Laura's ravings, since they are set up as the preferable kind of reaction.

Austen does not, of course, offer these heroines as serious models for us, but the idiom of disconnected imagery characterizes much of the juvenilia, and must somehow be accounted for as a persistent factor in Austen's incipient moral universe. Running mad is connected on one hand with remaining conscious of one's situation and on another with a kind of language that proceeds by episodic vignette rather than continuous narrative, and concatenated, diverse images instead of logically related ones. Such a language of disconnection is apt for conveying a capacious consciousness, in which one finds that the more one sees, the less one knows for sure, that the more one discerns, the less one decides. The mad consciousness and its speech turn away from decision and established relationships, which are grounded in a logic that excludes too many of the possibilities and ambiguities that make up reality. If Austen's fictions show individual minds moving towards increased awareness, then those fictions will be such as lead us away from decisive interpretations of them, and will deflect the reader from an understanding too demonstrable by simple logic or external evidence to acknowledge fully the unproveability of truth. The juvenilia offer intense, isolated scenes that cry out for interpretation, and resist it thoroughly. They invite us into their semblance of symbolism, and then undo whatever remnant of relationship could have given us a clue to the code.

Consider "The Adventures of Mr. Harley" (40). Mr. Harley's having become a naval chaplain, why is it important that "He accordingly cut his Hair and sailed"? Why this detail of preparation rather than another? The trivial detail, when it invades the plain narrative surface, becomes a provocative detail, partly because it sticks out, and partly because it links significant ideas to inappropriate objects. The juvenilia's texture is a float of such fetishes, of misdirected details ripe for the interpreter's obsessing. I find myself musing upon the connection between Mr. Harley's cutting his hair and his later encounter with "A man *without* a Hat [and] Another with *two*" (my emphasis). Is there some play of undersupplied and oversupplied males going on here, with Mr. Harley the Samson-figure between them, having cut his hair, and perhaps lost some of his mind, and if so, who is his Delilah? And was Emma's seat really a "Hogsworth"?

After all this hair and hat business, one cannot be surprised to learn that Harley's *head* has forgotten that he had married, and married the woman facing him. Whether it is sane or insane to be able to forget some of the basic items of one's biography is a question that must cede to the simple acknowledgment that facing the truth—in a stagecoach or elsewhere—usually requires a breakdown of mental routine akin to the breakdown that occurs when a neurotic attaches the wrong emotion to an irrelevant object. Seeing an unexpected truth interrupts normal mental processes as much as seeing a ghost does.

Here we can recall that what excited Freud about dreams was that they seemed to be formed by mental processes analogous to those his patients used to form symptoms. Sometimes they would displace an upsetting feeling from things or people with which it was originally connected, to things or people with which it was not. Sometimes they would make one person or object the symbol of several ambivalent, conflicting feelings. Both these processes—Freud calls them displacement and condensation—disguise some disturbing aspect of reality so that the neurotic, or the quite sane dreamer, can go on functioning or dreaming. A full understanding of our mental life requires us to untie these symbolic knots. To untie the knots, we repeat in our minds the tying of them.

Literature may be described as a web of knots, with people and places, events and objects, tied up in a way that lures us to untie and analyze their connections, but also guarantees we will never complete the task. Literature places us in an endless phase of deciphering symbols, in which we both move towards recognizing greater reaches of reality and are captured in the provisional insanity of the web itself. Part of the independent value of Austen's juvenilia is that they present the bare bones of what is literary: the unresolvable enigma. It is a narrative's resistance to interpretation that makes it literary, and its reader mad.

"The beautifull Cassandra," for example, like Mr. Harley, is attended by misappropriated Hats we are drawn to track. Cassandra falls in love with a Bonnet that her mother, "a celebrated Millener," has just finished for a countess.

Her theft of this status symbol recalls her father's claim to nobility through illegitimate descent, his "being the near relation of the Dutchess of ——'s Butler" (44). Having established the irregularity of the heroine's pedigree, Austen confirms her social autonomy by having her put the Countess' Bonnet "on her gentle Head"—"gentle" referring to her social class—and set out for her adventures not from her father's house but her mother's shop, deriving her identity from the commercial rather than the aristocratic, and from the distaff rather than the paternal, side of her family. The independence she attains by falling in love with a Bonnet rather than a Man is demonstrated in the next chapter, where she curtseys and walks on after meeting with an accomplished Viscount. Her transcendence of rising capitalist service industries is next shown in chapter 4: "She then proceeded to a Pastry-cooks where she devoured six ices, refused to pay for them, knocked down the Pastry Cook & walked away" (45). In the central adventure, she finds herself unprovided of money to pay the hackney coachman who has driven her to Hampstead and back. It is not clear why she feels bound to pay him but not the Pastry Cook: Austen has taught us to expect recklessness as the norm for her heroine. Perhaps the circular Quest in the cab has brought Cassandra to question her private resources, as the feast of ices did not. Whatever has transpired within the heroine, we know it is important, from her solving the problem by giving up the Bonnet to the driver. This versatile piece of headgear continues to mark significance without elucidating it. Perhaps Cassandra now feels convinced enough of her identity to dispense with its external emblem, even though her ability to meet the world's demands is compromised by her empty pockets.[2]

Her tremulous encounter with Maria in chapters 8 and 9 indicates the compatibility of uncertain resources with social relations. Both ladies manifest shock (about what we have no clue), yet neither requires any information to fill out the empty pockets of their meeting. Does their "mutual silence" (46) duplicate the antithematic conspiracy of an author and readers committed to neglecting what passes for normal objects of interest in society? Committed instead to analyzing the floating, nonspecific bonnet-objects that imply, without defining, the real but unacknowledged concerns that underlie our actions?

The oddity of head ornaments continues in chapter 10, where "the Widow, . . . squeezing out her little Head thro' her less window, asked her how she did." Again, the light context of a youthful work of nonsense does not fully account for the image's strangeness. On one hand, the little head and less window suggest a person of little wit and less perspective. On another, they form a birth image, referring to that contest between a new person and a narrow aperture that never ceases to disconcert people. Perhaps all identity is born of some such contest between emergent self and social pressure. Whether one goes this far in reading the widow at the window—and there is nothing to stop us from it—or reads her as the ubiquitous old lady of every neighborhood, whose own win-

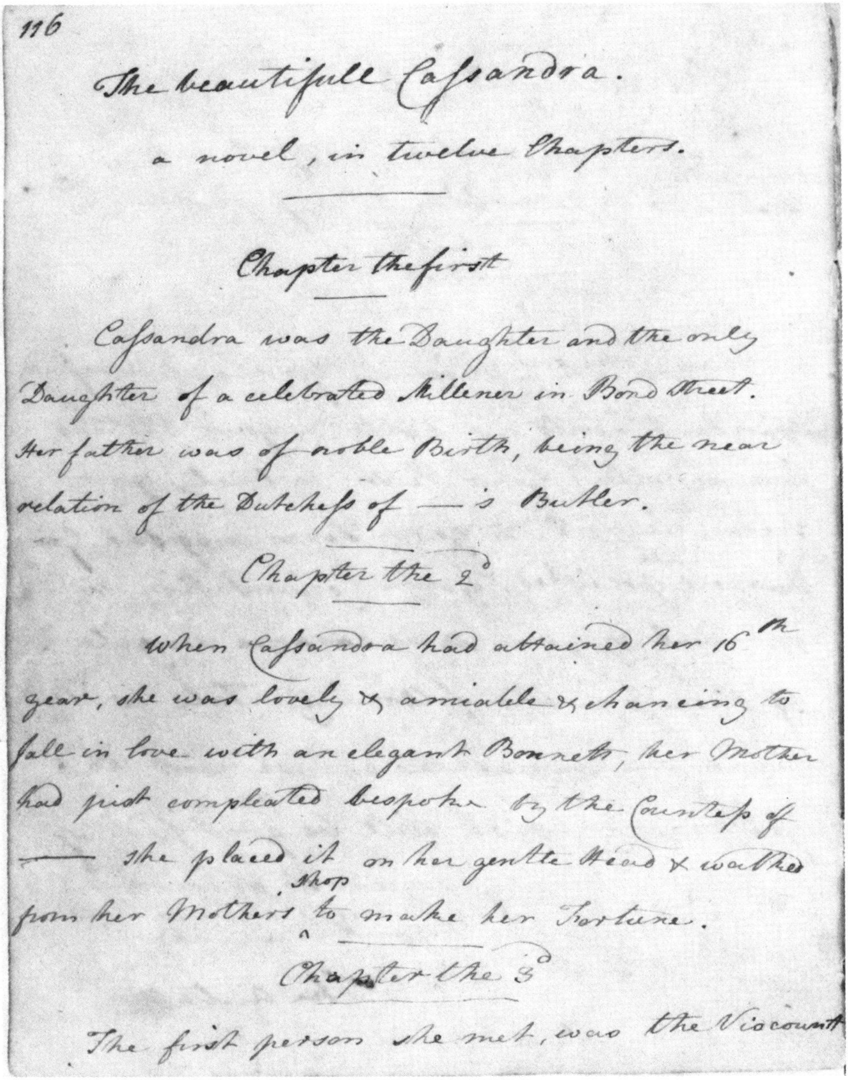

The beautifull Cassandra.

a novel, in twelve Chapters.

Chapter the first

Cassandra was the Daughter and the only
Daughter of a celebrated Millener in Bond Street.
Her father was of noble Birth, being the near
relation of the Dutchess of —— 's Butler.

Chapter the 2d

When Cassandra had attained her 16th
year, she was lovely & amiable & chancing to
fall in love with an elegant Bonnett, her Mother
had just compleated bespoke by the Countess of
—— she placed it on her gentle Head & walked
from her Mothers shop to make her Fortune.

Chapter the 3d

The first person she met, was the Viscount

Figure 8.   "The beautifull Cassandra: a novel, in twelve Chapters"
(Volume the First *MS; Courtesy The Bodleian Library, MS Don.e.*7)

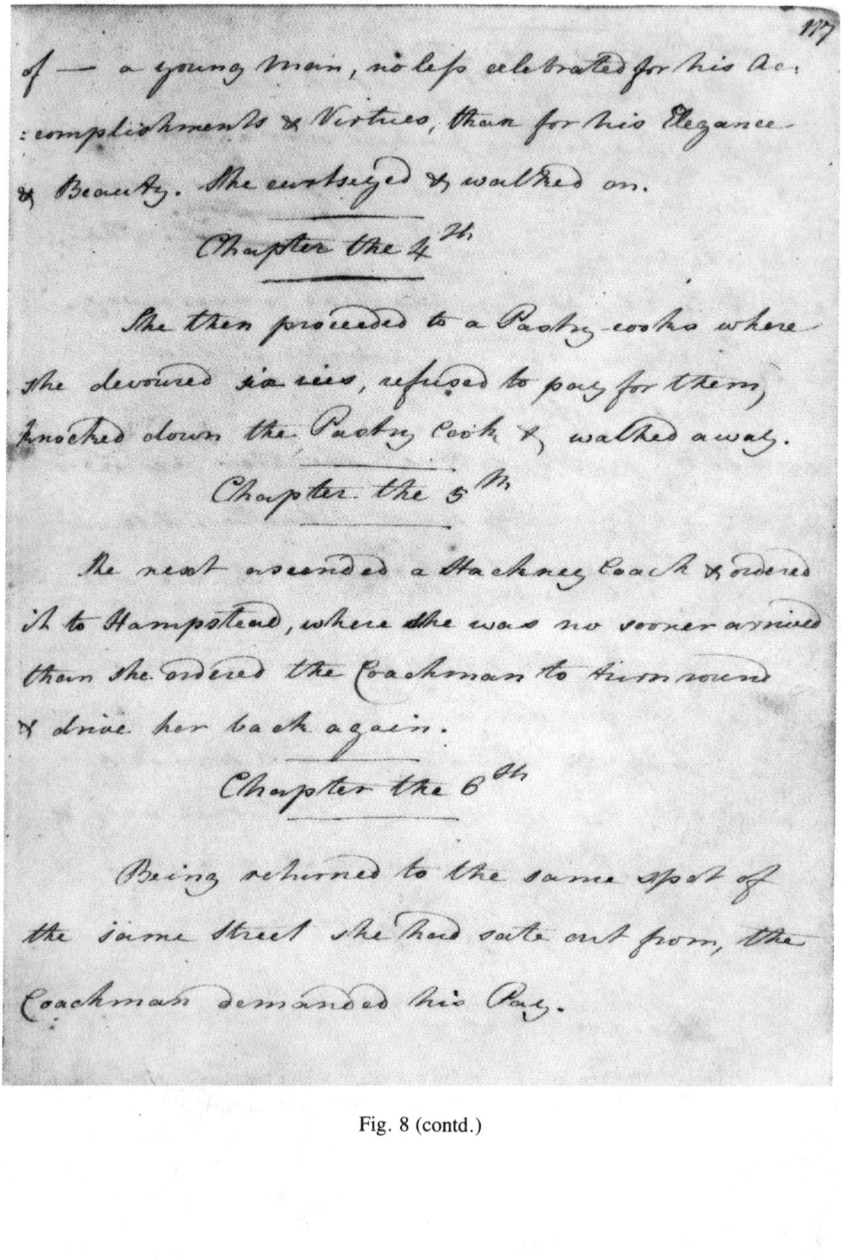

of — a young Man, no less celebrated for his Ac:
:complishments & Virtues, than for his Elegance
& Beauty. She curtseyed & walked on.

Chapter the 4th

She then proceeded to a Pastry-cooks where
she devoured ka-ries, refused to pay for them,
knocked down the Pastry Cook & walked away.

Chapter the 5th

She next ascended a Hackney Coach & ordered
it to Hampstead, where she was no sooner arrived
than she ordered the Coachman to turn round
& drive her back again.

Chapter the 6th

Being returned to the same spot of
the same street she had sate out from, the
Coachman demanded his Pay.

Fig. 8 (contd.)

Chapter the 7th

She searched her pockets over again & again;
but every search was unsuccessfull. No money
could she find. The man grew ~~impatient~~ impudent. She
placed her bonnet on his head & ran away.

Chapter the 8th

Thro' many a street she then proceeded
& met in none the least adventure till on
turning a Corner of Bloomsbury Square, she
met Maria.

Chapter the 9th

Cassandra started & Maria seemed surprised; they trembled, blushed, turned pale &
passed each other in a mutual silence.

Chapter the 10th

Cassandra was next accosted by her

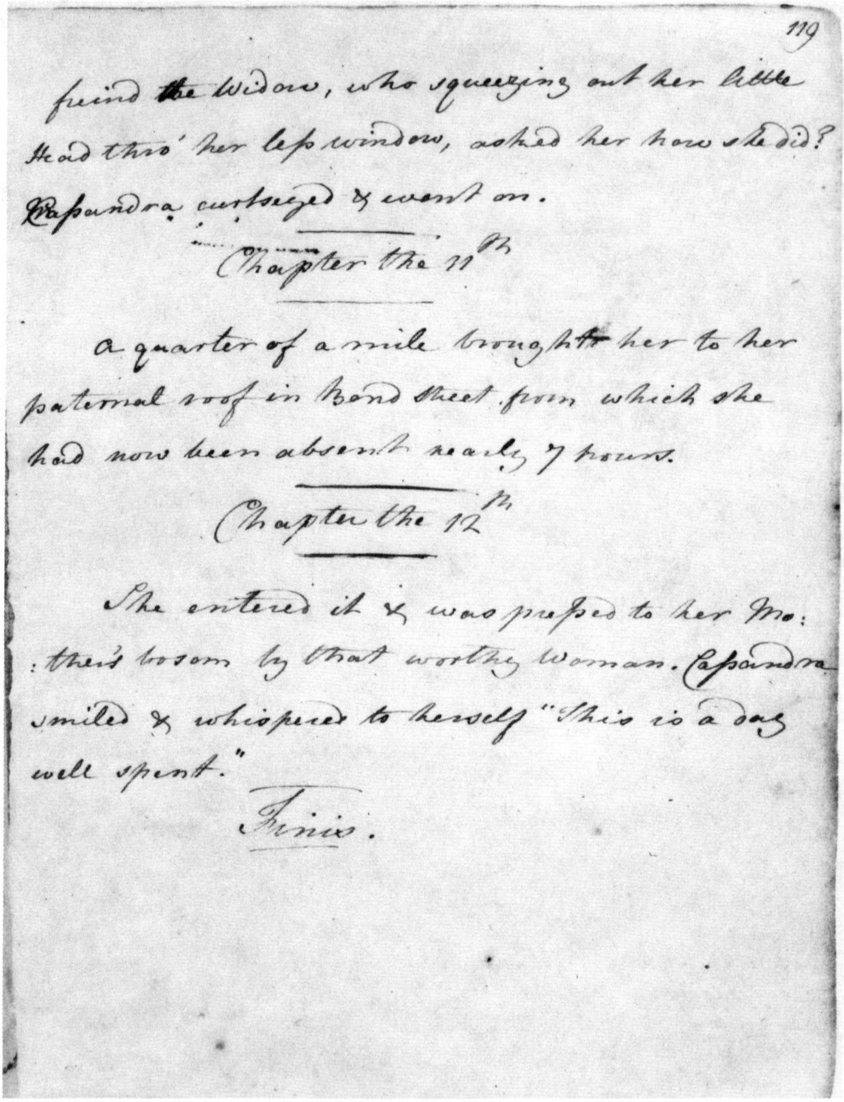

friend the Widow, who squeezing out her little
Head thro' her lep window, asked her how she did?
Cassandra curtseyed & went on.

Chapter the 11th

A quarter of a mile brought her to her
paternal roof in Bond Street, from which she
had now been absent nearly 7 hours.

Chapter the 12th

She entered it & was pressed to her Mo:
:ther's bosom by that worthy Woman. Cassandra
smiled & whispered to herself "This is a day
well spent."

Finis.

Fig. 8 (contd.)

dow's panorama is not enough for her good gossip's mind eager to judge of others' doings, she is a figure of more than literal dimensions by virtue of her remarkable appearance. And because of the spareness of this brief epic, the text gives no sure indication that we should or should not read her in any particular way. We shall all have different readings of her, yet we cannot disagree with each other, since none of us can prove either the invincibility of our own or the inappropriateness of someone else's interpretation: critical discourse becomes as mad as its text. Austen's bare-bones nonsense narrative embodies the perfect undecidability of meaning that characterizes rich, true literature. In its most naked presentation, where literary image and ornament stand apart from meaning or theme, it leads us into irrational, fanciful thinking, and in doing so, reminds us of our minds' first gestures at making (up) sense of things.

It may be useful to give formal names to the dislocated kind of image Austen sets loose in these early narratives. One way of describing literary language is to divide it into metaphor and metonymy. Metaphor is the figure based on some substantive similarity between two things. Burns writes "O my Luve's like a red, red rose" because his love and the rose share several traits: appearance, fragrance, a combination of fragility and power, of freshness and voluptuousness. Metonymy is based, not on natural similarities, but on simple juxtaposition or association. Thus we have Bogart's line to Bacall when he emerges from the shower in *Dark Passage:* "I'm glad there was a towel big enough to cover my embarrassment." Here the object is called by the emotion it evokes.

Metaphor is based on similarities that our reason and five senses can test. In eluding them, metonymies are both more exciting and more difficult to understand. The hats and bonnets of the juvenilia are symbols that have a life of their own, passing among the characters as emblems of meaning that bestow no meaning, but invite us to make connections between unlikely objects.[3] Austen's nonrepresentational aesthetic is mirrored by the drawings made during "A Tour through Wales," "which are very beautiful, tho' perhaps not such exact resemblances as might be wished, from their being taken as she ran along" (176). The rush of Austen's images seeks to be comprehensive, not comprehensible.

The ultimate example of unlikely connection, in fictions of society, is usually marriage. People in the juvenilia may end up with each other out of spiteful second-guessing, as in "The three Sisters," or out of sheer formal convention, as at the end of "The Visit," where Miss Fitzgerald declares, "Since you Willoughby are the only one left, I cannot refuse your earnest solicitations—There is my Hand" (54: a nice send-up of the common metonymy "giving one's *hand* in marriage").

"The Mystery: an unfinished comedy," as its title suggests, is the purest example of free-floating signs of meaning. The whispers and interruptions constituting its dialogue are emblems of our ignorance, and the playlet as a whole is an extended metonymy of the idea of an indiscernible idea. This obscure reach of mind is enacted at the end by Colonel Elliott's whispering of the secret to the sleeping Sir Edward. We witness the passage of meaning from imminent revelation to its final resting place in the sleeping part of our brain, the aristocratic unconscious, draped gracefully, even as silently, "in an elegant Attitude on a Sofa" (57).

The enigmatic texture of Austen's initial writing helps resolve the supposed problem of her limited scope, usually formulated in the terms, "She ignores the French Revolution." But the French Revolution, and other public cataclysms, are most often used in literature as metaphors for various passions the author sees in human nature. These events are in effect projections of either the author's or a character's concerns or qualities. This is a fairly romantic idea of history, seeing events as metaphors of oneself or human nature, and as such, is more likely to occur to a person of public power, a rich person, or a male. Austen's heroines are none of these. They cannot and do not view external events as reflections of themselves. (When Catherine Morland and Marianne Dashwood attempt to do so, they receive quite a reeducation of their imaginations.)

Private protagonists create significance in their lives by metonymic gestures that do not depend on a social frame. The heroine of "Catharine," for example, mentally links the bower behind her home with the absent friends who built it with her, and to this place apart, at the end of a retired garden walk, "she always wandered whenever anything disturbed her, . . . firmly persuaded that her Bower alone could restore her to herself" (193).

More humorously, the affable Mr. Gower of "Evelyn" carries around in his head, as a touchstone for his tastes and identity, a sort of detachable landscape in the form of

> a small circular paddock, which was enclosed by a regular paling, & bordered with a plantation of Lombardy poplars, & Spruce firs alternatively placed in three rows . . . unincumbered with any other Timber, the surface of it perfectly even & smooth, and grazed by four white Cows which were disposed at equal distances from each other. (181)

> . . . [F]our Rose trees served also to mark the quarters of the Shrubbery, by which means the Traveller might always know how far in his progress round the Paddock he was got—. (184)

This perfect symbol of Mr. Gower's cozy mental cosmos consoles him when he arrives at the castle of his deceased brother-in-law-to-be's family. Its "winding approach, struck him with terror," and "he thought it required the Paddock of Evelyn lodge" to counteract "an irregularity in the fall of the ground, and a profusion of old Timber" (187).

It is while walking the round of his paddock that Mr. Gower encounters a rose lying in the gravel, and is thereby abruptly reminded of his sister Rose, upon whose behalf he had been journeying when he was completely distracted by the user-friendly appearance of Evelyn. Where Burns's rose is a metaphor for a beloved and well-remembered lady, Mr. Gower's rose is a metonymy for the name of a sister he had utterly forgotten. For someone so abstracted and unchallenged, a metaphor simply will not do: it takes a very heavy pun to anchor Mr. Gower's disconnected mind.

Charlotte Lutterell, the great cook-correspondent in "Lesley Castle," pictures all significance as a form of meal, and translates all life's forces into menu and linen:

> Hervey had been thrown from his Horse, had fractured his Scull and was pronounced by his Surgeon to be in the most emminent Danger. "Good God! (said I) you dont say so? Why what in the name of Heaven will become of all the Victuals? We shall never be able to eat it while it is good. However, we'll call in the Surgeon to help us—. I shall be able to manage the Sir-loin myself; my Mother will eat the Soup, and You and the Doctor must finish the rest." Here I was interrupted, by seeing my poor Sister fall down to appearance Lifeless upon one of the Chests, where we keep our Table linen. (113)

To Charlotte, the great events are precisely those that transpire in her kitchen's precincts. People like Charlotte, Mr. Gower, and, more seriously, Catharine, do not see themselves mirrored metaphorically in the world, but carry their meanings around with them in personal metonyms like meals and bonnets, bowers and paddocks, husbands and wives.

Those who dispute Austen's awareness of public events may not have consulted her "History of England," in which she assigns value to rulers on the largely arbitrary basis of party alliance or portrait. The whole notion of a great narrative of causation linking events is regarded as inadequate by an artist devoted to sapping what passes for consequence and celebrating the connections made by the private, eclectic fancy. Significance is in the eye of the beholder, and Edward V is therefore "unfortunate" because he "lived so little a while that no body had time to draw his picture" (140). In the next sentence a misplaced modifier metonymically identifies his successor with an action: "He was murdered by his Uncle's Contrivance, whose name was Richard the 3d."

Austen takes no more account than Richard did of that primary factor of history, descent and affiliation. Illegitimacy hovers behind the beautiful Cassandra, Mr. Harley forgets his wife, Mr. Gower forgets his sister, and Lady Harcourt, in "Henry and Eliza," only accidentally realizes that the girl she found under a haycock and adopted over 18 years ago is her *real* daughter, and the same child Lord Harcourt in his turn had forgotten was to have arrived while he was on a journey to America. Lady Harcourt voices a parental amnesia that may be as true as it is whimsical: "Satisfied within myself of the wellfare of my Child, I soon forgot I had one, insomuch that when, we shortly after found her in the very Haycock, I had placed her, I had no more idea of her being my own, than you had" (39). Reality's only sure home seems to be in the metonymic Haycock. Lord Harcourt is willing to accept his wife's "rational & convincing Account" as sufficient proof of his child's identity. History consists less in what happens than in what is told; fiction is the accessible metonymy of an unknowable history.

The epistolary and dramatic formats of much of the juvenilia disrupt the mode of continuous historical relation, and suggest that Austen's narrative develops from conversation rather than plot. The stories do not depend deeply on causation or consequence, but express the blips in individual consciousness as new or latent ideas bubble up from the unconscious. Her plotting of mind rather than matter recaptures, and reinitiates the reader into the prerational origins of thought. It is the reduction and breakdown of causality and common sense into the metonymic names and objects we use to figure our desires that bring us so close to the inner workings of our and the characters' minds. The most interesting people all seem to be running mad, and we, their decipherers, can read their madness only by choosing to commit our own madness, in interpreting, in agreeing to make up at least half the meanings as we go along.

Notes

1. For fuller discussion of resistance to interpretation as the mark of both literature and madness, see Shoshona Felman, *Writing and Madness*, Ithaca, 1985. For another description of Austen's "anarchic" genius in the face of social ideals both "invaluable" and "insufferable," see John Bayley, *The Uses of Division: Unity and Disharmony in Literature*, New York, 1976, p. 22. On the resonance of metonymies, see the chapter on cosmic symbols in Angus Fletcher, *Allegory: The Theory of a Symbolic Mode*, Ithaca, 1964. For the metonymic quality of Austen's mature works, one should read the excellent essay "Austen: The Heroism of the Quotidian," in Irvin Ehrenpreis, *Acts of Implication: Suggestion and Covert Meaning in the Works of Dryden, Swift, Pope, and Austen*, Berkeley, 1980, pp. 112–45 (also in slightly abridged form as "Jane Austen and Heroism," *New York Review of Books* 26 (1979), pp. 37–43). Finally, for the workings of symbol- and symptom-formation, one should go to the horse's mouth and peruse Sigmund Freud's *Case Studies in Hysteria, The Interpretation of Dreams, The Psychopathology of Everyday Life,* and/or *Wit and Its Relation to the Unconscious.*

2. The possible psychoanalytic readings of empty pockets do not quite bear going into here. Suffice it to say that in the now-traditional sexual readings of them, the virginity or the barrenness they might represent pose no obstacle at all to the Janesque heroine's adventuring.

3. Austen seems to have retained her fondness for hats as metonymies of significance. She writes Cassandra in her letter of 27 October 1789 that she is making a bonnet, "on which you know my principal hopes of happiness depend."

"You, Who I Know will enter into all my feelings": Friendship in Jane Austen's Juvenilia and *Lady Susan*

Deborah J. Knuth

The following letter shows a praiseworthy combination of eager affection and patient resignation now that there can be no further communication between "Alicia" and what might appear to be her suitor:

> My dear Alicia
> I yeild to the necessity which parts us. Under such circumstances you could not act otherwise. Our friendship cannot be impaired by it; & in happier times, when your situation is as independant as mine, it will unite us again in the same Intimacy as ever. For this I shall impatiently wait. . . .[1]

The conventions of epistolary fiction enhance both the "impatience" of the forbidden correspondent and the serene assurance of constant affection. The nobility of these sentiments would seem to belie their context and significance, however, when we realize that the author is the calculating Lady Susan and the future "happier times" a reference to the death of her friend Mrs. Johnson's sickly husband. (The letter concludes, "Adieu, dearest of Friends. May the next Gouty Attack be more favourable. And may you always regard me as unalterably yours" [308].) But if, amid Austen's irony in this letter, we consider the sympathy between Lady Susan and Mrs. Johnson, we may find ourselves reconsidering the novel itself. The heroine accurately (and often) proclaims herself the mistress of verbal disguise: "If I am vain of anything, it is of my eloquence" (Letter 16, 268; see also Letter 25, 293 and Letter 33, 303), but her letters to Mrs. Johnson reveal her machinations and feelings unadorned. "I was never so enraged before, & must releive myself by writing to you, who I know will enter into all my feelings," confesses Lady Susan of this correspondence (Letter 22, 280). I want to suggest that reexamining the interplay of sentiment with irony in *Lady Susan* and Jane Austen's other early writings[2] may help us understand the complexity of Austen's subject in all her novels; my focus is on relations between women friends.

While friendship between women in Jane Austen's novels has engaged some critics, the novels themselves seem to direct us to consider such relationships unimportant precursors to the heroine's betrothal to the hero. Even though this last letter from Lady Susan assures her confidential friend that "I never was more at ease, or better satisfied with myself & everything about me, than at the present hour" (307), Marvin Mudrick goes out of his way to lament the waste of Lady Susan's passionate nature in marriage to Sir James Martin, "the greatest booby of all." He sees this vicious heroine as the novel's "ultimate, tragic victim. . . . The world defeats Lady Susan, not because it recognizes her vices, but because her virtues have no room in it."[3] But perhaps Mudrick's revision of this novel does not go far enough; it is only when we assume that the heroine's fulfillment must be in uniting with a worthy (intellectually, if not morally) man that *Lady Susan*'s conclusion remains dissatisfying. In fact, Austen omits such a desirable man from her narrative (the married Manwaring is left largely uncharacterized; the virtuous Reginald De Courcy seems gullible and spineless), but insists on the fervency of the frank partnership between Lady Susan and Mrs. Johnson.

Of course, Austen's earliest writings are no doubt in dialogue with and satirical of the cult of friendship in popular novels of the late eighteenth century. Characteristic sentimental excesses between friends recur in the juvenilia and find place in her later fiction whenever such hypocrites as Isabella Thorpe, Lucy Steele, or Mary Crawford profess instant "affection" for the heroines of *Northanger Abbey, Sense and Sensibility,* and *Mansfield Park* with motives that range from opportunism to malice and envy to creating a false persona. But this easy dismissal of one kind of "friendship" in her work need not mean that Austen sees women's friendship as unimportant, or even secondary, in comparison with marriage. Even when critics share Mr. Knightley's judgment of Emma's self-indulgent "interest" in Harriet Smith, they go on (as I think the novelist invites us) to deplore the failed friendship between Emma and Jane Fairfax.[4] And when women's friendship is permitted to influence the heroine, it is accorded much importance. Janet Todd refers to Jane Austen's "distrust of [female] friendship" in her later work,[5] and Lady Russell's inadvertent betrayal of Anne Elliot before the start of *Persuasion* usually comes in for more attention than lowly Mrs. Smith's corresponding care, so significant to the novel's denouement, for her mentor/protegée's best interests. In fact, according to some readers, the evils of Lady Russell's limited perspective are matched by the pernicious reticence of Mrs. Smith, who hesitates to reveal the antihero's treachery almost too long.[6] Mrs. Smith, however, might be most accurately viewed as significant to the novel because she provides a trustworthy, equal—in Janet

Todd's terms, "horizontal"—friend for Anne who is otherwise thrown upon her unsympathetic family and her short-sighted confidante Lady Russell.

It would seem that, to critics, female friendship can be exploitative, often silly, occasionally dangerous, but never, in the end, particularly significant. Even Rachel Brownstein, who writes sensitively of women's friendships in Austen's fiction, and who happily notes that "[t]wo things about Jane Austen's life are important . . . : she was a spinster, and a sister," concludes that "Austen's heroines, who must acknowledge that they are like other women, must in the end leave the company of their sex." She writes in the context of Emma's "foolish connection with simple Harriet Smith."[7] Emma's cultivation of Harriet is of course problematical, but I would like to reconsider such easy dismissals.[8]

Of course, the master plot of Jane Austen's novels, courtship, makes the female relationship an apparently marginal aspect of her fiction, as is appropriate: she wrote for readers who preferred their novels cut to pattern. But to see courtship as a flat design may be to miss the layers of Austen's exploration of relationships. The skeptical reader—one who suspects the author herself of some skepticism about pat fictional order—need not conspire with the obvious dictates of the form to the extent of ignoring the author's collateral focus, within her works' boundaries, on the importance of "sisterhood" in the lives of her woman characters.

The juvenilia and *Lady Susan* provide an ideal point of departure for a study of women's relationships. As an introduction to the body of Austen's work, these stories, plays, burlesques, novels, and fragments of novels can be seen as analogues to the first seven chapters in relation to the whole of *Pride and Prejudice*. The exclusively feminine company of the Bennets and Lucases before the introduction of Bingley, Darcy, and Wickham (and Collins) shows a society in which none of the girls seem really to be "out," as they discuss men and hats and friendship.[9] (The earliest indication of Caroline Bingley's treacherous nature, after all, is her palpably false friendship for Jane Bennet.) As the juvenilia date from the precourtship era of Jane Austen's own life, they admit a focus on friendship as a unique form of female experience. And the works themselves, though the majority are apparently about relations between men and women, often abandon a courtship pattern, as I suggest Lady Susan Vernon does in discussing her own destiny (Letter 39, above).

The title of "Frederic & Elfrida," among the earliest works from the juvenilia's *Volume the First,* suggests a romance, but the first two paragraphs describing the hero and heroine immediately give way to a digression about Charlotte, Elfrida's "intimate friend," whose suicide follows shortly, after a pair of neighboring sisters is introduced further to divert attention from the eponymous couple. The automatic quality of the courtship plot is satirized in the epistolary "Amelia Webster," also from *Volume the First*. This three-page bagatelle introduces six characters—to the reader, hardly to one another. One eventual bridal couple "meets" only because George Hervey has seen the heroine through a telescope: "[I] was so struck by your Charms that from that time to this [six days] I have not tasted human food." In the very next letter, these victims of love at first sight and two other couples are paired off with equal haste in the newspaper's list of marriages (47–49). In the course of two acts (and four pages) Austen's drama "The Visit" similarly manages to pair off its roster of available characters. Miss Fitzgerald concludes the plot by addressing Sir Arthur's silent nephew: "Since you Willoughby are the only one left, I cannot refuse your earnest solicitations—There is my Hand" (54).

"Love and Freindship" is more concerned with friendship than with courtship or marriage. This burlesque novel is in the form of the middle-aged Laura's letters describing her picaresque, romantic exploits to Marianne, the daughter of Laura's childhood friend. The spurious emotion and spontaneous attachment of false friendship are the butt of Austen's satire here, as they are in *Northanger Abbey, Sense and Sensibility,* and *Pride and Prejudice.* But it is important to see that friendships, however comically treated in the novel, have greater endurance than do marriages. Friendship is even the occasion for the novel's being written.

The primary pairing in "Love and Freindship" is between Laura and Sophia, the wife of her husband's best friend. While marriages in the novel seem to be prompted more by a desire to flout parental authority and economic prudence than by mutual attachment, the requirements for friendship are precise, if typical of sentimental (and mock-sentimental) fashion. When the penniless Edward elopes with Laura to his friend Augustus's seat, Laura is particularly grateful for the presence of Sophia; she has been "deprived during the course of 3 weeks of a real freind":

> Sophia was rather above the middle size; most elegantly formed. A soft Languor spread over her lovely features, but increased their Beauty. —It was the Charectaristic of her Mind—. She was all Sensibility and Feeling. We flew into each others arms & after having exchanged vows of mutual Friendship for the rest of our Lives, instantly unfolded to each other the most inward Secrets of our Hearts—. (85)

Young Laura has been especially relieved to find Sophia first with Edward's sister Augusta:

> There was a Disagreeable Coldness and Forbidding Reserve in [Augusta's] reception of me which was equally Distressing and Unexpected. None of that interesting Sensibility [marked] her Manners and Address to me which should have Distinguished our introduction to each other. Her Language was neither warm, nor affectionate, her expressions of regard were neither animated nor cordial; her arms were not opened to receive me to her Heart, tho' my own were extended to press her to mine. (82)

And Laura has met Lady Dorothea, who was Edward's father's preference as a daughter-in-law, another candidate for disdain: "She staid but half an hour and neither in the Course of her Visit, confided to me any of her Secret thoughts, nor requested me to confide in her, any of mine" (84). It is true that Edward and Augustus, whose meeting follows that of their wives, also "fl[y] into each other's arms" (86), sentimental behavior that "was too pathetic for the feelings of Sophia and myself—We fainted Alternately on a Sofa."[10] But flying and fainting notwithstanding, the male friendship hardly parallels the women's in importance. For one thing, Edward and Augustus promptly leave the scene, the latter arrested for debt (and possibly theft as well), and eventually they leave the story entirely when they are killed in a phaeton accident. Furthermore, despite the broad treatment of the friendship of Laura and Sophia, the two women prove resourceful to each other in crises, certainly more so than their husbands. Their adventures include a journey to Scotland; the discovery of their (mutual) grandfather; an experiment in matchmaking, as they prompt an elopement between an indifferent heiress and a fortune hunter; and the separate achievements of an elegy on the death of Edward (by Laura), and a virtuoso heroine's swoon (by Sophia), one that leads to a feverish death.

By the end of her absurd trials, Laura has learned sufficient vulgar prudence to submit to an income from her late husband's father, but notes plaintively that "the unsimpathetic Baronet offered it more on account of my being the Widow of Edward than in being the refined and Amiable Laura" (108). Here may be found the lesson that Laura would impart to young Marianne in her review of her story: society deems the feelings of women insignificant compared with the social and financial status of men. But Laura herself hardly seems to have adopted any lesson from her own story, nor does she seem to agree with the more sensible Isabel, Marianne's mother, in the first letter of the novel:

> How often, in answer to my repeated intreaties that you would give my Daughter a regular detail of the Misfortunes and Adventures of your Life, have you said "No, my freind never will I comply with your request till I may be no longer in Danger. . . . " You are this Day 55. If a woman may ever be said to be in safety from the determined Perseverance of disagreable lovers and the cruel Persecutions of obstinate Fathers, surely it must be at such a time of Life. (76–77)

Isabel, who evidently intends her friend's life to serve as an exemplum to an impressionable Marianne, would hardly be encouraged by Laura's summary at the end of "Love and Freindship": "My Adventures are now drawing to a close my dearest Marianne; at least for the present" (108). Laura never rejects the earliest sentimental values that would no doubt inform her further adventures. The only direct advice that she will concede to pass to Marianne is the dying speech of Sophia: "Beware of swoons Dear Laura. . . . A frenzy fit is not one quarter so pernicious; it is an exercise to the Body & if not too violent, is I dare say conducive to Health in its consequences—Run mad as often as you chuse; but do not faint—" (102).

As comical and apparently insignificant as this short novel may seem, its claim on our attention is assured when we consider the relationship between "Love and Freindship" and *Sense and Sensibility,* where one of the two heroines displays an excessive sentimentality quite reminiscent of Laura and Sophia.[11] Like them, Marianne, who bears the name of Laura's tutee, allows her romantic definition of "noble" behavior to obscure her moral judgment and her common sense; Marianne Dashwood's near fatal twilight walks cause an illness that is particularly communicable to sentimental young women, and Sophia has died of the same disease. But in *Sense and Sensibility* the shrewdly "sentimental" Lucy Steele provides a contrast with the genuine feeling of Marianne Dash-wood, making us unable to dismiss the latter for her excesses, even if she were not so important a friend to her sister Elinor, the representative of sense, throughout the novel.[12] The very last words of *Sense and Sensibility,* after all, pay tribute to the sisters' neighborly friendship as "not the least considerable" of their "merits and happiness."[13] Even in "Love and Freindship" and elsewhere in the juvenilia, the studied romantic dogma that may direct characters' lives can create frequent comedy and satire without forfeiting our serious attention. On the subject of Austen's attacks on sentimentality in her early work, A. Walton Litz reminds us that "burlesque and parody are not necessarily acts of rejection, and if they are then the rejection is likely to be of something within the writer's own nature."[14]

My blurring of the distinctions between friends and sisters is deliberate; many of the same issues that Austen addresses by comparing and contrasting friends often arise, especially in the juvenilia, between sisters instead—or in addition. The epistolary "The three Sisters," also from *Volume the First* is a gallery of the varied relations among women even as it is a satire on mercenary marriage. While Miss Stanhope busily negotiates her impending marriage's social and financial details, triumphing over her friends and rivals the Dutton sisters, she laments her fiancé's characteristics: "He is quite an old Man, about two & thirty, very plain *so* plain that I cannot bear to look at him. He is extremely disagreable & I hate him" (58). But if Mary dismisses this hapless Mr. Watts, her letter continues, not only will he become a prey to the Duttons, but to her own sisters, Sophy and Georgiana. Another perspective on these absurd calculations comes from young Georgiana's satirical descriptions to Anne, her spirited correspondent. Though the younger Miss Stanhopes concur with foolish Mary's estimate of Mr. Watts's attractions, they entertain them-selves with a clever rewriting of his description to fit the ambitions of their marriage-minded sister: "They say he is stingy; We'll call that Prudence. They say he is suspicious [jealous]. *That* proceeds from a warmth of Heart always excusable in Youth & in short I see no reason why he should not make a very good husband [for Mary]" (62). Georgiana's letter continues, "They will probably have a new Carriage, which will be paradise to her, & if we can prevail on Mr W. to set up his Phaeton she will be too happy. These things however would be no consolation to Sophy or me for domestic Misery" (63).

In providing herself with all "Three Sisters," Austen permits both friendly sympathy and competition within the Stanhope family, but the addition of sympathetic correspondents is more than an epistolary device; these women, and the Dutton family, show a rich circle of often insightful comrades, despite the stereotypical characterization of women as necessarily rivals. Georgiana Stanhope's irreverent commentary on the business of courtship and marriage prefigures Elizabeth Bennet's detachment from groups of dancers in chapters 3 and 6 of *Pride and Prejudice;* on these occasions she is less a wallflower than a satirist, sharing her deflations of Darcy and the others not with her sister Jane, but with her friend Charlotte Lucas.[15]

Of course, Austen builds into all her work evidence that some women can betray each other just as readily as some men betray women. The sisters Matilda and Margaret Lesley in "Lesley Castle" from *Volume the Second* parody any idealized vision of sisterly relations: "we are neither dull nor unhappy; on the contrary there never were two more lively, agreable or more witty Girls, than we are," Margaret assures her correspondent. "We read, we work, we walk and when fatigued with these Employments releive our spirits, either by a lively song, a graceful Dance, or by some smart bon-mot, and witty repartée. We are handsome my dear Charlotte, very handsome and the greatest of our Perfections is, that we are entirely insensible of them ourselves" (111). The recipient of this self-congratulatory letter is Charlotte Lutterell,who manages, in the intervals of her household tasks, to write often not only to Lesley Castle, but to her maliciously "confidential" friend Susan who coincidentally becomes these peerless Lesley sisters' new stepmother, and hence their economic rival. The double correspondence gives valuable comic perspective when the suspicions and assessments of both parties are contrasted. But the indefatigable device that permits this epistolary variety, Charlotte herself, excellent cook and manager that she is, is apparently deficient in sisterly sympathy. Her own sister Eloisa writes to a new friend,

> I once thought that to have what is in general called a Freind (I mean one of my own Sex to whom I might speak with less reserve than to any other person) independant of my Sister would never be an object of my wishes, but how much was I mistaken! Charlotte is too much engrossed by two confidential Correspondents of that sort, to supply the place of one to me, & I hope you will not think me girlishly romantic, when I say that to have some kind and compassionate Freind who might listen to my Sorrows without endeavouring to console me was what I had for some time wished for, when our acquaintance with you, the intimacy which followed it & and the particular affectionate Attention you paid me almost from the first,

caused me to entertain the flattering Idea of those attentions being improved on a closer acquaintance into a Freindship which, if you were what my wishes formed you[,] would be the greatest Happiness I could be capable of enjoying. (132)

The absurd situations and the consistent hyperbole in "Lesley Castle," not to mention the omnipresent food imagery, almost defy a reading that takes friendship between women—or anything else—seriously. But the theme of friendship is so persistent in all of Austen's early work that it seems inescapable, especially when it is present in such divergent, relatively mature productions as *Lady Susan* and "Catharine, or The Bower" from *Volume the Third.*

Lady Susan would appear to permit the most negative reading of women's relationships: one of the marriages that ends the story, after all, has pitted a mother as a rival to her own daughter for an eligible, rich, if foolish, young man. Even what I have suggested to be a relatively sentimental relationship between the heroine and her correspondent Mrs. Johnson can be dismissed as a matter of epistolary convenience for the plot. Surely Lady Susan herself presumes upon her friend's evident interest in maintaining the forms (at least) of propriety in the unsavory assistance she seeks, even to insisting that Mrs. Johnson entertain Lady Susan's one honorable suitor for an evening in order to leave her and her married lover Manwaring unmolested. At other times, the heroine complains of her friend's officiousness: "You are very good in taking notice of Frederica [Lady Susan's daughter], & I am grateful for it as a mark of your friendship, I am far from exacting so heavy a sacrifice. She is a stupid girl, & has nothing to recommend her. I would not therefore on any account have you encumber one moment of your precious time" (Letter 7, 252). The general tone of devotion between these correspondents, however, prevails, even when Lady Susan makes her most outrageous suggestion of a friendly service Mrs. Johnson might perform—that she undertake to worry Mrs. Manwaring to death. And though marriage to Manwaring, were he to become a widower, is Lady Susan's evident fantasy, her correspondent sketches an idyllic partnership that excludes men, when she anticipates a period of intimate visiting with Lady Susan: "Mr. Johnson leaves London next Tuesday. He is going for his health to Bath, where if the waters are favourable to his constitution & my wishes, he will be laid up with the gout many weeks. During his absence we shall be able to chuse our own society, & have true enjoyment . . . we may be always together" (Letter 26, 295–96). While this imagined felicity does not come to pass—the gout not being as convenient to the women's wishes as is planned here—this is a telling picture of female friendship (mischievously mingled, as in "Love and Freindship," with female conspiracy) that disregards the married state, happy or otherwise, of the correspondents. It suggests that even the hardhearted Lady Susan has some emotional needs that can be met neither by the devotion of men—suitors, husbands, lovers—nor even by her abundant self-admiration.

We may conclude our study of Jane Austen's exploration of the relationships of women with "Catharine, or The Bower," the last work in the formal juvenilia. Unlike the slightly later *Lady Susan,* this unfinished novel stresses the sentimental style over the broader comedy and satire that have competed with it throughout the early work.

Choosing to place her orphaned heroine in the unpleasant charge of a severe aunt, the author would appear to afford her few romantic possibilities. As we meet the young Catharine, she is afforded "constant releif in all her misfortunes" by "a fine shady Bower, the work of her own infantine Labours assisted by those of two young Companions who had resided in the same village—." Catharine's[16] "imagination was warm, and in her Freindships, as well as in the whole tenure of her Mind, she was enthousiastic. This beloved Bower had been the united work of herself and two amiable Girls, for whom since her earliest Years, she had felt the tenderest regard" (193). Clearly, it would seem, the description of the bower in the first pages of the story identifies Catharine as susceptible to sentimental cliché; her relation to the sisters Cecilia and Mary must be similarly silly. But just as the reader has settled into such a comfortable judgment, the sisters are hustled off the scene to varied unhappy fates which might have proved adventures for a more conventional kind of orphaned heroine. The reader is left behind with Catharine and her recourse to "this arbour . . . [which] encouraged . . . the tender and Melancholy recollections of hours rendered pleasant by" her lost friends (194).

Even as she will do in *Sense and Sensibility* and *Northanger Abbey* (whose heroine shares Catharine's name), Austen tempts her readers to an undiscriminating dismissal of the strong feelings of sentimental young women, only to present us with caricatures that complicate our response. In "Catharine," it is Camilla Stanley—whose family pays a visit to the heroine's aunt—who represents the ignorance and shallow artifice of false friendship and provides a contrast with the enduring ties, now kept by correspondence, between the heroine and the sisters who have left. Camilla's abuses of language and her taste in literature resemble Isabella Thorpe's, and when the reductive dialogues that pass for conversation with Camilla send Catharine to the haven of "her dear Bower," the reader is ready to adjust the value of that retreat (207). Despite her wishes that the arrival of Camilla can "in some degree make amends for the loss of Cecilia & Mary," Catharine is forced to conclude the contrary: "She found no variety in her conversation; She received no information from her but in fashions, and no amusement but in her performance on the Harpsichord . . . and when [Catharine] had learnt from her, how large their house in Town was, when the fashionable Amusements began, who were the celebrated Beauties and who the best Millener, Camilla had nothing further to teach ..." (198, 201–2). (Were the harp substituted for the "Harpsichord," the description might suit Mary Crawford.) Camilla's equally shallow mother applauds the stylish custom of friendship and correspondence between young women, while Catharine's aunt, less "modern," judges "a correspondence between Girls as Productive of no good, and as the frequent origin of imprudence & Error by the effect of pernicious advice and bad Example" (210–11). Austen is inviting us to mediate between the trivial, false "sensibility" of Camilla and her London friends and the equally extreme view of Catharine's guardian. Camilla is moved to remonstrate with her hostess, "'But who knows what you might have been Ma'am, if you *had* had a Correspondent; perhaps it would have made you quite a different Creature'" (211), and, for once, the reader is inclined to agree with her.

Camilla's one great advantage to Catharine would seem to be her possession of a brother, Edward Stanley, who arrives briefly to dance with and delight the heroine. But Austen soon removes Edward from the scene; and even before his departure, while Catharine is being electrified by his presence, she is busily assessing his defects and deciding whether they "merely preceded from a vivacity always pleasing in Young Men" or "testif[ied] a weak or vacant Understanding" (235–36).

When the novel breaks off, the possibility of a visit from Catharine's married friend Cecilia is the only likely change in the heroine's future. "Her bower," we are told, "alone retained its interest in her feelings," and though "perhaps that was oweing to the particular remembrance it brought to [Catharine's] mind of Edw[ar]d Stanley," generally the enduring relationship in the novel is that between Catharine and her old, now absent friends (239). Their fates, ultimately unknown, seem not to promise well: Cecilia has been sent out to India where she has, as designed, been married off to "a Man of double her own age, whose disposition was not amiable, and whose Manners were unpleasing, though his Character was respectable," but who may, as Catharine feelingly points out, "'be a Tyrant, or a Fool or both for what she knows to be the Contrary'" (194, 205). Mary, the younger sister, has gained the unenviable position of poor relation and ladies' companion to a pair of spoiled girls—friends, in fact, of Camilla—who spend most of the year in Scotland. Catharine assesses Mary's lot: "There was not indeed that hopelessness of sorrow in her situation as in her sisters; she was not married, and could yet look forward to a change in her circumstances" (195). Perhaps Catharine here unwittingly identifies the paradox of the courtship plot: that, while single women have little but marriage to hope for, marriage is the completely "hopeless" state—whether for good or ill—because it is the state in which a woman is fixed, even more firmly than Catharine is imprisoned by her aunt or Mary by her subservient position.

Austen makes the charms of the almost-hero of "Catharine, or The Bower" equivocal: Edward "had scarcely a fixed opinion on [any] Subject" (231), and he is, after all, Camilla's brother. Just when Catharine is preparing to overlook his faults, the author suddenly dismisses him altogether. Feminine accomplishments, on the other hand, endure and retain their value; Catharine's correspondence with Camilla soon ends, but the letters to Cecilia and Mary continue. The structure of the bower, moreover, that cooperative achievement of friendship, remains as the novel trails off, a symbol of the relative importance of women's relationships even in the society Austen describes. Though the subject of her later novels seems unequivocally "love" rather than "friendship," then, it may be useful to consider how Jane Austen, who never married herself but carried on important correspondences and friendships throughout her hardly hopeless life, might be undermining the sole importance of marriage in the lives of her heroines.

Notes

1. Jane Austen, *Lady Susan,* in *Minor Works,* volume 6 of *The Works of Jane Austen,* ed. R.W. Chapman, rev. Brian Southam, Oxford, 1954, Letter 39, p. 307. All citations from the juvenilia and *Lady Susan* are taken from this edition.

2. I assume the dating of *Lady Susan,* 1793–94, given by Brian Southam in chapter 3 of *Jane Austen's Literary Manuscripts,* Oxford, 1964; the debate over the dating of this novel is summarized by A. Walton Litz in *Jane Austen: A Study of Her Artistic Development,* Oxford, 1965, p. 40.

3. Marvin Mudrick, *Jane Austen: Irony as Defense and Discovery,* Princeton, N.J., 1952, p. 138.

4. See Ruth Perry, "Interrupted Friendships in Jane Austen's *Emma,*" *Tulsa Studies in Women's Literature* 5 (Fall 1986), 185–202, an essay read at the Colgate Feminist Theory Study Group in 1985. It has influenced much of my thinking about women's relationships in Austen's work.

5. Janet Todd, *Women's Friendship in Literature,* New York, 1980, p. 400. Generally Todd's views on friendship in Jane Austen's fiction seem harsh. For her approach's "biographical context," see pp. 396–402. On *Mansfield Park,* see pp. 249, 267–68.

6. See K.K. Collins, "Prejudice, *Persuasion,* and the Puzzle of Mrs. Smith," *Persuasions* 6 (1984), 40–43. In "Mrs. Smith and the Morality of *Persuasion,*" *Nineteenth Century Fiction* 30 (1975), 383–97, Collins reviews the traditional attacks on Mrs. Smith as either an awkward plot device or an opportunist who seeks merely to use Anne's influence with Mr. Elliot to gain her lost fortune.

7. Rachel Brownstein, *Becoming a Heroine: Reading about Women in Novels,* New York, 1982, pp. 105, 109; emphasis added.

8. Todd analyzes the relationship, in the tradition of Mudrick, as modeled on a "flawed marriage," p. 285; see also Perry, p. 199. My view would salvage some aspects of Emma's "use" of Harriet as virtues of friendship. For Sandra M. Gilbert and Susan Gubar, however, as with many critics, female friendship in Jane Austen's fiction is merely "female rivalry" for attention from men. See *The Madwoman in the Attic,* New Haven, 1979, p. 126.

9. I concede that my idyllic evocation of the Bennets at home is a direct contradiction of most views of that novel. In *Communities of Women: An Idea in Fiction,* Cambridge, Mass., 1978,

pp. 47–48, for example, Nina Auerbach deems that women "lead a purgatorial existence together" in all of Jane Austen's novels. See pp. 35–55.

10. In his notes to "Love and Freindship" in *Volume the Second,* Oxford, 1963, p. 211, Brian Southam points out that the alternating swoon echoes Sheridan's stage direction in *The Critic,* III, i.

11. On the relation of "Love and Freindship" to *Northanger Abbey* and *Sense and Sensibility,* see Juliet McMaster, "The Continuity of Jane Austen's Novels," *SEL* 10 (1970), 723–39.

12. Brian Southam too makes this point in *Jane Austen's Literary Manuscripts,* London, 1964, pp. 25–26.

13. Jane Austen, *Sense and Sensibility,* ed. R.W. Chapman, Oxford, 1933, rpt., 1982, p. 380.

14. Litz, p. 14.

15. I do not think that the idea of "sibling rivalry" is particularly important for an understanding of sisters in the juvenilia or elsewhere in Austen's fiction, even though certain characters, including Mrs. Stanhope of "The three Sisters" and of course Mrs. Bennet, encourage sisters in competition. Some readers do stress this point, however; see John Halperin, "Unengaged Laughter: Jane Austen's *Juvenilia,*" *South Atlantic Quarterly* 81 (1982), 286–99 [reprinted in this collection—Ed.]. Patricia Meyer Spacks focuses on the use of "bad" and "good" sisters in fiction as an opportunity for authors to "imagine the pleasures of self-indulgence as well as the rewards of self-restraint." See "Sisters," in *Fetter'd or Free? British Women Novelists, 1670–1815,* ed. Mary Anne Schofield and Cecilia Macheski, Athens, Ohio, 1986, pp. 136–51.

16. To reduce confusion, I shall use this name and spelling to refer to the character throughout, even though "Kitty" and "Catherine" recur in the text as alternatives.

Jane Austen's Manuscripts of the Juvenilia and *Lady Susan:* A History and Description

Mary Gaither Marshall

Jane Austen's literary manuscripts are exceedingly rare. Other than 150 letters and several autograph fragments, only a few works in her hand survive: a fair copy of *Lady Susan* (1793–94); an unfinished working draft of *The Watsons* (1803–4); a fair copy of *Plan of a Novel* (ca. 1815); two cancelled concluding chapters of *Persuasion* (July 1816); an unfinished first draft of *Sanditon* (January–March 1817); and three transcript volumes of the juvenilia, *Volume the First, Volume the Second,* and *Volume the Third* (written between 1787 and 1793). This dearth of original documents makes the extant manuscripts essential to the understanding of Jane Austen's literary development and techniques, particularly her editing and revising. The emergence and growth of one of England's literary geniuses can be seen through the study of the textual and publishing history of her earliest efforts: *Volume the First, Volume the Second, Volume the Third,* and *Lady Susan.*

Voluminous reading and continual writing are the best means of improving a writer's skills. The Austen home was the ideal atmosphere for the development of a budding literary talent, for the family had a tradition of reading aloud and of composing verses and plays for its own entertainment. Jane Austen's juvenilia spring from that tradition. Her letters confirm that her family spent many evenings with one member reading a book to the others: "My father reads Cowper to us in the evening, to which I listen when I can"; "Ought I to be very much pleased with Marmion?—as yet I am not.—James reads it aloud in the Eveng."[1]

In keeping with the family custom, Jane Austen loved to read to herself and to her family, particularly from novels. Although she wrote to James Stanier Clarke that she was "the most unlearned and uninformed female who ever dared to be an authoress,"[2] the evidence clearly confirms the irony of her self-deprecating words. In his "Biographical Notice" of 1818, Henry Austen noted Jane's love of reading: "It is difficult to say at what age she was not intimately acquainted with the merits and defects of the best essays and novels in the English language."³ Jane's letters confirm her bookish habits. She read Richardson, Fielding, Burney, and Johnson, among others. Literary references pervade her correspondence: "To-morrow I shall be just like Camilla in Mr. Dubster's summer-house" (Burney's *Camilla*); and "We have got the 2d vol. of Espriella's Letters, & I read it aloud by candlelight."⁴ Reading was such a routine part of Jane's life that when her friend Martha Lloyd requested that she bring books with her on an upcoming visit, she responded: "You distress me cruelly by your request about Books; I cannot think of any to bring with me, nor have I any idea of our wanting them. I come to you to be talked to, not to read or hear reading. I can do that at home."⁵

Jane Austen was skilled at interpretive reading and must have been one of the family's favorite entertainers. Henry records in his biographical notice, "She read aloud with very great taste and effect. Her own works, probably, were never heard to so much advantage as from her own mouth."⁶ Jane was not always satisfied, however, with the reading skills of others. In a letter to Cassandra, she described her mother's reading of *Pride and Prejudice:* "Our second evening's reading to Miss Benn had not pleased me so well, but I believe something must be attributed to my mother's too rapid way of getting on: though she perfectly understands the characters herself, she cannot speak as they ought."⁷ Anna Lefroy related a story to her aunt reading aloud from one of the earliest versions of *Pride and Prejudice:* "I have been told that her earliest Novels, certainly P. & P were read aloud in the Parsonage at Dean when I was in the room—& not expected to listen—that I did listen with all my might, was so much interested & talked so much afterwards about Jane & Elizabeth that it was resolved for prudence sake to read no more of the story aloud in my hearing."⁸ As Jane Austen's work matured and began to be published, she continued to read her compositions aloud to her family. She wrote to Cassandra in January 1813 about receiving the first copy of *Pride and Prejudice:* "Miss Benn dined with us on the very day of the books coming & in the evening we set fairly at it, and read half the first vol. to her, prefacing that, having intelligence from Henry that such a work would soon appear, we had desired him to send it whenever it came out, and I believe it passed with her unsuspected."⁹

In addition to works of the popular authors of the day, such as Cowper, Scott, and Lennox, Austen family members also read their own compositions aloud. James and Henry no doubt discussed and read selections from their weekly periodical *The Loiterer,* published at Oxford from January 31, 1789, to March 20, 1790. Her brothers' efforts, many of the same type of burlesque which she was already producing herself, undoubtedly encouraged the admiring Jane to listen to her muse and to write seriously.¹⁰ Beginning before her twelfth birthday in 1787 and continuing until after her eighteenth birthday in 1794, Jane composed plays, burlesques, and stories which later would fill three volumes. She probably created these early sketches to take her turn in the family entertainment. Although she dedicated stories and plays to family members and friends, those so honored may never have received copies, since no original manuscripts have survived. Jane perhaps copied the final draft of a sketch into one of the notebooks and then destroyed the original—not an uncommon practice for an author.

Initially, Jane Austen may have been content to read her works aloud for her family's amusement. Later, however, she sought the opinion of family members as to the merit of her creations. Her brother Henry wrote, "In the bosom of her own family she talked of . . . [her work] freely, thankful for praise, open to remark, and submissive to criticism."[11]

Textual evidence suggests that Jane Austen eventually used her early works as writers often use their journals—to collect story ideas, revise thoughts, write sketches for later use—that is, to practice her craft. She did not close the books of juvenilia during her eighteenth year, never to open them again; instead she returned to these volumes when she was working on her novels. Some of the same ideas, themes, characters, and names in the initial writings later appeared in her mature works. Jane's concern about manners, a major theme in her novels, is apparent in the juvenilia. The dialogues between Lady Greville and Miss Maria in "Letter the third From A young Lady in distress'd Circumstances to her freind," for example, foreshadow the conversations about social position and manners between Lady Catharine De Bourgh and Elizabeth Bennet in *Pride and Prejudice:*

> "Pray Miss Maria in what way of business was your Grandfather? for Miss Mason & I cannot agree whether he was a Grocer or a Bookbinder." I saw that she wanted to mortify me and was resolved if I possibly could to prevent her seeing that her scheme succeeded. "Neither Madam; he was a Wine Merchant." "Aye, I knew he was in some such low way." . . . She gave me such a look, & turned away in a great passion; while I was half delighted with myself for my impertinence.[12]

A. Walton Litz notes another example of the juvenilia as a precursor to the novels: " 'Evelyn' is a forerunner of *Northanger Abbey* and *Sense and Sensibility,* works in which Jane Austen explores the limits of the imagination while affirming its essential role in all moral judgments."[13] Jane also plays with names that appear in her later works: The name Annesley (Admiral) in "A Collection of Letters" appears again in *Pride and Prejudice* as Mrs. Annesley (a companion to Miss Darcy); in "A Collection of Letters," T. Musgrove writes to his love Henrietta; later, in *Persuasion,* the lovers' names are combined into Henrietta Musgrove.

Although the juvenilia notebooks reflect some editing and revising, most of the transcriptions in them are clearly fair copies, carefully and neatly written and containing errors only of the type made during monotonous duplication— words misspelled (e.g., "Magestically"); letters and words transposed (e.g., "Freindship"); wrong words written in the speed of transcription (e.g., "than" instead of "that"); and words omitted and repeated when reading ahead (e.g., copying "for" twice in " . . . her Sister's reign for famous for building" when the passage should read " . . . her Sister's reign was famous for building.")[14] The mistakes were generally erased or neatly corrected.

Although the juvenilia were organized in three separately bound volumes, the material contained in each did not appear in chronological order of composition, indicating that a finished piece was simply transcribed into any volume that was readily accessible. B.C. Southam determined that the majority of the works (12) were composed between 1787 and 1790. He dated the remaining nine from November 1791 to June 1793. Southam began to establish the chronology of the various pieces with Jane Austen's own dates on the manuscripts: "Love and Freindship," "13 June 1790"; "The History of England," "26 November 1791"; "Catharine," "August 1792"; and "A Fragment," "2 June 1793." Textual evidence, such as the dedications, also provided clues as to the time of composition: "Jack & Alice" and "The Adventures of Mr. Harley," both dedicated to Francis Austen while he was assigned to the ship Perseverance, from 1788 to 1791, clearly were written during those same four years. "Henry and Eliza" and "A Collection of Letters," both dedicated to "Miss Cooper," must have been composed before December 11, 1792, when that lady became Mrs. Williams. "The beautifull Cassandra," referred to in the dedication of "Catharine" as "The beautiful Cassandra," was completed before August 1792, the date Jane Austen noted at the end of the dedication to "Catharine." Southam calculated the chronology of the other juvenilia by comparing their styles to that of the already dated pieces.[15]

The times at which Jane Austen transcribed her early writings cannot be as readily determined as can the dates she composed them. Changes in her handwriting provide the best evidence as to the transcription chronology. Although many of the juvenilia pieces were not entered into the notebooks by date of creation, the first 11 in *Volume the First* were written in a childlike hand, indicating early composition. Those remaining were copied over a rather long time period (1787–1803) in a more mature hand, the last ones in a similar autograph to that seen in *The Watsons*.[16] The works contained in *Volume the Second* also reveal variations in Jane's handwriting: "Love and Freindship" and "Scraps" were in a copperplate script, "The three Sisters" in a middle hand, "Comedy" in a calligraphic hand, and other pages in a later script. The transcriptions in *Volume the Third* date from "May 6th 1792," inscribed on the first leaf of the volume, to approximately 1809. These pieces are written in the "middle hand."[17]

Evidence suggests, however, that both Jane Austen and her family remained interested in and continued reading the juvenilia after 1809. When she was revising *Sense and Sensibility* between 1809 and 1811, Jane was also editing sketches in the notebooks. As A. Walton Litz observed in "Chronology of Composition," "'Evelyn' (*Volume the Third*) is dated 'Augst 19th 1809,' while in a revision of 'Catharine,' Hannah More's *Coelebs* (first published in 1809) was substituted for a reference to Bishop Secker on the Catechism. Presumably, these late retouchings were connected with the general revival of Jane Austen's literary activity in 1809."[18] Also, in an 1814 letter to Cassandra, Jane made an allusion to "Love and Freindship": and sometime after her niece Anna Austen's 1814 marriage to Benjamin Lefroy, Jane allowed Anna to peruse *Volume the Third* and to write a continuation to "Evelyn," which appeared on three leaves inserted at the end of the volume.[19]

Lady Susan is a bridge between the juvenilia and the mature writings. In his preface to the first publication of *Lady Susan* (in the second edition of *A Memoir*), J.E. Austen-Leigh expresses his opinion of this early effort:

> The tale itself is scarcely one on which a literary reputation could have been founded: but though, like some plants, it may be too slight to stand alone, it may, perhaps, be supported by the strength of her more firmly rooted works. At any rate, it cannot diminish Jane Austen's reputation as a writer; for even if it should be judged unworthy of the publicity now given to it, the censure must fall on him who has put it forth, not on her who kept it locked up in her desk.[20]

Lady Knatchbull (Jane Austen's niece Fanny), who then owned the *Lady Susan* manuscript, gave James Austen-Leigh permission to publish the story. Either by accident or by guile of the publisher, *Lady Susan* had its title printed on the spine.

Lady Susan is one of only five manuscripts to have survived in total (the three volumes of juvenilia and *Plan of a Novel* being the others) and is the only complete manuscript copy of any of the epistolary novels. Because *Lady Susan* is a fair copy, containing only 12 minor corrections—most of the type that would be made when transcribing the manuscript, for example, "as soon as" for "as soon,"[21]—it reveals little about Jane Austen's techniques of revision. As the only existing manuscript (save for the title "Susan, A Novel in Two volumes" from *Northanger Abbey*) from the period in which she wrote the first versions of *Sense and Sensibility* (begun November 1797), *Pride and Prejudice* (begun October 1796), and *Northanger Abbey* (1798–99), however, *Lady Susan* is important in demonstrating the development of Jane Austen's writing.

Although the manuscript is undated, two leaves are watermarked with the

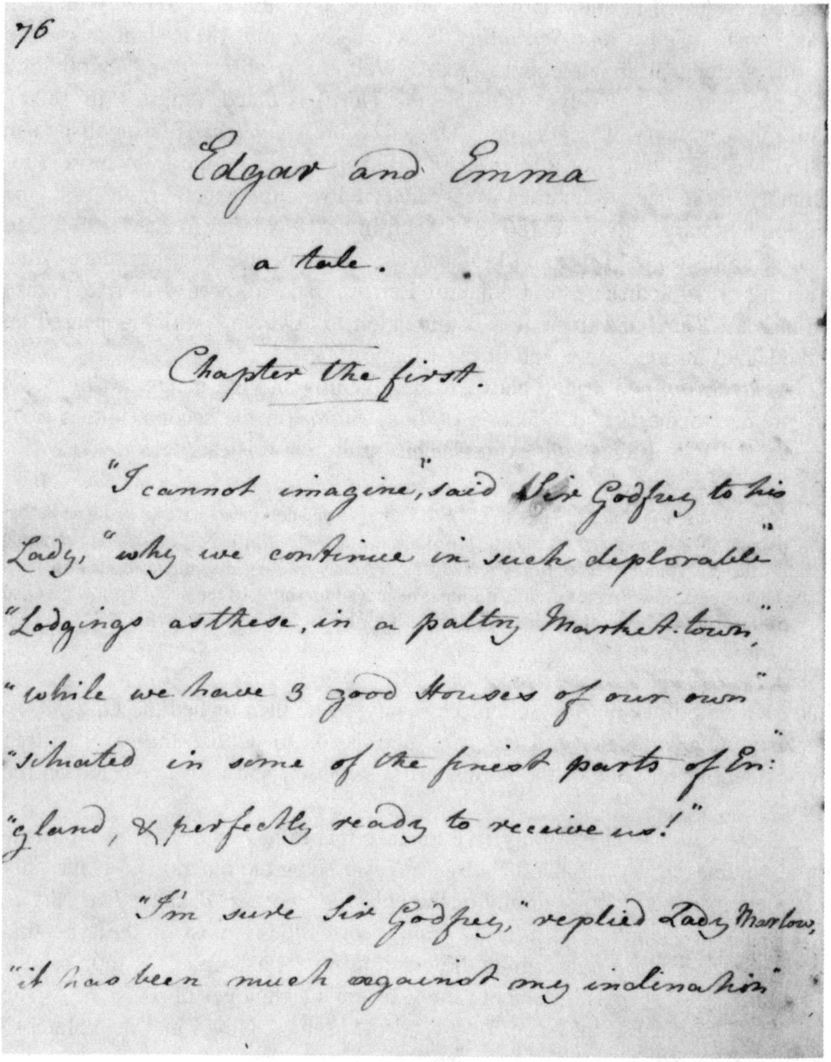

Edgar and Emma

a tale.

Chapter the first.

"I cannot imagine," said Sir Godfrey to his
Lady, "why we continue in such deplorable
"Lodgings as these, in a paltry Market-town,
"while we have 3 good Houses of our own
"situated in some of the finest parts of En:
"gland, & perfectly ready to receive us!"

"I'm sure Sir Godfrey," replied Lady Marlow,
"it has been much against my inclination"

Figure 9. First Manuscript Page of "Chapter the first," from
"Edgar & Emma: a tale"
(Volume the First *MS; Courtesy The Bodleian Library, MS Don.e.7*)

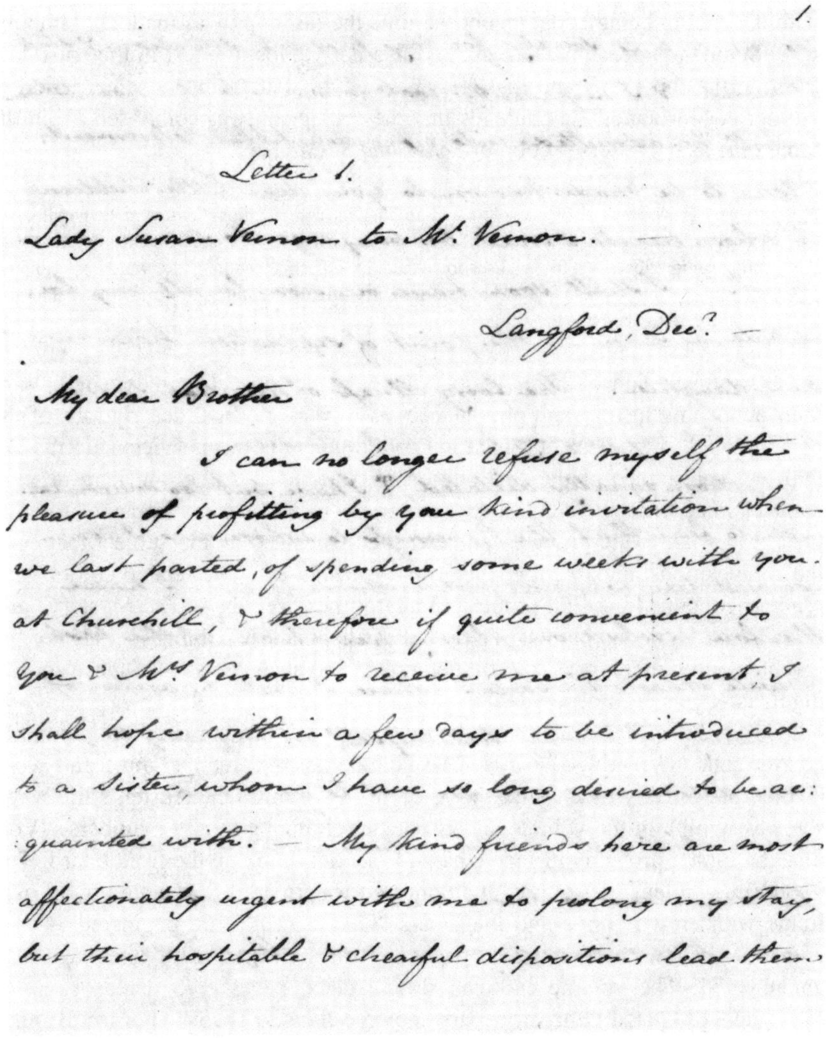

Letter 1.

Lady Susan Vernon to Mr Vernon. —

Langford, Dec.? —

My dear Brother

I can no longer refuse myself the pleasure of profitting by your kind invitation when we last parted, of spending some weeks with you at Churchill, & therefore if quite convenient to you & Mrs Vernon to receive me at present, I shall hope within a few days to be introduced to a Sister, whom I have so long desired to be ac=quainted with. — My kind friends here are most affectionately urgent with me to prolong my stay, but their hospitable & chearful dispositions lead them

Figure 10. "Letter 1: Lady Susan Vernon to Mrs. Vernon"
(Volume the First *MS; Courtesy Pierpont Morgan Library*)

year 1805, indicating a transcription after that time. According to family tradition, *Lady Susan* was "an early production."[22] R.W. Chapman concludes that the novel was written about 1805 because the story is "very unlike [that of] a novice."[23] Most scholars, however, believe a date of 1794–95 is more exact, with the ending being added about the time the fair copy was made.[24] Although B.C. Southam agrees that Jane Austen had not yet lost interest in the epistolary form during the 1790s and that *Lady Susan* was written in the same period as "Elinor & Marianne," he contends that the conclusion was composed about the same time as the letters section of *Sense and Sensibility*.

> Perhaps growing tired of the plot, and finding its complications awkward to handle, she abandoned the letters and rounded off the story, disposing of the characters and completing the action summarily. . . . This final section cannot have been added long afterwards. . . . [T]here is nothing in the "conclusion" which would argue a date of composition much later than that we assign to the body of the work.[25]

Any discussion of Jane Austen's early works should include a review of their publishing history and provenance, as well as physical descriptions of the extant manuscripts. The first mention of the juvenilia did not occur until 1870 with the appearance of the first edition of *A Memoir*. Although, here descendants claimed that Jane's initial attempts were "of a slight and flimsy texture,"[26] these Victorians were probably somewhat embarrassed by the subject matter of the compositions: intoxication, illegitimacy, death, etc. The second edition of *A Memoir* contained the first printing of any of the juvenilia—"The Mystery" and *Lady Susan*. With the publication by R.W. Chapman (beginning in 1925) of the juvenilia and minor works, the first complete and accurate texts of these surviving manuscripts became available.

Volume the First was transcribed into a 19.8 × 16 cm notebook bound in quarter calf and marbled boards. The volume has a defective spine and worn boards, presumably much of the wear occurring during Jane Austen's life when she was writing in the volume and circulating it among family members. "Volume the First," probably in Jane's hand, is set out in ink on the front board. The 92 untrimmed leaves, some with an undated watermark of Britannia in an oval frame with crown above and the letters "GR" beneath, are paginated 1–180, with the first two unnumbered, page 167 misnumbered 177, and page 175 unnumbered. The volume contains several dated pages: 173 dated "June 2d 1793" and 180 dated "End of the first Volume June 3d 1793." "For my Brother Charles" is written in pencil by Cassandra on the front pastedown endpaper. Cassandra, at a later date, placed on the front pastedown a scrap of paper on which she had noted in ink: "For my Brother Charles. [rule] I think I recollect that a few of the trifles in this Vol: were written expressly for his amusement. C.E.A."[27]

Volume the First remained in the Austen family through the descendants of Charles until 1933 when it was acquired for the Bodleian Library by The Friends of the Bodleian. That same year R.W. Chapman obtained permission to publish the notebook (including "The Mystery," which had previously appeared in *A Memoir*). *Volume the First* contained few revisions, but some passages had been expunged. Chapman deciphered these and printed them in brackets: for example, the passage "a woman (?) in such a situation is particularly off her guard because her head is not strong enough to support intoxication"[28] is deleted. B.C. Southam contends that *Volume the First* originally was intended as a "showpiece," with initial corrections being neatly made in an attempt to preserve the look of a fair copy. Subsequent revisions, however, were scribbled in dark ink with heavy cancellations. According to Southam, these later alterations "are the changes that Jane Austen probably made when she came to use the notebook as a handy collection of stories to read aloud to the family."[29] Yet it appears just as likely that by the time of these later revisions Jane was using the volume as a repository for future ideas or perhaps as a working manuscript for future publication rather than as a source for family entertainment.

Volume the Second (19.5 × 16 cm) is bound in white vellum, which has become heavily soiled. The notebook was a gift from Jane Austen's father, as indicated on the contents page—"Ex dono mei Patris." "Volume the Second" is inscribed in Jane Austen's hand on the front board, and the spine contains some illegible lettering.[30]

The work originally contained 139 leaves, 6.3″ × 7.7″, with a "Pro Patria" watermark similar to that in *Volume the First*. The pages were trimmed with some loss to the top letters of text. Twelve leaves were removed, leaving only stubs: one leaf between pages 64 and 67, the end of "Love and Freindship" and the dedication to "Lesley Castle" (no text seems to be missing according to the contents page); two leaves between page 186, the end of "The History of England" and the dedication to "A Collection of Letters"; three leaves between pages 200 and 201, towards the end of "Letter the second" (but once again no text appears to be lost); one leaf between pages 212 and 213, between the second and third pages of "Letter the fourth"; five leaves at the end of the notebook, after the last numbered page 252. The sheets were probably removed because they either were spoiled during transcription or were blank sheets and could be reused. All but one of them were taken out, probably by Jane herself, before the contents page was written.[31]

Jane Austen composed the pieces in *Volume the Second* between 1790 and 1793. She dated "Love and Freindship" "13 June 1790" and "The History of England" "26 November 1791." Cassandra contributed to this latter effort a series of 13 medallion watercolors of the kings and queens of England, each of which appears at the beginning of its respective section. (Cassandra did not, however, do a portrait of Edward V, because, as her sister notes in the work, "This unfortunate Prince lived so little a while that no body had time to draw his picture.") The eleventh section of "The History of England," contains portraits of both Elizabeth, with a rather ugly nose and mean expression, and Mary Queen of Scots, looking pretty and delicate. Although Cassandra has been criticized as an artist because of what has been considered a rather crude drawing of Jane, the original watercolors of the kings and queens are quite witty and appropriate as illustrations for her sister's work.

Beneath the dedication to "Lesley Castle" are several lines: "Mssrs Demand & Co-please to pay Jane Austen Spinster the sum of one hundred guineas on account of your Humbl. Servant. H T Austen. £105. 0. 0." This passage is not in the hand of Jane Austen and was perhaps added by her brother Henry.

In his critical edition of *Volume the Second,* Southam documents over 200 changes made by Jane Austen. Most consist of the correction of copying errors. At first, Jane apparently was trying to preserve the fair copy look of the volume by erasing and crossing out lightly. Later, however, when changes in style appear and she evidently was using the notebook for perfecting her craft rather than for the amusement of family members, she revised the manuscript in a darker ink and heavier hand:[32] for example, on page 39, she has crossed out "as it was a most agreable Drive," noted above it "from its wonderful Celebrity" and then cancelled that phrase, and finally written "although it was at a considerable distance."

After Jane Austen's death, *Volume the Second* passed to Cassandra along with the other manuscripts. Sometime between then and her own death in 1845, Cassandra inscribed in pencil on the front pastedown endpaper: "For my Brother Frank, C.E.A." A scrap of paper attached to the front pastedown has this same inscription in ink. This notebook remained in the family of Admiral of the Fleet Sir Francis Austen until 1977 when it was acquired at the July 6, 1977, Sotheby's sale by the British Library for £40,000.[33]

Volume the Second was first published under the title *Love & Freindship and other early works, now first printed from the original MS. by Jane Austen, with a preface by G.K. Chesterton* in 1922, while owned by Janet R. Sanders, granddaughter of Francis. B.C. Southam edited the best textual and critical edition of the work in 1963 after he was able to examine the manuscript, then in the possession of Mrs. Rosemary Mowll.[34]

Volume the Third is bound in a small quarto volume of vellum-covered boards, with a double blind rule border, measuring 19.5 × 16 cm. The front cover is titled "Volume the Third," with a calligraphic flourish, in Jane Austen's hand, and the spine is unintelligibly lettered. The notebook consists of 72 leaves of laid paper, some with undated watermarks similar to those in *Volume the First*. Someone has written, in pencil, on the inside front cover: "Effusions of Fancy by a very Young Lady Consisting of Tales in a Style entirely new." On

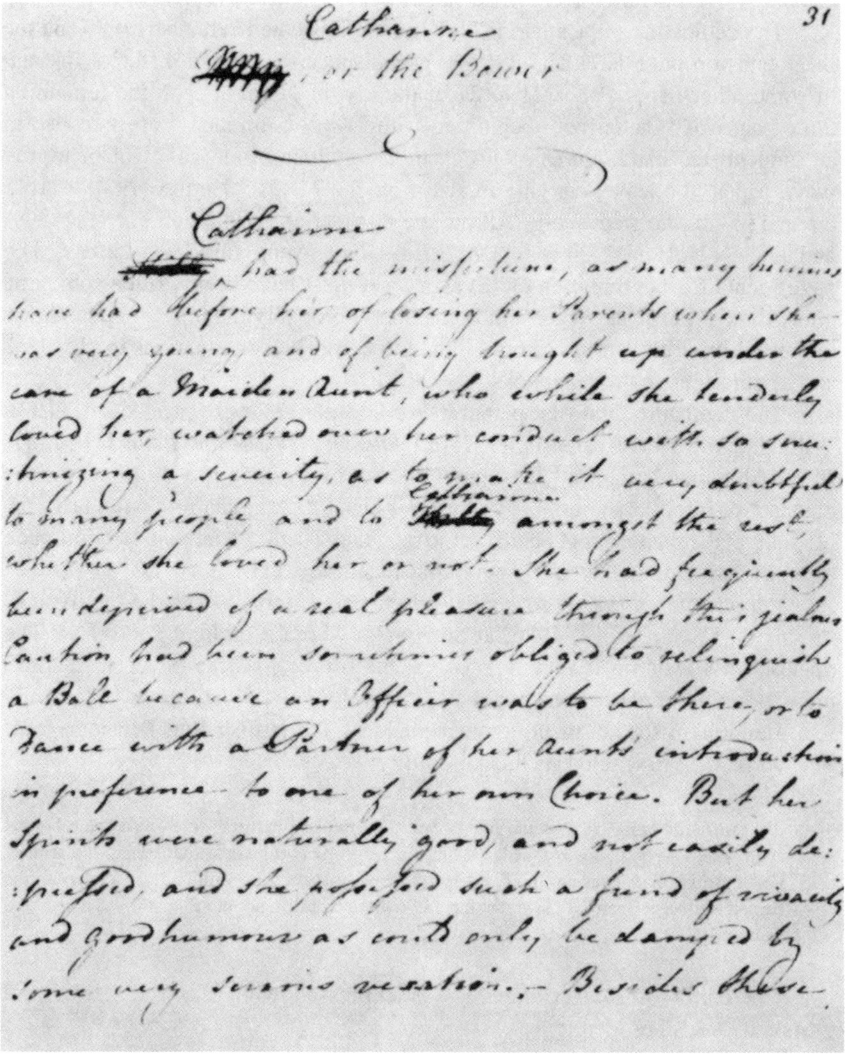

31

Catharine
~~Kitty~~, or the Bower

Catharine
~~Kitty~~ had the misfortune, as many heroines
have had before her, of losing her Parents when she
was very young, and of being brought up under the
care of a Maiden Aunt, who while she tenderly
loved her, watched over her conduct with so scru:
:tinizing a severity, as to make it very doubtful
to many people, and to ~~Kitty~~ Catharine amongst the rest,
whether she loved her or not. She had frequently
been deprived of a real pleasure through this jealous
Caution, had been sometimes obliged to relinquish
a Ball because an Officer was to be there, or to
Dance with a Partner of her Aunt's introduction
in preference to one of her own Choice. But her
Spirits were naturally good, and not easily de:
:pressed, and she possessed such a fund of vivacity
and good humour as could only be damped by
some very serious vexation.— Besides these

Figure 11. "Catharine, or The Bower"
(Volume the Third *MS; Courtesy Sotheby Parke Bernet & Co.*)

the first leaf Jane Austen has inscribed "Jane Austen—May 6th 1792." Also in pencil in an unknown hand is "for James Edward Austen Leigh." Cassandra probably wrote this inscription, as she did in *Volume the First* and *Volume the Second,* sometime after 1837 when James became Austen-Leigh.[35]

The dedication of "Catharine" to Cassandra is dated "August 1792" and the piece ends on page 127. The last few pages appear to be in a different ink and in some other hand. Pages 21 to 27 of the text of "Evelyn" and the remaining three pages of "Catharine," beginning with "Kitty continued," are likewise in an unidentified hand. *Volume the Third* also contains four leaves of blue-gray wove paper, the leaves varying in size from 14.7 × 15.7 cm to 19.4 × 15.5 cm and having no watermark. All but the last leaf are written on one side only, and the conclusion is signed "J.A.E.L."—Jane Anna Elizabeth Lefroy. The pages contain a continuation of "Evelyn" that must have been written sometime after Anna's marriage. Other family members, probably the nieces and nephews interested in writing, were also permitted to compose continuations to "Evelyn" and "Catharine" in the notebooks.[36]

The dedication and first paragraph of "Catharine" were printed in 1913 in William and Robert Austen-Leigh's *Jane Austen: Her Life and Letters.* In 1951, R.W. Chapman published the complete text of *Volume the Third,* from the manuscript in possession of R.A. Austen-Leigh.[37] Chapman noted the few corrections and revisions—generally of errors that occurred in transcription such as "for" corrected to "from"[38]—with brackets in the text.

Volume the Third, left to James Austen-Leigh, remained in the family until its sale on December 14, 1976, at Sotheby's, where it brought £30,000.[39] The manuscript's location is now unknown. One source lists the buyer as "anonymous"; another identifies the buyer as "Maxwell."[40] In all likelihood "Maxwell" is a pseudonym for an agent commissioned by the British Rail Pension Fund. *The Daily Mail* first suggests this possibility:

> A storm is building up over the fate of several national treasures which have been bought anonymously—probably as a hedge against inflation. It is rumoured that behind the secrecy is the British Rail Pension Fund which has recently spent £3.5 million. . . . Yesterday the British Railways Board . . . said that it could "neither confirm nor deny" that it had bought the manuscripts.[41]

The editor of *Book Collector* was impressed with Maxwell's taste and intrigued by his/her identity:

> The autograph sale was distinguished, for me, by the presence of a buyer, Maxwell, who had the unerring good taste to buy just those items I had marked in my own catalogue. He (or she) began with an elegant calligraphic letter from Nicholas Reynold to Ortelius (L180), went on with a fascinating letter from Thomas Paine to the president of the Directory, 28 December

1797 (L1600) and an excellent letter from the 22-year-old Ruskin to Henry Acland (L240), and then put down £30,000 for "Volume the Third." . . . I have never been so struck by "doppelganger effect" before, and I long to meet Mr. (Ms?) Maxwell.[42]

By the winter of 1978, however, that editor evidently realized that Maxwell probably had been acting as an agent. When a "Webster" bought the manuscript of *The Watsons* for £38,000, the *Book Collector* referred to him as "doubtless a stable-mate of the pseudonymous purchaser of *Volume the Third* in 1976. If, as is widely believed, these two manuscripts have gone to the British Rail Pension Fund, it is a pity that they cannot at least acknowledge their purchases, even if it is too much to expect them to let scholars use them."[43] Neither the former owner nor Jane Austen scholars know the whereabouts of *Volume the Third*. The notebook has simply disappeared, presumably into a bank vault. Maxwell was a "ghost" bidding for someone, probably the British Rail Pension Fund, which evidently does not want the location of the manuscript disclosed.

Lady Susan consists of 80 quarto leaves (158 numbered), measuring 19 × 15.5 cm, slightly trimmed, mounted, and bound in a Riviere binding of full orange morocco heavily gilt. The binding was added sometime before its sale at Sotheby's on December 17, 1898. Two of the leaves (the 44th and 55th) are watermarked 1805 and contain the name "Sharp."[44]

Cassandra bequeathed *Lady Susan* to Fanny Knight, later Lady Knatchbull. In 1882, Lady Knatchbull left the work to her son, Edward Knatchbull-Hugessen, first Baron Brabourne. The first auction sale of *Lady Susan* (from the library of Lord Brabourne) occurred at Puttick & Simpson on June 28, 1893, followed by a sale at Sotheby's on December 17, 1898, where the manuscript was purchased by Elliston for £22.10s. *Lady Susan* was next listed in a London bookseller's catalogue in 1900 for £100. Sometime between 1900 and 1925, the Earl of Rosebery purchased the manuscript, and on June 26, 1933, the work was again sold at Sotheby's as lot number 268 from the Rosebery library. Walter M. Hill, a Chicago bookseller, paid £2,100, almost 100 times the 1898 purchase price. The Pierpont Morgan Library, the present owner, purchased *Lady Susan* in December 1947 from James F. Drake, Inc., who had acquired it from Hill.[45]

Lady Susan was first published in the second edition of *A Memoir* in 1871. Unfortunately, the text was printed from an inaccurate copy because the original manuscript could not be found. The manuscript was eventually located in 1882 at the time of Lady Knatchbull's death.[46]

In 1925 R.W. Chapman was able to use the original *Lady Susan* manuscript, then in the hands of the fifth earl of Rosebery, to edit an accurate text. Chapman listed only 12 corrections in the manuscript but noted numerous errors made in the initial 1871 appearance of the text.[47]

Fate has decreed that four of the five Jane Austen manuscripts which survive in complete form are those of the earliest works: *Volume the First*,

Volume the Second, Volume the Third, and *Lady Susan.* The notebooks, whether intended for use as sources of entertainment for her family or as personal journals of story ideas, sketches, and experimental writing, constitute, along with *Lady Susan,* an invaluable legacy from Jane to her admirers. Through these earliest works, Jane Austen's development from an 11-year-old literary novice to an 18-year-old gifted author can be seen: her reliance on the burlesque in her early sketches, her experimentation with satire in the middle pieces, her emphasis on character and natural dialogue in the later works, and her polished and completed form in the epistolary novel *Lady Susan.*

Notes

1. *Jane Austen's Letters to Her Sister Cassandra and Others,* collected by R.W. Chapman, two volumes, Oxford, 1932, I, 39; I, 197. Hereafter referred to as *Letters.*

2. *Letters,* II, 443.

3. [Henry Austen], "Biographical Notice of the Author" in *Northanger Abbey: and Persuasion,* London, 1818, p. xv.

4. *Letters,* I, 9; I, 212.

5. Ibid., p. 89.

6. [Henry Austen], "Biographical Notice," p. xiv.

7. *Letters,* II, 299.

8. Anna Lefroy, *Jane Austen's Sanditon: A Continuation by Her Niece Together with "Reminiscences of Aunt Jane,"* ed. Mary Gaither Marshall, Chicago, 1983, p. 166.

9. *Letters,* II, 297.

10. Park Honan, *Jane Austen: Her Life,* London, 1987, pp. 59–62.

11. "Biographical Notice," p. xiv.

12. Jane Austen, *Volume the Second,* ed. Brian Southam, Oxford, 1963, p. 169.

13. A. Walton Litz, *Jane Austen: A Study of Her Artistic Development,* London, 1965, p. 35.

14. *Volume the Second,* pp. 40, 3, 16, 139.

15. Brian Southam, *Jane Austen's Literary Manuscripts,* Oxford, 1964, pp. 14–17.

16. Brian Southam, "The Manuscript of Jane Austen's *Volume the First,*" *The Library,* Fifth Series, 17 (1962), 232.

17. Southam, *Jane Austen's Literary Manuscripts,* pp. 16–17.

18. Litz, p. 49.

19. Southam, *Jane Austen's Literary Manuscripts,* p. 17.

20. James Austen-Leigh, *A Memoir of Jane Austen,* London, 1871. Hereafter referred to as *Memoir,* p. 201.

21. Jane Austen, *Lady Susan,* ed. R.W. Chapman, Oxford, 1925, p. 66.

22. *Memoir*, p. 201.

23. R.W. Chapman, *Jane Austen: Facts and Problems*, Oxford, 1948, p. 52.

24. Litz, p. 174.

25. Southam, *Jane Austen's Literary Manuscripts*, p. 46.

26. *Memoir*, p. 42.

27. David Gilson, *A Bibliography of Jane Austen*, Oxford, 1982, p. 383.

28. Jane Austen, *Volume the First*, ed. R.W. Chapman, Oxford, 1933, p. 33.

29. Southam, "The Manuscript of Jane Austen's *Volume the First*," p. 234.

30. Gilson, *A Bibliography of Jane Austen*, p. 372.

31. *Volume the Second*, pp. viii, 209–10.

32. Southam, *Jane Austen's Literary Manuscripts*, p. x.

33. Gilson, *A Bibliography of Jane Austen*, pp. 372–73.

34. *Volume the Second*, p. vi.

35. Gilson, *A Bibliography of Jane Austen*, p. 385.

36. Ibid., pp. 385–86.

37. Jane Austen, *Volume the Third*, ed. R.W. Chapman, Oxford, 1951, p. v.

38. Ibid., p. 38.

39. David Gilson, "Auction Sales," in *The Jane Austen Companion*, ed. J. David Grey et al., New York, 1986, p. 13.

40. Barbara Rosenbaum and Pamela White, *Index of English Literary Manuscripts*, London, 1982, pp. 21–31; "Austen Ms Brings £30,000," *Daily Telegraph*, December 15, 1976.

41. "Riddle of Nation's 'Lost' Treasures," *Daily Mail*, December 31, 1976.

42. "News and Comment," *The Book Collector* (Summer 1977), 247.

43. "News and Comment," *The Book Collector* (Winter 1978), 554.

44. Gilson, *A Bibliography of Jane Austen*, p. 375.

45. Ibid., p. 375 and Gilson, "Auction Sales," p. 13.

46. Gilson, *A Bibliography of Jane Austen*, p. 375.

Plots and Possibilities: Jane Austen's Juvenilia

Patricia Meyer Spacks

Toward the end of Jane Austen's early fragmentary novel, "Catharine, or The Bower," the heroine (variously called "Catherine" and "Kitty") speculates in high romantic vein about why a young man who has attracted her interest chose to depart for good early in the morning, without seeing her.

> In what anguish he must have left the house! Unable to see me, or to bid me adieu, while I, senseless wretch, was daring to sleep. This then, explained his leaving us at such a time of day—. He could not trust himself to see me—. Charming Young Man! How much must you have suffered! I *knew* that it was impossible for one so elegant, and so well bred, to leave any Family in such a Manner, but for a Motive like this unanswerable. (238–39)

The narrator goes on to comment on how "satisfied" this account of things leaves Kitty and to note the girl's failure to recollect, in arriving at her satisfying interpretation, "the vanity of young women."

The vanity allegedly characteristic of her age and sex has presumably contributed to Kitty's elaborate narrative of Edward Stanley's "unanswerable" motivation. Since the fragment breaks off a page later, we cannot know the true explanation of Edward's behavior, but we can guess that Kitty's version of things is false. In the fiction's economy, this episode calls attention to a crucial perplexity: what makes things happen within a fictional world? Austen's early authorial experimentation recurs insistently to this problem. Her explorations of motive and causality, internal and external, suggest a young writer's concern with possibilities of plot. Although we lack materials to construct a detailed chronology of individual pieces of juvenilia, we can see in the three volumes a consistent investigation of ways in which fictional plots generate themselves.

Not that Austen typically produces, in her early work, shapely or complete or plausible plots. On the contrary, few of these narratives make any kind of logical sense. Their author clearly takes pleasure in her absolute command over happenings on the page. No one forces her to make sense. She can ordain that a lover, struck with the charms of a "lovely Fair one" ("Amelia Webster," 49), refrain from food for five days; she can create a house consisting of two rooms and a closet for a man whose brother has conveniently offered to furnish precisely this amount of space ("A Tale"). She kills and resurrects characters at her convenience. She gives them incredibly abundant love affairs or deprives them of all lovers or makes them incapable of figurative language unless it concerns food. Much of the pleasure these tales and fragments create for the reader depends on the sheer arbitrariness of happening in them. They must have entertained their creator in just the same way.

The superficially neat plots that occasionally issue from Austen's structures of implausibility flaunt their defiance of social and moral cause and effect. My favorite case in point, from *Volume the Second,* is "A Letter from a Young Lady, whose feelings being too Strong for her Judgement led her into the commission of Errors which her Heart disapproved." In just over a page, Austen constructs a fantastic novel in miniature. She opens with a formulation familiar from dozens, if not hundreds, of eighteenth-century fictions concerned with young ladies possessed of feelings too strong for their judgments: "Many have been the cares & vicissitudes of my past life, my beloved Ellinor" (174). But the sentence ends less predictably: "& the only consolation I feel for their bitterness is that on a close examination of my conduct, I am convinced that I have strictly deserved them" (174–75). No other eighteenth-century heroine ever deserves her painful experience; young Jane Austen has formulated a revolutionary idea and made an important critical point. She generates her plot from the point, summarizing Anna Parker's career of murder, infidelity, perjury, and forgery and its reward in marriage to an inordinately wealthy man. We learn of no "cares" or harsh "vicissitudes." The fiction's final sentence underlines the protagonist's utter lack of remorse—indeed, of "feelings" of any kind. "I am now going to murder my Sister" (175), she blandly concludes. She suggests no motive.

The logic of the first sentence dictates the form of the tiny plot. A self-satisfied character who sees herself as a fictional heroine has behaved badly. The narrative action substantiates bad behavior and self-satisfaction. It does nothing more; it suggests the irrelevance of anything more. Such notions as "remorse" or "punishment" bear no connection to Anna's complacent self-absorption. She is a creation of fantasy; the freedom of fantasy allows outrageous acts to occur without penalty. Thus the logic of plot, in this instance and others, diverges from that of the world, in which aggressive action implies more complicated consequences. The simplification of consequence, the avoidance of morality, may comment on the avoidances in conventional sentimental fiction, but it also suggests the author's discovery that fiction can be purely fictional, operating by its own rules, allowed to evade restriction. Motiveless malignance thus may participate in comedy as well as tragedy. The maker of fictions exercises absolute dominion.

Reveling in this perception, the young writer produced extravagant stories that typically convey aggressive impulse, narrating the hostility of children to parents and of parents to children (e.g., the mother who rides horseback from England to Scotland, making her daughters run on foot beside her). They abound in sudden death and reversal of fortune. They foreshadow preoccupations of Austen's mature novels—love and money, of course, but also the tedium of conventional life.

That love and money generate plot hardly needs further demonstration. Austen's speculations about how the tedium of life can produce narrative have equally far-reaching implications, although such speculations do not, at this stage in her career, themselves produce compelling plots. "Memoirs of Mr. Clifford" (subtitled "An Unfinished Tale") uses the familiar narrative metaphor of the journey as structural principle for a story about a man who does nothing whatever of interest. Mr. Clifford, who lives at Bath, sets off to see London. The narrator reports the various kinds of carriages and horses he possesses, then begins to tell of his very slow journey, including such details as the boiled egg the protagonist shares with his servants at Devizes. This kind of detail is essential, since, although Mr. Clifford suffers five months of fever beginning the fourth day of his trip, essentially nothing happens to him from beginning to end. The fragment breaks off in the midst of a catalogue of places passed. Mr. Clifford appears to possess neither inner nor outer life. Similarly, "The beautifull Cassandra" ("A Novel in Twelve Chapters") reports the adventures of "the only Daughter of a celebrated Millener in Bond Street" (44). She sets out to make her fortune, curtseys to a viscount, knocks down a pastry cook (without internal or external consequences) after refusing to pay for her ices, takes a hackney coach to Hampstead, runs away from the coachman who demands pay, passes "thro' many a street" without "the least Adventure" (46), meets, in two successive chapters, two women, and returns home, whispering to herself "This is a day well spent" (47). Little more happens in "Amelia Webster," in which newspaper announcements of marriages substitute for accounts of courtship. "Lesley Castle," an unfinished epistolary novel, sketches a competitive situation between a stepmother and two stepdaughters but emphasizes the absence of happening through which the women can dramatize their desires. "A Collection of Letters" opens with a letter from a mother excited by the prospect of her daughters' entrance into society. Gradually we come to realize that "society"— consistently referred to as "a World"—consists of a drawing room inhabited by one other mother and her single daughter.

Such small fictions construct themselves from nonhappening rather than happening. Stressing poverty of experience, they force the reader to attend to nonplots. And they call attention to the young author's awareness of a problem implicit in any notion of fictional realism—especially, perhaps, for women writers of the gentry class, to whom, by clear social convention, nothing was supposed to happen.

By the end of the eighteenth century, the well-established difference between romances (reprehensible reading) and novels (conceivably defensible) depended on mimetic criteria. Traditional romances made no claim of realism. They depicted "unmixed" characters, flawless or villainous, and fanciful events. Novels, on the other hand (some called them "modern romances"), purported to render the texture of actual experience and at least to suggest the complexity of actual character. Although their neat resolutions and their frequent reliance on ideas of Providence distance them from twentieth-century notions of "real life," eighteenth-century readers often praised their probability. As Clara Reeve's spokeswoman in *The Progress of Romance* puts the point, "The Novel is a picture of real life and manners, and of the times in which it is written. The Romance in lofty and elevated language, describes what never happened nor is likely to happen."[1]

Austen's juvenile works often turn on jokes about, parodies of, romance, but the writer also explored other possibilities. In the narratives just summarized, she has not abandoned arbitrary happenings or events devoid of consequence, but she works with ostentatiously mundane raw material. And she confronts the fact that the substance of everyday life provides little obvious data for compelling fiction. Fictional young women in eighteenth-century novels frequently complain that nothing happens in their lives, they have nothing to write letters about. One can read the little story about the mother introducing her daughters into "the world" as a covert complaint of the same sort. Where can plot come from if fiction is to imitate a realm of actuality in which very little happens?

It can come only from the implications of character. Late eighteenth-century novelists reveal ever more explicit consciousness of the necessary intertwining of plot and character; Austen's juvenile fiction shows her working out implications of that consciousness. She does so partly by mocking her predecessors' notions of character. "Tho' Benevolent & Candid, she was Generous & sincere; Tho' Pious & Good, she was Religious & amiable, & Tho' Elegant & Agreable, she was Polished & Entertaining" (13). The joke of this sentence from "Jack & Alice" turns on the common fictional device of creating logical antitheses of character, antitheses implying potential consequences. Austen, displaying her sequence of *false* antitheses, in which each term duplicates the import of the adjective structurally opposed to it, calls attention to the arbitrariness of attributed meaning in fiction. The construction of character, like that of sentences, derives from the will to create significance. To follow out the consequences of asserted character (or for that matter, the consequences of sentences) produces plots, the primary medium of significance in fiction. But in her juvenile efforts,

Austen often contradicts this fundamental principle of fiction-making, creating plots instead by *denying* the consequences of her assertions. Thus Lady Williams, the woman described as generous, sincere, pious, "Agreable," drives Alice into a frenzy by harping on her drunkenness, offers malicious portrayals of her friends to a new acquaintance ("I am sorry to say too that I never knew three such thorough Gamesters as they are, more particularly Alice" [23]), and gives double messages to those about her ("I shall be miserable without you— t'will be a most pleasant tour to you—I hope you'll go; if you do I am sure t'will be the Death of me" [24]). Finally Lady Williams marries the youthful male paragon for whom at least two younger women have pined in vain.

These early works, of course, do not purport to be realistic. Fictions about fiction, they call attention to their own operations and to the relation of those operations to the workings of fictional precursors. Indeed, the true subject of all Austen's juvenilia is the resources and the limits of the imagination in creating characters and their stories. As the young writer tests imaginative possibility, she foretells principles of plot-making she will later choose to follow.

The most frequently recurrent plot-generating characteristic of persons in the juvenile fiction is relentless self-interest: what we might call *narcissism*. The tales I have termed "arbitrary" and "fantastic" often turn on an imagining of character in these terms. The young woman who without a qualm murders and cheats her way to marital happiness, for instance, displays a parodic version of narcissistic self-obsession. Typically, characters in these fictions possess virtually no awareness of the possible needs or desires of others. Laura, in the third letter of "Love and Freindship," like the murderer describes herself as pained by her own feelings: "A sensibility too tremblingly alive to every affliction of my Freinds, my Acquaintance and particularly to every affliction of my own, was my only fault, if a fault it could be called. Alas! how altered now!" The alteration, it turns out, involves clarification of focus. "Tho' indeed my own misfortunes do not make less impression on me than they ever did," Laura explains, "yet now I never feel for those of an other" (78). Speaking in this miniature self-portrait for many of her fictional fellows, she incidentally accounts for most of the happenings in "Love and Freindship," a work in which non sequiturs and inconsistencies make sense in relation to the self-focused consciousness of their creators. The clearly obvious irrelevancies abounding in the text derive also from human solipsism. A family sits around the fire. They hear a violent knocking on the door. No one answers; instead, they discuss whether or not the noise they have heard actually issues from someone's knocking, whether or not someone should respond to the summons, who that someone should be. Everyone considers only his or her own feelings and reactions; the person at the door remains purely hypothetical. The Ionesco-like scene concludes when a servant admits a young man who informs his audience "that he was the son of an English Baronet, that his Mother had been many years no more and that he had a Sister of the middle size" (80). The inconsequentialities and incongruities of this statement once more reflect the self-absorbed workings of an essentially uncensored consciousness.

The disturbing comedy of the entire work derives from such phenomena as the ferocious hostility of children toward parents; the greedy entitlement of the young, who steal what they want and resent the very possibility that anyone should object; the self-congratulation and utter selfishness of youthful lovers; the total rejection of moral consequence. If Austen here mocks clichés of the sentimental novel, she also calls attention to the foundation of narcissism that underlies such clichés. Only by taking herself with blind, obsessive seriousness can a character expect the world to interest itself in every detail of her emotional life. The conventions of fiction, Austen hints, often falsify the relationship between feeling and action as well as the true nature of self-proclaimed fine feeling. When the "noble Youth" who comes in from the cold toward the beginning of "Love and Freindship" recounts his initial defiance of his father, his auditors admire "the noble Manliness of his reply." His father, on the other hand, as he reports, comments, "Where Edward in the name of wonder . . . did you pick up this unmeaning Gibberish? You have been studying Novels I suspect" (80–81). The falsifications of feeling that Austen mocks indeed derive from novels. She implicitly intends to substitute more accurate renditions of motive and impulse, consequently more accurate structures of plot.

In most of these stories only one motive emerges, only a single source for plot. Margaret Lesley's first letter in "Lesley Castle" summarizes the situation of herself and her sister: "We are handsome my dear Charlotte, very handsome and the greatest of our Perfections is, that we are entirely insensible of them ourselves" (111). We can hardly be surprised to discover her reaction when she goes to London: "In short my Dear Charlotte it is my sensibility for the sufferings of so many amiable Young Men, my Dislike of the extreme Admiration I meet with, and my Aversion to being so celebrated both in Public, in Private, in Papers, & in Printshops, that are the reasons why I cannot more fully enjoy, the Amusements so various and pleasing of London" (135). The implications of this kind of self-regard emerge in the next sentence: "How often have I wished that I possessed as little personal Beauty as you do" (135–36). No concern for the feelings of others impedes Margaret's self-congratulations, direct and indirect. Miss Lutterell, recipient of the two letters quoted above, operates on comparable principles. Compulsively preoccupied with cooking and her skill in it, she responds to the death of her sister's fiancé by complaining obsessively over the labor she has wasted in producing the wedding feast. Several letters dwell on the subject and on her expedience for getting rid of the food. Vanity about one's competence or about one's appearance: both produce moral blindness. "Lesley Castle," in which, as I have already suggested, little happens, extends to a length of 28 pages simply by comically elaborating the unawareness that afflicts all its characters.

"Evelyn," probably a late composition from the juvenile years, provides an especially interesting example of the plot of narcissism because it creates a situation in which narcissism meets only the slightest obstacles. Austen's usual method, in these early works, depends on bringing the self-obsessed into conjunction with one another. In "Evelyn," Mr. Gower stands alone in his customary solipsism. At his first appearance in the text, he seems not particularly self-absorbed. He asks the landlady at an alehouse whether the parish contains any houses to be let. When she fails to answer, his spirits are weighed down by "the agonizing pain of Doubt & Suspence" (180). The landlady then responds that no one wishes to leave the parish because of its remarkable "sweetness of . . . Situation, & the purity of the Air, in which neither Misery, Illhealth, or Vice are ever wafted" (181). One family, however, from sheer generosity might rent their house. When Mr. Gower goes to visit them, they overwhelm him with food, drink, and money, offer him their house as a gift, and bestow their daughter on him, with a fortune of 10,000 pounds.

Gower's role as recipient makes him feel endlessly entitled. He allows his benefactors to remain in the house for a half hour, then settles into a regime of perfect happiness, interrupted only when, after some months, he accidentally remembers the sister on whose behalf he originally came into this part of the country. Afflicted "by Greif, Apprehension and Shame" (185)—his forgetfulness has briefly caused him to think badly of himself—he writes the sister, learns of her death, but goes anyhow to the castle owned by the father of the man she loved. "Mr Gower was a perfect stranger to every one in the Circle but tho' he was always timid in the Dark and easily terrified when alone, he did not want that more necessary and more noble courage which enabled him without a Blush to enter a large party of superior Rank, whom he had never seen before, & to take his Seat amongst them with perfect Indifference" (187). He demands to know of the lord of the castle whether, if the lord's son and Mr. Gower's sister were still alive, he would have consented to their marriage. The lord finds the question meaningless. Mr. Gower, furious, complains that "not even the death of your Son can make you wish his future Life happy" (188). Austen's part of the manuscript breaks off with his return home; some member of her family completed the narrative.

This depiction of a man whose behavior becomes ever more inappropriate, given his situation of having all needs and desires fulfilled, exemplifies one of Austen's central concerns. Mr. Gower's indulgent wife and her indulgent parents make Gower believe himself a natural recipient of indulgence from all. Such a belief effectively incapacitates him. The lord responds rationally to his foolish question: "No one can more sincerely regret the death of my Son than I have always done, and it gives me great concern to know that Miss Gower's was hastened by his—. Yet to suppose them alive is destroying at once the Motive for a change in my sentiments concerning the affair" (188). But Gower's self-regard has eliminated his capacity for rationality. The result of narcissism is non sequitur: so many of Austen's early plots suggest. The self-obsessed man or woman does not think of outcomes, does not deal in cause and effect. When someone says no to him, Gower can only depart in a rage. He cannot discuss, he cannot plan, he cannot sustain a course of action. He typifies his kind.

Such a discussion of a ridiculous character in a ridiculous fictional sketch may verge on the ridiculous itself because it appears to treat as a "realistic" rendition something that makes not the slightest claim of realism. Probability, that shibboleth of eighteenth-century novel critics, has nothing to do with such a work as "Evelyn." Mr. Gower is hardly a "character" at all. His quite showy fictionality—comparable to that of many other figures in Austen's early work— is far more manifest than his relation to human beings in the world outside the text. Like Sir William Mountague, eponymous protagonist of another early fragment, he functions mechanically. Sir William begins his career by falling in love with all three Miss Cliftons, and continues to love every female he meets. When his first fiancée suggests the opening day of the hunting season as their wedding day, he abandons her—he can always find a wife, but a day of hunting lost is lost forever. He has no trouble locating other objects for his affections, although he has to shoot the lover of one in order to persuade her to accept him. The comic plots in which such characters participate—which, in- deed, they generate—suggest that Austen has already discovered Henri Bergson's principle of comedy: when a human being acts, and keeps acting, like a machine, it's funny. Mr. Gower and Sir William and their fellows possess a single principle of action: self-interest. (Even Gower's apparent concern for his sister proves only an extension of self-interest.) They figure in fictions whose jerky, inconsequential sequences of event both dramatize and mock the limitations of such a principle.

If the plots and characters thus created bear little relation to "probability" and claim no "verisimilitude," they can yet be construed as indicating something of their author's attitude toward the world she inhabits. Paul Ricoeur has sug- gested that the fortunes of convention in fiction must for any adequate history of the novel be investigated in conjunction with those of verisimilitude.[2] The issue of convention also assumes considerable importance in the history of an individual novelist. Austen makes fun of numerous conventions of the eigh- teenth-century novel in her earliest works. She calls attention to the falsities of sentimentality, the ridiculousness of romance. Most especially, she mocks the claim of sensibility endemic among earlier fictional heroines. *Her* heroines make it clear that no genuine feeling need attend such a claim. The heroine of "Love and Freindship" who declines visiting her husband in prison because the scene would too greatly exacerbate her feelings typifies a troop of comparable figures. And these figures call attention to the new conventions that Austen offers in parody of and substitution for the old.

Foremost among her conventions, in the juvenilia, is that of the utterly self-absorbed character. A tumult of unimportant happenings issues from his or her nature. These characters lack all sense of responsibility to others; Austen uses her plots to objectify that lack by freeing their actions from moral consequence. Although a minor figure in "Jack & Alice" is removed from the scene by being hanged, more typically no one is punished for deviant behavior. The woman who murders her relatives receives only reward; the man who kills a woman's lover in order to get her for himself—gets her; the characters of "Love and Freindship" flourish on their ill-gotten gains. Such characters lack the development and complexity that long-established literary convention has led us to expect in fictional renditions of the human. Yet they possess a strange energy on the page. It is the energy of obsession, their own and their author's. Comparing Mr. Gower with his wife, who exists only to make him happy, or comparing the avaricious young folk in "Love and Freindship" with their elders, most often relegated to the role of fruitless rebukers, one realizes how shadowy, in these sketches, figures *not* completely absorbed in themselves become. Unable to complete many of the narratives she initiates (or losing interest in them), Austen consistently invents sequences (not logical sequences, only the one-thing-after-another kind) of violent, haphazard action, as if to say that no pattern of resolution can issue from people unable to acknowledge the importance of anyone besides themselves.

For a time, it seems, Austen could only imagine people of this sort. That's what I meant by suggesting the presence of obsession in author as well as characters. Setting out to parody literary genres that had given her pleasure but that seemed based on conventions grotesquely false to actual experience, she insistently offers a single alternative "truth": most people care only about themselves. The insistence itself makes us laugh. The woman who solves her problems by committing crimes and getting rewarded for them, the girls who learn from their experience that running mad is safer than fainting (equally dramatic, less likely to lead to fatal illness)—verbal evocations of such figures appeal to the universal desire to be freed from the rules that inevitably govern human life, the life of people situated among other people. Jane Austen's early characters don't play by the rules. We laugh to see them thrive—laugh because they are so ostentatiously only fictions.

Yet fictional convention, like all convention, renders a view of reality. The convention of character on which the young Austen relied suggests a depressed, an essentially chilling view. There are other ways to make jokes about sentimental and romantic fiction. As early as 1752, Charlotte Lennox, in *The Female Quixote*, constructed a full-length novel around the figure of a young girl deluded by her reading of fiction into hope for her own public significance. The girl, predictably, learns better in the end, but along the way she provides an instrument not only to make fun of the falsity of earlier conventions but to call attention to the kind of truth to which they attest. Arabella, the heroine, charms others within the text and has charmed generations of readers. Although she, like Austen's early characters, possesses an imagination obsessed with her own importance, she demonstrates also the capacity to interest herself compassionately and intelligently in other people and to respond, finally, to the rational intervention of another. As a figure in fiction, she reminds us that parody and mockery, even if it focuses on literary falsification, need not imply so bleak a view of character as that suggested—even though we laugh—by "Jack & Alice" or "Love and Freindship."

Austen's experiments in constructing plots on the basis of self-obsessed character could not go much farther than she took them. One obvious aspect of the juvenile sketches is the relative absence in them of anything one might call coherent plot. Some appear to start in the direction of such coherence, only to abandon it. Some reject it outrightly from the beginning. Only by imagining the narcissistic figure in a context of others less radically self-absorbed—others who, acknowledging the necessity of human connection, allow the possibility of the coherent connections of cause and effect that make plot—could the novelist make novels. And this, of course, is exactly what Jane Austen proceeded to do. Her mature novels all concern the situation of the modest or generous person (Catherine Morland, Elinor Dashwood, Fanny Price, Anne Elliot) surrounded by narcissists, or the struggle between self-obsession and self-awareness (Emma Woodhouse, Elizabeth Bennet, Marianne Dashwood). Even in the juvenilia, we can see her beginning to discover and to develop a more adequate literary convention for dealing with the subject of self-obsession.

"Catharine" stands last in the third volume of the juvenilia, although it was probably not composed last. Its position seems appropriate, for here Austen abandons parody and pastiche and explores more complex, less obsessive possibilities of character, hence of plot. The quotation that opens this essay illustrates the new element in this work. Although the narrator makes gentle fun of Kitty's interpretation, although the reader is surely intended to smile at it, we see in the character's effort to make sense of her experience a new energy of plot. The fully self-absorbed ask few questions. What has happened to my husband? a young woman may wonder, but she will not wonder long or hard. If a new man comes along, she will happily, if only temporarily, merge her destiny with his. If all else fails, she will tell her story to some hapless auditor. She will not devote herself to working out any problems: she resents the very existence of problems.

Kitty, or Catharine (she appears as Catharine in the first paragraph, as Kitty thereafter), prefigures Catherine Morland in her ignorance about the world and her eagerness to take a part in life. Represented as having many virtues—loyalty, good nature, warm affections, sociability, a lively spirit, even considerable willingness to comply with the often unreasonable demands of her maiden aunt—she promises a plot, in the literary sense, by the conjunction of her virtues with the kind of self-concern characteristic of her time of life. (Like many another heroine, she is 17.) At the point in the narrative where she performs her act of interpretation, she has encountered a young man similarly constructed although perhaps more foolish than she. He possesses wit, warmth, and social grace, and much more knowledge of the world than Catharine. Ominously, though, his degree of self-absorption prevents his compliance with social convention. He appears to concern himself little with the needs of others, beyond their attributed need to be charmed by him. Catharine's self-concern prevents her awareness of his. Encouraged by his sister's report of the young man's parting conversation, she readily believes herself the object of his affections.

It is easy to imagine the kind of plot that might be forthcoming, a plot based on collisions of character and of desire. Catharine's capacity for friendship (she remains loyal to the girls with whom she earlier built her "bower," although they have fallen on hard times) might war with her yearning for love. Her aunt's fearfulness about sexuality might limit the girl's opportunities even to encounter a would-be lover. Her putative lover's lack of consideration for others might make Catharine declare him inappropriate. Camilla Stanley, a comic precursor of Isabella Thorpe, might create obstacles. One could go on: here, as in none of the other juvenile works, possibilities for satisfying plot seem abundantly manifest because character has been complexly rather than monolithically imagined.

I suggested earlier that Austen's juvenilia can be read as fiction about fiction, explorations of the resources and limits of the imagination; I have ended by discussing character. But the subject has not really changed. For Austen, it seems—and this is, to my mind, the most exciting implication of the juvenilia—no separation divides the psychological from the technical aspects of fiction-making. To conceive plot is to conceive character, and conversely. What makes things happen in fiction? For Austen, the imagined feelings of imagined persons: "the vanity of young women," and the desire; the intersecting hopes and fears and angers of characters. The improbabilities of action in earlier romance and sentimental fiction, which Austen elaborately parodies, derive from falsities or inadequacies in the conception of character. In a sense Austen appears to have known this from the beginning. In another sense, she discovers it in the writing of her parodic early fiction, beginning fully to realize the implications of her insight in her experimentation with "Catharine."

Notes

1. Clara Reeve, *The Progress of Romance through Times, Countries, and Manners* (1785), two volumes in one, New York, 1970, I, 111.

2. Paul Ricoeur, *Time and Narrative*, volume two, trans. Kathleen McLaughlin and David Pellauer, Chicago, 1985, pp. 10–11.

Teaching "Love and Freindship"

Juliet McMaster

Do the juvenilia belong in the classroom at all? is a fair question, given the scarcity of time in most courses for covering great works of literature. If you have a chance to teach *Pride and Prejudice* or *Mansfield Park,* dare you jettison it for a selection of items from *Volumes the First, Second,* and *Third*? Put this way, the question possibly requires the answer "No." I am too confirmed an admirer of the six great novels to miss any opportunity of teaching them when it arises. I have taught *Pride and Prejudice* to grades 10 and 12 and to university freshmen, and *Emma* to freshmen and in survey courses on the English novel. And from time to time—O frabjous day!—I have the chance to teach all six novels to a specializing honors student, or in a graduate course. In these last cases, I make time for some of the juvenilia, and particularly for "Love and Freindship," as a way into the novels. Graduate students, who have some knowledge of the sentimental tradition that it parodies, are bowled over by it. And even in teaching Jane Austen at the lower and less specialized levels, I usually get in "Love and Freindship," if only in the form of some selected readings, as a way into the Jane Austen novel at hand.

But though by these means I have managed to teach "Love and Freindship" several times, I confess it has always been as an adjunct to teaching the major novels. So far, that is. But my experience has brought me to the conclusion that in the right context it can stand alone as a teaching text. A course in romanticism, for instance, could include it as a succinct critical text, since it is a marvelously pointed and intellectually acute reaction to romanticism, and a codification of its conventions. With its brevity and concentration, its control of diction and mastery of burlesque, it would be a joyful addition to courses in composition and rhetoric at both basic and advanced levels. Recently Sandra Gilbert and Susan Gubar have chosen "Love and Freindship" as the representative work by Jane Austen in *The Norton Anthology of Literature by Women,* and so it is not only newly available as an accessible text, but also likely to receive new prominence in courses in women's literature.[1]

One great advantage that this work has, and shares with the other juvenilia, as a text for a teaching to young people is that it is written by one of themselves. In teaching at high school and freshman levels in particular, where the English instructor is apt to be faced by a number of students more or less resistant to literature, it is a shrewd move in the game to beat the generation gap by infiltrating the opposition forces with an author who shows so many signs of sharing *your* concerns, while being on *their* side of the gap. This kid with the marvelous control of language and assured command of an extensive vocabulary, this writer with an intense and exuberant involvement in other literature, is a mere teenager, a 14-year-old. Some sharp cookie. Totally awesome, man. Perhaps, suspects the resistant student who may yet become a convert, there is something in literature after all.

The approach one takes in teaching "Love and Freindship" will of course vary according to the context in which it is taught. If it is a part of a course on romanticism or the history of the novel, then the emphasis will naturally fall on the war of ideas and the burlesque of the novel of sensibility. If it is a text in a course in composition and rhetoric, clearly the language and narrative technique will be to the fore. And when I am teaching it as an adjunct to the teaching of Jane Austen's other works, then it is useful to focus on the intimations of things to come, the themes and technical concerns that are to be developed in the great novels. By way of giving some coverage to all these possibilities, I will divide this essay into three parts, roughly on past, present, and future: one on the burlesque element as a reaction to literature that has gone before, one on "Love and Freindship" as a text standing on its own, and one on this little work as looking forward, a pointer to the novels yet to come.

Looking Back: The Burlesque

For the informed graduate student who comes to it via wide reading in the eighteenth-century novel and the novel of sensibility, "Love and Freindship" has a particular and unrivaled delight—something like it must have had for its first readers, Jane Austen's sister and brothers, who were steeped in the unselected and uncanonical fiction of the day. To come to young Jane Austen's reaction via *The Man of Feeling* or *The Fool of Quality,* or even *Clarissa* or *Evelina,* is to feel a bracing breeze of wit after a cloistered absorption in emotion.

But fortunately the wit is accessible to the less specialized student too, for you don't have to wade through *Laura and Augustus*[2] and the other novels that are being parodied to get the point. Their conventions and narrative procedures are brilliantly and unfairly generalized, selected and lampooned for us. As A.

Walton Litz points out, "The juvenilia are remarkably self-sufficient, and most of the burlesque passages are self-explanatory."[3]

Even the unsophisticated student may learn from the text itself—from Sir Edward's speech, carefully planted early in the work—that it bounces off other texts. Sir Edward is reacting to the romantic effusions of his son: "Where, Edward in the name of wonder (said he) did you pick up this unmeaning Gibberish? You have been studying Novels I suspect" (81).[4] For the reader uninitiated in the fiction Jane Austen was burlesquing, it can become a stimulating exercise to deduce the characteristics of the novels young Edward has been studying.

How would an intelligent but not necessarily widely read student respond to such a question on "Love and Freindship"? It reads, let us say, "Making clear the evidence on which you base your conclusions, deduce the major characteristics of the kinds of novel Sir Edward suspects his son of reading." First, the student would need to look carefully at what young Edward has just been saying. I quote here from his mini-autobiography, delivered on the first night of his acquaintance with Laura and her parents, which includes the dialogue with his father:

> "My Father . . . is a mean and mercenary wretch—it is only to such particular freinds as this Dear Party that I would thus betray his failings. Your Virtues my amiable Polydore (addressing himself to my father) yours Dear Claudia and yours my Charming Laura call on me to response in you, my confidence." We bowed. "My Father, seduced by the false glare of Fortune and the Deluding Pomp of Title, insisted on my giving my hand to Lady Dorothea. No never exclaimed I. Lady Dorothea is lovely and Engaging; I prefer no woman to her; but know Sir, that I scorn to marry her in compliance with your Wishes. No! Never shall it be said that I obliged my Father."
> We all admired the noble Manliness of his reply. (80–81)

The tirade received with such admiration by its later audience is designated "unmeaning Gibberish" by Sir Edward. This already points to two symmetrically opposed sets of values among the characters of the work; and with some close reading or some helpful guidance the student may align these values with Sense and Sensibility, in their extreme forms. Young Edward's values (as deducible from this passage alone) include a vaunted scorn for material considerations, an opposition on principle to fathers, a determination to be independent of parental guidance even at the cost of his own comfort and convenience, an extraordinary readiness to form instant intimacies beyond his family, and a strong propensity to talk about himself: we are already well on the way to the values of Sensibility (at least of Sensibility as here exaggerated and satirized), which are to be more elaborately adumbrated in the rest of "Love and Freindship"; and these are the values, clearly, that are enshrined in the novels that his father suspects Edward of reading. Since the same values are also articulated at large by the heroine, Laura, the student may expand from Edward's mini-narrative to his wife's larger one, and may move also from thematic concerns to technical ones. Laura, as heroine of sensibility, gives us a version of the novel of sensibility, with its routine gestures of sighing and swooning, prodigious coincidences, birth-mystery plot, embedded life-histories of different characters, and improbable layout in epistolary form. All this and much, much more (as the brochures say) the intelligent but unread student can deduce for herself from an attentive reading of the text, because of the vivid exaggeration of Jane Austen's parody.

The more fully initiated graduate student, meanwhile, may receive more recondite pleasure from the same passage, the pleasure of recognition. "Love and Freindship" is one more document in the ongoing eighteenth-century debates on true and false sensibility, marriages of interest and romance, the disinterestedness of true friendship, and the proper extent and limits of parental authority. Richardson's Clarissa Harlowe, for instance, had already delivered such a lecture as Sir Edward would have approved to her friend Anna, who was inclined to despise her sensible and eligible suitor because, like young Edward's Lady Dorothea, he was unexciting: "[You] have nothing to do [Clarissa tells her friend] but to fall in with a choice your mama has made for you, to which you have not, nor can have, a just objection: except the forwardness of our sex . . . makes it one that the choice was your mama's. . . . Perverse nature, we know, loves not to be prescribed to; although youth is not so well qualified . . . to choose for itself" (Letter 73).[5] Clarissa puts it mildly; her uncle Anthony's phrase, "a most horrid romantic perverseness" (Letter 32.4), might be closer to describing young Edward's reaction to Lady Dorothea. For the well-read seeker after sources, of course, "Love and Freindship" provides a veritable Happy Hunting Ground. Where shall we find the original for the wonderful recognition scene, in which poor Lord St. Clair is reunited with four grandchildren (all by separate mothers, and unaware of each other) in as many minutes? (91–92). In Fielding's *Joseph Andrews* ("I have discovered my son, I have him again in my arms!")?[6] In Smollett's *Humphry Clinker* ("You see, gentlemen, how the sins of my youth rise up in judgement against me")?[7] In Sheridan's *The Critic,* as Walton Litz suggests?[8] Or (my candidate) in Fanny Burney's *Evelina,* where Sir John Belmont, introduced to the girl who claims to be his daughter, responds with a dry irony worthy of Mr. Bennet, "It is not three days since, that I had the pleasure of discovering a son; how many more sons and daughters may be brought to me, I am yet to learn, but I am already perfectly satisfied with the size of my family"?[9] Fourteen-year-old Jane, familiar with these and many more, generalizes and caps them all with Lord St. Clair's bevy of supernumerary grandchildren. Well may he enquire nervously, "But tell me (. . . looking fearfully towards the Door) tell me, have I any other Grandchildren in the

House"—and, after dealing out banknotes all round, beat a hasty and permanent retreat (92).

An undue emphasis on "Love and Freindship" as burlesque of other novels has the danger of giving the impression, particularly to the unsophisticated student, that Jane Austen despised the fiction of her day. Henry Tilney can help here. Although he is the hero in a novel largely devoted to parody of the Gothic novel, and is an able parodist himself of Mrs. Radcliffe, he declares, "The person . . . who has not pleasure in a good novel, must be intolerably stupid. I have read all Mrs. Radcliffe's works, and most of them with great pleasure" (*NA*, 106). This intimate relation of admiration with mockery needs to be understood as informing "Love and Freindship" too. Reading novels and critically reacting to them were clearly the great delights of young Jane Austen's life. And her delight needs to emerge as well as her mocking judgment when we teach her youthful burlesque.

Suppose that "Love and Freindship," instead of being written by a 14-year-old girl for the small circle of her family, had been written by Byron—as it well might have been, in the same wicked mood in which he wrote "English Bards and Scotch Reviewers": it would surely have been published in its own day, and read, and laughed over, and quoted, and become part of the canon. B.C. Southam, who is careful to acknowledge the occasional and fugitive nature of Jane Austen's juvenilia, nevertheless calls it "the most amusing and incisive of all eighteenth-century attacks upon sentimental fiction."[10] For acute perception of the flaws in a certain mode, and the limber articulation of them, are not only remarkable for a 14-year-old girl, they are remarkable for *anybody*. This document in the history of ideas is the product of a first-class mind as well as of an agile creative imagination. The tenets of the cult of sentimentality, many of which were common to the romantic movement, are marvelously grasped, dramatized, and reduced to absurdity. In fact Jane Austen uses the logical strategy of *reductio ad absurdum* with brilliant consistency. Each treasured position of the sentimentalist is identified, exaggerated, and pursued to the point where it becomes a reversal of itself. Laura, Edward, Sophia and Augustus, the adherents to the cult, are like a comic version of Milton's Satan, who can produce a fine intellectual argument in support of his insanely perverse proposition, "Evil, be thou my Good."

Romantic individualism, chiefly manifested here in the rejection of social sanctions as epitomized in parental advice, becomes ultimately self-annihilating; as we have seen, Edward can't consider marrying Lady Dorothea, even though he likes her, because his father advises it. In the same way other treasured watchwords of the sentimental cult are consistently turned upside down. Sensibility itself, the capacity to feel tenderly for others, becomes callousness: at the outset Laura admits that though her sensibility was at one time "too tremblingly alive to every affliction of my Freinds," she now feels for nobody's afflictions but her own (78). Sophia enacts this hyper-refinement of the emotions: "Alas, what would I not give to learn the fate of my Augustus! to know if he is still in Newgate, or if he is yet hung. But never shall I be able so far to conquer my tender sensibility as to enquire after him" (97). Romantic reverence for the beauties of external nature becomes one more way of turning in upon the self:

> "What a beautifull Sky! (said I) How charmingly is the azure vained by those delicate streaks of white!"
> "Oh! my Laura (replied she hastily withdrawing her Eyes from a momentary glance at the sky) do not so distress me by calling my Attention to an object which so cruelly reminds me of my Augustus's blue sattin Waistcoat striped with white!" (98)

"The world is too much with us," wrote Wordsworth, giving memorable voice to the romantic's rejection of a hyper-civilized society and of things worldly; "late and soon,/Getting and spending, we lay waste our powers." Laura and her fellow romantics believe that they live according to the spirit of this rejection. Edward scorns his father, the representative of social authority, as "a mean and mercenary wretch," and expects to live the life of the lilies of the field, who toil not, neither do they spin. But as our students quickly notice, this innocent assumption that the world owes them a living leads directly to various acts of theft and embezzlement, and numbers of banknotes are "gracefully purloined" (88) with some skill by these untaught children of nature. Decades later, Dickens was to render this sinister reversal of a vaunted indifference to material things in the figure of Harold Skimpole, a character based on another romantic, Leigh Hunt. Skimpole confesses proudly "to two of the oldest infirmities in the world: one was, that he had no idea of time; the other, that he had no idea of money." He claims, "I covet nothing. . . . Possession is nothing to me." But he proceeds cheerfully on the assumption that others must support him, and like his forebears, Laura and her associates, he elevates his freeloading into a moral principle. "I almost feel as if *you* ought to be grateful to *me*," he tells his benefactor, "for giving you the opportunity of enjoying the luxury of generosity."[11] Jane Austen's Sophia can similarly turn the moral tables on her benefactor when, being caught in the act of "majestically removing" his banknotes to her own purse, she angrily calls their owner the "culprit" (96).

This pattern of turning romantic principles into their own reversal is most fully and inventively developed in the presentation of freedom of choice: Laura and company believe that they are free spirits, children of nature, living a life of spontaneous response, rejecting the hardened conventions of their parents' society, and expressing themselves habitually by the "spontaneous overflow of powerful feelings" that is Wordsworth's definition of poetry. That is their conception of themselves. As Jane Austen exposes them, however, we see them as the veritable slaves of their own convention of freedom. Their responses are rigidly codified, their language is a prescribed jargon, their attitudes as such are *de rigueur;* their very swoonings are performed with a paramilitary precision, "alternately on a sofa" (86). Far from being free individual spirits living lives untrammeled by the stultifying conventions of society, they conduct their lives by a code so rigid and exacting that it extends to the name (it must be classical like "Laura" and "Augustus," not homegrown like "Bridget"), stature (it must be above the middle height), and the color of the hair (it must be auburn).

All this comes most comically to the fore in the episode at Macdonald-Hall, where Laura and Sophia, who have hitherto been exiles from society, become authority figures themselves. The 15-year-old Janetta Macdonald proves malleable, and her new role models, with considerable zest, set about her conversion from Sense to Sensibility. She is engaged to Graham, but Laura and Sophia take things into their own hands. "They said he was Sensible, well-informed, and Agreable; we did not pretend to Judge of such trifles, but as we were convinced he had no soul, that he had never read the Sorrows of Werter, & that his Hair bore not the least resemblance to auburn, we were certain that Janetta could feel no affection for him, or at least that she ought to feel none" (93). Laura and Sophia, with their own rigid notions of propriety, prove to be even more arbitrary and tyrannical than conventionally tyrannical parents; and they symmetrically reverse the requirements of such parents as Clarissa Harlowe's by detaching Janetta from the prudent suitor and marrying her to an opportunistic fortune hunter.

To identify, exaggerate, and reduce to their own absurd opposites these tenets of the dying cult of sentimentality, from which the new cult of romanticism, phoenixlike, was about to rise, and to do all this in the dramatic form of a brief narrative, is surely to have achieved something considerable in the history of those movements, as well as to have produced a marvelously funny pastiche. "Love and Freindship" as burlesque, as a reaction to previous and contemporary texts, deserves a place in courses on the eighteenth century and romanticism.

The Text Itself

Although "Love and Freindship" inevitably makes its first impact as a burlesque, it also deserves attention for its own intrinsic value, and for its internal ironies. Students in a course on composition would have plenty to learn from the control of language and the narrative structure of this brief but eventful story.

The series of letters that constitutes "Love and Freindship" sets it up as a narrative of instruction. Isabel asks Laura, the friend of her youth, to recount "the Misfortunes and Adventures of your Life" for the moral benefit of her daughter, Marianne (76). Laura quickly assumes that she is to appear in her own story as the positive moral example: "may the fortitude with which I have suffered the many Afflictions of my past Life, prove to her a useful Lesson," she prays (77). But the attentive student who matches the beginning with the ending will notice that Isabel is far from admiring the youthful Laura's conduct. When they meet in the stagecoach which coincidentally contains all the surviving personages of the story, Laura delivers an oral version of her life story, but Isabel tends to be disapproving. "[F]aultless as my Conduct had certainly been during the whole course of my late Misfortunes and Adventures, she pretended to find fault with my Behavior," notes Laura indignantly (104). Isabel, it appears, has gone through some moral evolution in the course of the narrative: having been once the bosom "Freind" of Laura and the chosen companion of her youth, she learns from her friend's experience and her recounting of it that Sense is morally preferable to Sensibility. Hence her scheme in eliciting Laura's written narrative is to provide her daughter Marianne with a *negative* example, not the positive one that Laura fondly assumes. Marianne as reader is to learn to *avoid* Laura's sentimental excesses, and is so to be converted from Sensibility to Sense, as her mother was before her. Although Jane Austen doesn't labor the point—in fact she merely tosses it in—there are intricacies and ironic possibilities in this narrative setup that are worthy of a more elaborate tale.

Laura herself is immune from any moral benefit to be derived from her experience: the only moral she can draw from it is the one she relays from the dying Sophia, about the imprudence of willful fainting fits (102). She remains satisfied that since "I had always behaved in a manner which reflected Honour on my Feelings and Refinement," she must be irreproachable, and so have nothing to learn (104).

The many interpolated narratives within Laura's narrative suggest that the young Jane was meditating (though certainly not solemnly) on narratology. What is narrative *for*? All the characters, whether on the side of Sense or Sensibility, clearly lap it up. On that memorable coach ride between Edinburgh and Stirling, the characters deliver autobiographies at an astonishing rate. First, at Sir Edward's entreaty, Laura tells the story of his son's death; next, Laura "related to them every other misfortune which had befallen me since we parted"; next, Isabel gives Laura "an accurate detail of every thing that had befallen her since our separation"; finally, Augusta supplies "the same information respecting herself, Sir Edward & Lady Dorothea" (104–5). Laura's curiosity for such personal narratives is insatiable. After this marathon of telling and listening, while the others are regaling themselves with "green tea and buttered toast," Laura seeks out her cousins, and "we feasted ourselves in a more refined and Sentimental Manner by a confidential Conversation" (106)—consisting, of course, in further "entertaining Narration" (108). Apparently Laura actually lives off people's lives and adventures. To keep her supplied with this verbal grist to her mill can be exhausting, and poor Edward may be said to have died from the effort:

> "Oh! tell me Edward (said I [when his phaeton has overturned]) tell me I beseech you before you die, what has befallen you since that unhappy Day in which . . . we were separated—."
> "I will" (said he) and instantly fetching a deep sigh, Expired—. (100)

What, besides a substitute for toast and tea, do Laura and the others get out of each other's stories? It seems that the morally approved characters, Sir Edward and his ilk, get moral enlargement and some matter for thought: the raw data can be sifted, interpreted, judged; it conduces to more than itself. But for the Sensibility crew, a life history is mere food for curiosity. Laura *telling* a story proposes to "gratify the curiosity of [Isabel's] Daughter" (77); Laura *hearing* a story desires Isabel only "to satisfy my Curiosity" (104). For such people a story begins and ends with itself, or rather with *the* self, and no mental or moral growth is involved in the transmitting of it. The teller gratifies the self, and slakes the listener's curiosity (or the "degrading thirst after outrageous stimulation" that Wordsworth was to complain about in the preface to *Lyrical Ballads*). Jane Austen was to pursue the distinction between kinds of discourse in her later novels. Henry Tilney can rise to conversation, stimulating the mind beyond the individual and the particular toward exchange at a shared and general level; John Thorpe is capable only of talk. "All the rest of his conversation, or rather talk," the narrator discriminates in *Northanger Abbey,* "began and ended with himself and his own concerns" (*NA,* 66). Thus Sir Edward wants Laura to tell him of Edward, a third party. But Laura makes Edward's death only an episode among her own adventures, for she can proceed no further than the I-thou narrative.

The two species, with their opposed sets of assumptions about appropriate behavior and appropriate discourse, have their own distinct languages. And identifying these languages, or the kinds of *patois* common to a group, or particular to an individual, can be a useful exercise in a course in composition and rhetoric. The conversation between Edward and his sister Augusta, representatives respectively of Sensibility and Sense, is a good starting point. Augusta has just suggested that Edward may need to apply to his father for the support of his new wife, Laura:

> "Never, never Augusta will I so demean myself. (said Edward). Support! What Support will Laura want which she can receive from him?"
> "Only those very insignificant ones of Victuals and Drink." (answered she).
> "Victuals and Drink! (replied my Husband in a most nobly contemtuous Manner) and dost thou then imagine that there is no other support for an exalted Mind (such as is my Laura's) than the mean and indelicate employment of Eating and Drinking?"
> "None that I know of, so efficacious." (returned Augusta). (83)

The whole conversation is longer, but even from this extract one can tell that the two interlocutors speak in two different registers; and if one's students in rhetoric can become sensitive to tonal register, much is gained. Edward adopts the grand style for the expression of his elevated emotions of scorn and indignation. Augusta calls him "you," but he calls her "thou," and his archaism is intended to capture the dignity of chivalric romance. His characteristic syntax is exclamatory ("Support!" "Victuals and Drink!") and histrionic. Augusta on the other hand is down-to-earth and colloquial, to match her practical concern with creature comforts. She speaks economically in sentence fragments, supplying only the noun phrases that answer his rhetorical questions (he means them to be rhetorical). And she, like her father, can handle irony ("None that I know of, so efficacious"), whereas it is characteristic of the adherents of sensibility that they are as incapable of using irony as of understanding it. Their speeches may of course be ironic for the *reader,* however. Here, for instance, Edward's outrage at the notion that Laura will need support from his father can be matched against the circumstances of the ending, when the widowed Laura retires on an allowance of £400 a year, supplied by Sir Edward (108).

An exercise in practical criticism of such a passage can alert students to different verbal styles. And because Jane Austen is here being deliberately crude and hyperbolic, even the unawakened freshman can get the point. The marvelous nuances and finely discriminated tones in the quite recognizable speech patterns of John Thorpe, Mrs. Jennings, Mary Bennet, Mr. Woodhouse, and the rest are yet to come. But meanwhile we still have broad burlesques by way of developing the student's ear, such as Laura's speech when mad. It is a takeoff of Ophelia, even to being for much of its length in iambic pentameter. For instance:

> Give me a violin—. I'll play to him
> & sooth him in his melancholy Hours—
> Beware ye gentle Nymphs of Cupid's Thunderbolts [a hexameter
>   this time],
> [A]void the piercing Shafts of Jupiter. (100)

A full study of Jane Austen's language is not possible here, but I touch on what seem to me useful starting points, by way of suggesting how much is there to follow up. One kind of sensitivity that is particularly surprising in so young a writer is her fine ear for what is hackneyed and outworn. Laura and Sophia talk in catchwords, in ready-made clichés: "She was all Sensibility and Feeling. We flew into each others arms & after having exchanged vows of mutual Freindship for the rest of our Lives, instantly unfolded to each other the most inward Secrets of our Hearts" (85). So much is compacted into one sentence— the physical action, the content of the vows, the invoking of lifetimes, the unfolded secrets—that the sentence structure itself conveys the emptiness of the claims. The two heroines could as well be conducting their meeting by semaphore, like Girl Guides, waving successively the Sensibility flag, the Eternal Vow flag, and the Inmost Secret flag. And one of the sharp weapons in Jane Austen's verbal armory comes into wicked play: the adverb. The fact that those inmost secrets are unfolded "instantly" utterly devalues them. Likewise we get the comedy of the ladies' fainting "alternately" on the sofa, a preview of the more subtly controlled irony, to be encountered hereafter, of Charlotte Lucas's deliberate setting out to meet Mr. Collins "accidentally" in the lane (*PP*, 121).

Jane Austen's major novels are famous for their restraint, for their delicacy, for their miniaturist's craftsmanship, etcetera. Not so the juvenilia. The juvenilia are wild and rowdy, full of extravagant exaggeration, exuberant jokes, nonsense, slapstick, and anarchic humor. "Love and Freindship" is the kind of work that provokes belly laughs. And like other funny books—*Pickwick Papers* for instance[12]—it has a plot that is subordinated to the jokes. It's not easy to remember the sequence of the action of such works. Laura and her lovers and friends rocket about between London, Wales, and Scotland in a manner that is as difficult for the readers as for the characters themselves to keep track of. But of course this very chaos is intentional. "It would be almost impossible to summarize the action of 'Love and Freindship,'" Litz points out, "since one of Jane Austen's aims was to satirize the intricate and unnatural plots of contemporary fiction."[13] She has, for instance, a birth mystery plot of an intricacy to dazzle and dismay. But one of the pleasures for the close reader of this wild text is that in the midst of the anarchy it has its own order and consistency. For years I have admired the revelation scene in which Lord St. Clair discovers his four separate grandchildren for its mere craziness: "Acknowledge thee!" exclaims the Venerable Stranger to Laura, "Yes dear resemblance of my Laurina & my Laurina's Daughter, sweet image of my Claudia and my Claudia's Mother, I do acknowledge thee as the Daughter of the one & the Grandaughter of the other" (91). Surely no one can follow such stuff! But lately, when I had to set the passage as an exercise in practical criticism, I tried constructing a family tree, and found to my delight that it all works. Moreover, in working out Lord St. Clair's and other families, I found that a chart demonstrates a balanced familial symmetry among the figures of Sensibility and Sense. In supplying this chart, I claim to be the first genealogist who has taken Lord St. Clair's family tree seriously.

I have indicated the characters of Sense in straight caps, and the characters of Sensibility in italic caps. This makes it clear that while the heroine has a pedigree of unblemished Sensibility, the hero's family members are symmetrically divided. Sensibility needs the opposition of Sense to define itself. Sir Edward and Philippa, brother and sister, represent Sense and Sensibility respec-

Laura's and Sophia's Family

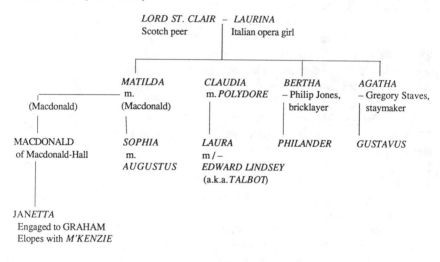

LORD ST. CLAIR – *LAURINA*
Scotch peer | Italian opera girl

MATILDA   *CLAUDIA*   *BERTHA*   *AGATHA*
m.   m. *POLYDORE*   – Philip Jones,   – Gregory Staves,
(Macdonald)   (Macdonald)   bricklayer   staymaker

MACDONALD   *SOPHIA*   *LAURA*   *PHILANDER*   *GUSTAVUS*
of Macdonald-Hall   m.   m / –
             AUGUSTUS   *EDWARD LINDSEY*
                       (a.k.a. *TALBOT*)

JAN*ETTA*
Engaged to GRAHAM
Elopes with *M'KENZIE*

Edward's Family

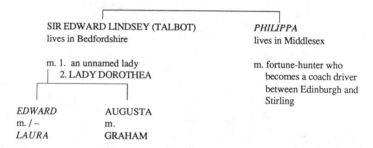

SIR EDWARD LINDSEY (TALBOT)   *PHILIPPA*
lives in Bedfordshire   lives in Middlesex

m. 1. an unnamed lady   m. fortune-hunter who
    2. LADY DOROTHEA   becomes a coach driver
                             between Edinburgh and
                             Stirling

EDWARD   AUGUSTA
m. / –   m.
LAURA   GRAHAM

Marianne's Family

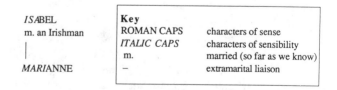

ISABEL
m. an Irishman

MARIANNE

Key	
ROMAN CAPS	characters of sense
ITALIC CAPS	characters of sensibility
m.	married (so far as we know)
–	extramarital liaison

Figure 12. The Genealogies of "Love and Freindship"

Figure 13.   " . . . tell me, have I any other Grand-Children in the House"
(*From "Love and Freindship," page 92; Illustration by Juliet McMaster*)

tively; the same is true of the next generation, Augusta and Edward. Sophia (Sensibility) is likewise opposed to her cousin Macdonald (Sense). And there is a similar symmetry among the morally mobile younger generation. Young Janetta Macdonald, who begins by espousing Sense, is converted by Laura and Sophia to Sensibility, and the sequence of her two suitors, Graham and M'Kenzie, confirms this. Young Marianne, for whom the letters are written, is presumably mobile in the other direction (if her mother's plan works), being converted by the moral action of this narrative from Sensibility to Sense.

The wild implausibility of the birth mystery plot and its revelation, and the other unlikely relationships, turn out to be not random and chaotic, but neatly patterned, to reinforce the major thematic oppositions of the tale.

And in the same way as the theme provides structure and pattern for the family tree, so the moral oppositions provide shape for the story. Browning is said to have claimed that if Jesus Christ had not existed, we would have had to invent him: the myth is so aesthetically à propos for the state in which humanity finds itself. Similarly, I sometimes think that if morality hadn't existed, Jane Austen would have found a way to invent it. For those sharp antitheses (between sense and sensibility, or between the self-centered and the outward-looking, or between wisdom and folly), those clean oppositions in "Love and Freindship" and the major works too, are there not just for didactic purposes, but because they supply form, a tense, and delightful aesthetic structure.

Looking Forward: Intimations of the Major Novels

To discover Sense and Sensibility as located in siblings is to lead to the relation of "Love and Freindship" to the major novels.

Laura's chosen friend, Sophia, from fainting in the grass as the evening dew is falling, contracts "a violent pain in her delicate limbs, accompanied with a disagreeable Head-ake" (101), and presently dies, delivering the memorable advice about avoiding fainting-fits that is the overt moral of "Love and Freindship." I like to recall that the recipient of this advice is called Marianne, for it is Marianne Dashwood in *Sense and Sensibility* who contracts a violent cold ("with a pain in her limbs") after twilight walks in dew-wet grass, which proves almost fatal. And the two Mariannes are both educated from Sensibility towards Sense. This is only one of dozens of connections between "Love and Freindship" and the major novels. And if one is teaching it as an adjunct to the teaching of Jane Austen's major works, clearly the ongoing theme of Sense and Sensibility makes the most obvious starting point. "Love and Freindship" leads most clearly and directly to *Sense and Sensibility*. But the contrast between Sense and Sensibility, varied as the rival claims of reason and emotion, remains a central structuring idea in all the novels. The conventions of the cult of Sensibility, without the sensibility itself, are insincerely adopted by Isabella Thorpe in

Northanger Abbey; Marianne Dashwood has the genuine article, and in her sensibility is sympathetically treated, though regarded as excessive in its manifestation. And Elinor, who has sense, is educated in the direction of sensibility. This movement is continued in *Pride and Prejudice,* which presents a woman and a society too apt to be governed by the head and to neglect the affairs of the heart. Fanny and Mary Crawford in *Mansfield Park* are recognizable variations on Marianne and Elinor. In *Emma* the theme goes underground, as it were, and emerges explicitly only at the end. Emma, with her eagerness and her outspokenness and her readiness to promote romance, first strikes us as belonging on the sensibility side of the pale; while the undemonstrative Jane Fairfax, proper and controlled and apparently a cold fish, looks like the representative of sense. But by the end we have learned that Jane, guiltily cherishing a secret passion, is the uncontrolled romantic, while Emma, who hasn't even recognized whom she's in love with, emerges as strong in the head, but rather weak in the heart. Anne Elliot, we know, completes the pattern. "She had been forced into prudence in her youth, she learned romance as she grew older" (*P,* 30). From "Love and Freindship" to *Persuasion* we can see Jane Austen go through much the same evolution.

An alternative clue, planted in "Love and Freindship" and running as a strongly uniting thread through the other novels, starts with Sir Edward's pregnant conclusion, when faced with his son's romantic outburst, "You have been studying Novels I suspect" (81). This leads not only backward into the novels Jane Austen was burlesquing, but forward into the novels she was to write herself. That is, we can go beyond the activities of parody and burlesque to the more interesting and dominant idea of literature as model for life. Jane Austen's characters, like Don Quixote, are intently engaged in a quest to make experience conform to literary precedent.[14] Again, students of the whole canon can trace this idea as developed with increasing subtlety through Catherine's Gothic fantasies in *Northanger Abbey,* and Marianne's sense of entrapment in hackneyed language and hackneyed responses at the very moments that she is practicing them, to the elaborate fictions that Emma imposes on life. Many of Emma's most serious errors arise from the assumption that fictional conventions are transferable to life. Her preconception that Harriet Smith, of unknown parentage, is a fit wife for a gentleman is ultimately traceable to the same conventions that Jane Austen parodied in the Lord St. Clair episode in "Love and Freindship": because there's a birth mystery about Harriet, Emma concludes she must be of noble parentage. The theme is dear to the hearts of Jane Austen and other well-read novelists (Cervantes, Fielding, Sterne, Thackeray, George Eliot, and James come especially to mind), because it is born of a consuming love of books. These are writers who *live* their literature, and are wryly conscious of the propensity. And they are sophisticated, too, being fully aware, long before Oscar Wilde told the rest of the world, that "Life imitates Art far more than Art imitates Life." Jane Austen's fictions, from her juvenilia on, demonstrate a constant and amused concern with the complex and sometimes hilarious interaction of life and literature.

"Love and Freindship" is as visible a step toward the mature novels in matters of technique as of theme. Jane Austen's giant step from the eighteenth century to the nineteenth involved for her a weaning from the epistle. *Sir Charles Grandison* and *Evelina* were undoubtedly habit-forming: "Love and Freindship" ("a novel in a series of letters"), "Lesley Castle" ("An unfinished novel in letters"), "A Collection of Letters," and *Lady Susan* lead to "First Impressions" and "Elinor and Marianne," the lost first epistolary versions of mature novels. And in those novels themselves the letter continues to be of crucial importance. What "Love and Freindship" shows in this evolution is Jane Austen's power of self-examination. It is easy to slip into a convention; but a finely conscious artist in the making already has a weather eye on the potential absurdities in a medium. In the opening she brilliantly conflates two separate conventions in order to burlesque both. She combines the convention of the perfect heroine, necessarily described in the third person by an omniscient narrator, with the first-person narrator of the epistolary novel, with hilarious effect: "Lovely as I was," writes Laura modestly, as though she were someone else, "the Graces of my Person were the least of my Perfections. Of every accomplishment accustomary to my sex, I was Mistress . . . " and so on (77–78). In other ways the letters draw attention to their own absurdity; for they aren't written, according to the Richardson formula, while the mind is in the midst of present distresses; they are recollected in tranquility, long after the event, and sent away in arbitrarily chopped-off chunks. Here is the self-critical creative mind at work. Full self-awareness belongs rather to sense than to sensibility, after all.

"That [M'Kenzie] certainly adores you (replied Sophia) there can be no doubt" (94). Sophia is here in the process of detaching teachable young Janetta from her old suitor and attaching her to a new one, as Emma is later to do with Harriet Smith. The passage is pregnant with other concerns that are to be lasting in the Jane Austen canon: not only the propensity to arrange reality according to a preconceived pattern, as Emma the imaginist does, but also the indoctrination and manipulation of one human being by another. The impress of a formed consciousness upon a relatively unformed one is the stuff that some of the best novels, but especially Jane Austen's, are made of. The pedagogic enterprise is a dangerous and fascinating one, and it may turn out well, like Henry Tilney's with Catherine, or disastrously, like Sophia's with Janetta or Emma's with Harriet. "We all love to instruct," comments Elizabeth Bennet in a moment when she is aware her practice doesn't measure up to her preaching, "though we can teach only what is not worth knowing" (*PP,* 343).

But to return to our own students, and our pedagogic enterprises on their behalf (and our own). There is only so much we can tell them: the rest they must discover for themselves. And "Love and Freindship" is a text that will do much towards teaching itself. Although it is the product of subtle perceptions, and shows a subtle artist in the making, it is itself gloriously obvious. And unlike the self-centered romantics it parodies, it leads attention beyond itself, by its reach for other literature, by its healthy mockery of the unending circle of self, and by its exuberant play of mind.

Notes

1. Sandra M. Gilbert and Susan Gubar, eds., *The Norton Anthology of Literature by Women: The Tradition in English,* New York and London, 1985, pp. 206–32. Professors Gilbert and Gubar's close and revealing study of "Love and Freindship" in *The Madwoman in the Attic,* New Haven and London, 1979, pp. 113–19, is an excellent feminist reading.

2. Marvin Mudrick has plausibly argued that Elizabeth Nugent Bromley's *Laura and Augustus: An Authentic Story: In a Series of Letters,* three volumes, London, 1784, is the most likely candidate as the single butt of "Love and Freindship." *Jane Austen: Irony as Defense and Discovery,* Berkeley and Los Angeles, 1968, pp. 5–12.

3. A. Walton Litz, *Jane Austen: A Study of Her Artistic Development,* London, 1965, p. 18.

4. References to the major novels are by page number to Chapman's edition.

5. Samuel Richardson, *Clarissa* (1747–48), ed. Angus Ross, Harmondsworth, 1985, p. 291.

6. Book III, chapter 16.

7. Volume III, letter for October 4.

8. Litz, p. 21.

9. Letter 78.

10. Brian Southam, *Jane Austen's Literary Manuscripts,* Oxford, 1964, p. 3.

11. *Bleak House,* chapter 6.

12. G.K. Chesterton, in his preface to the first printing of "Love and Freindship," also makes this connection: Jane Austen's inspiration, he says, "was the inspiration of Gargantua; it was the gigantic inspiration of laughter." *"Love and Freindship" and Other Early Works by Jane Austen,* New York, 1922, p. xv.

13. Litz, p. 19.

14. I have elaborated on this concept at more length in *"Pride and Prejudice:* Acting by Design," chapter 2 of *The Novel from Sterne to James,* by Juliet McMaster and Rowland McMaster, London, 1981, 19–36.

Money Talks: Jane Austen and the *Lady's Magazine*

Edward Copeland

Judging from what we find in the juvenilia, Jane Austen met the *Lady's Magazine* (1770–1832) early. Short tales, simply plotted, high-tuned to cliché, internally organized into three clear divisions—this is the structure of Austen's parodies and the heart of *Lady's Magazine* fiction. As to theme: first, a courtship problem, almost invariably economic; second, a plot elaboration of that problem; finally, a quick resolution of the economic problem by the arranging hand of the author. Again, Austen nails it. This simple formula was the mainstay of *Lady's Magazine* fiction, nourished monthly for 50 years, from 1770 to 1820.[1] "Everybody" read the *Lady's,* too, though "everybody" embraces a relatively narrow group in the population: the families of gentry down through the families of prosperous artisans and tradesmen—the masses provided no market for fiction in the late eighteenth century.[2] *La Belle Assemblée,* better known for its elegant fashion illustrations, came late to the scene (1806–32) and was only an intermittent supporter of fiction. It was the *Lady's Magazine* that held sway with an inclusive readership made possible through a bookseller's market that, before 1820, had not moved into the class stratification of the nineteenth century.[3] In fact, from 1770 to 1820, most of the *Lady's* fiction appears to have been provided by the readers themselves, gratis.[4] A *bargain,* as the editors regularly reminded the readers—"the plates worth *four* times the price charged for this Magazine" (Jan. 1819). The *Lady's Magazine* found its widest audience, however, not in sales, but through the circulating libraries, available there to anyone with a subscription in yearly volumes, indexed and bound. The *Lady's Magazine:* cheap, omnipresent, and written for women—there's no wonder that the young Jane Austen sharpened her pen on it.

The frontispiece for 1789 features an "elegant Female Figure," her bound collection in hand, "seated in her Library, contemplating the Beauties of the LADIES MAGAZINE" (fig. 14). This young woman, the editor explains, repre-

Figure 14. Frontispiece from the *Lady's Magazine*
(Lady's Magazine, *January 1789*)

sents "Study, who is crowned by Wisdom, in the Character of Minerva, with a Chaplet of Laurel, assisted by Cupid, displaying the Torch of Hymen." The plate reveals a different message. With its elegantly imagined "Library" and well-turned-out reader, a better title would be, "Consumer Desire Ministered to by Sentimental Love and a Show of Education."

Of course the great joke in the juvenilia is Austen's youthful discovery of the paradoxical affinity of sentimental literature and consumerism. "What a beautifull Sky!" cries Laura, the heroine of "Love and Freindship"; "How charmingly is the azure varied by those delicate streaks of white!" "Oh, my Laura," replies Sophia, "do not thus distress me by calling my Attention to an object which so cruelly reminds me of my Augustus's blue sattin Waistcoat striped with white" (98). In "Lesley Castle," the news of the death of her sister's bridegroom and the cancellation of the wedding feast overwhelms Miss Charlotte Lutterell: "'Good God! (said I) you dont say so? Why what in the name of Heaven will become of all the Victuals? We shall never be able to eat it while it is good. However, we'll call the Surgeon to help us—'" (113). The innocence of the joke hangs on in *Sense and Sensibility* with Nancy Steele and her beaux and clothes, and in *Northanger Abbey,* where the thrills of Blaize Castle depend on a reliable gig and horse, and the circulating library provides "horrid" fiction for the price of a subscription ticket. Isabella Thorpe's sentimental cant, that she "should not have a wish unsatisfied" if her marriage to James Morland could "take place now upon only fifty pounds a year" draws on the monthly grist of the *Lady's Magazine* to disguise a lust for consumer display: "a carriage at her command, a new name on her tickets, and a brilliant exhibition of hoop rings on her finger" (*NA,* 122).

The other great joke in the juvenilia has to do with consumerism as well. Nothing is funnier to the youthful Austen than finding the lower ranks in fiction. In Austen's "Jack & Alice," a "lovely young Woman lying apparently in great pain beneath a Citron-tree" begins her childhood history: "I am a native of North Wales & my Father is one of the most capital Taylors in it" (20). Or, in "The beautifull Cassandra" we find that "Cassandra was the Daughter & the only Daughter of a celebrated Millener in Bond Street. Her father was of noble Birth, being the near relation of the Dutchess of——'s Butler" (44). Laura, the heroine of "Love and Freindship," recounts her "unhappy story": "My Father was a native of Ireland & an inhabitant of Wales; My Mother was the natural Daughter of a Scotch Peer by an italian Opera-girl . . . " (77). We also find two sentimental characters in "Love and Freindship" driving a stagecoach from Edinburgh to Stirling for their living: "It has only been to throw a little money into their Pockets (continued Augusta) that my Father has always travelled in their Coach to view the beauties of the Country since our arrival in Scotland—for it would certain have been much more agreable to us, to visit the Highlands in a Post-chaise than merely to travel from Edinburgh to Sterling & from Sterling to Edinburgh every other Day in a crouded & uncomfortable Stage" (105).

We ignore a key to Jane Austen's world, if we dismiss the juvenilia as nothing more than amateur target practice. The *Lady's Magazine* was a worthy adversary for the young Jane Austen, an enemy strong enough and dangerous enough to attract her attention. First, there is the astonishing fact that, potentially, every month of the year (and a "Supplement" in January) the magazine circulated to every middle-class household in Britain. Second, that it was fun to read, really appealing. Austen probably found an echo to her own tastes within its covers. The *Lady's* offered a tempting variety of consumer features: sheet music in frequent issues, plates with specific notes on fashion ("Turbans are still the fashion. Some wear them with the part before that used to be behind. . . . The colours of ribbands are marigold and oxblood, mostly striped and shaggy" (See fig. 15 [March 1802]), recipes, patterns for filigree work, for aprons—in fact the very topics that make so large a part of Austen's letters to Cassandra. In 1798, a review of *Lovers' Vows* appeared, accompanied by an illustration of the entire cast, Frederick and Agatha (Henry Crawford and Maria Rushworth) in warm embrace.[5] In April 1800, there was an account, again with picture, of Mrs. Leigh-Perrot, Austen's aunt, and a description of her trial for allegedly stealing lace from a shop in Bath.[6] Finally, there was the fiction itself, relentlessly, remorselessly, month by month, tuned to its only subject, the trials of Everywoman, and regularly illustrated in provocative plates "by the Best Hands." It is no exaggeration to claim that in its first 50 years, the *Lady's Magazine* defined women's issues for two generations of women from the middling ranks.

Austen's most obvious response in the juvenilia focuses on the disparity between formal realism and the sentimental conventions of the *Lady's*. "Jack & Alice" (1787–90), for example, with its adventures in Pammydiddle, its jointures, titles, estates, and faintings, an estate in North Wales, and an exile as the "favourite Sultana of the great Mogul" make it a highly seasoned ragout of short tales from the *Lady's*. But, Austen's engagement with the magazine is more complex than the sparkle of comic mockery can suggest. The ephemera of the market play a part in Austen's fiction as formative as her obligation to the "great tradition." And, no surprise: the consumer revolution forced an uncomfortable sisterhood. Women's economic vulnerability in a male-dominated system weighed equally upon the magazine writers and Austen as well. Both the *Lady's* stories and Austen's youthful parodies cast women in an impossible dual role, as consumer and commodity at once, often in the same transaction. Austen's tale, "The three Sisters," provides an excellent example of the economic dilemma. Three young women and their mother argue over a wealthy suitor: while two of the sisters attempt to dodge their position as negotiable commodi-

Figure 15.   "Paris Dress"
(Lady's Magazine, *October 1802*)

ties in the market, the third tries to raise the bargaining price—"Remember the pinmoney," she says, "two hundred a year" (64). In effect, Austen's juvenile work, and her mature work as well, join the *Lady's Magazine* at a central crossing: consumerism, where middle-class women of all ranks faced an especially dangerous passage.

The similarities and the differences between Austen's economic fictions and those in the *Lady's* sort themselves out, in one major respect, in terms of rank. Austen writes with her own class, the rural elite, at the center of her fictions: resident landowners of the aristocracy and gentry, of course, but also men in the gentlemanly professions, the clergy, officers of the army and navy, and even lawyers, retired merchants, and rentiers with respectable country connections—the "pseudo gentry," as David Spring calls them, "gentry of a sort, primarily because they sought strenuously to be taken for gentry."[7] The *Lady's Magazine* has its fair share of heroines with fathers from this group, "the wealthy owner of an estate in the West of England," but the more prominent sources of income in the *Lady's* stories come from groups that Jane Austen's heroines could never know socially: tradesmen, small farmers, petty clerks, solicitors, physicians, unofficered members of the military, impoverished curates, and at the grander end of the income scale, manufacturers, and wealthy nabobs just returned from India and the West Indies. In the *Lady's Magazine* as in Austen's novels, all sources of income are prominently displayed for the readers' consideration:

Clarinda was a daughter of a neighbouring farmer. ("The Budget," Oct. 1783)

George Davison, a very fashionable young fellow, . . . had only a small post under the government. ("The Careless Lover," Aug. 1788)

Mr. Horton [had] gone out to India some years before and very rapidly made a fortune. ("The Deserted Infant," March 1794)

My father, whose name was William Seymour, lived in the city of Bristol, and followed merchandise. ("The History of Amelia Stanford," June 1797)

Mr. Betterton . . . was the proprietor of a large, and apparently flourishing, manufactory. ("The Widow," July 1803)

Agnes Williamson [was] the daughter of a tradesman whose dissipated habits had reduced [him] to a state of insolvency. ("The Young Widow; or the Secret Benefactor," June 1817)

With its focus on the social aspirations of the lower middle ranks, the *Lady's Magazine* also assumes that its readers appreciate the advantages of boarding school culture. In fact the editors promote the *Lady's* to headmistresses as suitable for use in the schools. The issue for September 1771, the second year of publication, presents a plate depicting girls earnestly engaged in the business of needlework, reading, and dancing. In story after story, old school fellows meet to produce plots for their authors. "The Surprise" (April 1779), a simple example, features a happy couple who begin their career at a ball "in which the pupils of the different seminaries were brought together."

The juvenilia display Austen's pointed contempt for such useful seminaries: "Isabel had seen the World," claims Laura in "Love and Freindship"; "She had passed 2 Years at one of the first Boarding schools in London; had spent a fortnight in Bath & had supped one night in Southampton." Among her own most regretted "misfortunes," Laura admits, is the inevitable fading of her school-learned accomplishments: "I can neither sing so well nor Dance so gracefully as I once did—and I have entirely forgot the *Minuet Dela Cour*" (78). In "Lesley Castle," Miss Margaret Lesley, four years out of school, writes Miss Charlotte Lutterell ("two such tender Hearts, so closely linked together by the ties of simpathy and Freindship") of her current daily engagements: "We read, we work, we walk and when fatigued with these Employments releive our spirits, either by a lively song, a graceful Dance, or by some smart bon-mot, and witty repartée" (111). Austen's Lady Susan uses a school in London as the dumping ground for an unwanted daughter. The debunking continues in *Northanger Abbey* with Mrs. Allen and her "former school fellow and intimate," Mrs. Thorpe, who, until their joy at an accidental meeting in Bath, "had been contented to know nothing of each other for the last fifteen years" (*NA*, 32). In *Sense and Sensibility*, she memorializes the institution in the decorations of Charlotte Palmer's girlhood bedroom, where "over the mantlepiece still hung a landscape in coloured silks of her performance, in proof of her having spent seven years at a great school in town to some effect" (*SS*, 160). Mrs. Goddard's school in *Emma* gets off with casual approval—the girls are "not screwed out of health"—and Anne Elliot has some pleasant relief at a school that's out of reach of her unfeeling father and sister, but Mrs. Goddard's student, Harriet Smith, presents no great model of brain power, and Anne's old school intimate, Mrs. Smith, has not exactly turned out well.

Austen lines out her territory by this social mockery. We laugh with her, but we have to recognize that the fiction she targets represents a strong, active tradition of female writing that she attacks with reason. She and they are indeed at odds. In the *Lady's Magazine* ("The Budget," July 1783), it is the son of a wealthy baronet who seduces the farmer's daughter, whereas in Austen's novels, we find villains in Lucy Steele, the niece of a schoolmaster from Plymouth, or Augusta Hawkins, the daughter of a merchant, "he must be called," from Bristol, or even poor Harriet Smith who nearly ruins Emma's life, and who finally turns out, of course, to be the illegitimate daughter of a tradesman. By challenging the features she found most objectionable in the *Lady's Magazine*, its lingo of consumerized sentiment and its sympathetic address to the social aspirations of the lower ranks, the youthful author could establish, first, her right to belong to a higher literary tradition—that of Richardson, Fielding,

Burney, and Edgeworth, which she specifically lays claim to in *Northanger Abbey*—and, second, her own social claims, as a writer, to the respectable upper ranks of society.[8]

Even so, the fiction of the *Lady's Magazine* offered something that Jane Austen did understand and appreciate: a lively consideration of women's economic plight. For example, a story from the *Lady's* (the "Supplement" for 1794) entitled "The Ship-wreck" reveals two proper names that "Milton wd have given his eyes to have thought of" (*Letters*, 402): a Mr. *Brandon*, "a truly respectable gentleman with a large estate in the west of England," and a Mr. *Willoughby*, a youth possessing a heart of "manly sensibility," but a much smaller estate. "One could live upon" such names "for a twelvemonth," as Austen wrote in another context (*Letters*, 420). The Willoughby of the *Lady's Magazine* falls in love with the respectable Mr. Brandon's only daughter: "He quickly loved, sincerely and ardently loved; and she as quickly perceived his passion, which she met with complacence and approbation." But, "the delight they felt in each other's company," the author notes, "prevented them from reflecting, as yet, on the formidable obstacle that must oppose their union," a considerable difference in fortune. They comfort each other with the following bromide: "What is the value of that wealth which only administers to luxury, or what the evil contained in that poverty which still furnishes all the necessaries and even the reasonable conveniences of life?" Readers of Jane Austen's *Sense and Sensibility* must surely prick up their ears: Brandon? . . . Willoughby? . . . Willoughby's inferior fortune? . . . And doesn't Marianne Dashwood say something about "the value of wealth"?—"What have wealth or grandeur to do with happiness?" (*SS*, 91).

A disparity in fortune, an obdurate parent, arbitrary economic power, a single woman in the eye of the storm: it sounds familiar. The women in *Sense and Sensibility*—Marianne Dashwood, Eliza Williams (Colonel Brandon's first love), her daughter of the same name, even Elinor Dashwood—all get entangled in analogies with the tale from the *Lady's*. The Mr. Brandon of the *Lady's Magazine*, for example, forbids his daughter, "rent by conflicting passions, and shedding torrents of tears," to marry young Willoughby. The father embarks with her on a ship out of Bristol to deliver her to a wealthy Irish suitor. No sooner does the ship leave the Bristol quay, however, when a "wave broke over the vessel, and [Miss Brandon], being deprived by her fear, of all strength and presence of mind, was hurried by it into the raging deep." A young man appears from the crowd, flings himself into the water, and "found, swam with his beauteous prize" until a wave casts the heroine upon a rock, which her rescuer reaches soon after: "What was her surprize, when she had fully recovered her senses, to perceive that the man to whom she owed her life was no other than him on whom she had bestowed her affections, the generous, the constant Frederick Willoughby!" (fig. 16). The rejoicing father, Mr. Brandon, searches the crowd for his daughter's "preserver." "Her preserver," as the anonymous author terms him a second time, "appeared, and announced himself to be Willoughby, that Willoughby who . . . would not hesitate to encounter a thousand times the same danger he had now braved to shield her from harm." Austen's readers will not forget the enthusiastic response of Margaret Dashwood, Marianne's younger sister, to her older sister's rescue from a tumble on the Downs: Margaret insists on calling the Austenian Willoughby "Marianne's preserver," an expression, as Austen remarks, displaying "more elegance than precision" (*SS,* 46).

In most respects, of course, Austen turns the *Lady's Magazine* story on its head. Austen's dashing young Willoughby does *not* save Marianne Dashwood from the economic storm that overwhelms her—the older, sedate Colonel Brandon does; Austen's Colonel Brandon does *not* devalue feeling for money, as does Mr. Brandon in the *Lady's Magazine.* On the other hand, the moral affixed to the *Lady's* story seems to meet the general turn of events in *Sense and Sensibility:* as the Mr. Brandon of the *Lady's Magazine* confesses when he presents his daughter's hand to the constant Frederick Willoughby, "I feel now that useless wealth and tinsel honours cannot enter into competition with the generous emotions of the heart, and real virtue." The inconstant John Willoughby of Jane Austen's novel arrives at the same conclusion: "I have, by raising myself to affluence, lost every thing that could make it a blessing" (*SS,* 321). In addition, Mrs. Ferrars, the John Dashwoods, and the Hon. Miss Morton make a handsome illustration of "useless wealth and tinsel honours." In short, Austen does not reject the *Lady's Magazine* tale out of hand in *Sense and Sensibility.* She selects; she grafts. What had previously been thought marginal, may indeed be central.[9] Her allusion to the story, probably no more than a private joke shared with Cassandra, signals the running presence in her fiction of a covert engagement with women's sentimental fiction.

The implicit consumerism of *Lady's Magazine* fiction announces itself in the illustrations. For example, compare poor Miss Brandon's sad disarray in figure 16 with the well-dressed woman in figure 17. Practiced readers of the *Lady's* would recognize at once that the waves and shore in the two illustrations are, as emblems, one and the same—a common illustration in the *Lady's* of the either/or economics of female survival. Jane Austen draws on it in *Sanditon* when Mrs. Parker gently complains that the house Mr. Parker has built in coastal Sanditon is unpleasantly exposed to the winter storms. Persuasive hints in the plot suggest that the Parkers are headed for financial storms as well. In "The Patriotic Parting," the heroine waves her husband farewell as he leaves on a dangerous military campaign; she must wait in suspense, says the text, for "the summit of all her wishes." That "summit," the story claims, is her husband's safe return, but the illustration suggests an important addition. The husband departs (hardly a glance backward awarded him by the illustrator); the fashionable outfit remains. The heroine's smart hat, dress, and glove blowing in the

Figure 16. "The Ship-wreck"
(*Supplement*, Lady's Magazine, *1794*)

breeze stay in the reader's visual memory to confirm the success of her wait—the prize money from the campaign that will support such consumer elegance. Miss Brandon, however, lies overwhelmed by the same waves that bring prosperity to the woman in "The Patriotic Parting." The rules of an economy controlled by male interests have destroyed her, or so it seems: cast upon her rock, lashed by the threatening waves, no Willoughby in sight, alone and desolate, scarcely dressed at all, she, too, is Everywoman, a woman "deprived by her fear, of all strength and presence of mind." "The Ship-wreck" slips into *Sense and Sensibility* more strongly than Austen might admit, either to Cassandra or to herself. As an emblem, its illustration easily prefigures Marianne Dashwood's plight in *Sense and Sensibility*. Marianne's brush with death derives from a fever caught by walking on wet grass, but the situation that drives her to take the dangerous walk cannot be laid to her own doing—that *her* Willoughby proves inconstant, that he refuses to rescue her, and that he abandons her to the storm for Miss Grey, an heiress with 50,000 pounds.

The *Lady's Magazine* conjures up a world mesmerized, terrorized, and enchanted by consumerism. The Gothic battlements overlooking the shoreline in "The Patriotic Parting" lend support to Terry Lovell's intriguing suggestion that the enthusiasm for Gothic fiction and for consumer goods at the end of the eighteenth century originates in a common source, the demands of early consumer capitalism.[10] Economic oppression is never far off in the *Lady's*. A tabulation of five frequently recurring plot motifs in the *Lady's Magazine* from 1793 to 1815 (Austen's writing years) reveals the development of a woman's literature created around a hostile economy (fig. 18). Each decade brings a new plot. In the last years of the old century, the magazine's tales suggest the helplessness of women before the new economy. Stories in which parents or guardians tyrannically insist that the heroine marry for money crowd the columns in the 1790s (they occur even more frequently earlier, in the 1770s and 1780s), but taper off to practically nothing by 1800. Similarly, stories in which marriage is the only salvation from a life of poverty wax strong in the 1790s, and then all but disappear by the second decade of the new century. Men turn feckless in the second decade: failed businessmen, gamblers, poor providers, vicious, moody, undependable. As a corollary, stories in which women assume economic responsibility show a marked rise. The same is true of plots that feature women's skill with housekeeping and the domestic budget: there is almost nothing about this earlier, but it becomes a dominant theme in the new century.

Without suggesting a picture of Jane Austen at the door of Chawton Cottage, casting her eyes anxiously up and down the High Street for the next issue of the *Lady's Magazine,* the table indicates that Austen's plots share with the *Lady's* the same economic pattern. Two of Austen's novels conceived in the 1790s, for example, *Sense and Sensibility* (1795) and *Pride and Prejudice*

Figure 17.   "The Patriotic Parting"
(Lady's Magazine, *July 1782*)

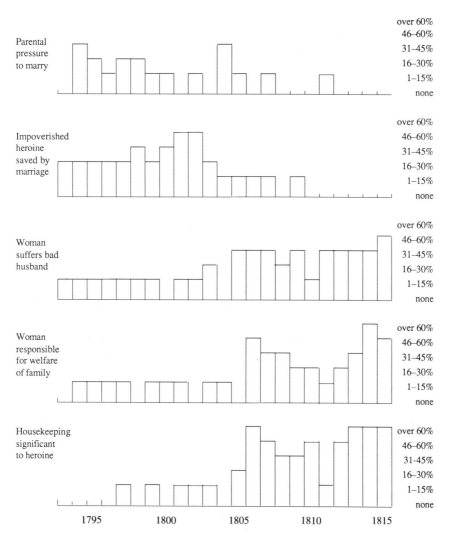

Figure 18.   Plot Frequencies in the *Lady's Magazine*, 1793–1815

(1796–97), feature plots in which Austen's heroines either marry or face poverty in the same sudden-death economic world inhabited by the *Lady's Magazine*'s heroines.[11] Consumer Gothic specifically thickens the plot in *Northanger Abbey,* another 1790s novel (1798–99): the matchmaking ambitions of that consumer enthusiast, General Tilney, display Gothic villainy at the high end of the income scale; John Thorpe, the other consumer-mad male in *Northanger Abbey,* takes the lower end—"Mr. Thorpe only laughed, smacked his whip, encouraged his horse, made odd noises, and drove on" (*NA,* 87). In the novels conceived in the second decade of the new century, *Mansfield Park* (1811–13), *Emma* (1814–15), and *Persuasion* (1815–16), the plots demand stronger exertions from their heroines in far more complex economic worlds. Fanny Price reflects bitterly that Mary Crawford's domestic budget and Edmund Bertram's income will never square; Emma Woodhouse performs her duties to the poor with sympathy, supplies Miss Bates and her mother generously with pork, and faces awkwardly the ordeal of new consumer show in the impertinent Coxes, the rising Coles, and the intrusive Mrs. Elton. Anne Elliot ponders the meaning of furniture: her sister Mary's ill-chosen finery at Uppercross Cottage; the elder Musgroves' mix of old and new at the Great House; the Harvilles' cozy fittings at Lyme Regis; her sister Elizabeth's rented elegance at Bath; Mrs. Smith's squalid lodgings in the same city.

But what hangs on most insistently from Austen's juvenile experimentation with the short fiction of the *Lady's* is the power of the genre itself: the fable. Austen may graft the *Lady's Magazine* fiction onto her own for her own purpose, but the *Lady's* fiction grafts its energies onto Austen's in return.[12] As Susan Suleiman explains in her study *Authoritarian Fictions* (1983), fables make implicitly restrictive demands on their readers: "the reader need not actually recognize [herself] in the subject of the fable; it is sufficient if [she] merely imagines the possibility of such recognition."[13] Once the recognition is accomplished, the reader is implicated in the "lesson" embedded in the story. In such a context, Everywoman lives, in spite of the complexity of Austen's fictional worlds. Austen parodies the tradition in dedicating a parcel of juvenile pieces "To Miss Jane Anna Elizabeth Austen," her infant niece: "I dedicate to You the following Miscellanious Morsels, convinced that if you seriously attend to them, You will derive from them very important Instructions, with regard to your Conduct in Life" (71). *Northanger Abbey* offers a later expression of the problem: "I leave it to be settled by whomsoever it may concern," writes Austen at the conclusion of her novel, "whether the tendency of this work be altogether to recommend parental tyranny, or reward filial disobedience" (*NA,* 252). But it is a tradition she cannot avoid: *Sense and Sensibility* is burdened with the "Ship-wreck" whether Austen wants it or not.

"Self-Conviction" (October 1816), a tale of female self-control and good domestic management, illustrates the operation of this wider discourse in rela-

Figure 19. "Self-Conviction"
(Lady's Magazine, *October 1816*)

tion to one of Austen's mature works. The accompanying plate (fig. 19) reveals a well-dressed woman in an elegant library, just turning from her Bible, her hand outstretched in pitying forgiveness over a man who grovels on the floor, his hat forlornly fallen onto the rug and his hand futilely outstretched to touch the base of the stand that holds her Bible. We turn to the story for an explanation of the interesting scene. The lady is Mrs. Howard, who lives "in a pleasant village in the Vale of White Horse . . . a lady but little known to her neighbours, except by her virtues, and extensive charity to the poor." Her husband, the man on the floor, has abandoned her, the tale explains, on a suspicion of her infidelity. He leaves her without a word, for years, while he goes to Switzerland to be bitter. A traveling neighbor meets him by accident in Geneva, explains all, and Mr. Howard hastens home to "solicit forgiveness from her he had so cruelly injured."

> He perceived his wife in a situation which deprived him of sensation. She was contemplating the miniature of her husband; her whole soul seemed wrapped in her meditation! conviction rushed to his bosom;—the sight was too much for Howard; with a faint voice supplicating forgiveness he sunk to the ground—and expired.

The plate gives us the perspective we need for an interpretation. The first thing we notice is a new Everywoman, an assured well-turned-out matron, who has replaced Miss Brandon, distraught and abandoned to the waves. The economy seems to have come round: the room is handsome, with a bookcase, a painting on the wall, a carpet, and solid furniture. The husband/lover has returned, and nothing seems to have fallen apart in his absence. Mrs. Howard is sad, but she has her house, her books, her carpet, and a miniature of Mr. Howard in happier days. The author has no use for him at all: he "expired." Mrs. Howard will obviously sail on, still "known to her neighbours" by her "virtues" and her "extensive charity to the poor." It is blasphemous to mention Anne Elliot and Frederick Wentworth here, but I will chance it. The monological texts of the *Lady's Magazine* make it a comic comparison, but the outline of the situation is there: Wentworth leaves in a pique, abandons Anne, stays away for years (to be bitter), comes back, asks forgiveness, and finds that Anne has been wearing his miniature in her heart all the time. We remember that Anne is also known in her neighborhood for her charities to the poor, her sound presence of mind, her reading, and to Lady Russell's certain knowledge is a good hand at household management. She does not approve of Sunday travel.

In *Emma*, Austen addresses the *Lady's Magazine* again, this time directly. A story from the *Lady's* entitled "Guilt Pursued by Conscience" (Nov. 1802) sparks a rich development of satire. Indeed, *Emma* might well be read as a revisiting of the old issues of the juvenilia with a more complex consciousness of their implications. The *Lady's* story begins with eerie familiarity:

Mr. Knightley, a country-gentleman of not very large fortune, but such as was amply sufficient for his mode of living—as he rarely visited the capital, and had an aversion to the expensive pleasures of dissipated life—had married, from the purest affection, and an esteem which grew with his knowledge of its object, . . . a deserted orphan [left] at a boarding-school near the residence of a relation of his whom he sometimes visited. As by this union he made no addition to his property, nor formed any advantageous connexion, he was by some blamed, and by other ridiculed. He however found himself amply compensated, both for the censure and the sneers which he encountered, by the amiable qualities and virtues of his wife; who, like himself, despised ambition, and sought only the genuine enjoyments of domestic happiness.

The interesting orphan's true parentage of course is discovered at the conclusion to be monied and respectable, and she to be the heiress to a considerable fortune.

Here we have Emma Woodhouse's destructive fantasies at their source: first, her complacent assumption that Harriet Smith, her boarding school protégée will of course be of respectable birth; second, her horrified belief that *her* Mr. Knightley will, in spite of public ridicule, marry Harriet. Again, as in "The Ship-wreck," the parable is "corrected." With Austen's guidance, we judge Harriet Smith's most ambitious fantasy, marriage to Austen's Mr. Knightley, as reprehensible pride: "But now I seem to feel that I may deserve him; and that if he does choose me, it will not be any thing so very wonderful" (*E*, 411). And we weigh the plausibility of Emma Woodhouse's fiction-primed imagination: "It was horrible to Emma to think how it must sink him in the general opinion, to foresee the smiles, the sneers, the merriment it would prompt at his expense. . . . Could it be?—No; it was impossible. And yet it was far, very far, from impossible" (*E*, 413).

In *Emma*, Austen plays with reflections and echoes of the *Lady's Magazine* large and small. Social ambition and consumer acquisition in the novel—the Coles' new dining room, Jane Fairfax's piano, Mr. Perry's new carriage (the rumor), Mr. Weston's new house—fit the ideology of the *Lady's Magazine* like a new pair of French gloves. Nor does Mrs. Elton have any need to thumb through French prints for her shepherdess costume: most any volume of the *Lady's Magazine,* in any year she might choose, could provide her with the consumer inspiration: "Lysidas and Elfrida" (March 1777) features a particularly fetching shepherdess bonnet. Harriet's long waist in Emma's drawing is standard equipment for heroines in the *Lady's:* see the frontispiece for the year 1789 (fig. 14). Mr. Elton's language, "Precious deposit!" is *Lady's* slang in "Family Anecdotes" (April 1806). For years, the *Lady's* featured a monthly charade. The citizens of Highbury become fantasists by rules of its world: Emma assigns one "orphan," Harriet Smith, first to Mr. Elton, then to Frank Churchill; Mrs. Weston puts Jane Fairfax, the real orphan, with Mr. Knightley; the odious Mrs. Elton provides Jane with an up-to-date *Lady's Magazine* conclusion—female satisfaction through employment. In Jane Austen's conclusion, however, we find a provocative paradox: Harriet gets Mr. Martin the farmer, which actually is a common middling-rank marriage in *Lady's Magazine* fiction; and Jane Fairfax gets the suddenly rich Frank Churchill, another classic *Lady's* story in the romantic vein. Under Austen's wry control, we laugh at one and sigh apprehensively at the other; but we are caught in the very ideological trap which she persuades us that we escape, complicit in accepting both these shopworn endings. Here is "commodity fiction" with a vengeance. The most disturbing implication that hides behind Austen's whole enterprise is that the *Lady's Magazine* might be right. Mr. Knightley might just as well marry Harriet as not. Emma, with the right amount of money and the right social rank, gets Mr. Knightley, but the resolution is the same: a winner-take-all prize in a sparring match with magazine fiction.

Austen finds an alien language, an "other" class, a despised literary tradition in the *Lady's Magazine*—and, strikingly, the same economic crisis for women that drives her own fictions. The *Lady's Magazine* asserts its presence in the juvenilia and hovers over the later works, I think, because it so guilelessly represents for Austen the contemporary obsession with a new consumer world. Its monthly offerings were ephemeral, but omnipresent as air. It touched the aspirations and fears of women from every one of the middling ranks, high and low. In addition, its publication in yearly volumes had the effect of establishing it as a standard. In fact, when the new series, beginning in 1820, announced the editors' intention to replace the fiction contributed by readers with fiction from professionals only, a grass-roots forum for women came to an end.

Milan Kundera writes in *The Art of the Novel* (1988) that, "the novel's spirit is the spirit of complexity."[14] One expects that Jane Austen would agree. The authoritarian spirit of the *Lady's Magazine* leaves no room for a novelist like Austen to negotiate novelistic complexity—as she knew from the beginning. But then neither does an intransigent, authoritarian economy. We find Austen caught in a familiar Derridean bind, in "a certain relationship, unperceived by the writer, between what [she] commands and what [she] does not command of the patterns of the language that [she] uses."[15] Austen both "takes in" and "takes on" the *Lady's Magazine,* simultaneously. She, however, may be clearer about her relationship than we think. When her niece Anna asked for advice on a fledgling novel, Austen spelled out her notion of the difference between popular literature and her own: "Devereux Forester's being ruined by his Vanity is extremely good; but I wish you would not let him plunge into a 'vortex of Dissipation.' I do not object to the Thing," she tells Anna, "but I cannot bear the expression;—it is such thorough novel slang" (*Letters,* 404). The "Thing," Devereux Forester's "ruin" (economic ruin, of course), satisfies Austen immensely: Let it be. As for the style: Consider the source.

Notes

1. Robert D. Mayo, *The English Novels in the Magazines, 1740–1815,* Evanston, Ill., 1962, p. 223, sees this short fiction as continuing in vogue until 1815. In *Lady's Magazine,* short tales, however, are common until 1820, when the magazine began a new series.

2. Terry Lovell, *Consuming Fiction,* London, 1987, p. 49.

3. James J. Barnes, *Free Trade in Books: A Study of the London Book Trade since 1800,* Oxford, 1964, pp. 2–18.

4. Alison Adburgham, *Women in Print: Writing Women and Women's Magazines from the Restoration to the Accession of Victoria,* London, 1972, pp. 148–50, 218–35. See also, Cynthia L. White, *Women's Magazines, 1693–1968,* London, 1970, pp. 31–32, 35–36.

5. The Jane Austen Society, *Report for the Year 1973,* Alton, Ill., 1974, p. 23.

6. *The Lady's Magazine,* pp. 171–76. David Gilson, *A Bibliography of Jane Austen,* Oxford, 1982, p. 454.

7. "Interpreters of Jane Austen's World," in *Jane Austen: New Perspectives,* ed. Janet Todd, London, 1983, pp. 56–63.

8. See Mary Poovey, *The Proper Lady and the Woman Writer,* Chicago, 1984, pp. 180–82.

9. Jonathan Culler, "Grafts and Graft," in *On Deconstruction: Theory and Criticism after Structuralism,* Ithaca, N.Y., 1982, pp. 134–56, discusses the Derridean implications of "grafting" a "minor unknown text . . . onto the main body of the tradition." He writes, "the marginal graft works with these terms to reverse a hierarchy, to show what had previously been thought marginal is in fact central" (pp. 139–40).

10. Lovell, p. 35.

11. A. Walton Litz, "Chronology of Composition," in *The Jane Austen Companion,* New York, 1986, pp. 47–52.

12. Jonathan Culler, *On Deconstruction:* "The concentration on the apparently marginal puts the logic of supplementarity to work as an interpretive strategy: what has been relegated to the margins or set aside by previous interpreters may be important for precisely those reasons that led it to be set aside. Indeed the strategy of the graft is double" (p. 140).

13. Susan Suleiman, *Authoritarian Fictions,* New York, 1983, p. 53.

14. Milan Kundera, *The Art of the Novel,* trans. Linda Asher, London, 1988. Quoted by Gabriel Josipovici, "The Ironist Aloof," *TLS* (24–30 June 1988), 695.

15. Jacques Derrida, *Of Grammatology,* trans. Gayatri Chakravorty Spivak, Baltimore, 1976, p. 158.

The Juvenilia: A Family "Veiw"

Joan Austen-Leigh

In many ways Jane Austen must be considered singularly blessed. The manner in which from generation to generation her descendants respect her memory is, we imagine, precisely that which she would have chosen for herself—and she would have been hard to please.

Virginia Woolf

There is something captivating in the notion of a young Jane Austen—"not at all pretty and very prim, unlike a girl of twelve," in the words of her cousin Philadelphia Walter[1]—seated at her table in the parsonage at Steventon in the dressing room with the chocolate-brown carpet, head bent, scratching away, committing to paper the creations of her fertile mind to present to her family and her friends.

Their humble servant, she called herself, sometimes their obedient humble servant, in the dedications of the juvenile pieces, dedications which themselves parodied the grandiose style of the day. (One has only to think of Dr. Johnson and Lord Chesterfield.) To Martha Lloyd: "As a small testimony of the gratitude I feel for your late generosity in finishing my muslin Cloak," for "Frederic & Elfrida" (3). To Francis William Austen: "Midshipman on board his Majesty's Ship the Perseverance," for "Jack & Alice" (12). To Mrs. Austen: "An interesting & well written Tale is dedicated by Permission . . . ," for "Amelia Webster" (47). To Cassandra: "If the following Tale will afford one moment's amusement to you, every wish will be gratified," for "The beautifull Cassandra" (44). To James Austen: "The following Drama . . . will I hope afford some amusement to so respectable a *Curate* as yourself," for "The Visit" (49).

"Amusement" is the key word; to entertain, the object. The dedications include most of her brothers; the two Lloyd sisters; her cousins, Jane Cooper and the Comtesse de Feuillide; and both her infant nieces, Anna and Fanny—the two latter accompanied by teasing admonitions to their parents concerning their future education. It is fortunate for us that Jane so dedicated her early works. It gives us that tiny extra bit of information—greedy detectives as we have ever been—second names of her brothers supplied, the date Frank joined the navy, and most important of all, the years in which she began to write, information which might otherwise have eluded us.

Yet the family in later generations have been, in the opinion of many, curiously reluctant to release these works to the public, "writings which the authoress had not chosen to publish herself."[2] And, indeed, given Jane Austen's love of "pewter" it would seem that there was an opportunity missed. The conclusion must follow that she considered these works unworthy to appear in print.

When I say "the family" were reluctant, it is my own branch of the Austens, the Austen-Leighs to which I refer. For it is we who in the main have been the custodians in succeeding generations not only of the reputation, biography, and letters of our aunt, but also of the chief of the surviving manuscripts, *Lady Susan, The Watsons, Volume the Third*—the last of the works to be published—and *Charades;* and it is we who have released them to the public.

Jane's brothers had various occupations; and most of the brothers, or their descendants, had some share in increasing our knowledge of her life. Henry wrote the Biographical Notice (a rather sickening affair to modern taste) that was affixed to the posthumously published *Persuasion* and *Northanger Abbey.* Edward Austen (Knight) was a landowner, a country gentleman, uninterested in literary matters. His grandson, Fanny's son, Lord Brabourne, did publish the first edition of the *Letters* (1884). Charles and Frank were sailors, away from home, though Frank's grandson and great-granddaughter produced *Jane Austen's Sailor Brothers* (The Bodley Head, 1906). But it was James's descendants, beginning with his son James Edward Austen (-Leigh in 1837) who were scholars, writers, clergymen, and publishers who in each generation took their degrees at Oxford or Cambridge, and added to the stock of information available on Jane Austen.

James Edward Austen-Leigh, my great-grandfather, Jane's favorite nephew, at the age of 72 wrote the *Memoir of Jane Austen,* published appropriately enough on her birthday, December 16, 1869, by Richard Bentley. (The title page of this first edition bears the date "1870.") It is the only such work by one who knew her. His sister, Caroline Austen had transcribed her own memories two years previously and James Edward drew from these. They were eventually published as a separate work by the Jane Austen Society at Alton as *My Aunt Jane Austen,* 1952. James Edward's daughter, Mary Austen-Leigh, at the age of 82, wrote *Personal Aspects of Jane Austen* (John Murray, 1920). His

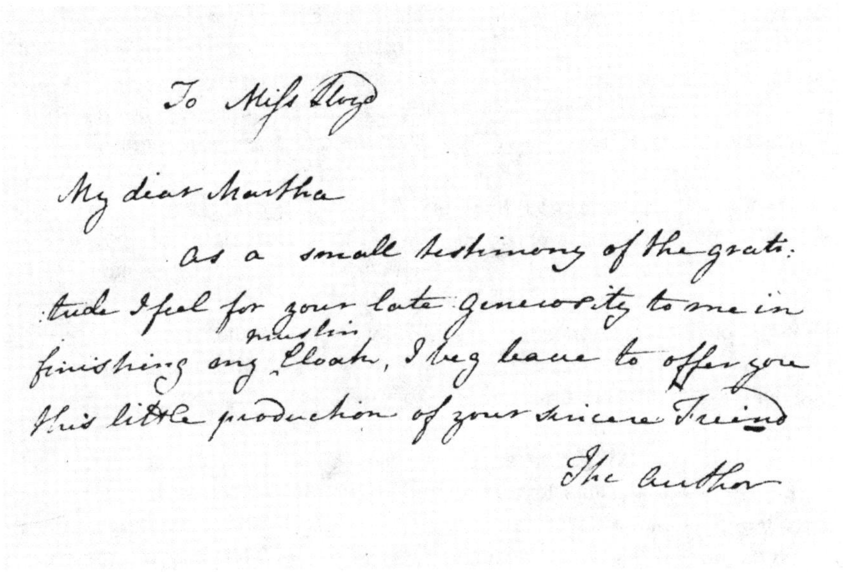
To Miss Lloyd

My dear Martha

As a small testimony of the grati:
:tude I feel for your late generosity to me in
finishing my muslin Cloak, I beg leave to offer you
this little production of your sincere Freind
The Author

Figure 20. "To Miss Lloyd," Dedication to "Frederic & Elfrida"
(*From a collotype of* Volume the First *in the 1933 Clarendon Press limited edition*)

son, William, and his grandson Richard A. Austen-Leigh produced *Jane Austen: Her Life and Letters* (Smith Elder & Co., 1913), an accurate, objective, factual work on which all other biographies are, or should be, based. In fact in *Etoniana,* the (unsigned) obituary of Richard A. Austen-Leigh (d. 1961) states, "Nor can we forget his works on his relative, Jane Austen, which laid the foundation of modern Janian scholarship, before the days of R.W. Chapman. . . . "

Thus the history of the release to a clamorous public of the manuscripts in general and the juvenilia in particular is one of a gradual, one might almost say grudging, relinquishment.

In the second edition of his *Memoir* James Edward Austen-Leigh published *Lady Susan* and *The Watsons* (to which he had given the titles, according to Chapman) and a portion of *Sanditon.* This in 1871. The volume was actually issued with "Lady Susan" printed on its spine, as Chapman remarks, "by inadvertence or cunning." Mary Austen-Leigh discusses the regret and dismay felt by James Edward: "He foresaw the disappointment of its readers when they should discover the nature and brevity of the story [*Lady Susan*], and still more did he feel to put forward, as though on a par with her other works, a character sketch which she never intended to give to the world would not appear on his part to be showing due respect to the memory and judgment of his aunt."[3] Even before the book appeared he felt it necessary to state a disclaimer in the notice he wrote prior to its publication. "If it [*Lady Susan*] should be judged unworthy of the publicity now given it, the censure must fall on him who has put it forth and not on her who kept it locked up in her desk."[4]

Mary Austen-Leigh has also given an explanation of how so young an author could possibly record so evil a character as Lady Susan. Jane's great friends Mary and Martha Lloyd (who in later life married two of Jane's brothers) were the granddaughters of "the cruel Mrs. Craven" who, according to family tradition, treated her own five daughters (of whom Mrs. Lloyd was one) as despicably as Lady Susan did Frederica. It is of interest that Mrs. Craven's husband was at one time governor of South Carolina.

It was another 50 years before the first notebook of the juvenilia (*Volume the Second*) appeared under the title "Love and Freindship," published by Chatto and Windus in 1922, and taken from a copy in the Bodleian Library which had been purchased from Charles's descendants. R.W. Chapman tells us, "The spelling 'Freindship' is not eccentric. Boswell once wrote 'freind' and Jane Austen habitually wrote 'neice' and even 'veiw'." *Volume the First* followed in 1933 and *the Third* in 1951.

Chapman, the editor of the [complete] *Works of Jane Austen* in his preface to Volume VI, *Minor Works* (1954), declares, "These immature or fragmentary fictions call for hardly any comment" (v). But do they? With our avid interest in everything pertaining to Jane Austen today, how do we feel about these writings that she "had not chosen to publish herself"? That is the question. Why did she not so choose?

I believe it would take a person very much obsessed with her own importance (which Jane assuredly was not—Jane, who for so long kept her anonymity, and even after her name was disclosed never put it on her books or made any effort to encounter anyone in the literary world) to feel that the effusions of her youth, the playful, boisterous *jeu d'esprits* written to amuse her family would be of the smallest interest to the public at large. Considering her views about *Pride and Prejudice* being "too light, bright and sparkling," is it not possible she was even ashamed of these early writings?

Could my ancestors, the worthy, scholarly, upright Austen-Leighs have foreseen the voracious appetite of her fans for anything pertaining to or even remotely connected—one might say to a ludicrous degree—with their aunt, would their attitude to the publication of the minor works have been different? I believe not. I think they would have been even more particular. As it is, recently discovered correspondence[5] shows how averse both Edward and Caroline were to the publishing of the last verses of "Venta" written two days before Jane Austen died, as not being "worthy" of her as she was perceived by the public.

One cannot help but feel that many of the earliest scraps would never have seen the light of day if they had been by another hand. An example is the foolish play, "The Visit." Precocious, for a schoolgirl, but is that not all that there is to be said?

One can argue that in these early writings one discerns the flexing of her muscles, Jane Austen in training for her future task. In the maneuverings of Lady Susan we detect a future Wickham. In "Catharine, or The Bower," we see the beginnings perhaps of Catherine Morland; the wit and charm of Henry Tilney is a palimpsest of Mr. Stanley. But of this tale the authors of the *Life* state, "The story is at times amusing, but obviously immature, and we need not regret that it was never finished."[6] The later Jane is visible, undoubtedly: the wit, the cynicism, the unexpected twist that raises a smile. Quotable phrases abound even at her tender age. He came "of a very ancient Family & possessed besides his paternal Estate, a considerable share in a Lead mine & a ticket in the Lottery" (31). Or, "like many other sensible People, they sometimes did a foolish thing" (30). And, most famous of all, "She was nothing more than a mere good-tempered, civil and obliging Young Woman; as such we could scarcely dislike her—she was only an Object of Contempt" (100–101). *That* from "Love and Freindship" was finished June 13, 1790, written when, unbelievably, she was 14½ years old. Of course one thinks of Mozart; his early works were not suppressed. But his boyhood tunes were simple, not over-ornamented, while Jane Austen's early writings are very much so.

Naturally it is interesting to observe how Jane Austen refined her art; how she learned that less is more. In the period of the juvenilia, for example, the vulgarity of such a phrase as "Come Girls, let us circulate the Bottle" (54), would not have been uttered. Moreover, the occasion would never have arisen for uttering it, even by Lucy Steele, in the six novels. There are many references to drunkenness in the juvenilia, but comparatively few in the novels, only Mr. Elton drinking "too much of Mr. Weston's good wine" and a young Lucas crying out that if he was as rich as Mr. Darcy he would drink a bottle a day.

Although hardly meant to be taken seriously, death is another subject introduced to excess. People die or are murdered right and left at the convenience of the plot. One of the charms of Jane Austen's novels is that no character who has appeared on stage dies, only those in the wings whom nobody cares about, such as Mr. Norris and Mrs. Churchill.

Is it heresy to say the juvenilia should not have been published? In the six novels, I am sure the reader of these words will agree, there is never a dull sentence, never a superfluous word. But in *Lady Susan,* for example, there is many a tedious reiteration of circumstances already known to the reader. G.K. Chesterton in his introduction to "Love and Freindship" declares that Lady Susan is "comparatively dull," describes the works as "nursery jests," and remarks he would willingly have left Lady Susan in the wastebasket in exchange for "Love and Freindship" (ix).

Life and Letters states "Mr. Harley" was written about 1788 when Frank was a midshipman.[7] Jane was only 12 (remembering that she was born at the very end of the year). That few of us at age 12 or 14 or 25 could write as "well," with such style and in such pure English, is begging the question. There are people, I am not one of them, who find Miss Bates tedious. How much more so is the fifth letter in "Love and Freindship" which devotes a much longer space than that taken by any of Miss Bates' speeches simply to a knock at a door. The early writings are concerned with marriage, titles, and estates, without the interaction of character which animates the later novels; and although they are leavened by wit, they are not often leavened by wisdom.

Many avid devotees of Jane Austen who have read her works times without number have never sat down and plodded their weary way through the complete juvenilia, and for good reason. I confess to being one of that number until very recently. The juvenilia, I believe, could well have been left, not in the wastebasket but in a drawer, for study by scholars, who I venture to suspect are pretty much the only people who ever really peruse them.

We mustn't forget Jane's own advice to her niece Caroline, advice quoted in the *Memoir* and sent in a message from Winchester. Caroline was herself 12 when Aunt Jane suggested that she should read more and write less until she was 16, and wished she had done so herself in the "corresponding years" of her life.

To R.W. Chapman must remain the final word. Writing in his preface to

Volume the First (1933), when *Volume the Second* had already been published and *Volume the Third* had not, he says, "It will always be disputed whether such effusions as these ought to be published; and it may be that we have enough already of Jane Austen's early scraps. The author of the *Memoir* thought a very brief specimen sufficient. But perhaps the question is hardly worth discussion. For if such manuscripts find their way into great libraries, their publication can hardly be prevented. The only sure way to prevent it is the way of destruction, which no one dare take."[8]

Notes

1. William and Richard Arthur Austen-Leigh, *Life and Letters of Jane Austen,* London, 1913, p. 59.

2. Mary Augusta Austen-Leigh, *James Edward Austen Leigh: A Memoir,* n.p., 1911, p. 265.

3. Mary Augusta Austen-Leigh, *Personal Aspects of Jane Austen,* London, 1920, pp. 98–99.

4. James Edward Austen-Leigh, *A Memoir of Jane Austen,* second edition, London, 1871, p. 201.

5. Deidre Le Faye, "Jane Austen's Verses and Lord Stanhope's Disappointment," *The Book Collector* 37:1 (Spring 1988), 86–91.

6. William and Richard Arthur Austen-Leigh, p. 56.

7. Ibid., p. 57.

8. R.W. Chapman, Preface to *Volume the First,* Oxford, 1933, p. ix.

Lady Susan:
The Wicked Mother in Jane Austen's Work

Barbara Horwitz

"What a woman she must be!"[1] writes Reginald De Courcy to his sister, Catherine Vernon, about Lady Susan. And *Lady Susan* is an achievement principally because she is so compelling a character. Her effectiveness does not lie merely in her beauty and charm, as her enemies notice, but in her "artfulness," a word they often use to describe her. I maintain that her use of art, like that of her creator, Jane Austen, primarily involves language. When she confides in a friend, she writes in aphorisms, the voice typically Austenian: "I have never yet found that the advice of a Sister could prevent a young Man's being in love if he chose it" (258).

On the occasions when she is addressing those "respectable people" who are her adversaries, she speaks their own language, the language of the conduct books. These books on female education and conduct, enormously popular during the late eighteenth and nineteenth centuries, were strongly influenced by the educational theories of John Locke and the moral teachings of the Evangelicals. These writers, often women, paint a portrait of the good mother since the only universally accepted reason for educating women at all was to train them to be good mothers.

Although most of these books are simple manuals of advice, many of them are cast in the form of letters and several take the form of novels. Regardless of their literary form, they are grounded in the theories of perception and cognition found in John Locke's *An Essay concerning Human Understanding* (1690) and given practical application in his *Some Thoughts concerning Education* (1693), a very detailed guide to bringing up children. In this work, Locke defines the primary goals of education as the inculcation of virtue, wisdom, breeding, and learning. To achieve these goals he advises the conscientious parent to study the behavior of his child and tailor an education to the child's nature. Although Locke's precepts were originally meant for a young gentle-men, he wrote later that with only very minor changes, they could serve equally well for the education of young ladies.[2]

For advice on that score, however, parents had been referring to the work of Abbe Fénélon who wrote *Traite de l'education des filles* (1687). This book remained so influential that James Boswell consulted it for advice over a 100 years after it first appeared. Some of the most widely disseminated works based on the principles of Locke and Fénélon were written by Sarah Fielding, John Gregory, Richard and Maria Edgeworth, Mme De Genlis, Hannah More, Clara Reeve, Jane West, and Mary Wollstonecraft. With the exception of Wollstone-craft, all of these writers were sternly conservative politically and highly ortho-dox theologically.

It is probable that Jane Austen was familiar with all or most of them. Madame De Genlis' *Adelaide and Theodore* is alluded to in *Emma* (461); and she, Hannah More, and Jane West are explicitly mentioned in the *Letters* num-bers 25, 48, 125, 73, and 101. Also, these ideas were shared by most writers and thinkers of the time. Jane Austen agrees in many respects but her tone is never rigidly moralistic as theirs tends to be, possibly because she understands that the mind cannot, and indeed should not, always control the heart. Most important, she believes the goal of education for women is not to produce good mothers, but to achieve self-knowledge, just as it is for men.

Like the writers of the conduct books, Jane Austen does concern herself with the duties of mothers. Mothers or mother figures play highly significant roles in the novels and in the juvenilia, but the only good mothers are dead; the rest are either ineffectual, like Mrs. Morland in *Northanger Abbey* (suggesting Catherine read an essay to cure her broken heart), or offensive like Mrs. Bennet and Lady Catherine De Burgh. Lady Russell gives Anne Elliot very bad advice in *Persuasion* and Mrs. Turner, who had adopted Emma Watson in *The Wat-sons,* reneges on her commitments to the penniless young girl and sails off to Ireland with a new husband (Captain O'Brien), lust overpowering her sense of duty to Emma. In the juvenilia, Catherine's aunt in *Catharine, or The Bower* is stern and unloving. The "Worthless Louisa" in "Lesley Castle" is far worse. She deserts her husband and baby daughter to run off with another man (110). The Lesleys' new stepmother, too, has very little use for the Lesley children. As the "disagreable woman" says, "I have once in my life been fool enough to travel I dont know how many hundred Miles to see two of the Family, and I found it did not answer, so Deuce take me if I am ever so foolish again" (138). However, only one natural mother or mother figure in any of Jane Austen's work is thoroughly and purposely malignant—Lady Susan.

Where did she come from? John Halperin believes she is based on the character of Eliza de Feuillide, Jane Austen's cousin who married a French aristocrat and was rather flirtatious. Her husband was guillotined during the

Reign of Terror.[3] Other biographers identify her with Lady Craven, the grand-mother of Jane Austen's friends Martha and Mary Lloyd, whose behavior to her daughters was so brutal as to have become notorious.[4] Some critics have insisted Lady Susan is a figure based on literary antecedents rather than a real person. They see her as a figure out of Restoration comedy—bright, beautiful, and entirely unprincipled. Warren Roberts identifies her with the heroine of Choder-los de Laclos's *Les Liaisons dangereuses*. Roberts suggests that Eliza de Feuil-lide may have brought a copy of the French novel to Steventon when she visited there.[5] Whatever Lady Susan's origins, she remains a unique figure in Jane Austen's novels. No other female character in the later novels possesses Susan's combination of beauty, charm, energy, intelligence, and malevolent drive for power.

Outwardly Lady Susan seems absolutely perfect. According to Catherine Vernon, who dislikes her, Lady Susan is "excessively pretty," "sweet," "clever and agreable," and possesses "a happy command of Language" (251). Mrs. Vernon admits that even she was nearly deceived by her writing. "She has already almost persuaded me of her being warmly attached to her daughter, tho' I have so long been convinced of the contrary. She speaks of her with so much tenderness and anxiety, lamenting so bitterly the neglect of her education, which she represents however as wholly unavoidable" (251).

Lady Susan not only brings up her daughter improperly and cruelly, obvi-ously ignoring the spirit of the conduct books, she uses their own form of discourse to justify her misconduct. This woman has absolutely no use for moral values. She has been a bad wife who despised her husband when he was alive. She flirts with other men, causing pain to their wives and misery to their sweethearts. Otherwise completely uninterested in her daughter, she uses her to show her own power, particularly over men. Sir James Martin will do what-ever she asks and she wishes to put Sir Reginald De Courcy in the same position. She acknowledges, "There is exquisite pleasure in subduing an insolent spirit, in making a person predetermined to dislike, acknowledge one's superiority" (254).

Lady Susan recognizes, however, that paying lip service to the strictures of the moralists not only makes her seem respectable, "that great word" (245), but allows her to do whatever she pleases. The wonderful irony that permeates this work has its foundation in the fact that quoting books on the duties of mothers provides Lady Susan with the rationale for mistreating her daughter at will. Lady Susan is quite conscious of her ability to appropriate the language of those whose ideas she has no notion of accepting. She does not exaggerate as she explains why she expects to get her way with the Vernons and Sir Reginald; she possesses "command of Language" (268).

Readers may sense that they are reading an *anti*-conduct book. Is it possible that Jane Austen is trying to show the reader the worst possible mother as the

writers of the conduct books tried to describe the best possible mother? *Lady
Susan,* however, is by no means merely a parody of a conduct book: this
anti-heroine does not simply behave in a manner directly contrary to the way
the books say she should. Instead, she attempts appearing to behave exactly as
they recommend by using their very words to justify her behavior. She paints a
false picture of herself with the language of the conduct books. Jane Austen
shows her using this language so artistically that we are forced to admire Lady
Susan's technique as much as we do that of Jane Austen.

In the tradition of Jane Austen's other insincere but charming villains—
Willoughby, Wickham, and the Crawfords—Lady Susan succeeds in appearing
to be an estimable human being for a time—at least in the eyes of the male
characters. The books on female conduct would condemn her goals, but they
could not disapprove of her conversation or conduct at Churchill, the Vernons'
home. There she behaves with complete circumspection, particularly in the
company of Sir Reginald. Certainly, concern for the education of her daughter
seems genuine. Although the reader never believes "the sacred impulse of
maternal affection" (245) burns within her, she is most convincing to the other
characters as she demands:

> Can you possibly suppose that I was aware of her unhappiness? that it was my object to make
> my own child miserable, & that I had forbidden her speaking to you on this subject, from a
> fear of your interrupting the Diabolical scheme? Do you think me destitute of every honest,
> every natural feeling? Am I capable of consigning *her* to everlasting Misery, whose welfare it
> is my first Earthly Duty to promote? [289]

Of course, Lady Susan insists she wants the best possible education for
Frederica. This, according to the conduct books, involves the inculcation of
virtue, first of all. Virtue is taught, according to John Locke and the other
writers on education who followed his lead, primarily by insisting on absolute
obedience. Lady Susan is outraged at Frederica's disobedience in running away
from school because it has upset her plans; thus she is able to express her outrage
even to her enemies. She ought to be enraged at Frederica's disobedience.
Frederica has run away from school because she is afraid—with good reason—
that she will be forced to marry Sir James. While the moralizers advise against
forcing one's children to marry against their will, they are far more adamant
about not allowing one's children to disobey. Hannah More believes that "habit-
ual restraint" is necessary to educate girls properly. She also believes female
education should inculcate a "submissive temper and a forebearing heart."[6]
Even Mary Wollstonecraft warns against ever allowing a child to have her own
way.[7] Clara Reeve goes so far as to insist that laxity in this regard will ruin not
only one's children, but the nation, and even mankind.[8]

Lady Susan attributes Frederica's misbehavior to the fact that she "was a spoilt child" (288). Spoiling a child by indulging his whims or failing to insist on perfect obedience condemns him to a life of self-indulgence and libertinism. Other novelists agree. Lovelace, the villain of Samuel Richardson's *Clarissa* (1748) was a spoiled child and the perfect example of the amoral monster an overindulgent mother could create. In Jane Austen's novels, too, the elopements of Lydia Bennet and Maria Bertram are a direct consequence of the fact that they were spoiled by their mother or aunt. Tom Bertram has been spoiled because he is the heir to Mansfield Park, and, before his illness, is a wastrel.

Lady Susan blames her daughter's disobedience on the fact that she was spoiled by Frederica's late father whose memory she pretends to revere. Mrs. Vernon, too, tries to explain Frederica's faults by referring to her early miseducation. Similarly, Reginald, Mrs. Vernon's brother and Lady Susan's prey, tries to explain Lady Susan's faults to Mrs. Vernon by imputing "her errors" to her neglected Education & early Marriage" (256). Lady Susan insists her own lack of accomplishments is due to the fact that she herself was "so much indulged in [her] infant years" that she never had to learn anything (253). This admission would explain her true character to the readers of the time. Of course she is a villain; that is what spoiled children become. It is true that the writers on women's education advised against forcing one's child to marry wholly against her wishes, so to her friend Lady Susan explains, "I could not answer it to myself to force Frederica into a marriage from which her heart revolted; & instead of adopting so harsh a measure, merely propose to make it her own choice by rendering her thoroughly uncomfortable till she does accept him" (253–54). To her enemy, Mrs. Vernon, Lady Susan offers a slightly more acceptable excuse: she says she firmly believed that Frederica had no rational objections to Sir James (289). She realizes, however, that her excuse is a very weak one, and hastens to change the subject.

The writers would have agreed with Lady Susan on yet another count. They maintained that it was wrong for a woman to fall in love with a man before he fell in love with her. Both John Gregory[9] and Jane West[10] warn against such behavior. Of course, the narrator of *Northanger Abbey* laughs at this ignorance of the human heart and she demonstrates in the case of Catherine Morland that falling in love with a man can actually attract him; but the writers of the conduct books insist that such behavior exposes a young lady to ridicule, and even, as Lady Susan writes, shows "indelicate feelings" (282).

Lady Susan is clever enough to blame herself for any deficiencies in Frederica when she speaks to the Vernons and Reginald. She insists she simply does not know her child (288). Locke and the other writers on education insist a parent must be thoroughly familiar with a child's nature. To accomplish this, a parent must spend a good deal of time winning his child's love and trust so that the child will be open and frank with him. It is noted in *Mansfield Park* that Sir Thomas Bertram is an inadequate parent because his children find him daunting and spend as little time as possible in his company. Eventually, he takes responsibility for not educating them properly. Lady Susan, on the other hand, is so skillful a manipulator that she manages to convince Sir Reginald that her poor relationship with Frederica is the girl's fault. He explains, "Frederica does not know her Mother—Lady Susan means nothing but her Good—but Frederica will not make a friend of her. Lady Susan therefore does not always know what will make her daughter happy" (287).

She does admit that because she feels unequal to the task of educating Frederica herself, she intends sending her to school. Whether a child should be educated at home or at school, and under what conditions, was a matter thoroughly discussed. The writers insisted that children needed an excellent education but they realized that some mothers were not capable of educating children properly and talented governesses could be very difficult to find. Schools would have been considered the obvious solution to the problem were it not for the fact that the age was convinced, with Locke, that the child's tutor had to study his character and know him really well.

Locke attacked boarding schools because they failed to teach virtue and could not remedy character defects since the masters had such large numbers of boys to supervise. Mme De Genlis, Mary Wollstonecraft, and Jane West also censured such institutions for instilling vanity and providing only superficial accomplishments. This was the standard charge laid against girls' schools. Jane Austen blames the self-centered vanity of the Bingley sisters in *Pride and Prejudice* on their education at a fashionable school.

Jane West recognized that parents who cannot find proper teachers for their daughters must send them to school, as Lady Susan does, but she warns them that when their daughters are at home they must devote themselves to "repressing their vanity, encouraging their virtues and winning their friendship in order to influence their behavior." Of course Lady Susan has no intention of doing this.

Some writers who were directly involved in running girls' schools were suspicious of them.[11] Fénélon, the spiritual advisor at a convent school, insists that the best education takes place at home because no one can study a child and remedy defects in his character so effectively as his parents.[12] A school can, however, provide skilled masters. The presence of other children must insure healthy competition and a loss of shyness. Since Lady Susan wants the best masters for her daughter (and also complains of Frederica's shyness) she cannot be considered culpable for choosing to send her to school. Even Catherine Vernon, who has considerable moral authority, believes Frederica belongs in school. Of course she sees school as shielding Frederica from her mother's sorry example and malign influence (247).

Then, too, Lady Susan is sending Frederica to a "private" (244) school—a small establishment in which the students are well supervised. The writers on education did not object to such establishments and neither did Jane Austen. Indeed, her father kept such a "school" and, for a short time, she and her sister Cassandra attended another such school.

Jane West stresses one other major consideration which Lady Susan might have borne in mind. Girls, as they reach adolescence, must be more carefully supervised to prevent "sexual misconduct" because "if the breath of calumny blow upon the tender foliage of female fame, it is blasted forever."[13] It is not surprising that Jane West's sentiments are echoed by Mary Bennet in *Pride and Prejudice* when she sermonizes on her sister Lydia's disgrace in running off with Wickham. Madame De Genlis, for example, considers a woman's most important attribute her reputation, her person, and her charm in that order.[14]

Lady Susan is just as aware of the paramount importance of reputation as any moralist. She conciliates Reginald in order to protect her reputation (292). Earlier, when she had to explain to Reginald why she tried to prevent the marriage of his sister, Catherine, to her brother-in-law, she mentioned that she heard rumors detrimental to Catherine's reputation. Reginald uses that information to defend Lady Susan's actions as well as her reputation. If Catherine Vernon, "in the security of retirement" could be slandered, one "living in the World & surrounded with temptation" should not be condemned if "she should be accused of Errors" (264). Two points have been made very effectively and very economically. Lady Susan is not to blame; Lady Susan is not to *be* blamed! Lady Susan establishes her reputation as firmly as possible.

Jane Austen, of course, is far less doctrinaire than Lady Susan or the writers of the conduct books on the subjects of reputed or actual sexual misconduct. For one thing, she shows us that girls who are not at school, such as Lydia Bennet, are in at least as much danger of seduction as those who are at school. She blames some schools for encouraging certain character defects but she does not blame them for encouraging sexual license. She uses the Bingley sisters in *Pride and Prejudice* to exemplify Jane West's belief that schools tend to create "fine ladies," women who think far too much of themselves and their possessions.[15] The Bertram sisters in *Mansfield Park* could not blame their miseducation on a school, and of course, Anne Elliot in *Persuasion*, a product of a school, grew to be almost "too good." To what extent does Jane Austen agree with Lady Susan and the writers on education about the crucial importance of reputation? In *Pride and Prejudice*, Lydia overcomes the obloquy of her liaison with Wickham because they marry. Maria, in *Mansfield Park*, is not so fortunate. Hannah More[16] and Jane West[17] would agree that both women deserved lifelong ostracism. Mary Wollstonecraft would urge society to be more charitable.[18] It is an indication of Lady Susan's hypocrisy that she echoes the sentiments of the most rigid writers and thinkers, as she says, commenting on the harm Manwaring's attentions might do to her reputation: "Those women are inexcusable who forget what is due to themselves & the opinion of the World" (269).

Lady Susan mentions that the school to which she sends Frederica is terribly expensive. Presumably, Frederica will make rich friends. The writers on education considered the connections girls might make at school. Jane West writes that in schools, without adequate supervision, girls are likely to choose unsuitable friends whose influence may be harmful.[19] Even in the early works this problem does not arise for Jane Austen, and her later heroines (Catherine Morland, for example) make unworthy friends even though they are not in school.

Although readers and thinkers of the time might have disapproved of sending Frederica to school, still they would not have faulted Lady Susan for choosing a school for her daughter if she herself were genuinely unequal to the task of educating Frederica. Lady Susan does, however, reveal her wickedness to the readers of the time when she chooses a *London* school for Frederica. All writers on education, in fact, recommend bringing children up in the country. This idea gained particular currency in the eighteenth century through the influence of Rousseau. Madame De Genlis has her exemplary parents, the D'Alamanes, flee to the country in the middle of the night with their children so their friends cannot dissuade them from leaving Paris. Lady Susan's choice of a London school would sound a jarring note to the nineteenth-century reader.

The writers on education believed young people need to learn useful social and domestic skills as well as virtue and fortitude. Lady Susan agrees. She is annoyed at Frederica's "artlessness" and is certain it must lead to ridicule. In fact she accounts for Mrs. Vernon's partiality to Frederica by maintaining that Mrs. Vernon wants "to have all the sense & all the wit of the Conversation to herself; Frederica will never eclipse her" (274). Locke writes at length on insuring strength of body and mind. Lady Susan, quite conscious that fortitude is a socially approved virtue, maintains that she herself must show it—when separated from her daughter (245). Her actions are far from admirable but her facility in using the language of her enemies is remarkable.

Academic learning was the least important aspect of education. The course of study that Lady Susan wishes Frederica to follow is not exactly what was recommended, but many would agree with her in not approving of anything more than a superficial education for women. Lady Susan believes her daughter ought to know how "to play & sing with some portion of Taste, & a good deal of assurance, as she has *my* hand & arm, & a tolerable voice" (253). She does not approve of "the prevailing fashion of acquiring a perfect knowledge in all the Languages Arts & Sciences; it is throwing time away; to be Mistress of French, Italian, German, Music, Singing, Drawing &c. will gain a Woman some applause, but will not add one Lover to her list. Grace & Manner after all are of the greatest importance" (253).

Writers such as Mary Wortley-Montague and Jane West believed that study could be a compensation for the lack of lovers, or, less positively, could frighten prospective lovers away. Mary Wortley-Montague asserted that the educated woman should "conceal whatever learning she attains, with as much solicitude as she would hide crookedness or lameness."[20] Dr. Gregory[21] and Jane West[22] concurred. Hester Chapone too, fears to see any girl she loves "remarkable for learning."[23]

Jane Austen agrees with Hester Chapone, Hannah More, and Mary Wollstonecraft, who recommend a course of serious reading as the most effective method of female education. (This is how she herself as well as most of her heroines received their education.) Frederica shares that experience. Despite the neglect and ill treatment she has received, Frederica is not ignorant, "being fond of books & spending the chief of her time in reading" (273). She may even owe her good character to this habit. It is true she is shy, but under the kind tutelage of Mrs. Vernon she begins to overcome her timidity. We certainly believe Mrs. Vernon when she insists "There cannot be a more gentle, affectionate heart, or more obliging manners" (273) than Frederica's.

Mrs. Vernon is, of course, the kind of mother of whom the writers on education approve. She is a devoted daughter, wife, and mother—polite, virtuous and well-read. She is also the only character besides Frederica to see through Lady Susan. Since Mrs. Vernon will help to educate her and since Reginald De Courcy must fall in love with her, Frederica will be as happy as she deserves to be. Will her undeserving mother be equally happy married to the rich but silly Sir James Martin? The narrator reminds us explicitly that the only factors that can prevent Lady Susan's second marriage being happy are "her Husband, & her Conscience" (313). Both of which, as we know, are negligible.

A knowledge of the books on female education and conduct demonstrates just how talented Lady Susan is in using the language of conventional morality to gain her less-than-moral aims. It is no accident that she is so often referred to as "artful" in contrast to her daughter who is described as "artless." She is an artist who, like her creator, is adept at using language. It may be that because we admire Jane Austen's artistry with language we cannot hate Lady Susan. Indeed, the reader (as well as many critics) attempts to find excuses for her cruelty on the grounds that she lives in an age hostile to women, especially those who are not rich enough to be independent. The fact that the reader finds it difficult to hate Lady Susan, but can certainly hate the hypocrisy of the age, demonstrates once again the remarkable quality of Jane Austen's irony. Even in this work, written when she was not yet 20, Jane Austen's irony is remarkably sharp without ever being unpalatably bitter. It allows us, in the words of the elder Sir Reginald, to admire Lady Susan's "Beauty and Abilities without being blinded by them to her faults" (262).

Notes

1. R.W. Chapman, *The Works of Jane Austen,* vol. V, *Minor Works,* ed. R.W. Chapman, rev. B.C. Southam, London, 1972, p. 248. All internal notes refer to this volume or to *Jane Austen's Letters to Her Sister Cassandra and Others,* Oxford, 1932.

2. John Locke, *Letter to Mrs. Clarke,* February 1685, *The Educational Writings of John Locke,* ed. James L. Axtell, Cambridge, 1968, p. 344.

3. John Halperin, *The Life of Jane Austen,* Baltimore, 1984, p. 48.

4. Jane Aiken Hodge, *Only a Novel: The Double Life of Jane Austen,* Greenwich, Conn., 1973, pp. 42, 55.

5. Brian Southam, *Jane Austen's Literary Manuscripts,* pp. 45–52; J.A. Levine, "'Lady Susan': Jane Austen's Character of the Merry Widow," *Studies in English Literature, 1500–1900,* 1:4 (1961), 23–35, cited in Warren Roberts, *Jane Austen and the French Revolution,* New York, 1979, p. 215.

6. Hannah More, *Strictures on the Modern System of Female Education with a View of the Principles and Conduct Prevalent among Women of Rank and Fortune,* Dublin, 1800, p. 106.

7. Mary Wollstonecraft, *Thoughts on the Education of Daughters* (1786), Princeton, N.J., 1972, p. 6.

8. Clara Reeve, *Plans of Education with Remarks on the Systems of Other Writers* (1792), New York, 1974, pp. 36, 132, 34.

9. Jane West, *Letters to a Young Lady in which the Duties and Character of Women are Considered* (1806), New York, 1974, III, 104.

10. John Gregory, *A Father's Legacy to His Daughters* (1774), New York, 1974, p. 104.

11. West, *Letters,* III, 227–28.

12. H.C. Barnard, *Fénelon on Education: A Translation of the 'Traite de l'education des filles' and Other Documents Illustrating Fénelon's Educational Theories and Practice,* Cambridge, 1966, p. 97.

13. West, *Letters,* III, 224.

14. Felicité De Genlis, *Adelaide and Theodore or Letters on Education,* London, 1796, p. 36.

15. Jane West, *The Advantages of Education* (1793), New York, 1974, p. 35.

16. More, pp. 37, 7.

17. West, *Letters,* I, 242, 247.

18. Mary Wollstonecraft, *A Vindication of the Rights of Women,* London, 1796, p. 6.

19. West, *Letters,* III, 26.

20. Lady Mary Wortley-Montague, *Selected Letters,* ed. Robert Halsband, London, 1970, p. 237.

21. Gregory, pp. 31–32.

22. West, *Letters,* III, 4.

23. Hester Chapone, *Letters on the Improvement of the Mind Addressed to a Young Lady* (1777), London, 1822, p. 139.

The Unmasking of Lady Susan

Beatrice Anderson

In his discussion of *Lady Susan,* A. Walton Litz remarks that Jane Austen, as her observation matured, realized that women like Lady Susan are ideal creatures as remote from reality as the Man of Feeling, and no believable character could possibly be as self-assured and so free from illusion.[1] I wholly disagree with Mr. Litz; for not only is Lady Susan a believable character but she is an excellent model for a personality disorder that has been documented in psychological literature for over a century and a half. Unlike schizophrenia and other psychoses, however, the disorder is often not readily discernible, leaving its bearer active among us, just as Lady Susan remains a viable part of her society. First labeled psychopathy, the antisocial behavior that Lady Susan exhibits has more recently been called sociopathy.

Jane Austen, a brilliant observer of the human personality in all its variations, was ahead of her time in documenting so accurately the psychopathic (or sociopathic) personality which we see in Lady Susan. We have no proof, however, that one person existed in Jane Austen's experience to serve as the model for Lady Susan as some critics believe. For instance, A. Walton Litz suggests two possibilities for the origin of Lady Susan: Jane Austen's cousin, later sister-in-law, Eliza de Feuillide; or a lady with characteristics similar to those of Lady Susan who was known to the author through family gossip. And Louis Kronenberger, perhaps referring to the latter lady, says of Lady Susan: "she was plainly suggested by the grandmother of one of Jane Austen's connections—a wicked, beautiful society woman named Craven and known as the terrible Mrs. C., who, all tenderness to her children in public, in private beat and starved and locked them up."[2]

Even though we cannot prove one person was the model for her heroine, Jane Austen most likely took the characteristics for Lady Susan from life rather than from the scientific studies of the psychopath which were just beginning in her time. Adolf Guffenbühl-Craig explains that psychiatrist Philippe Pinel (1745–1826) was the first to describe psychopathy as a psychiatric phenomenon. His work was followed by that of his student Jean Etienne Dominique Esquirol (1772–1840), who introduced the concept of "alteration of intention and feeling where the intelligence retains its integrity," and later by the work of English psychiatrist James Richard (1786–1848), who wrote of "moral imbecility."[3] When Jane Austen made her fair copy of *Lady Susan* in or after 1805, she probably had not heard of, nor knew the specific characteristics of a psychopath, yet she created a creature that might have served as a model case study.

Before beginning a discussion of Lady Susan's characteristics, I would like to more fully clarify the definitions of both psychopath and sociopath, noting how the terms denote very similar characteristics which all easily coincide with Lady Susan's traits. According to H.M. Cleckley, author of the most famous work on the psychopath, *The Mask of Sanity* (1964), these are the chief character traits of the psychopath: superficial charm, adequate intelligence, absence of anxiety, insincerity, lack of remorse or shame, antisocial behavior, poor judgment, selfishness and egocentricity, lack of capacity for love, unemotional sexual behavior, lack of long-term life plans, and rarely, if ever, suicidal attempts.[4]

And under the personality description of the sociopath, Professor Wolman says: "All of them are exceedingly selfish, overdemanding, manipulative, and exploitative."[5] Sociopaths have no superego, remorse or guilt feelings, leaving them free to lie, cheat, and take advantage of those around them without self-retribution. Always ready to justify their dishonest behavior, sociopaths are sensitive to their own pain but not to the pain of others, and never blame themselves but, instead, tend to be hostile and to believe themselves innocent victims of adverse conditions and/or hostile environments. They justify their own hostile attitudes by the need to defend themselves, and, in most situations, seek attention and approval by portraying themselves as victims. "Every sociopath," says Professor Wolman, "is selfish and manipulative. They care only for themselves and use others as tools for their own satisfactions. . . . They are bent on immediate gratification of their needs and exercise very little, if any, self-criticism."[6]

Finally, as Lady Susan so closely fits the description which Vernon W. Grant adds to the basic definition of psychopaths in *The Menancing Stranger,* I would like to bring in his discussion. Grant notes that psychopaths at their sociable best may be amiable, outgoing, and often attractive people with a talent for living totally in the present, a trait that others often envy and admire. Free spirits and adventurers, psychopaths are often of normal intelligence or far above it. But although they are intelligent, they are usually sharp, clever, or shrewd rather than wise. Outstandingly self-centered, psychopaths tend to perceive those around them as objects rather than as "selves" with feelings and motives with which they can identify. They may become vexed and peeved, showing moods of spite, vanity, and self-pity, but they do not feel mature, wholehearted anger, true or consistent indignation, honest, solid grief, sustaining pride, deep joy, or genuine despair. Even in situations of great distress or misfortune, their emotional responses are not as expected; for they do not grieve as others grieve.[7]

In light of these definitions, let's discuss *Lady Susan*. In *A Rhetoric of Irony* Wayne Booth uses *Lady Susan* as one of two prime examples of dramatic irony, commenting that Jane Austen reveals Lady Susan's hypocritical nature in juxtaposed letters (Letter 2 contradicts the feelings she expresses in Letter 1, for instance). He says: "the basic dramatic irony that builds throughout the work toward Lady Susan's final unmasking needs no interpreter: the reader with his eyes open cannot lose his way."[8] Unquestionably, then, the reader recognizes Lady Susan's devious behavior. But I would like to bring out some specific places that clearly show the individual characteristics of the psychopath (or sociopath) in Lady Susan.

The first traits I cited in my discussion of the psychopath, using Cleckley's definition as my guide, can be seen in Lady Susan in the first few letters of the novelette: superficial charm, adequate intelligence, absence of anxiety, insincerity, lack of remorse or shame, antisocial behavior, and poor judgment. Lady Susan's first meeting with Catherine Vernon is notable for showing the heroine's superficial charm. "I was certainly not disposed to admire her," Mrs. Vernon writes to Lady De Courcy of Lady Susan, "tho' always hearing she was beautiful; but I cannot help feeling that she possesses an uncommon union of Symmetry, Brilliancy and Grace" (251). Thus, even though the astute Mrs. Vernon knows of her sister-in-law's faults, at least in part at this point, she cannot help but remark on her charisma. Articulate, persuasive, and charming, Lady Susan behaves well, leaving Mrs. Vernon to report her manners as "gentle, frank and even affectionate" (251). Yet, we know from the beginning that this "gentle, frank" lady has come to Churchill as a last resort, feeling no goodwill toward her hosts. Thus, not only do we see her superficial charm immediately but her insincerity and hypocrisy as well. In other words, Lady Susan feigns beliefs, feelings, or virtues she does not possess and behaves falsely and without sincerity. For she writes her friend Alicia Johnson that if there were another place in England open to her she should prefer it. She says: "Charles Vernon is my aversion, and I am afraid of his wife" (246). This insincere, deceptive woman, however, pretends to come with "affection."

That she shows adequate intelligence is too obvious to warrant a discussion; for the imaginative justifications she invents for her past behavior to change Reginald De Courcy's opinion of her undoubtedly reflect a sharp, crafty intelligence. And her absence of anxiety is pointedly brought forth in a number of places, but most notably in the beginning in Letter 2 as she speaks of the uproar she has caused in the Manwaring household. With no sign of anxiety, remorse, or regret, she tells Alicia that she has distinguished no one's attentions but those of Manwaring and, of course, those of Sir James Martin, but his only for her daughter's sake and then only to detach him from Miss Manwaring. In saying this, she adds the evidence of her antisocial behavior and poor judgment. For certainly, we cannot consider it socially proper or in good judgment to engage the affections, as Reginald De Courcy puts it, "of two Men who are neither of them at liberty to bestow them—and all this, without the charm of Youth" (248). Thus, we see Lady Susan almost immediately as a charming, intelligent, anxiety-free woman, whose crafty but hypocritical behavior storms forth shamelessly, without proper judgment and without regard for those she hurts. Though no longer young, as Reginald De Courcy points out, she cleverly utilizes her beauty and finely tuned charm to manipulate those around her.

The final traits I listed from Cleckley's description are: selfishness and egocentricity, lack of capacity for love, unemotional sexual behavior, lack of long-term life plans, and a rare occurrence of suicide attempts. We see Lady Susan's selfishness and egocentricity in almost everything she does. One fine example is her behavior in trying to prevent the Vernons' marriage in addition to preventing her husband from selling the family estate to his brother. She says: "Could Matters have been so arranged as to prevent the necessity of our leaving the Castle, could we have lived with Charles and kept him single, I should have been very far from persuading my husband to dispose of it elsewhere . . . " (249). She adds, speaking of the Vernons' marriage and subsequent abundance of children: "what benefit could have accrued to me from his purchasing Vernon?" (250). Transparently demonstrating her selfishness, she deems no act necessary that will not benefit her directly. Her egocentricity, moreover, causes her to think and act always with a view of herself as the center of all experience and keeps her from seeing the justice of her brother-in-law's purchasing Castle Vernon as well as his feelings in wishing to retain the family estate. She displays sensitivity only to her own feelings. Writing to Mrs. Johnson about the sale of the castle, she notes that "it was a trying circumstance," and adds, "and everybody ought to respect the delicacy of those feelings [her own], which could not endure that my Husband's Dignity should be lessened by his younger brother's having possession of the Family Estate" (249).

Lady Susan's capacity for love is unmistakably deficient. She shows no affection for her daughter. Insisting that Frederica marry a man whom she herself finds loathsome, she hopes to humiliate the young girl into submission by keeping her in school. She tells Mrs. Johnson: "School must be very humiliating to a girl of Frederica's age; and by the bye, you had better not invite her anymore on that account, as I wish her to find her situation as unpleasant as possible" (253). She also tells Alicia Johnson that Frederica is a stupid girl with nothing to recommend her. And upon discovering that her daughter has left school, Lady Susan is agitated, but Mrs. Vernon suspects no real feeling behind her exhibition, saying: "I am afraid of being ungenerous or I should say she talks *too* well to feel so very deeply" (267). Finally, when Mr. Vernon arrives with Frederica, Mrs. Vernon notes that although Lady Susan had previously been "shedding tears," she hardly speaks to her daughter, and when the young girl begins to cry, immediately whisks her off to another room. Mrs. Vernon concludes: "I am led to believe as heretofore that the former has no real Love for her daughter" (270). Not only does Lady Susan behave dismally toward Frederica, pushing her to marry the loathsome Sir James and expectantly relishing victory because of the young girl's suffering and humiliation at school, but she displays no love, no affection, no compassion, and no motherly concern for her daughter on her anguished arrival at the Vernons, thus, displaying classic psychopathic tendencies in her inability to love. Further, not only does Lady Susan fail to love Frederica but she also shows no signs of having loved her husband. The next question is, what about Manwaring?

In writing to Alicia about her feelings toward Reginald De Courcy, she explains that she cannot ever feel more than friendship for him, adding: "On *my* side, you may be sure of it's never being more, for if I were not already as much attached to another person as I can be to any one . . . " (258). We need go no further, for in that statement she discloses the proof of her inability to experience deep feelings—deep enough to be called love—even for Manwaring. She enjoys Manwaring, however, because he is handsome, polished, and flattering. She compares Reginald De Courcy to Manwaring, saying of Reginald: "He is less polished, less insinuating than Manwaring, and is comparatively deficient in the power of saying those delightful things which put one in good humour with oneself and all the world" (258). She favors Manwaring for his spirit and immorality which so resemble her own. A good match for her in these traits, he carries on a flirtation with the beautiful coquette in his own home before the notice of his own wife. But Lady Susan does not love Manwaring. He is only a man, enough like herself, to bring her amusement.

In considering Lady Susan's ability to engage in unemotional sexual behavior, we might recall that she married and had a child with a man she did not love. In addition, she repeats this behavior in ultimately marrying Sir James Martin, who she has always found "contemptibly weak" (245), thus continuing to show this ability.

That she has no long-term life plans is also evident. From Sir Reginald's letter to his son, we learn that Lady Susan not only previously neglected her husband while encouraging other men but that "her extravagance and dissipation were gross and notorious" (260). Now, having to a great extent squandered most of her fortune, she is without a home and yet unconcerned not only with

56

But she shall be punished; she shall have him.—
I have sent Charles to Town to make matters up if
he can, for I do not by any means want her here.
If Miss Summers will not keep her, you must find
me out another school, unless we can get her married
immediately. — Miss S. writes word that she could
not get the young Lady to assign any cause for her
extraordinary conduct, which confirms me in my own
private explanation of it. —

Frederica is too shy I think, & too much in
awe of me, to tell tales; but if the mildness of her
Uncle should get anything from her, I am not a-
fraid. I trust I shall be able to make my story
as good as his. — If I am vain of anything, it is of
my eloquence. Consideration & Esteem as surely follow
command of Language, as Admiration waits on Beauty.
And here I have opportunity enough for the exercise
of my Talent, as the chief of my time is spent in

Figure 21. "Letter 16: Lady Susan to Mrs. Johnson," from *Lady Susan*
(Lady Susan *MS; Courtesy Pierpont Morgan Library*)

conversation. Reginald is never easy unless we are
by ourselves, & when the weather is tolerable we pace
the Shrubbery for hours together. I like him on the
whole very well, he is clever & has a good deal to say,
but he is sometimes impertinent & troublesome.
There is a sort of ridiculous delicacy about him which
requires the fullest explanation of whatever he may
have heard to my disadvantage, & is never satisfied
till he thinks he has ascertained the beginning & end
of everything.

This is one sort of Love — but I confess
it does not particularly recommend itself to me.
I infinitely prefer the tender & liberal Spirit of
Manwaring, which impressed with the deepest conviction of my merit, is satisfied that whatever I
do must be right; & look with a degree of contempt on the inquisitive & doubting Fancies of that
Heart which seems always debating on the reason-
                                        : ableness

immediate plans but with the long years ahead as well. We find her in the process of living off friends and relatives, where she remains until she exhausts her last possibility and decides to marry Sir James.

The last item on Cleckley's list of psychopathic traits refers to the low incidence of suicide attempts in psychopaths. Would Lady Susan ever attempt suicide? Not likely. In her final letter to Alicia Johnson—with everything having gone against her wishes and all her schemes thwarted, with Reginald De Courcy angry with her and her friend Alicia forced to abandon their friendship, and with her plan for Frederica to marry Sir James as yet unfulfilled—she writes cheerfully to Mrs. Johnson that their friendship will remain unimpaired and they will unite again in happier times (after the death of Mr. Johnson), "meanwhile," she says, "[I] can safely assure you that I never was more at ease, or better satisfied with myself and everything about me, than at the present hour" (307).

That Lady Susan is unquestionably a sociopath according to Professor Wolman's list of characteristics is also easy to prove. She is overdemanding (demanding Frederica's marriage to a man neither she nor her daughter can tolerate); manipulative (amending Reginald De Courcy's view of both her past and present behavior by persuading him that a mistaken belief about his sister had guided her conduct in attempting to prevent the Vernons' marriage and convincing him of her devoted maternal love for Frederica as her only motive for arranging a marriage between her daughter and Sir James); and exploitative (exploiting the Vernons and Manwarings). In addition, she lies (to everyone but Alicia Johnson, and especially to Reginald De Courcy to elicit his good opinion); cheats (deciding immediately she has no intention of paying Frederica's school costs even before she places her with Miss Summers); justifies her dishonest behavior (in her explanations to Mrs. Johnson); and demonstrates insensitivity to the pain of others, especially Frederica.

Instead of understanding her daughter's reluctance to marry a man she loathes, Lady Susan sees herself as the injured party. She tells her friend Alicia: "She shall find that she has poured forth her tender Tale of Love in vain, and exposed herself forever to the contempt of the whole world, and the severest Resentment of her injured Mother" (282). She is also, of course, insensitive to the pain she causes Miss and Mrs. Manwaring through her flirtations with each lady's gentleman. In fact, she finally suggests to Mrs. Johnson that her friend might hasten Mrs. Manwaring's death by irritating her already violent feelings.

Moreover, Lady Susan never blames herself for anything that goes amiss in her life, but shifts the blame to those around her or calls bad luck the culprit. This is not to imply that she is self-deceived, however. For Lady Susan always knows her self and her feelings well, knows she acts a part when manipulating others to suit her own wishes, and not only knows she hurts others but feels justified in doing so to attain her own ends. But when her schemes fail, she accuses others because they have eluded her manipulations, refusing to cooperate. And thus she deems uncooperative people or unfortunate circumstances the cause of all her unfulfilled endeavors. In the episode of her life we are privy to witness, for instance, she is vexed with those who have thwarted her plans: Mr. Johnson for enlightening Reginald; Reginald for not standing by her and believing another of her fabrications; and Frederica for her uncooperativeness in refusing to marry Sir James. Lady Susan tells Mrs. Johnson in her final letter that she abhors Mr. Johnson, despises Reginald, does not care if Frederica whimpers and the Vernons storm, but she will insist on her daughter's marriage to Sir James. She says: "I regard them not. I am tired of submitting my will to the Caprices of others—of resigning my own Judgement in deference to those, to whom I owe no Duty, and for whom I feel no respect. I have given up too much—have been too easily worked on . . . " (308). Thus, although she is not self-deceived, understanding herself well, she does see things from her own viewpoint, with herself at the center of everything. Because everyone else is an "object" to her that she hopes to manipulate for her own purposes, she judges that she has given up too much if the "objects" fail to perform as she intends.

She not only blames others, however, but also perceives that her plans fail due to bad luck. For instance, Mrs. Manwaring's visit to Mr. Johnson, which immediately precedes Mr. De Courcy's entrance, is unfortunate. Alicia Johnson writes Lady Susan to explain the circumstances, saying: "She came to this house to entreat my Husband's interference, and before I could be aware of it, everything that you could wish to be concealed, was known to him. . . . All is by this time known to De Courcy, who is now alone with Mr. Johnson" (303). Upon receiving Mrs. Johnson's letter, Lady Susan responds: "How unlucky that you should have been from home" (303).

Although Lady Susan realizes her own immorality—though she would not label it so negatively—she never feels guilt, regret, or repentance when truths about her emerge to thwart her plans. Instead, she accuses others (the "objects" in her life) for circumventing her plans and/or unfortunate circumstances. Mrs. Manwaring's visit to Mr. Johnson would have instigated no problem, of course, if Lady Susan had not much to hide. But she sees only the ill-timed visit and subsequent disclosures as her enemies, instead of her own faulty behavior.

In our previous discussion of Lady Susan we covered many of the traits that Vernon W. Grant talks about in *The Menancing Stranger*: Lady Susan's attractiveness; her knack of living in the present as a "free spirit," an adventuress without responsibilities or long-term life plans which depend upon diligent, consistent, and ethical behavior; her intelligence; and her egocentricity. And in her lack of compassion for those around her, it is plain that she thinks of others as "selves" without feelings and motives with which she can identify—as "objects," in fact. The last trait, however, we have not discussed, that her vexation with others falls short of wholehearted anger as she is as incapable of deep anger as she is of love. In addition, she fails to feel consistent indignation, honest grief, sustaining pride, deep joy, or genuine despair. Mrs. Vernon's last letter to her mother reflects how easily Lady Susan springs back from disappointment. According to Catherine Vernon, Lady Susan, who has just left, had arrived "looking all chearfulness and good humour" (309), despite defeat of her two primary endeavors: to marry Reginald and to marry Frederica to Sir James.

She is only peeved, moreover, at having to break off her friendship with Alicia Johnson. And in response to Mrs. Johnson's letter in which Alicia reports the meeting between Reginald and Mr. Johnson where all is disclosed, Lady Susan only says: "This Eclaircissment is rather provoking" (303). Even in her argument with Mr. De Courcy about Frederica's marriage to Sir James, she maintains her calm while deeply provoked. She tells Alicia: "At length he left me, as deeply provoked as myself, and he shewed his anger *more*. I was quite cool, but he gave way to the most violent indignation" (282). Unable to feel emotions to any depth, she only becomes temporarily provoked, peeved, vexed, or irritated. In fact, she never experiences any depth in any of the normal human emotions.

Lady Susan, as a classic psychopath or sociopath, plays a game in life. If her schemes fail, she reassesses her options and moves on to an alternate game plan—in the instance we witness, to marrying Sir James. As readers, we realize that Lady Susan thwarts her own plans through her immoral behavior and lack of conscience. For when she chooses, she can act a part with precision, behaving as a normal human being, mimicking behavior she observes in others, and following accepted social rules. But her flaw is that she can only do this for a short time before her selfish tendencies break through, revealing her true nature to others. As a psychopath or sociopath who is unaffected by the injuries she inflicts, as we see in her heartless behavior toward Frederica and Miss and Mrs. Manwaring, she is less than fully human, missing an essential part of the normal personality—a conscience. What is more, the convincing facade of normalcy which hides her treacherous instincts makes her even more dangerous. For almost everyone around her, unsuspecting the truth at first, is at the mercy of her unscrupulous behavior. As a fictional creation, Lady Susan is not an ideal creature, however, or remote from reality. She is a well-documented type, a psychopath or sociopath, that exists among us at the rate, according to Remi J. Cadoret, of from 2.4% among small town dwellers to 3.1% among those living in inner suburbs and 5.7% of city inhabitants.[9]

Jane Austen's Lady Susan is highly credible as a psychopath or sociopath. As a beautiful, well-bred, charming, sexually alluring, intellectually vivacious woman, she enslaves almost any man she selects (her husband, Manwaring, Sir James, and temporarily, Reginald De Courcy). To achieve her ends, she behaves with utter disregard for others and with callous, cold-blooded, manipulative guile. Because, in addition, she feels no anxiety, remorse, or regret, she operates freely with an abundance of insincerity and hypocrisy, skillfully fabricating stories and feigning emotions without experiencing the usual accompanying self-reproach. Her selfishness and egocentricity often lead her to poor judgment and antisocial behavior, however, shown clearly in her response to her brother-in-law's wish to purchase Vernon Castle and her behavior at Langford. And Lady Susan has no capacity for love—not even maternal love. She justifies her actions towards others on the basis of her own inclinations, is able to behave sexually without emotion (often as one means to her ends), and never feels despondent or suicidal when all goes amiss, but immediately bounces back with a new game plan.

Lady Susan is a remarkable woman, defective as a moral human being, insensitive, entirely selfish, believing she is never at fault and laying the blame for aborted plans on unfortunate circumstances or uncooperative people in her life. And although her adventuress spirit, beauty, and cleverness make her potently attractive, she is more dangerous because of these traits which effectively conceal the evil human being lying beneath the lovely shell. Self-seeking, self-indulging, without a speck of compassion for others, and no hint of a conscience, she is malevolent at the very core of her being.

We may never know if Jane Austen conceived of Lady Susan based on any one character she knew in life, but we can be sure that the creature she presents in Lady Susan comes from the author's deep understanding of the many facets of the human personality.

Notes

1. A. Walton Litz, *Jane Austen: A Study of Her Artistic Development*, New York, 1965, p. 41.

2. Louis Kronenberger, *The Polished Surface: Essays in the Literature of Worldliness*, New York, 1969, p. 135.

3. Adolf Guggenbühl-Craig, *Eros on Crutches: Reflections on Psychopathy and Amorality*, trans. Gary V. Hartman, ed. Mary Helen Gray, Irving, Tex.,1980, p. 49.

4. Benjamin B. Wolman, *The Sociopathic Personality*, New York, 1987, p. 96.

5. Ibid., p. 42.

6. Ibid., pp. 42–43.

7. Vernon W. Grant, *The Menancing Stranger: A Primer on the Psychopath*, Oceanside, Calif., 1977, pp. 50–52.

8. Wayne C. Booth, *A Rhetoric of Irony*, Chicago, 1974, pp. 65–66.

9. Remi J. Cadoret, "Epidemiology of Antisocial Personality," *Unmasking the Psychopath: Antisocial Personality and Related Syndromes,* ed. William H. Reid, Darwin Dorr, John I. Walker, and Jack W. Bonner, III, New York, 1986, p.29.

Lady Susan: Sport or Cinderella?

Hugh McKellar

There is one glory of the sun, and another glory of the moon, and another glory of the stars; for one star differeth from another star in glory.

St. Paul employed this version of separate-but-equal in his attempt to explain the resurrection of the dead to the contentious Corinthians—who repaid his efforts by becoming, of all the fledgling churches he counseled, the only one to disintegrate completely. And I may accomplish no more than he by attempting to show that *Lady Susan* does not deserve out-of-hand dismissal merely because it offers readers a different kind of pleasure than Jane Austen's longer works.

Granted, it fits into the Austen canon no more neatly than Aesop's bat fit in with the birds or with the beasts who sent him packing when he tried to claim kin with them. It shares epistolary form with the juvenilia, but eschews the exaggeration which either distinguishes or dominates them. Unlike *The Watsons* or *Sanditon,* it satisfies Aristotle's requirement of having a beginning, a middle, and an end—though the ending necessarily reflects the disappearance of practically all the characters' original reasons for communicating by letter. Internal evidence for dating is thus frustrating if not contradictory, while external evidence is in scant supply.[1] Nowhere in her surviving letters does Jane Austen mention working on *Lady Susan,* let along submitting it to a publisher. We have only a fair copy innocent of a title, in her handwriting, on paper watermarked 1805—which could have lain for some time in the shop before she bought it, or in her desk before she used it.

At least nobody has sought, to my knowledge, to cut the Gordian knot by suggesting that Jane, in 1805 or thereafter, obligingly copied out a sequence of letters composed by Cassandra Senior or Junior. But if authorship could be attributed, even tentatively and erroneously, to some other member of that talented tribe, we would have to stop asking questions which have thus far proved fruitless anyhow, and grapple with the possibility that the little story is not trying to be *Emma* and failing, but trying to be something quite different— and succeeding.

Granted, anyone capable of transmuting the letters which allegedly comprised "First Impressions" into *Pride and Prejudice* could presumably have worked a similar miracle on *Lady Susan* had she wished. But we are the ones who wonder why she failed so to wish, and who assume that, having made the fair copy, she gave *Lady Susan* up for a bad job. Have we created a problem where she saw none? Did she leave *Lady Susan* alone because she thought it was all right in its way as it stood, or felt that extensive changes were less apt to improve it than to spoil it?

However she reasoned, one obvious consideration would deter her from sending it near a publisher: only by padding it till all the effect of its pace was ruined could she have produced the wherewithal for a volume bulky enough to persuade a potential purchaser of getting his money's worth, whereas it is a shade too long to fit into a single issue of a literary magazine.[2] What becomes of a script which is the wrong length for any medium within your reach, and yet too tightly knit for easy expansion or contraction? You investigate serial publication, or set about producing enough other material to make up a marketable volume; if you never get round to doing either, or if your relatives find it so hilarious that they make a pet of it and won't let it go, your story remains within your family circle.

This was, of course, the fate of *Lady Susan,* which reached the public as an appendix to J.E. Austen-Leigh's 1871 *Memoir.*[3] But who was likely to read the *Memoir* without some previous acquaintance with one or more of the six novels? And could any such reader easily have remained unaware of Thackeray's *Vanity Fair,* which had been selling well for two decades? How, then, could the first non-Austens to encounter Lady Susan help seeing her in terms of Becky Sharp? Readers enamored of Elizabeth Bennet, Emma Woodhouse, or Anne Elliot were unlikely to open their arms to Lady Susan, given their generation's concentration on character as opposed to craftsmanship. Neither was James Edward the biographer to dispel the impression that dear Aunt Jane once tried to depict a Bad Woman, but found the task so distasteful that she quit half way through. For the peace of mind of all concerned, Lady Susan had to be declared a cuckoo in the Austen nest, with her existence explicable only on the assumption that her creator had not yet put away childish things.

Might we, whose professed standards for female conduct diverge from those of Queen Victoria—who was yearning about 1871 to horsewhip Bertrand Russell's mother for proposing that women should vote—entertain the possibil-

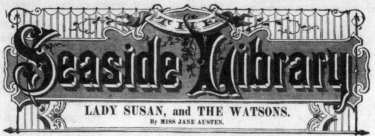

The Seaside Library

LADY SUSAN, and THE WATSONS.
By MISS JANE AUSTEN.

This Number contains two Complete Stories, Unchanged and Unabridged.

Vol. LXV.   SINGLE NUMBER.   GEORGE MUNRO, PUBLISHER, Nos. 17 to 27 Vandewater Street, New York.   PRICE 10 CENTS.   No. 1313

The Seaside Library, Issued Daily.—By Subscription, $36 per annum.
Copyrighted 1882, by George Munro.—Entered at the Post office at New York at Second Class Rates.—August 7, 1882.

LADY SUSAN,
AND
THE WATSONS.

By MISS JANE AUSTEN.

JANE AUSTEN.

NEW YORK:
GEORGE MUNRO, PUBLISHER,
17 to 27 VANDEWATER STREET.

Figure 22.   Title Page to the First American Edition of *Lady Susan* and
The Watsons
(*From The Seaside Library; Courtesy the Library of Congress*)

ity that *Lady Susan* is vintage Jane Austen, even if an unfrequented corner of her vineyard produced its grapes?

Whereas affection may ripen quickly or slowly, a flirtation can go on for only so long before the principals decide to move either closer together or farther apart. Even if they are able and inclined to learn from experience, they have hardly time to make or digest many significant discoveries about themselves or the world around them. Hence the chronicle of a flirtation, which is all *Lady Susan* pretends to be, must concentrate on what the characters do, rather than on what they are or become—on their deployment of the personal resources they already have rather than on their development of new ones.

While Jane Austen continued to create static characters, in the novels she uses them somewhat like fixed stars against whose predictability we can measure the personality changes in the characters she obviously likes.[4] Fascination with the possibilities of contrapuntal interplay between static and dynamic characters could easily have inclined her to leave *Lady Susan* alone; any development in the characters, even if the time span allowed of it, would endanger completion of the plot, which is the story's mainstay. Frederica and Reginald are young enough and bright enough to grow in understanding, but, if they do, they may not yield to the manipulations of Catherine Vernon and her mother as readily as they did to those of Lady Susan. Thus Jane Austen had cause to feel about these brain-children much as Pope Pius VII later did about the Jesuits: "*Aut sint ut sunt aut non sint* (Let them be as they are or else not at all)."

Novels-in-letters were assuredly more popular in the eighteenth century than they have been since; but abandonment of an unfashionable form does not automatically entail artistic advance, if that form will effectively accommodate what one wants to say. The juvenilia show Jane Austen displaying the weaknesses of epistolary form: a letter written to fill up the sender's time and directed to an acquaintance with small reason to care about its content is bound to seem artificial.[5] *Lady Susan* demonstrates that she also learned the form's strengths: each of its letters has a specific purpose. The sender always has information which the recipient wants or needs (even if a good deal of emotional unburdening is mixed in), and the postal service provides the most efficient available way of conveying it.

Since almost every letter is addressed to a relative or close friend of long standing, economy of expression can be achieved on two fronts. No one has to waste time and energy on constructing, or on penetrating, facades; these people can spell out what they think and intend. Neither does any writer drag in by the hair, for readers' benefit, masses of information which the recipient could hardly help having already. We accumulate as much background knowledge as we need to follow the plot, but we are deemed intelligent and alert enough to pick up and fit together scattered details mentioned in passing by various writers. For example, Catherine Vernon tells her mother that Lady Susan can use financial help; Sir Reginald recalls hearing of her "extravagance and dissipation"; and eventually she reveals that her husband had to sell his estate, though she prevented its purchase by his younger brother. Thus we deduce, without realizing quite how, that her money problems are of her own making. This fabric of information is woven so carefully that if you try to rearrange the details, casually strewn though they look, you start the whole thing raveling. The texture is as tight as the time frame, and yet nothing seems strained or implausible. Epistolary form may have worked in "First Impressions" or "Elinor and Marianne" no better than it does in much of the juvenilia; but, having made it work superbly here, Jane Austen apparently heeded the adage, "If it ain't broke, don't fix it."[6] Perhaps she thought of it as a mere exercise, treading the path laid down by Richardson, Smollett, and Fanny Burney, but no less capable of giving pleasure than that high-spirited derivative sequence by another brilliant teenager, Felix Mendelssohn, who undertook to enhance with music an amateur production of *A Midsummer Night's Dream*. Having elected to march for once to the beat of a different drummer than usual, she walked tall.

I am by no means championing *Lady Susan* at the expense of the six novels, any more than I would advise music lovers to eschew *Fidelio* and the *Choral Symphony* and embrace the arrangements of Scottish folksongs and German peasant dances which Beethoven made from time to time. But when a major creative artist descends from the mountain tops where hardly anyone else can tread with assurance to the more thickly populated tablelands, s/he still manages to beat most of the smaller-scale practitioners at their own game; Beethoven's folk-tune arrangements are more satisfying than most other people's. And we, as readers and listeners, occasionally lack the energy to accord to great art the response which we can usually give, and which we know it deserves; at such times, minor works absorb all the appreciation we can muster, and give us as much enjoyment as we can take until we are once again hitting on all cylinders. We hurt only ourselves by "despising the day of small things."

Yet such "small things" as *Lady Susan* may arouse in us a kind of disquiet unknown to Jane Austen's first readers. They lacked the technical means to render many aspects of the world around them predictable and controllable, although they imposed order where they could: their intricate system of social stratification provided ready-made guidance for any two people meeting for the first time and uncertain how to behave towards each other. But they had barely begun to standardize production of consumer goods, or of occupational roles; hence they did not expect consistency in either things or people to anything like the extent that we do,[7] simply because most of the time we get it. They were no less fond of neat pigeonholing than are we, but were able to apply it to far fewer areas.

Only as machines became more reliable, and the use of their standardized products more widespread, could the notion develop that human beings, including writers, might well become similarly predictable, at least in regard to what they offer the public: people have a right to know what they can expect from you, and to complain if they get something different. However well this principle may work in a society whose members regard it as axiomatic, it becomes rather awkward when applied retroactively; practically any page of the British Library's *Catalogue of Printed Books* will feature at least one writer who stepped into one furrow and stayed there, as well as one whose range of subject matter is wide enough to make us label him a popularizer or a dilettante. For we have grown more suspicious than our ancestors of a person who seeks, let alone achieves and displays, competence in a field unconnected with his livelihood; if he were a solid citizen who truly meant business, he would surely keep his nose to his chosen grindstone. And that grindstone may be even genre fiction: Agatha Christie kept faith with her legions of admirers not only by retaining for her detective stories the surname of a husband whom she shed in short order, but also by publishing under the name of "Mary Westmacott" the romances she occasionally felt like writing.[8] Having trained her readers to count on "a new Christie for Christmas," she forbore to tax their little gray cells by making them change over, during her long and happy second marriage, to "a Mallowan for midsummer"; when they asked for "a Christie," they got the superbly plotted thriller they expected. Lest they feel cheated, she never used her fame to palm off on them a romance, even though her heroines are more diligent and single-minded in pursuit of their quarry than either Poirot or Miss Marple. Despite full awareness that Jane Austen had nothing to do with the publication of *Lady Susan* as we have it, do we still feel somehow entitled to Christie's kind of fair warning that, for once, we cannot expect a story of the maturing of a young woman faced with a moral choice?

And have we come, by way of "Mary Westmacott's" young huntresses, back to Lady Susan Vernon, who can hardly be trusted to recognize a moral choice if she saw one, or at least to admit it?

Admittedly, she likes attention and admiration from men—a taste, however reprehensible, prevalent among some two billion of the planet's current inhabitants. But does she like men, or does she need for herself all the liking of which she is capable? Is she, perhaps, a charter member of the company of Austen solipsists headed by Lady Bertram and Mr. Woodhouse? Like them, she intends no harm to other people, who simply do not register on her consciousness strongly enough to resent; like them, she takes for granted that any demands she makes on others will be met, as most of the time they indeed are, without her having any need to reciprocate. But she cannot be as indolent as they, for staying home with Pug or Mr. Perry would appall her; no more than Sir Walter Elliot can she manage without an audience. He requires constant reassurance that his looks, and she that her charms of face and tongue, have lasted better than anyone else's; but whereas he can afford to maintain Mrs. Clay as resident reassurer, she has to make do with Manwaring, or whatever personable man comes within reach.

And still the people around her take fright, perhaps less at what she actually does than at the feelings they project onto her from within themselves. Invariably, she wreaks less havoc than lies within her power; are the onlookers dimly but uncomfortably aware that they, if possessed of such power, might exercise less restraint?

Reginald could save himself and his family much worry by remembering how he characterized her before they ever met: "the most accomplished Coquette in England. As a very distinguished Flirt, I have always been taught to consider her" (248). Unwittingly, he came close to specifying the category whose championship she wanted; having won it, she has but to defend her title, for she shares the sentiments if not the poetic proclivities of Muhammad Ali.[9] She need not even, except to Alicia, exult, "I'm the greatest," for she has taken good care to maintain a base from which she can put her specialized skills on public display whenever she pleases. Her first husband was too "milky," as she puts it, and her second is too silly, to bring her to heel as Mr. Johnson can do with Alicia. Even while acknowledging the expediency of Alicia's counsel to marry Reginald if possible, she parries it, explaining that "dependence on the caprice of Sir Reginald would not suit the freedom of my spirit" (299). She speaks often of wanting "dominion" over Reginald's will, but not over his inheritance—or his body.

If Sir Reginald, who reminds his son of "her neglect of her husband, her encouragement of other Men," had heard so much as a rumor of infidelity on her part, could he forbear to mention it? His daughter apprehends no danger to Charles Vernon; and not even Alicia contemplates Lady Susan's eloping with Manwaring, although he has accepted "dominion" to the point of believing that whatever she does is right. All available evidence thus suggests that the most she wants from any man is docility; but such a voluntary limitation of objectives is beyond the comprehension of Mrs. Manwaring—and perhaps of many readers in our own day.

We have heard so much, during the past quarter-century, about men's tendency to regard women as possessions that we can easily fail to appreciate how prevalent the reverse situation has been in the past, to say nothing of the present. If ownership and property rights obsess all the people you know, will you not likewise grasp, and cling to tenaciously, whatever your society allows you to hold? As the law of England stood throughout Jane Austen's lifetime, the marriage ceremony effectively transferred any money or real estate a bride might have into her husband's control; however affluently she walked into church, she walked out a pauper. (Ironically, the law of czarist Russia, from 1649 on, protected the assets a woman brought into a marriage—although, since the vast majority of Russians, female or male, owned precious little at any stage of their careers, its benefits were hardly widespread.) To what, then, could she claim clear title, if not to her husband—even "a poor thing, sir, but mine own"? Nor, despite passage of the Married Women's Property Act, had attitudes changed appreciably by 1871—and perhaps less than could be wished by 1971.

Hence readers are well equipped to understand the attitude of Alicia, who displays about as much affection for Mr. Johnson as does Charlotte Lucas for Mr. Collins ("But still he would be her husband" [*PP*, 122]), and advises Lady Susan to annex Reginald while she can, much as Charlotte says of Jane Bennet, "When she is secure of [Bingley], there will be leisure for falling in love as much as she chooses" (*PP*, 22). They can see what motivates Mrs. Manwaring: although Mr. Johnson washed his hands of her when she insisted on marrying a man of whom he disapproved, she appeals to him to make Lady Susan stop trespassing on her turf, confident that he will rally to the defense of her property rights if not of her happiness. (Of course, if her defiant marriage jeopardized her prospects of an eventual inheritance from Mr. Johnson, and Manwaring was imprudent enough to take her on anyhow, other manifestations of his lack of wisdom are only to be expected.) She seems to feel that any failure of hers to hang onto a husband, unsatisfactory though he may be, will reflect on her guardian as well as on herself—somewhat as Sir Thomas Bertram feels responsible for Tom's extravagance.

But what are we to make of Lady Susan, who reveals no wish either to be owned by a man, or to own one? Does she, by any chance, exemplify the degree of autonomy which women are now supposed to strive towards achieving, but which actually scares most people, regardless of gender, out of their wits?

Queen Victoria, during her state visit to Paris in 1855, quite intentionally reduced her hostess, the Empress Eugénie, to quivering jelly. Eugénie, whose youth had been spent in poverty, was shaken to the core by noticing that the Queen, when she went to sit down, never looked round to make sure that her chair was in place, because she had no experience of chairs not being exactly where she wanted them. Such complete confidence, wailed Eugénie, was beyond her, and would remain so; but it is not, as regards men if not chairs, beyond Lady Susan. She need not look round for a deferential man, because in her experience one or another has always been there. Since most people's sense of security is closer to Eugénie's than to Queen Victoria's, an encounter with total assurance, even in a fictional character, can easily unnerve them.

And perhaps Lady Susan, rather like Henry Higgins in *Pygmalion*, has never concerned herself with other people enough to realize that emotional connection matters far more to most of them than it does to her. Though preferring her daughter's room to her company, she has contrived, without benefit of military training, to assert her authority over Frederica quite as firmly as General

Tilney does over Eleanor, and she tries as hard as she might with an unwanted kitten to find her a good home. Why should Sir James Martin, if he can be brought to do her bidding, not become Frederica's meal ticket instead of Miss Manwaring's—indeed, what else is he good for? She can barely imagine, let alone empathize with, the impotent fury of Miss Manwaring at seeing her hopes of an establishment, and her chance at a title, vanishing in the wake of an older woman who has borne all her life a title which she cannot lose. (For her Christian name, rather than her maiden or married surname, to follow her title directly, her father must have been at least an earl—a distinction she shares only with Lady Catherine de Bourgh and Lady Anne Darcy, who likewise kept her title after marrying a man who had none.) As for Frederica, what should she want or expect beyond food, clothing, and shelter, seeing how great a catch she isn't?

Lady Susan shares also the confidence, not entirely misplaced, of Lady Catherine and Emma that they can arrange other people's lives better than the recipients of their attention could do for themselves; but while her manipulations resemble Emma's, she grows as angry as Lady Catherine when people presume to deviate from the script which she has prepared for, if not shared with, them. How dare Sir James visit Churchill except at her behest? How dare Frederica not only appeal to Reginald for help, but make her liking for him obvious? Inconveniencing Lady Susan, or pointing out the limitations of her "dominion," cries out for condign punishment. Even Alicia prefaces her announcement that their correspondence must end with a plea that Lady Susan will not be angry with her for what is clearly Mr. Johnson's fault.[10]

Do we manifest that same tendency when we reproach Jane Austen for not bringing *Lady Susan* into line with the expectations her longer novels have aroused in us? Since she, for whatever reason, made no effort to bring this book before the public, we are in a way eavesdroppers, and must risk being surprised or displeased by what we were not supposed to hear. Probably the finale of Alicia's valediction expresses the attitude we might best adopt: "I dare say you did all for the best, & there is no defying Destiny."

Notes

1. In the first edition of *Lady Susan* that R.W. Chapman prepared for Oxford University Press (1925), he put its date at "about 1805"; in *The Works of Jane Austen*, vol. VI, *Minor Works*, London, 1954, rev. 1975, Brian Southam prefaces *Lady Susan* with his reasons for believing that it was written between 1793 and 1795. Since the sole extant manuscript cannot reveal how many predecessors it had, neither eminent scholar may be entirely mistaken.

2. *Lady Susan* did make its American debut in a periodical, albeit an unusual one: *The Seaside Library* 65:1313, New York (1882), carried it (pp. 3–13) along with *The Watsons*. See David Gilson, *A Bibliography of Jane Austen*, Oxford, 1982, p. 370, item F1.

3. Though omitted from the *Memoir*'s first edition (1870), it appeared the next year in the second edition, whose spine was lettered, "Lady Susan." See Gilson, *A Bibliography,* p. 495, item M130.

4. For example, the movement of Elizabeth Bennet's viewpoint towards congruence with Darcy's becomes traceable as, after her return from Kent, she finds her mother's behavior increasingly hard to bear, although Mrs. Bennet had displayed no better judgment the previous autumn. Similarly, readers sense more quickly than Mary Crawford that her appeal to Fanny Price to regard Henry's flight with Maria Rushworth as forgivable will be futile, because Fanny's self-confidence and moral standards have been rising, whereas Mary's have at best stood still.

5. Notably "Letter the Ninth" of "Lesley Castle," which Mrs. Marlowe laboriously composes merely to keep her promise to the depressed girl into whose company she had been thrown at Bristol.

6. In the column she published during March 1988 to mark the thirty-first anniversary of her syndication, Ann Landers claimed credit for enriching the language with this admonition.

7. No one, apparently, thought worse of Henry Austen for successively taking up three unrelated occupations; perhaps, in an age when parents often chose occupations for their children, drastic career changes were only to be expected. Unless the consistency and predictability of mass-produced articles had come to be quickly and generally appreciated, William Morris and John Ruskin would hardly have troubled to inveigh as fervently as they did against uniform machine-made goods.

8. *Giant's Bread* (1930); *Unfinished Portrait* (1934); *Absent in the Spring* (1944); *The Rose and the Yew Tree* (1947); *A Daughter Is a Daughter* (1952); *The Burden* (1956).

9. In case Jane Austen's fame outlasts the renown of this gentleman (b. 1942), posterity may care to know that as Cassius Clay, he won the world heavyweight boxing championship in 1964, only to be stripped of his title in 1967, allegedly for refusing induction into the American army—though neither his change of name on becoming a Black Muslim or his habit of taunting would-be challengers in distinctly unsportsmanlike verse had gained him much sympathy. After the U.S. Supreme Court ruled in 1971 that he had been unjustly deprived of his title, he regained it in 1974 and held it, except for a few months, until he retired in 1979. His autobiography (with Richard Durham), *The Greatest: My Own Story,* New York, 1975, displays modesty and tact comparable to Lady Catherine de Bourgh's.

10. See *Lady Susan,* Letter 38, opening paragraph.

Jane Austen's Epistolary Fiction

Susan Pepper Robbins

Jane Austen began her career as an epistolary novelist, but by the mid-1790s she had broken away from that eighteenth-century form of narrative in letters to speak in the voice that carries her heroines to the last chapters where one—Anne Elliot—is seen writing a letter to Captain Wentworth who is only across the crowded room.

For Austen, letters could present the world of the good parent and ordered community. Her earliest fictions—"Frederic & Elfrida," "Henry and Eliza," "A Tour through Wales—in a Letter from a Young Lady—," "Evelyn," and "Catharine, or The Bower"—use the epistolary form in essentially the same ways Samuel Richardson and Henry Fielding had. This kind of letter narrative is an eighteenth-century form which presents a world of stable parents whose children must grow up. In Austen's mature work, however, the letter is embedded in the narrative voice and functions in a different, nineteenth-century way to present a world of weak parents who have nerves, eat carefully, avoid drafts, depend on tall mirrors and The Baronetage. These weak parents rely entirely on their children for moral support.

Austen's view of social and family order changed. After 1794, the families in her stories have greater difficulties, and ones that could not be represented in letters. We are told in *Emma*, "Nobody, who has not been in the interior of a family, can say what the difficulties of an individual of that family may be" (146).

The family structure which is based on superior children like Elizabeth Bennet, who minister to parents, is not found in Austen's earliest epistolary fiction. Those early parents in the epistolary works like "Edgar & Emma" are "guided by Prudence & regulated by discretion" (30). Austen's technical genius is obvious when we study "Love and Freindship," written entirely in letters in 1790, and *Lady Susan* which was begun in letters in 1793, but concluded abruptly in a narrative voice in 1794. Austen abandons letters, a mode of narration which does not accommodate her changing view of the world and develops a mode that does—novels with embedded letters.

The seven years between the epistolary "Love and Freindship" and the revision of the epistolary "Elinor and Marianne" into the narrated *Sense and Sensibility* were the years when Jane Austen was finding and establishing her method of telling a story with letters embedded in it, a story wherein "the child is the father to the man." In *Sense and Sensibility,* a mother is described as "the most rapacious of human beings . . . the most credulous; her demands are exorbitant" (120); and in the later *Mansfield Park,* we hear of the mother who thinks "more of her pug than her children." Children, also, are different from their early portraits in Austen; indeed, Catherine Morland rebels against sex-roles imposed on girls' play. She was "fond of all boys' play, and greatly preferred cricket to . . . dolls" (*NA,* 13). In this "new" kind of story of new kinds of children and parents, Austen like her contemporaries in poetry, Wordsworth, Coleridge, Byron, Keats, and Shelley, accomplished a revolution in form. After her, there are no great epistolary novelists; Trollope in *Dr. Thorne* looks back with nostalgia at the novel of letters: "There is a mode of novel-writing which used to be much in vogue, but which has now gone out of fashion" (chapter 38). If we examine Jane Austen's early years of writing, the 1790s, we can see why she closed the curtains on the epistolary novel.

The parents in Austen's major novels are best remembered for their failings: the Bennets' sharing of only one true mind between them, and that one flawed by cynicism; Mr. Woodhouse's small concerns with drafts from open windows and light suppers; Mr. Price's inebriated "Saturday condition"; Sir Walter Elliot's dependence on tall mirrors. The children of these parents, however, are remembered for their sparkling intelligence, cleverness, sober virtue, and self-effacement. This family structure in which children are superior and minister to their parents is not found in Austen's earliest fiction. There, she creates wise and protective parents who are cursed with stupid and ungrateful progeny. The early parents are "very sensible people" like Sir Godfrey and Lady Marlow (*EE,* 30). Austen associated the world of the good parent and its implications of community order with epistolary fiction. When she began to alter the nature of the families in her fiction in the period of the late juvenilia (1793–97),[1] she discarded the documentary function of the letter found in traditional epistolary fictions and developed new functions for letters as literary devices embedded in narration. Although Jane Austen never published a novel written in letters, the epistolary fiction of the eighteenth century was the point of departure for her writing career, and much of her juvenilia is epistolary. During the last decade of that century, she rejected the "pure" epistolary novel for the novel that incorporates letters whose function is the presentation of the "new" family where the child is father to the man or, in Austen's case, a daughter is both mother and father to the whole family.

By 1797, Austen had completed her career as an epistolary novelist. "Love and Freindship," written entirely in letters during the "middle" period of the juvenilia was finished around 1790. Although she later copied it into a note-book, *Volume the Second,* she never revised it.[2] She must have felt satisfied with it or felt that it could not be reworked or translated out of its epistolary casting. However, two other epistolary compositions of this decade were later reworked into the narrated *Sense and Sensibility* and *Pride and Prejudice.* It is very helpful to examine the break in *Lady Susan* from letters to narrative to understand Austen's sensitivity to form. Austen accomplished a revolution in the form of the novel and the function of the letter as a narrative device by transforming the traditions she had inherited from eighteenth-century novelists. This is not to say that there had never been narratives that included letters before 1797. Her own early narratives had letters. In *Tristram Shandy,* Walter Shandy writes to his brother Toby to explain the mysteries of women. What Austen did was change the function of the letter from an eighteenth-century "effective document," a sign of the ordered community, fixed character and stable family to a nineteenth-century device of "affective gesture" wherein changes in social structures are reflected.

What I mean when I say letters are "effective" is that they document a world where parents are the source of goodness and value, a world where communication is possible from point A to other points. In the narrated "Frederic & Elfrida," one of the early juvenilia written between 1787 and 1790, the wisdom of Elfrida's parents gives structure and stability to the tale. One letter appears in the story: Elfrida commissions her friend Charlotte to buy a bonnet to suit her complexion. The narrator tells us that Charlotte "brought her Freind the wished-for Bonnet, & so ended this little adventure, much to the satisfaction of all parties" (4–5). The narrator's closure—"so ended this little adventure, much to the satisfaction of all parties"—confirms the "effectiveness" of the letter. Its function is to document request-compliance in a stable commu-nity. Communication is an unquestioned and given verity of the social group.

Another short narrative of the juvenilia, "Henry and Eliza," demonstrates the compatibility of the world of the good parent and the effective function of the letter. Eliza writes a letter to her patroness that documents the new situation in the plot in a summarily lucid way: "Madame, We are married and gone" (36). At the end of the story, Eliza is rescued by people who reveal themselves to be her real parents and whose generosity she had repaid by stealing 50 pounds. In the very short epistolary story, "Amelia Webster," seven letters bring about marriages; here in the juvenilia, letters and social order are in perfect harmony.

In the late juvenilia, we begin to see the crisis in family order that will be fully presented in the mature fiction. There is an accompanying crisis in the epistolary form. Parents desert their children, or they are mean to them. A mother divides a pair of slippers between her daughters in "A Tour through Wales—in a Letter from a Young Lady—." Louisa Lesley in "Lesley Castle" is an adulteress who "wantonly disgraced the Maternal Character" (110). Her neglected daughter is a forerunner of the wunderkinder of the later novels— "Just turned two years old; as handsome as tho' 2 and 40" (111). Sir George Lesley, the patriarch of the castle, "still remains the Beau, the flighty stripling, the gay lad, and sprightly Youngster that his Son really was about five years back, and that he has affected to appear ever since," as his daughter writes. It is significant that "Leslie Castle" which Austen began writing in letters was left unfinished. Southam rightly says that as a "whole, the work lacks unity" (32). We can conclude that for Austen the epistolary form could not give shape to the world of irresponsible parents and shaken community order where fathers act like striplings.

In "Evelyn" of the same period, parental generosity and sibling loyalty are ridiculed. The four letters embedded in the narrative function describe the confusion in the family; the letters are "ineffective." Their function is not to bring about resolutions because the relationships they seem to represent do not exist, except as shams. For instance, the hero writes to his first wife's parents to tell them that their daughter is dead. He assures them in the same letter that he is happy with his new wife. They answer in a letter, thanking him for his "unexampled generosity in writing to condole us on the late unhappy accident" (191) and enclose 30 pounds as a wedding gift. Only 10 days have passed since their daughter's death. When family loyalties and, by extension community ties, break down letters cannot be effective. Letters depend on the assumption of a stable world of honored family relationships.

Another piece of late juvenilia has for its heroine an orphan who finds the letters from her best friends (orphans too) "always unsatisfactory." Here in "Catharine, or The Bower," family and community are threatening. The isolated bower is the only safe place in such a world. "Solitude & reflection: are the only restoratives Catharine seeks. The only subjects suited to correspondence are trivia like a "bonnet & pelisse."

For Richardson and other eighteenth-century authors, verisimilitude and the imitation of Nature were the great duties of art; their task, as Dr. Johnson described in *Rambler* 4, was to engage "in portraits of which every one knows the original, and can detect any deviation from exactness of resemblance." Writers were "just copiers of human manners." Other standards for art, however, replaced imitation, and Austen's shift from letters to narratives reflects the profound revolutions that were reshaping the minds and lives of men and women. In short, her change in form is—to use M.H. Abrams's title—from the letter or "mirror" to the voice of the guiding narrator, the "lamp."

Austen's debt to Samuel Richardson is well known; her knowledge of his works was "probably such as no one is likely again to acquire."[3] She knew that Clarissa's letters were documents in the case against Lovelace. As John Preston says of the letters in Richardson, "They do not refer to a situation, they *are* the situation.[4]

To find the Emma behind the dangerously witty and articulate Miss Woodhouse is the new realm Jane Austen explores. She does not write, after the juvenilia, in what Geoffrey Tillotson describes as the general mind of the eighteenth century which believes "that what is real and important is what is public and 'normal' rather than private and singular."[5] Richardson in the preface to his *Familiar Letters on Important Occasions* defines the letter as a formal model of other social interactions; in his words, he intended the letters as "rules to think and act by as well as forms to write after."[6] In Austen, letters do not function as public vehicles, as rules or models. For her, the letter included in the novels is an instrument to help present the disruption of social and family order. Austen wants to tell the story of the reinterpretation by the private consciousness of that disorder.

Why did Jane Austen revise her epistolary novels—"First Impressions" into *Pride and Prejudice* and "Elinor and Marianne" into *Sense and Sensibility*? It is not going too far to say that Austen evolves a new literary genre in the sense that E.D. Hirsch defines: "When an author evolves a new literary genre . . . he not only extends existing conventions but combines old convention systems in a new way."[7] Wolfgang Iser, who discusses the new genres created at the end of the eighteenth century, bypasses Austen's achievement, skipping from Smollett to Scott.[8] Ian Watt pays tribute to Austen's "technical genius" which combined the realism of presentation—the letter—and the realism of assessment— the wise narrator. These two "realisms" were the narrative problems to which Richardson and Fielding had only partial answers. By embedding letters in her narratives, she merged the presentational and assessing perspectives. In fact, she mixed the genres of the epistolary novel and the narrated novel so finally and brilliantly that the novel in letters was made, after 1800, an archaic genre to which authors such as Henry James could only whimsically return.

Lady Susan begins as an epistolary novel as I have said, but ends as a narrated one. The interruption of the correspondence by the voice of a narrator makes *Lady Susan* most important in a discussion of the incompatibilities of the novel in letters and Austen's emerging themes of the threatened and developing self and family in an increasingly unstable society—however wonderfully stable it seems to us today! The differences between the use of the letters in "Love and Freindship" and the function of letters in *Lady Susan* demonstrate the change in Austen's vision.

In "Love and Freindship," the epistolary structure is successful because the violence of the plot never, for all its stagey virulence (kidnappings, chases, thefts, elopements, deaths), disrupts social order. The letters are effective documents of all that they describe; furthermore, they direct the violence toward positive community ends. Their function is public: the education and protection of the young person. However, in *Lady Susan,* the letters do not direct or control the new kind of violence with which Austen is dealing, a violence Southam defines as "the disruption of personal and family relationships" (47). The epistolary structure is not a congenial medium for such violence, the violence Austen was hearing about as she wrote *Lady Susan,* the Reign of Terror under Robespierre in which her cousin's husband was executed.[9]

In "Love and Freindship," parents represent at least some semblance of a moral order which contains and controls the excesses of the young people, Laura and Sophia. In *Lady Susan,* however, collapse is inevitable—and the abandoned letter narrative reflects this collapse. Parental order at the center of this work is deeply disturbed. Lloyd K. Brown defines the dilemma this way: "On the one hand, Lady Susan's selfish vitalism thrusts against the established norms of moral conduct. Yet, on the other, the moral is threatened from within by its putative champions," the Vernons.[10] Supposedly concerned for their niece Frederica, the Vernons are motivated by a prurient voyeurism as they watch the girl suffer in their own home. Lady Susan calls her daughter a "devil." The protective parent and trust in the family are the norms Austen sets her parody of sentimentality against in "Love and Freindship." In response to Isabel's request to write to her daughter Marianne, Laura writes 15 letters giving a "regular detail of [her] Misfortunes and Adventures" (76). Isabel intends Laura's letters to be a "useful lesson" to young Marianne. We can hear in Isabel's first letter the controlling comic note of the good parent. This letter reverses Laura's pompous and sentimental foolishness. Isabel, the wise parent, can risk having the outrageous Laura write to her daughter because she is perfectly confident of her own parental authority and strength. Isabel appeals to Laura's infatuation with her own suffering and deflates it slyly. "You are this day 55. If a woman may ever be said to be in safety from the determined Perseverance of disagreable Lovers and the cruel Persecutions of obstinate Fathers, surely it must be at such a time of Life" (77). In the penultimate letter, we hear the unspoken maternal intentions of Isabel under the loud assertions of Laura's sanctimony: "faultless as my Conduct had certainly been during the whole Course of my late Misfortunes and Adventures, [your mother] pretended to find fault with my Behaviour in many of the situations in which I had been placed" (104). Obviously, the mother is right to find fault with Laura, and she knows that Laura's letters will expose the faults to young Marianne. The protective mother puts all the misfortunes and excesses to educational purpose when she asks Laura to write letters giving a regular detail of her life. Thus, all chance, misfortune, and misdirection are turned to direction and instruction for the child in good eighteenth-century fashion.

All the parents in "Love and Freindship" are morally superior to their children. Austen ridicules the rebellions of the young, and her parody reduces their rebellions to irrational antics. Brissenden makes this point: "Jane Austen's loving couples are absurd because they defy and disobey their parents *when there is no need to*" (132). All the violence in the story is contained and controlled within the hierarchical structure of the family. The letters as educators maintain and transfer this order. Parents are wiser than children; children rely on them for their education as well as "those very significant supports of Victuals and Drink." Young Edward says as he steps into his father's carriage to escape his "domination," "It is my greatest boast that I have incurred the Displeasure of my Father!" (85). Laura's misfortunes are settled at last, and she lives on a pension handed down through the orderly ranks of family. She never reinterprets her past as Anne Elliot will so painstakingly do in *Persuasion*.

The violence in *Lady Susan* cannot be converted to good purpose as it was in "Love and Freindship." Here the family can not absorb the threats to its stability, nor can the letters reshape the chaos into education as they do in the earlier work. The epistolary form of the novel is truncated—the letters halt, and a narrator affixes a conclusion to them. Whereas the parents in the epistolary story had provided everything for the children, even the carriages for them to run away in, in *Lady Susan,* the parents provide nothing except bad examples and anguish for their children. Austen had evidently begun to feel in the three years between the two works that the epistolary novel was not suited to the world of revolution, where power was seized and the old moral orders violated by individuals like Lady Susan. It is the narrating voice that concludes the story of Lady Susan and her daughter that brings to rest all the havoc caused by the wicked parent. This voice is the formal replacement of the lost ordering of the world represented in the good parent and the letters that documented such a stable world.

There is familial confusion from the beginning of *Lady Susan*. Enmity exists between the Vernons and Lady Susan. Her visit almost destroys the Manwaring marriage. "The whole family are at war" (245). Lady Susan sees her daughter as little as possible and calls her "the torment of my life," and "that horrid girl of mine." Mother and daughter are rivals for Reginald. The daughter, kept in a prison-like room, is in every moral way superior to her mother. Only her complexion and wit are inferior to Lady Susan's.

In such a society where mother is set against daughter, hostilities prevent language from working in its customary way, that is, in a public way. Codes and private uses of language must work to protect the values of civilization. The letter, emblem of public meaning, is inappropriate to this dangerous world. Hypocrites do not write letters, or if they do they . . . shred . . . them, and Lady Susan is the consummate hypocrite who can "make Black appear White" (251). Given the confusions, the problem is how to communicate.

Frederica writes only one letter in the book; it is addressed to Reginald who loves her mother. He is the one person her mother did not expressly forbid her to write. She writes, "I am afraid my applying to you will appear no better than equivocation, and as if I attended only to the *letter* and not the spirit of Mama's command" (279). Ironically, it is this letter that she must rely on, not the spirit of her mother. It is an ineffective form; it does not document her distress as Clarissa's did. Reginald is momentarily moved by the letter, but soon forgets it.

Nevertheless, Frederica's letter, written into the void where "the whole family are at war," is a new kind of letter. In *Persuasion,* this new function of the letter will be brought to perfection when Wentworth proposes by letter. He relies on a traditional form to encase a private gesture. In *Lady Susan,* the letters are ineffective; the plot stagnates as the letters fail to bring any order out of the confusions in the families. The dilemmas and problems that prevail at the beginning of the story continue at the end of the last letter; there has been no change. Only Frederica's letter is different in kind from the other letters. It is gesture framed in a letter, a plea in this case. But the gesture, so ephemeral, is the one the narrator takes up and develops in the narrated conclusion. In other words, the gesture made by Frederica in her letter—a gesture which is ignored by the receiver in the epistolary part of the novel—is "protected" and validated by the narrator, for Frederica does marry the unworthy Reginald. Her gesture encased in the letter resonates in the narrated conclusion.

Austen has redefined the function of the letter. No longer a document, it is a private, often hopeless, gesture. Such a letter of private gesture needs the support or "environment" of narration which offers what has been lost: the authority of effective language. The answer to a letter of gesture is implication carried in the narrating voice—that Reginald will marry Frederica. Her letter had seemed to fail; yet, it is the only one that will bring some moral order out of the warring families. Alone, the letter can not resolve the hypocrisies and machinations of a bad and powerful mother. It is only a desperate and hopeless gesture too weak to salvage the plot. A narrator must rescue the story from its epistolary casting and, in doing this great deed, change the function and status of the letter from public property to private intangible.

At the end of the letters, Lady Susan's power over her daughter is still absolute. She takes her to London with her, away from even the dubious protection of her Uncle Vernon. The destructive powers of the mother are flourishing when the letters end. The truth that will save Frederica (that her mother is wicked, that she ruined the Manwaring marriage and persecutes her daughter) is not communicated to her would-be rescuer, Reginald, by letter. Even after Reginald has learned the worst about Lady Susan, there is little indication in the letters that he will act to save Frederica. As Lukacs says, "any form must contain some positive element in order to acquire substance as a form" (123).[11] Truth is excluded from the epistolary part of the story; Frederica's letter is the only one that contains a "positive element," but the voice of the narrator must bring about the rescue of Frederica.

Lady Susan, then, written during the time when the original version of *Sense and Sensibility* was being revised out of its epistolary form into a direct narrative, provides a time and place to study Austen's genius for composition, fitting form to story.

Austen uses a narrator who, *in loco parentis,* directs confusion toward resolution into harmony and organizes diverging points of view. B.C. Southam sums up Jane Austen's achievement, "In the later novels, she evolved a mode of presentation which unites and reconciles the different points of view that can divine relationships and comprehend meanings far beyond the range of epistolary fiction" (50). The lost parental authority finds ample compensation in the voice of the narrator whose tone of amused tolerance in the conclusion to *Lady Susan* assures us that all is well, if not right, in the new world presented in the book. Lady Susan marries Sir James, the man she stole from Miss Manwaring for Frederica to marry. Only the wise narrator could sort out the tangle of relationships:

> Whether Lady Susan was, or was not happy in her second Choice—I do not see how it can ever be ascertained—for who would take her assurance of it, on either side of the question? . . . She had nothing against her, but her Husband, & her Conscience. Sir James may seem to have drawn an harder Lot than mere Folly merited. I leave him therefore to all the Pity that anybody can give him. For myself, I confess that *I* can pity only Miss Manwaring, who coming to Town & putting herself to an expence in Cloathes, which impoverished her for two years, on purpose to secure him, was defrauded of her due by a Woman ten years older than herself. [313]

Behind the astringence of the irony in this conclusion are the clear moral judgments. The narrative voice has indeed become a source of order and value; it is the voice of the lost good parent who speaks instead of writing letters.

Notes

1. Brian Southam, *Jane Austen's Literary Manuscripts: A Study of the Novelist's Development through the Surviving Papers,* London, 1964, p. 16.

2. Ibid., p. 17.

3. James Edward Austen-Leigh, *Memoir of Jane Austen,* Oxford, 1951, p. 89.

4. John Preston, *The Created Self: The Reader's Role in Eighteenth-Century Fiction,* New York, 1970, pp. 46–47.

5. Geoffrey Tillotson, *Eighteenth-Century English Literature,* New York, 1969, p. 4.

6. Samuel Richardson, *Familiar Letters on Important Occasions,* London, 1902, I, xxvii.

7. E.D. Hirsch, Jr., *Validity in Interpretation,* New Haven, 1967, p. 106.

8. Wolfgang Iser, *The Epistolary Novel in the Late Eighteenth Century: A Descriptive and Bibliographic Study,* Eugene, Oregon, 1940, p. 9.

9. Donald Greene, "The Myth of Limitation," *Jane Austen Today,* Athens, Georgia, 1975, pp. 143–75, and R. F. Brissenden, "La Philosophie dans le boudoir; or, A Young Lady's Entrance into the World," *Studies in Eighteenth-Century Culture,* Cleveland, Ohio, 1972, II, 117 and 125.

10. Lloyd K. Brown, *Bits of Ivory: Narrative Techniques in Jane Austen's Fiction,* Baton Rouge, La., 1973, p. 153.

11. Georg Lukacs, *The Theory of the Novel,* trans. Anna Bostock, Cambridge, 1971, p. 119.

A Panel of Experts

Edited by Susan Schwartz

JULIET   This is the occasion in which you, the audience, are the stars. I will
be introducing the panelists first, and they will speak briefly about the
issues they're particularly interested in; but we are not limited to those.
After that we're going to turn it over to you, to ask questions of whomever
you choose, and also to make comments. This is the time that the floor has
the floor. Just briefly to introduce our speakers, starting on my right here:
Regina Barreca has been at the City University of New York, and she's
recently been appointed to the University of Connecticut. Her most recent
book is on the threshold of publication. It's called *Women and Comedy;*
so I take it that to Gina we may address both the bitter and serious questions
about injustice to women, and all those irreverent and wild questions about
what's funny. That gives you quite a range. **Rachel Brownstein** teaches
at Brooklyn College and at the City University of New York. She teaches
the eighteenth-, and especially the nineteenth-century novel, and she's the
author of *Becoming a Heroine: Reading about Women in Novels.* She's
ready to instruct us, of course, on that interesting art of how it is that you
become a heroine—I hope in life as well as in fiction. She tells us that she's
been noticing in the juvenilia there is a very definite preoccupation with
the subject of age. I give you this brief example from "Frederic & Elfrida":
"Mrs. Fitzroy did not approve of the match on account of the tender years
of the young couple, Rebecca being but 36 and Captain Roger little more
than 63. To remedy this objection, it was agreed that they should wait a
little while till they were a good deal older." Now I'm hoping that Rachel
may tell us not only how to become a heroine, but how to *stay* a heroine.
And **Jan Fergus** on my left, used to teach at Brooklyn College, but is now
at Lehigh University. She is the author of *Jane Austen and the Didactic
Novel;* so she is full of good moral instruction for us. I don't think it's

going to be limited to theories of the solemn. She tells me that she has noticed that in the juvenilia, particularly, we have many images of women doing all those things—and doing them with zest—that women are not supposed to do, like having affairs, and getting drunk, and so forth. Here we see the young and sprightly and outrageous Jane Austen. All in the cause of good morality, I am sure. **Donald Stone** teaches at Queens College of the City University. He's the author of *The Romantic Impulse in Victorian Fiction* and *The Novelist in the Changing World*. He told me that his first article ever (and that must be the first of very many indeed), was on Jane Austen, on the subject of her use of language; so I think we ought to consider him our local language expert tonight, ready to talk about Jane Austen's mastery of words. I am hoping that since he's written about the whole issue of romanticism and what it is to be a romantic, he might be able to deal with that interesting subject of where we place Jane Austen in the literary tradition. Do we, like many people, consider her a throwback to the Augustans? Or do we consider that she is passionate and revolutionary enough to make the Brontës look pretty tame? I'm **Juliet McMaster.** I'm currently the editor of *Persuasions*. My own work has been mainly with nineteenth-century novelists—Thackeray, Trollope, Jane Austen, and Dickens (most recently); but currently I'm just shifting gears to the eighteenth-century novel. I now turn to our panelists.

GINA   One of the things I found most interesting in the last couple of weeks is that I've just finished teaching *Sense and Sensibility* to a class of juniors and seniors at U. Conn., some of whom are English majors, some of them not. A few came from places where these are some of the first books they've actually read all the way through, they admitted. "I read this one without the Cliff notes," someone said. This was an enormous achievement. I posed a question on the end of *Sense and Sensibility:* should we consider this a happy ending? We've got 360 pages of Marianne's devotion and passion for another man, and then suddenly we learn two paragraphs from the end that she finally fell in love with Colonel Brandon. Should we accept that kind of ending? I found the same kind of difficulty with the ending in *Lady Susan*—are we meant to accept it, really? What are we to think? How can it ever be ascertained whether Lady Susan is happy or not? I'm not convinced that this is a happy ending. I'd like to hear your responses as to whether you think she judges Lady Susan an evil woman who must go off with this appalling man we can't like, or whether Lady Susan does pretty well at the end of the book, and in fact sets out and achieves all the goals that she's wanted. She gets a man, she gets some money, she gets a little power, she keeps her position in the world, and she can flirt all she wants. Doesn't she achieve every goal that she sets out to accomplish?

And therefore shouldn't we in some way (to lead into Rachel), applaud her as some kind of heroine, as opposed to the evil, vicious vampire woman who's at the heart of the text? So I'd like to kind of talk about endings, and how we finish up with this book.

RACHEL   Well, I want to throw out just two things, one in order to segue out of the heroine thing. Isn't it interesting that in the first novel Jane Austen brought to publication, the mother of the heroines, Mrs. Dashwood, is about the same age as Lady Susan—and also about the same age as Colonel Brandon—and there's absolutely no question of her remarrying, although she is a widow? Why do you suppose Jane Austen had it that way? The second thing I've been thinking about for a long time; I just want to hear what other people have to say. I want to read what Patricia Spacks read this morning, Lady Susan's comment to her friend Mrs. Johnson that, "if I am vain of anything, it is of my eloquence. Consideration and esteem as surely follow command of language, as admiration waits on beauty." That reminds me of a passage from, of all things, John Locke's *Essay concerning Human Understanding,* which I'll read to you: "Eloquence," writes Locke, "like the fair sex, has two prevailing beauties in it to suffer itself ever to be spoken against, and it is in vain to find fault with those arts of deceiving wherein men find pleasure to be deceived." The connection of deceit and eloquence and the fair sex, and the idea that an eloquent woman must be a deceitful woman, a woman who does not say what she thinks, that eloquence is deceit, and that men "find pleasure in being deceived" interests me. Also interesting is the question of what this thinking must have felt like to a woman who considered herself gifted with eloquence and yet not disposed to be deceitful.

JAN   As Juliet said, one of the things that I loved about the juvenilia is the energetic side of Jane Austen's imagination—and the energy that goes into the creation of a character like Lady Susan and the outrageous characters of the juvenilia. There are women about to murder their sisters, or kill off everybody else in their families, or like the character Alice in "Jack & Alice" who flies to her bottle to console herself for the pangs of disappointed love. I start my students on the juvenilia. I remind them how young Jane Austen was when she wrote the pieces that I assign. Their response is overwhelming. They love it. They love the juvenilia in a way that allows them to appreciate more of the complexities of the later novels—more of the complexities in the presentation of characters—than I found when I didn't use the juvenilia. In spite of Juliet's introduction of me as somebody who emphasizes the morals of Jane Austen, I want to say that I'm delighted to report that I ask my students, who are of course the age of Frederica in the novel, where do their sympathies lie in *Lady Susan*? Is Lady Susan somebody to be reprobated for her terrible behavior to her daughter? Where do they feel that the emotional center of this matter rests? "How do you feel about Lady Susan as a person?" As one, they say she's wonderful!—and male and female in the audience really feel, "Go for it, Lady Susan!" And this brings us back to the question that Gina raised: does she get what she wants in the end? How do we read that ending?—is it a punishment of Lady Susan, or is it a triumph for her?

DONALD   Well, I have actually two things, two very different sorts of topics that struck me as I was listening to the other panelists. First of all, don't be intimidated by the question of Jane Austen and language. That was an article I wrote many years ago. I was fascinated by her use of language for reasons I'll come to in a moment. (I have a colleague who loves to boast that he knows 32 languages, all of them Yiddish.) Austen has, from a very early age—one can see in her burlesques—a huge enjoyment in picking up on the jargon of the period. It's one of the things that makes the juvenilia so fresh. You imagine you can hear every television commercial or read every trashy novel written today and be able to pick up the same kind of clichés, the same kind of cant, the same kind of stereotypes, the same kind of manipulation of language. We all know that words can be made to mean whatever one wants them to mean. I was going to read two passages, but actually Rachel read one already. Lady Susan is described by Mrs. Vernon as talking very well, "with a happy command of Language, which is too often used, I believe, to make black appear white." For an author who has such pleasure, from a very early age, in playing with other people's language, and yet who is herself in the process of developing a language that means something, we have to ask ourselves when we read these pieces, what did she say? Who is she saying them for? *Lady Susan* obviously was written for her family. It was one of the family entertainments. Did the fun for the family lie in the fact that they were somehow enjoying a complicity *with* Lady Susan?—or did it lie in the fact that they were seeing *through* Lady Susan? There are different kinds of sophistication that are involved. Must we necessarily find Lady Susan sympathetic in order for the novel to have "modern" appeal?—when maybe it's the manipulation of language on her part (as we all know people manipulate language) that also adds to the appeal of the book?

JULIET   I invite questions from the audience.

Q   It seems to me that addressing how Jane Austen and her family reacted to *Lady Susan* really hinges on the question of whether or not it was written in indignation about an actual case that came to Jane Austen's attention. If it was an actual case, then it's fairly obvious that we are not supposed to sympathize with Lady Susan.

RACHEL   You're speaking I suppose of the Mrs. Craven who locked up her daughters; but suppose there's another biographical germ behind this novel. Suppose Eliza Hancock de Feuillide, the cousin who married Henry Austen and was 12 years older than he (just as Lady Susan would have been that much older than Reginald)—suppose she also was in the background. Suppose there was not only the story of Mrs. Craven, but also the story of Eliza to whom Jane Austen had dedicated "Love and Freindship"? Suppose there were both the negative source, Mrs. Craven, and the positive, or once-positive source, Eliza. That would account, wouldn't it, for a kind of double response to Lady Susan—if we're going to believe in the biographical sources of character?

Q   Lady Susan is probably not so much different from a lot of parents who are trying to influence their children, especially their daughters, into marriage; so that it is conceivable that she was commenting on a very broad social question.

GINA   I think that in acting on what she would justify as her daughter's behalf, she was fulfilling that role of a mother. That was important. At least part of her charm—the reason I'm very much seduced by this character—is that she is like the devil in *Paradise Lost*. She was being a good mother in trying to provide for her daughter, although trying to provide really along the wrong lines; but the man she chose for Frederica turned out to be good enough for *her*. So was she in fact erring so widely? If it's good enough for me, it's good enough for you! So was she in fact being so evil and awful? Wasn't she simply acknowledging the way the world went at the time?

Q   Would the panelists comment on the maternal inadequacies of Mrs. Bennet vs. Lady Susan?

GINA   You don't feel the same kind of criticism of Lady Susan in the text as you do of Mrs. Bennet. I know a lot of mothers who are quite indignant at the treatment of Mrs. Bennet in *Pride and Prejudice,* and I, at least, when I read *Lady Susan,* don't feel that, even though she is manipulating her daughter, and using her as a way of arranging her life for herself more comfortably. Still, in spite of all of the comments of Catherine Vernon on this terrible behavior, one doesn't feel the same. You feel embarrassed *with*

Elizabeth when her mother behaves so badly at Netherfield, and Elizabeth's humiliation is something really felt; whereas you don't feel that for Frederica—at least I don't, and my 17-year-old students didn't feel it. Somehow that's not where your concern seems to be directed.

RACHEL   But isn't Mrs. Bennet different from Lady Susan in that Mrs. Bennet is a mother first of all and only, whereas Lady Susan is out for her own unmentionable purposes? In *Sense and Sensibility* it's simply not a question of whether 36-year-old Mrs. Dashwood will look for another husband. That simply doesn't come up. She's supposed to take care of her daughters, period; whereas, what Lady Susan does is certainly more shocking.

GINA   Because there's some kind of competition, sexual competition, between the mother and daughter in a very obvious way.

JULIET   I feel that a kind of contract exists between the character and the reader; and in the case of Lady Susan, we know perfectly well we do not *esteem* this woman, and I don't think we *love* her exactly either. We have some *sympathy* for this woman, who's got this wonderful bouncing-back power and resilience, and she's center stage all the time. But I don't think we are bamboozled by her. We know just how bad she is. We know just how awful it would be to be her daughter. Nevertheless, Jane Austen knows how to separate those two elements of sympathy and judgment, and to be fascinated with the interaction of the two.

RACHEL   Doesn't that have to do though with what Donald was talking about, the language, and our pleasure in being deceived by Lady Susan, our pleasure in her eloquence, which is similar to Mr. Bennet's? Remember Mr. Bennet says that Wickham is his favorite son-in-law. That kind of feeling, that you *like* Lady Susan, the way he likes Wickham.

DONALD   There's a pleasure in her use of outrageousness. I was looking through my edition of the *Minor Works,* which I bought in my student days, and found myself erasing in the margin references to Ionesco and the Absurd which 20 years ago would have been modish, but in 1987 seem rather silly. But one of my favorites of her works of the juvenilia is "The History of England." Her description of Queen Elizabeth, that "disgrace to humanity, that pest of society," and so forth. She has a lot of fun with characters—what the British call a lot of "guying" that goes on—so that she can treat an outrageous character with a certain amount of humor and sympathy as long as it's within the bounds of literary burlesque. In the same way Jane Austen can take characters who were sympathetic and pretend for the moment that they are unsympathetic, outrageous and so forth.

JAN   One of the nearest things she can make fun of is her own sympathies. As we all know, she loved Mary Queen of Scots and she makes a joke of that love. We are aware of Jane Austen's marginalia in her copy of Goldsmith—how much she loved the Stuarts. I think it was her father's book, but she jokes about it. It's that wonderful duality that she has from the time she was 11 years old, that keeps me enthralled, I think, and stunned a lot of the time; especially the sophistication of those early works—it's staggering.

Q   Did you hate Lady Susan all the way through? Did you find her despicable? Weren't you taken in a bit by her attractions?

DONALD   There's a distinction between being a good mother and being a good character with good characterization. Think of the people who watch Joan Collins—not exactly thinking that she's a moral paragon. Jane Austen is playing with a similar kind of characterization.

Q   I love the way Jane Austen uses language. Is it Jane Austen's use of language or her character's use of it that's so deceptive?

RACHEL   But Lady Susan's a special case because she's the one who's speaking so well, and it's because she speaks so well that she can do all this home wrecking and manipulating; so that raises a real question of whether eloquence is in fact okay.

Q   Is it Jane Austen, or isn't it?

RACHEL   Well, Lady Susan takes power by speaking so well. She seduces Reginald De Courcy by talking to him, after all more effectively than other women talk. So all these ladies are in competition, not only over men. They're also in competition as to who can be smartest and who can manipulate language the best, raising the question of how to be attractive through language—as a writer, or as a woman.

DONALD   Returning to the question of language that you raised before: when I was working at my romantic impulse book, which is about 60 to 70 percent devoted to women writers in the Victorian period, a question one comes back to again and again when dealing with Austen, with Charlotte Brontë, with Elizabeth Gaskell, with George Eliot—the main figures I deal with—whether they have a right to be writing at all; whether the writing of fiction is lying; and the question of dissimulation becomes a great moral problem. In Gaskell's novel, *Ruth,* for example, the fact that the character lies (the heroine's son lies at one point) is treated as a terrible moral infringement; and yet—if you know *Cranford*—in *Cranford,* the whole community is kept together because of lies: you know, elegant economy, euphemisms. In Austen's world, you establish your identity by your speech, by your language. You do things for the family or for your readers, but they also consist of lying. There's a real dual attitude, as we know in Austen, and by the time we come to *Mansfield Park,* I think that's really where the conflict becomes very outspoken, in her outcry against theatricals, for example. What is so terrible about theatricals? People pretending to be what they're not. Obviously, it's a real issue.

RACHEL   The idea of woman as seducer goes back to Adam and Eve—the one who's going to create the Fall. The tradition of the talking woman, the eloquent woman, as a source of evil is a concept that goes back to Medieval tradition—the monkish tradition that it was through women's advice that men fell. That tradition identifies women's eloquence in a particular way. So when women are writing, there is an overconcern with the issue. Is writing lying, dissimulation?

Q   Lady Susan is supposed to be a very beautiful woman. What is the impact of beauty and how does it work?

DONALD   The only case I can remember where Jane Austen makes fun of beauty—she does on a number of occasions—is in "Jack & Alice." She satirizes the hero, who is so beautiful that his very eyes when he comes to the ball—all he has to do is stare at people, and they fall over dead! That's not to say that beauty in itself means rather less than some inner quality.

GINA   I wanted to raise one point that Jan had made that I thought was wonderful. What if we didn't have Lady Susan's letters, if we didn't hear her inner voice and know how evil she was, how would *we* react to her? Wouldn't we be like Reginald in wanting to somehow believe her as the wronged? If someone comes to us with their true story of themselves, as opposed to what we've heard from everybody else, doesn't it again draw us into that inner circle and so make us want to believe them? I think the ending of *Lady Susan* was just playing.

JULIET   We must let Phyllis Ann Karr [the writer of an extended version of *Lady Susan*] answer this one. Was she playing rather than being serious in this?

PHYLLIS   She might well have been. It reminds me of the old Alfred Hitchcock show: at that time the television code said you cannot show the criminal triumph, so there were dramatizations where the woman killed her husband with a frozen leg of lamb and Hitchcock comes in at the end to say the next time she was caught.

Q   It occurred to me that one exercise that is sometimes recommended for writers is to take some crime or some philosophy you think heinous, or a character you absolutely hate, just above the lowest of the low, and then you try to get inside the character, try to understand the character, in taking the story from this character's viewpoint. It's an experiment for a writer: understand why this character would do such things. Lady Susan could be such an experiment; the whole theatrical scene of *Mansfield Park* could be such an experiment.

Q   I don't think it's fair to judge *Lady Susan* any differently from other novels and say Jane Austen was "playing."

GINA   And don't you get the same kind of problem with the ending of *Mansfield Park*?—where you have words to the effect that "However long it *should* take for these two people to fall in love, that's how long it did take." It's like the author again walks out on the end: "Let other pens dwell on guilt and misery," etc. "I'm not going to do this, I'm going to give you a happy ending because that's what you demand"—and it's almost as if she's running out to sum up.

JULIET   I don't want to stop the discussion, which is so lively, but I also want to hear about other things than *Lady Susan*. I don't know if others of you do. "Catharine," "Love and Freindship," "The History of England"— are you ready for that? It would mean a change of gear. I just feel that *Lady Susan* has got very good coverage by this time.

Q   If Jane Austen had written nothing else but the juvenilia, what would be her literary reputation? What would we think of them? Would we still regard them so highly?

JAN   I feel very strongly that they would be hailed as a brilliant comic discovery, and there would be statements on the sadness of the fate of this writer. But suppose that they were found in the cookie box, would they be identified, do you think, as the work of a woman or as the work of a man?

DONALD   I think we take for granted that Austen's readers were by and large women; but in fact in the Austen family there were far more males that she wrote for than there were women. In the nineteenth century, judging from the Victorian response to her work, it was through male critics like George Henry Lewes, for example, that Austen's reputation really grew. Lewes wrote to Charlotte Brontë, and insisted that if she wanted to become a great craftsman, to perfect her style, she should read Austen's novels. Lewes and George Eliot, when they were living together and Eliot was writing novels, would read Jane Austen to each other every night. It was both a pleasure and a kind of stimulus.

JAN   I had a colleague once who was an eighteenth-century scholar, and Jane Austen was the only female writer that he could bear to read. I think he saw the eighteenth century wrongly as purely male, and he saw Jane Austen as a male writer, and I think in some ways the tradition of liking Austen that you speak of is very much in that tradition. She has a male mind, a male sense of irony, and it's an impossible question to answer. What we're doing now is showing what the feminist reading of Austen indicates—that her vision is distinctly female, although unusual, different from her contemporaries' in lots of ways.

RACHEL   That's what I was going to say. It's not really that she's writing for an audience of women, but that she's writing *about* women, about the sentimental tradition. She's writing about novels about young girls. She's poking fun with what some take to be masculine strength of mind at the kind of sentimentality of novels about your girls of sensibility: maybe that's where the gender confusion comes in.

GINA   But I've found it interesting doing some reading on the idea of women in comedy, or looking over histories about comedy in English literature—usually with modest titles like *A History of Comedy in English Literature* (I mean things that say they are going to encompass everything!). Often Jane Austen was the only writer mentioned; and she was often dismissed pretty early on in the book. As J.B. Priestley wrote in the *History of English Humor,* Jane Austen can be considered one of the few women humorists in the tradition, but that you knew what you were in for when you read Jane Austen: a lot of "feminine small potatoes," and that was it. And Priestley said it without apology; so that she was just dismissed as dealing with the girls; "but *we're* talking about *real* humor—you know, men's humor." I think that she is coming against a tradition that really doesn't know what to do with her. The male humorist tradition doesn't know where to put Austen.

Q   Before this meeting I dined with an old friend of 30 years who is a psychotherapist; and the question of the gender of the attendees at this conference came up. And he found it absolutely extraordinary that it was mostly women. Jane Austen is a strong writer and there should not be a sexist reaction.

JULIET   Why are there not more of you here? You would be very welcome, you know that. Of course such a thing will operate not only with Jane Austen but with Charlotte Brontë, too. But we also have all those women Trollopians and Dickensians. Why don't we all bring our husbands and sons, for a start?

Q   I would like Jan Fergus to name two or three other pieces from the juvenilia to start my husband reading Jane Austen.

JAN   I guess I think any of them will do, but I always assign "Frederic & Elfrida" because the only time I ever saw my brother laugh out loud, enjoying Jane Austen, was when he read "Lovely and too charming fair one, notwithstanding your forbidding squint, your greasy tresses and your swelling back, which are more frightful than imagination can paint or pen describe, I cannot refrain from expressing my raptures at the engaging qualities of your mind." My brother loved that; my students love that. It's just wonderful. And I also assign "Jack & Alice" because of Alice running off to the bottle. And *Lady Susan* definitely; and "The History of England," which is so hilarious. I also want to refer to the comment Rachel made. Literary historians would revel in the juvenilia as a record of a contemporary reader's response to literature. I mean, in itself it would be valued, and literary historians wouldn't let it die for that reason; but I think it's the kind of writing that people would want to insert (if it were suddenly discovered) into courses on the eighteenth century, to show that this kind of critical spirit was widespread—that you don't look only at the major writers for the criticism of sentimentality. You look at what they would assume would be an extraordinarily talented young person. It would be looked upon with great interest—probably with more energy than it's looked upon now. Many people ignore the juvenilia, because the major works, the great novels, are so wonderful. I think if all we had were the juvenilia, we'd pay a lot more attention to them. But not all the panelists agree with me and they should have their say.

GINA   I was going to say that in the back of my mind is a comment that I'm not even sure I should make: which is that if we were going to discover the gender of the writer, somehow there were "very few dates in history," and that would give it away as somehow written by a woman. We're going to get into personalities.

JAN   That's the joke on Goldsmith's history, you know, the famous fact that Goldsmith's history did not include more than the occasional date per chapter. I'm not sure that anybody could maintain that stereotype there.

DONALD   It does seem to me (going back to what I said before): of course part of the pleasure is knowing that, yes, this is *Jane Austen* who wrote this, and we can see connections between these works and the later works. We can read "Catharine," which is my favorite of the juvenilia, and think of *Persuasion,* which comes so many years later: *Persuasion,* which is supposed to mark a new romantic element in Austen; and yet we see in "Catharine" that it was there from the very beginning. But again, shall we say from a modern point of view (and I mean a modern point of view that will always be modern, whether now or 100 years from now), she instantly zeros in on whatever is the reigning fashion of the moment, the jargon of the moment, the cant of the moment. It's for that reason that she adored Dr. Johnson, for example. You can feel certain that every time you watch or listen to a politician and know that the person is saying something absolutely fake—that means something else—then *that's* when you get the Jane Austen spirit, which is not just male-female, but a kind of universal, shall we say, satirical honest spirit. I was thinking of that wonderful line of Mort Sahl's quoted in the *Times.* "Well, what was the whole fuss about the Joe Biden scandal? It was only a case of one man's ghost writer stealing from another person's ghost writer." That's a perfect Jane Austen kind of remark.

RACHEL   To get back to *Lady Susan* for a moment: I think that one of the things that's most pleasurable in that book, in the letters, is the change of voice, where you have Lady Susan speaking terribly well, very softly, and then switching into how she *really* talks when she's writing to Mrs. Johnson. You have a sense of very different voices coming out of that one woman: and it's that kind of complexity that makes it all interesting. I also want to add a dissenting voice about the juvenilia. I agree with everything that all of you have said: I think that literary historians would certainly have found the juvenilia invaluable and I agree that she pokes at convention and the sense of Jane Austen gleefully satirizing all of the cant of her day makes it fun. But I must say I had a terrible pang when Jan said, "If we had that and nothing else." I think that you read all this, the juvenilia and *Lady Susan* and even *Sanditon* too—*I* do anyway—with a sense of their thinness. I mean, there are so many miles between them and the novels that . . .

JAN   I disagree with you about *Sanditon*. I think *Sanditon* is enormously complicated and conceived on a larger scale.

RACHEL   . . . I said even *Sanditon*. I like all of them, and am very fond of "Catharine," and I *do* see them as prefiguring a lot; but I guess I agree with Mrs. Leavis that the finished novels were products of accretion; and the density is what I miss in the juvenilia, and in *Sanditon,* and in "Catharine"—although I see the beginnings there of what was going to come. I think the minor works are most interesting as evidence of what a very, very precocious genius would have produced. It's fascinating stuff, fascinating because you have read the other novels, and you look back and you see intimations and glimmerings and that sort of thing. Maybe I'm the only one—I just don't read the minor works in the same way. The prose begins to sound tinny—even *Lady Susan*. I have to keep going back and rereading; whereas I don't have this problem, ever, even reading *Emma* for the seventy-fifth time.

JULIET   But you have gone back to read *Emma* 75 times.

RACHEL   Yes I have, for a different reason.

Q   Wouldn't she be laughing at us taking these so seriously?

DONALD   She would have laughed at us taking any of her work seriously.

Q   Weren't the early ones just that—early ones?

JAN   But you have to remember, she was tinkering with them years later.

Q   But she didn't feel they were finished and she didn't feel they were professional, or I don't *think* she thought they were worthy of publication; and I think she'd be laughing now.

JAN   She wasn't sure that *Northanger Abbey* was worthy of publication, and it's not even clear that she thought that way about *Persuasion* either. Remember where she says, "I have a something ready for publication, which may perhaps come out." (She's not totally satisfied with it) and

"Miss Catherine,"—one of the titles of *Northanger Abbey*—"is put on the shelf for the present. I don't know whether she felt, especially with *Northanger Abbey,* that that was ever done to her satisfaction, in her mature judgment, even though she was ready to publish it earlier.

Q   Yes, the endings of all of them seem so perfunctory, don't they?

JAN   But isn't that what we've been talking about all along? That's true at the end of *Lady Susan,* it's true at the end of *Sense and Sensibility,* of *Mansfield Park.* . . .

JULIET   I suppose we can agree that one thing we miss in the juvenilia is the continuing narrative. We don't get the developed character and the developed incident, but we get jokes thick and fast—a Monty Python kind of experience. I like the bit in *Northanger Abbey* where she says, "We ought to stick together. If the heroine of one novel be not patronized by the heroine of another, where are we?" You could say that she is *parodying* Anne Radcliffe and the Gothic novel there; but at the same time she is expressing a degree of solidarity with her fellow female novelists. She says, "The men get praised and anthologized—with a scrap of a *Spectator* and a chapter from Sterne, but we who write *Camilla* and *Belinda,* we *women* novelists, are scarcely noticed." It's already strong in *Northanger Abbey.* You don't have to wait until *Persuasion* to hear that voice, do you?

JAN   And again, her family was very fond of novels, all of her brothers were great novel readers, and as she said in one of her letters, they're not ashamed of being so. Remember Henry Tilney in *Northanger Abbey* saying that men read nearly as many novels as women, and he had snatched the copy of *Mysteries of Udolpho* away from his sister, and kept her from finishing it, because he couldn't bear to wait until she came back from seeing to a caller to go on.

Q   Isn't it awful that Jane Austen really feels it necessary to reply to these ideas on novels in *Northanger Abbey?*

DONALD   The thoughts extended I think beyond more than just *novels* in the early part of the nineteenth century. One thinks of Lord Byron's remarks to Lady Blessington about the reasons that he was such an unfit husband: it was that his mind was always dwelling in a world of the imagination, which made it somehow more difficult for him to deal with reality and domestic matters.

RACHEL   But Byron said that his wife had been Clarissa Harlowed by her parents into such a paragon—that in effect the novels had made Annabella so prim.

GINA   If you haven't yet read a book that's just come back into print, which was a favorite of Jane Austen, called *The Female Quixote,* by Charlotte Lennox, I would imagine that you would like it. I think Jane Austen read it three times. It's about a young woman who is raised in isolation from society, and brought up reading only French romantic novels. So we have a lot of this material that Jane Austen is later to discuss. The problem is Arabella, who's at the center of this text. She is this wild heroine who's always jumping off horses and crying rape if she sees someone who's 40 feet away from her; and she wants men to duel over her; and she wears only gowns that were based on Grecian heroines. In fact she's absolutely the smartest, best character in this book. And in fact two men duel over her at the end, almost as though they don't know what they're doing; they have swords in their hands and they're saying, "Why are we doing this?" Somehow she has in fact managed to impose her novel world on reality. So you have to start to wonder who's right—all the people who are telling her, "You can't do this," or Arabella—who's in fact managing to do this very ably.

DONALD   But again the model for that is Cervantes.

Q   I'd like to go back to the question of what makes a heroine.

RACHEL   Well, a novelist *makes* a heroine; and the convention was to choose a young, unmarried girl and to make the story of her marrying the story that made her into the heroine of the novel. That's one reason why *Lady Susan* is so interesting, because it takes a woman who is not only not young, and unmarried, but who is really a wrecker of families, rather than a melder of families as a young girl would be. She not only divides her husband from his brother but causes all sorts of other family rifts. Charlotte Lennox's suggestion is that what makes a heroine is having read enough novels to have an idea of oneself as a heroine, which one then acts on. Once you know what a heroine is, you become one because a heroine's are the terms in which you see the world around you. And if you see clearly enough, you can impose your view on other people.

Q   I've recently taken a seminar on sentimental films of the 1930s called "Women's Films," and with an audience of men and women, and this is an interesting parallel to the question of who reads novels.

JAN   I'm doing some research on the eighteenth-century reading public in England, and so far as I can tell, at least up till about 1780, men read more novels than women, at least according to these records.

JULIET   I would like to add "Love and Freindship" to the catalog of the works that you should use to introduce Jane Austen. With some of my students I start on that as an introduction to Jane Austen, when I'm working up to *Emma*. I give them a little prehistory of the burlesque, and that continuing theme—the Don Quixote theme—according to which life is imitating other people's art. Emma feels that anybody who's been rescued by a man has got to fall in love with him, because that's the convention. With "Love and Freindship," I start with that knocking at the door, when nobody's going to open it. "Is there somebody knocking at the door?" "Yes, I'm sure it's somebody knocking at the door," the characters go on. She has that technique of repeating a joke often enough that you just are carried away by it. It's the "Laugh-In" technique. Say "Sock it to me" often enough and you've got a whole population laughing with you. Jane Austen knew that technique, and in "Love and Freindship" she used it superbly. The *pieces* of it are so marvelous. It's hard afterwards to recount the story; but that's not the kind of thing it is. It's wonderful *pieces,* which fit together. I also found that teaching "Love and Freindship" in the context of a graduate course in the Romantics has worked well; because it is such a spot-on reaction to so many of the romantic conventions, and it is so brilliant as an intellectual response to the Romantic movement.

Q   Does the panel consider anyone else's juvenilia—I can only think of the Brontës'—as worthwhile as Jane Austen's?

DONALD   Gaskell, George Eliot, Trollope—really—when *they* wrote their first novels, they were in their late thirties. Gaskell was close to 40 when she wrote her first work of fiction. In the case of the Brontës and Austen, you have an exceptional matter. Some of you know a recent paperback edition, which selects about 150 pages of the Brontë juvenilia, and prints it alongside about 150 pages of the Austen; it makes marvelous counter-reading. I'm not so sure that the Brontës' reputations would be all that secure if only their juvenilia existed and *Jane Eyre* and *Villette* had somehow vanished; but one feels that at least the Austen juvenilia would remain of interest to the literary historians. Carl Lansbury once complained that Trollope only wrote 45 novels and it was such a loss that he died before he could write another 35. If Austen had lived on. . . .

Q   Jane Austen's juvenilia were so hilarious—but aren't we being too solemn and pompous? Will they bear the weight of all this dissection?

JULIET   Do you feel that's what we're doing? I agree that a good joke can be spoiled by explanation, but don't you think that any work of literature expands by close examination? I have a lot of students who feel that a work of literature's like a flower—you take it apart and it's dead; but so far as I'm concerned that's not the case. The more you find out about it, the more is there.

JAN   I'll get back to the question about other juvenilia. I just finished the juvenilia of Matthew Lewis. I don't know if any of you ever heard of him, but he wrote that truly astonishing novel, *The Monk*. It doesn't include the line "the worms crawled in, the worms crawled out." It ought to. The whole Gothic, with nuns being seduced and raped, and vaults with moldering bodies beside them! It couldn't be further from Jane Austen. When he was 16 he wrote a parody of the sentimental novel. It's amusing, it's interesting to look at, but it doesn't have that wonderful style of Jane Austen, the language. If you put it beside "Love and Freindship," it doesn't hold a candle to it. It's just not that witty, not as funny. There are moments in it that are quite hilarious and that might make many of us laugh aloud, but it's not the same. It's not in the same category at all. What we're doing here is celebrating the juvenilia and delighting in Jane Austen's amazing virtuosity. It's astonishing what she has accomplished in these pieces— staggering. I keep asking myself as I read them, what could make a 19-year-old write something like *Lady Susan*? I look around at the 19-year-olds I've known, and think, how could any of them perform like that?

RACHEL   They're more often like Charlotte Brontë, aren't they? They're sober and solemn and pouring their hearts out, and the idea that a 19-year-old could cast such a cold eye is astonishing, let alone a 14-year-old.

JULIET   Our time is up now, and we have indeed been celebrating the juvenilia and *Lady Susan* this entire five-day-long weekend. Thank you very much. We had a superb "graduate seminar" here, with superb graduate students.

Jane Austen's Juvenilia and *Lady Susan:*
An Annotated Bibliography

David J. Gilson and J. David Grey

Asterisked entries indicate those works to which reference is made in the articles included in this collection. References made to works other than the *J* and *LS* are not included in this bibliography. Since this bibliography is intended to be exhaustive, the compilers would appreciate learning of any omissions.

Further reference may be made to David Gilson, *A Bibliography of Jane Austen* (The Soho Bibliographies 21), Oxford: Clarendon Press, 1982, reprinted 1985, 877 pp. Additional details concerning the manuscripts and publication history of the juvenilia and *Lady Susan* may be found in Section F; Section M (Biography and Criticism) covers studies published up to 1978, but virtually all such items appear in the present list. Researchers are also directed to Barry Roth and Joel Weinsheimer, *An Annotated Bibliography of Jane Austen Studies, 1952–1972*, Charlottesville: University Press of Virginia, 1973, 271 pp., and its continuation by Barry Roth alone, *An Annotated Bibliography of Jane Austen Studies, 1973–1983*, Charlottesville: University Press of Virginia, 1985, 359 pp.

A., G.E.P. "Jane Austen's 'Love and Freindship and Other Early Works,'" *Notes and Queries* 156 (1929), 349–50.

   Shows that the words "Yes, I'm in love I feel it now" are adapted from a song by F. Whitehead with music ascribed to Handel.

Adams, Oscar Fay. *The Story of Jane Austen's Life*. Chicago: A.C. McClurg and Company, 1891.

   A section called "Earliest Attempts at Writing," pp. 37–42, includes a reprint of "The Mystery."

Allen, M.H. "Love and Freindship," produced and adapted by M.H. Allen, BBC Regional Service, 17 August 1936.

Allen, Walter. "The Virtues of the Epistolary Novel," *Times Literary Supplement,* 26 January 1973, 98.

Apperson, George Latimer. *A Jane Austen Dictionary.* London: Cecil Palmer, 1932.

> The first of many "alphabets." Includes references to characters in *Volume the Second.*

Auerbach, Nina. *Communities of Women: An Idea in Fiction.* Cambridge, Massachusetts and London: Harvard University Press, 1978.

> *Lady Susan,* p. 50; "History of England," p. 54.

Austen, Caroline Mary Craven. *My Aunt Jane Austen: A Memoir.* Alton: The Jane Austen Society, 1952.

*Austen-Leigh, James Edward. *A Memoir of Jane Austen.* 2nd ed. London: Richard Bentley and Son, 1871.

> The first publication of *Lady Susan,* pp. 203–364, with a prefatory note by J.E. Austen-Leigh, p. 201. Also first published in this volume was the play, "The Mystery," pp. 43–45. A passage on *Lady Susan* from a review of the *Memoir* in *Spectator* 44 (1871), 891–92, attributed to Richard Holt Hutton, is reprinted by B.C. Southam in his *Jane Austen: The Critical Heritage,* vol. 2, 1870–1940, London: Routledge & Kegan Paul, 1987, pp. 171–73.

*Austen-Leigh, Mary Augusta. *Personal Aspects of Jane Austen.* London: John Murray, 1920.

> Chapter 6, pp. 98–110: *Lady Susan.*

Austen-Leigh, William, and Austen-Leigh, Richard Arthur. *Jane Austen: Her Life and Letters.* A Family Record. London: Smith, Elder & Co., 1913.

> The juvenilia are discussed, pp. 53–58, with a text of "The Mystery," a summary of "Catharine, or The Bower," and titles of other stories; *Lady Susan* is discussed on pp. 80–81.

B., B. "Jane Austen's 'Lady Susan,'" *Notes and Queries,* 11th series, 7 (1913), 388.

> Asks if *Lady Susan* has been printed; an editorial note refers to the *Memoir.*

Babb, Howard Selden. *Jane Austen's Novels: The Fabric of Dialogue.* [Columbus]: Ohio State University Press, 1962.

> The juvenilia are discussed, pp. 33–37.

*Bailey, John Cann. *Introductions to Jane Austen.* London: Oxford University Press, 1931.

> Chapter 8, pp. 112–47, deals with *Lady Susan, The Watsons,* "Love and Freindship," and *Sanditon.*

*Baker, Ernest Albert. *The History of the English Novel.* Vol. 6: "Edgeworth, Austen, Scott." London: H.F. & G. Witherby, 1935.

> "Early Stories," pp. 65–69.

Barker, Gerard A. *Grandison's Heirs: The Paragon's Progress in the Late Eighteenth-Century English Novel.* Newark: University of Delaware Press, 1985.

"Sir Charles Grandison or the Happy Man," "Jack & Alice," "Evelyn," and "First Impressions" are discussed, pp. 146–50.

Barton, John. "The Hollow Crown: An Entertainment by and about the Kings and Queens of England." London: French-Harrap, 1962.

Contains a selection from "History of England."

*Bayley, John. *The Uses of Division: Unity and Disharmony in Literature.* London: Chatto & Windus, 1976.

*Beer, Frances. *The Juvenilia of Jane Austen and Charlotte Brontë.* Harmondsworth, Eng.: Penguin Books, 1986.

The introduction discusses Jane Austen's juvenilia, pp. 9–19.

Bellman Nerozzi, Patrizia. *Jane Austen.* Bari: Adriatica, 1973.

Chapter 2, pp. 55–87: "I Juvenilia"; Chapter 6, pp. 183–212: *"Lady Susan, The Watsons, The Plan of a Novel."*

Bertinetti, Roberto. *Ritratti Di Signore: Saggio Su Jane Austen.* Milano: Jaca, 1987.

Chapter 1 discusses "Jack & Alice," "Frederic & Elfrida," "Love and Freindship," and *Lady Susan,* pp. 13–23.

Birkhead, Edith. "Sentiment and Sensibility in the Eighteenth Century Novel," *Essays and Studies by the English Association* 11 (1925), 92–116.

*Birrell, Augustine. *More obiter Dicta.* London: William Heinemann Ltd., 1924.

"Elementary Jane," pp. 36–42, is a reprint of a review of the 1922 *"Love & Freindship" and Other Early Works.*

Black, Frank Gees. *The Epistolary Novel in the Late Eighteenth Century: A Descriptive and Bibliographical Study.* Eugene, Oregon: University of Oregon Publications, 1940.

See pp. 100–108 on the juvenilia.

Blum, B.M. "A Study of Jane Austen's Juvenilia as a Response to Late 18th-Century Fiction and in the Light of Her Later Work." M.Phil. thesis, University of Oxford, 1979.

Bok, H. Abigail. "A Dictionary of Jane Austen's Life and Work," in *The Jane Austen Companion,* ed. J. David Grey et al., New York: Macmillan Publishing Company, 1986, pp. 399–493.

Exhaustive; includes everybody and everywhere in everything.

*Booth, Wayne Clayson. *A Rhetoric of Fiction.* Chicago: University of Chicago Press, 1961.

*_____ . *A Rhetoric of Irony.* Chicago and London: University of Chicago Press, 1974.

On *Lady Susan,* pp. 64–66.

Bradbrook, Frank Wilson. "Jane Austen and Choderlos de Laclos," *Notes and Queries* 199 (1954), 75.

Suggests that Eliza de Feuillide introduced Jane Austen to *Les liaisons dangereuses* and that the novelist derived some aspects of *Lady Susan* from this work.

*_____ . *Jane Austen and Her Predecessors.* Cambridge: Cambridge University Press, 1967.

Bradbrook, Muriel Clara. "The Elegant Eccentrics," *Modern Language Review* 44 (1949), 184–97.

See p. 193 for a parallel between the Ladies of Llangollen (Lady Eleanor Butler and Miss Sara Ponsonby) and Laura and Sophia in "Love and Freindship."

*Brissenden, Robert Francis. *Virtues in Distress: Studies in the Novel of Sentiment from Richardson to Sade.* London: Macmillan, 1974.

See especially chapter 5: *"La Philosophie dans le Boudoir;* or, A Young Lady's Entrance into the World," pp. 268–93.

*Brophy, Brigid. "Jane Austen and the Stuarts," *Critical Essays on Jane Austen,* ed. B.C. Southam. London: Routledge & Kegan Paul Ltd., 1968; New York: Barnes & Noble, Inc., 1969, 21–38.

About "The History of England."

*Brown, Julia Prewitt. *Jane Austen's Novels: Social Change and Literary Form.* Cambridge, Massachusetts and London: Harvard University Press, 1979.

*Brown, Lloyd Wellesley. *Bits of Ivory: Narrative Techniques in Jane Austen's Fiction.* Baton Rouge: Louisiana State University Press, 1973.

The juvenilia are discussed on pp. 141–45 and *Lady Susan* on pp. 145–55.

*Brownstein, Rachel. *Becoming a Heroine: Reading about Women in Novels.* New York: The Viking Press, 1982.

Brüggemeier, Luise-Marie. *The Journey of the Self: Studien zum Reisemotiv im Roman Jane Austens.* Frankfurt am Main: Peter D. Lang, 1981.

For material on the juvenilia, see pp. 48–60.

*Bush, Douglas. *Jane Austen.* New York: Macmillan, 1975.

Chapter 3, pp. 41–54, "Early Writings," discusses the juvenilia and *Lady Susan.*

*Butler, Marilyn. *Jane Austen and the War of Ideas*. Oxford: Clarendon Press, 1975.

> The juvenilia are discussed on pp. 168–72.

C., B.W. "Author Wanted," *Notes and Queries* 195 (1950), 305.

> Seeks the author of the motto to "Love and Freindship" ("Deceived in Freindship & Betrayed in Love"), cf. Dodds, Chapman (1952) and Shipps.

Cecil, Lord David. "Jane Austen's Lesser Works." Address given at the Annual General Meeting 1964. *Collected Reports of the Jane Austen Society 1949–1965*. London: Wm. Dawson & Sons Ltd., 1967, pp. 273–81.

_____ . *A Portrait of Jane Austen*. London: Constable, 1978.

> Youthful writings, pp. 59–63.

Chapman, Robert William. "Jane Austen," *Notes and Queries,* 12th series, 11 (1922), 67.

> Asks for identification of "Delamere" and "Emmeline," referred to in "The History of England."

_____ . "Preface" to *Lady Susan*. Oxford: Clarendon Press, 1925, pp. v–vi.

_____ . "Preface" to *Volume the First*. Oxford: Clarendon Press, 1933, pp. v–ix.

*_____ . *Jane Austen: Facts and Problems*. Oxford: Clarendon Press, 1948.

> See "Index," p. 219.

_____ . "Preface" to *Volume the Third*. Oxford: Clarendon Press, 1951, pp. v–ix.

_____ . *"Volume the Third," Times Literary Supplement,* 8 June 1951, 357.

> Confesses a minor error in the volume just published.

_____ . "Jane Austen's Minor Works," *Notes and Queries* 197 (1952), 106.

> Seeks the same information as B.W.C. (1950), cf. Shipps (1977).

*Chesterton, Gilbert Keith. "Preface" to *"Love and Freindship" and Other Early Works*. London: Chatto & Windus, 1922, pp. ix–xv.

Chillman, Dawes. "Jane Austen's Juvenilia as a Key to the Structure of Her First Three Mature Novels." Ph.D. dissertation, University of Texas, 1963.

> See *Dissertation Abstracts* 24 (1963–64), 724–25.

Church, Richard. "Introduction" to *Shorter Works by Jane Austen*. London: The Folio Society, pp. vii–x.

*Collins, K.K. "Prejudice, *Persuasion,* and the Puzzle of Mrs. Smith," *Persuasions* 6 (1984), 40–43.

Cope, Sir Zachary. "Who Was Sophia Sentiment? Was She Jane Austen?," *Book Collector* 15 (1966), 143–51.

Suggests Jane Austen's contribution to *The Loiterer;* cf. John Gore and Elizabeth Jenkins in response.

Cornish, Francis Warre. *Jane Austen.* London: Macmillan, 1913.

Lady Susan is discussed in chapter 9, pp. 220–25.

Davie, John, ed. *Northanger Abbey, Lady Susan, The Watsons* and *Sanditon* (The World's Classics). Oxford: Oxford University Press, 1980.

The introduction deals with *Lady Susan* on pp. xiv–xvi.

Davies, Simon. "Laclos dans la littérature anglaise du XIXe siècle," *Laclos et la libertinage, 1782–1982: actes du colloque du bicentenaire des "Liaisons dangereuses."* Paris: Presses Universitaires de France, 1983, 255–64.

See especially pp. 256–58 on Jane Austen and *Lady Susan,* with parallels between Lady Susan and Madame de Merteuil.

De Rose, Peter. *Jane Austen and Samuel Johnson.* Washington, D.C.: University Press of America, 1980.

De Rose, Peter, and McGuire, S.W. *A Concordance to the Works of Jane Austen.* 3 vols. New York & London: Garland Publishing, 1982.

Includes *Lady Susan* but not the juvenilia.

Devlin, David Douglas. *Jane Austen and Education.* London: Macmillan, 1975.

See pp. 29–34 on "Catharine, or The Bower," pp. 36–42 on *Lady Susan.*

Dodds, Madeleine Hope. "'The School for Jealousy' and 'The Travelled Man,'" *Notes and Queries* 193 (1948), 61.

Seeks information regarding these two plays, mentioned in the dedication to "The Visit."

Drabble, Margaret, ed. *Lady Susan, The Watsons, Sanditon* (Penguin English Library). Harmondsworth, Eng.: Penguin Books,1974.

Ms. Drabble's "Introduction" discusses *Lady Susan* on pp. 8–15.

*Duckworth, Alistair McKay. *The Improvement of the Estate: A Study of Jane Austen's Novels.* Baltimore and London: The Johns Hopkins Press, 1971.

Dunn, Catherine H. "Jane Austen: Her Family and Her Early Life and the Relationship between Her Juvenilia and Mature Novels." M.A. thesis, Boston University, 1948.

Ehrenpreis, Anne Henry. *"Northanger Abbey:* Jane Austen and Charlotte Smith," *Nineteenth Century Fiction* 25 (1970–71), 343–48.

Parallels between Charlotte Smith's *Ethelinde* (1789) and Jane Austen's "Catharine, or The Bower," as prototype of *Northanger Abbey.*

*Ehrenpreis, Irvin. *Acts of Implication: Suggestion and Covert Meaning in the Works of Dryden, Swift, Pope and Austen.* Berkeley: University of California Press, 1980.

Epstein, Julia L. "Jane Austen's Juvenilia and the Female Epistolary Tradition," *Papers on Language and Literature* 21 (1985), 399–416.

Etall, Margaret. *"Lady Susan,"* arranged and produced by Margaret Etall, 4 parts, BBC Radio 4, 26 December 1972–29 December 1972.

*Evans, Mary. *Jane Austen and the State.* London and New York: Tavistock Publications, 1987.

*Farrer, Reginald. "Jane Austen, *ob.* July 18 1817," *Quarterly Review* 228 (1917), 1–30.

*Forster, Edward Morgan. *Aspects of the Novel.* Edward Arnold & Co., 1927.

Frank, Maude Morrison. *Great Authors in Their Youth.* New York: Holt, 1915, pp. 265–91.

G., E.P. "Jane Austen MSS," *Notes and Queries* 194 (1949), 84.

Asks for whereabouts of the MSS of the juvenilia.

*Gilbert, Sandra M., and Gubar, Susan. "Shut Up in Prose: Gender and Genre in Austen's Juvenilia," *The Madwoman in the Attic: The Woman Writer and the Nineteenth Century Literary Imagination.* New Haven and London: Yale University Press, 1979, pp. 107–45.

_____ . eds. *The Norton Anthology of Literature by Women: The Tradition in English.* New York and London: W.W. Norton, 1985.

"Love and Freindship" is reprinted on pp. 206–32.

*Gillie, Christopher. *A Preface to Jane Austen.* London: Longman, 1974.

The juvenilia are discussed in chapter 4, pp. 24–34.

*Gilson, David John. *A Bibliography of Jane Austen.* Oxford: Clarendon Press, 1982.

See comments at beginning of this bibliography.

_____ . "Postscript" to *Four Pieces from Jane Austen's Juvenilia.* New York: The Jane Austen Society of North America, 1987, [p. 9].

Publication, on the occasion of the Society's AGM, includes "The Adventures of Mr Harley," "Sir William Mountague," "Memoirs of Mr Clifford," and "Amelia Webster."

Gleason, George Donald. "Dramatic Affinities in the Life and Work of Jane Austen." Ph.D. dissertation, Iowa State University, 1956.

"Love and Freindship" heavily influenced by Sheridan's *The Critic*.

Glennon, Gordon. *"Lady Susan."* 1970.

Produced at the Theatre Royal, Windsor, 16 March 1970–4 April 1970.

*Gooneratne, Yasmine. *Jane Austen*. Cambridge: Cambridge University Press, 1970.

Chapter 3, pp. 31–48, discusses "The Minor Works."

Gore, John. "'Sophia Sentiment': Jane Austen?" *The Jane Austen Society Report for the Year, 1966*, in *Collected Reports of the Jane Austen Society 1966–75*. Folkstone: Wm. Dawson & Sons Ltd., 1977, pp. 9–12.

In response to Cope (1966); cf. also Jenkins.

Goubert, Pierre. *Jane Austen: étude psychologique de la romancière*. Paris: Presses Universitaires de France, 1975.

Many index references to the juvenilia and *Lady Susan*.

Goudie, Marjorie Evelyn. "An Enquiry into the Language of Jane Austen as Exemplified in *Lady Susan*." M.A. thesis, University of Cape Town, 1946.

Gray, Donald J., ed. *Pride and Prejudice: An Authoritative Text, Backgrounds, Reviews and Essays in Criticism*. New York: W.W. Norton & Company, 1966.

"A Norton Critical Edition," here reproduced contains selections from the juvenilia: "from 'Jack & Alice,'" "from 'A Collection of Letters'" and "from 'Catharine,'" pp. 271–79. These lead into a discussion of, first, Leavis, then, *Pride and Prejudice*.

*Greene, Donald J. "Jane Austen and the Peerage," *PMLA* 68 (1953), 1017–31.

*Grey, John David, ed. *The Jane Austen Companion*. New York: Macmillan; London: Athlone Press [as *The Jane Austen Handbook*], 1986.

See especially, "Juvenilia" by Brian Southam, pp. 244–55, and *"Lady Susan"* by Ruth ap-Roberts, pp. 256–60.

Griffin, Cynthia. "The Development of Realism in Jane Austen's Early Novels," *ELH* 30 (1963), 36–52.

The discussion includes "Love and Friendship."

*Halperin, John. "Unengaged Laughter: Jane Austen's Juvenilia," *South Atlantic Quarterly* 81 (1982), 286–99.

   Reprinted in this collection.

*_____ . *The Life of Jane Austen*. Baltimore, Eng.: The Johns Hopkins University Press; Brighton, Eng.: Harvester Press, 1984.

   Discusses the juvenilia, pp. 35–47, and *Lady Susan,* pp. 47–49.

Halperin, John, ed. *Jane Austen: Bicentenary Essays*. Cambridge: Cambridge University Press, 1975.

Halperin, John, and Kunert, Janet. *Plots and Characters in the Fiction of Jane Austen, the Brontës, and George Eliot*. Hamden, Conn.: Archon Books; Folkestone: Wm. Dawson & Sons Ltd., 1976.

   Plot synopses of *Lady Susan,* pp. 61–63, and "Love and Freindship," pp. 65–66; cf. also: "Characters," an alphabet, pp. 205–82.

Hardwick, Michael. *The Osprey Guide to Jane Austen*. Reading: Osprey Publishing, 1973.

   "Love and Freindship," pp. 67–75, *Lady Susan,* pp. 85–97 (chiefly plot summary).

Harris, Jocelyn. "'All the Impassioned, & Most Exceptional Parts of Richardson': Jane Austen's Juvenilia," *The Interpretative Power: Essays on Literature in Honour of Margaret Dalziel,* ed. by C.A. Gibson. [Dunedin]: Department of English, University of Otago, 1980, pp. 59–68.

Helm, William Henry. *Jane Austen and Her Country-House Comedy*. London: Eveleigh Nash, 1909.

   Lady Susan is discussed, pp. 149–52.

*Hodge, Jane Aiken. *Only a Novel: The Double Life of Jane Austen*. New York: Coward, McCann & Geoghegan, Inc., 1972.

   Chapter 3, pp. 35–45, treats the juvenilia and *Lady Susan*.

Holbrook, Joanne. "*Lady Susan,*" produced by Mary Hope Allen, BBC Home Service, 25 July 1948. q.v. above.

Honan, Park. "Sterne and the Formation of Jane Austen's Talent," in *Laurence Sterne: Riddles and Mysteries,* ed. by Valerie Grosvenor Meyer. London: Vision Press Ltd.; Totowa, New Jersey: Barnes & Noble Books, 1984, pp. 161–71.

   Mention is made of several pieces from the juvenilia.

_____ . "Richardson's Influence on Jane Austen (Some Notes on the Biographical and Critical Problems of an 'Influence')," in *Samuel Richardson: Passion and Prudence,* ed. by Valerie Grosvenor Meyer. London: Vision Press Ltd.; Totowa, New Jersey: Barnes & Noble Books, 1986, pp. 165–77.

"3. An Apprenticeship with 'Sir Charles Grandison,'" pp. 171–76.

*_____ . *Jane Austen: Her Life*. London: Weidenfeld and Nicolson, 1987; New York: St. Martin's Press, 1988.

Discusses the juvenilia, pp. 70–77, and *Lady Susan,* pp. 101–2.

*Hopkins, Annette Brown. "Jane Austen's *Love and Freindship:* A Study in Literary Relations," *South Atlantic Quarterly* 34 (1925), 34–49.

Jackel, David. *"Leonora* and *Lady Susan:* A Note on Maria Edgeworth and Jane Austen," *English Studies in Canada* 3 (1977), 278–88.

Parallels.

Jarvis, William. "Lady Susan," *The Jane Austen Society Report for the Year 1984*. Alton: The Jane Austen Society, [1985], pp. 11–12.

Announces the republication of a series which includes *Lady Susan* (the 1925 Chapman Clarendon Press edition), London: The Athlone Press Ltd., 1984, with a "Foreward" to the Jane Austen Library by Lord David Cecil and a "Publisher's Preface" by B.C. Southam. Republication of *Volume the First* followed in 1985.

*Jenkins, Elizabeth. *Jane Austen: A Biography*. London: Victor Gollancz, 1938.

The juvenilia are discussed in chapter 3, and *Lady Susan* in chapter 12.

_____ . "A Footnote to 'Sophia Sentiment.'" *The Jane Austen Society Report for the Year, 1966. Collected Reports of the Jane Austen Society 1966–1975*. Folkstone: Wm. Dawson & Sons Ltd., 1977, pp. 12–13.

See Cope and Gore, both 1966.

*Johnson, Claudia L. "The Operations of Time, and the Changes of the Human Mind: Jane Austen and Dr. Johnson Again," *Modern Language Quarterly* 44:1 (1983), 25.

*_____ . *Jane Austen: Women, Politics, and the Novel*. Chicago: The University of Chicago Press, 1988.

Johnson, Reginald Brimley. *The Women Novelists*. London: W. Collins, 1918.

See pp. 105–16: "A 'Most Accomplished Coquette'" [i.e., Lady Susan].

_____ . *Jane Austen*. London: Sheed & Ward, 1927.

Discusses the juvenilia, pp. 92–109, and *Lady Susan,* pp. 110–15.

_____ . *Jane Austen: Her Life, Her Work, Her Family, and Her Critics*. London: J.M. Dent; New York: E.P. Dutton, 1930.

Chapter 5, "Folly Burlesqued," pp. 62–89, discusses the juvenilia and *Lady Susan*.

———— . *Lady Susan,* with an introduction by R. Brimley Johnson. London: Philip Earle, 1931.

The introduction occupies pp. ix–xxvi.

———— . "Introduction to *Sanditon, The Watsons, Lady Susan and Other Miscellanea.*" London: J.M. Dent & Sons Ltd., 1934, pp. ix–xiii.

Karr, Phyllis Ann. *Lady Susan: Based on the Unfinished Novel by Jane Austen.* New York: Everest House, 1980; London: Corgi Books, 1984.

A narrative rendition.

*Kaye-Smith, Sheila, and Stern, Gladys Bronwen. *Talking of Jane Austen.* London: Cassell and Company Ltd., 1943; New York: Harper & Bros., 1944 [as *Speaking of Jane Austen*].

*———— . *More about Jane Austen.* New York: Harper & Brothers, 1949; London: Cassell and Company Ltd., 1950 [as *More Talk of Jane Austen*].

Killalea, Geraldine. *"Love and Freindship" and Other Early Works.* New York: Harmony Books, 1981.

See "Introduction," pp. vii–x.

*Kirkham, Margaret. *Jane Austen, Feminism and Fiction.* Brighton, Eng.: The Harvester Press; Totowa, New Jersey: Barnes & Noble Books, 1983.

Klinkenborg, Verlyn. *British Literary Manuscripts* [in the Pierpont Morgan Library]. *Series II: from 1800–1914.* Catalogue by Verlyn Klinkenborg, checklist by Herbert Cahoon, introduction by Charles Ryskamp. New York: Pierpont Morgan Library, 1981.

Lady Susan is No. 16.

Kreuzer, Paul Geoffrey. "The Development of Jane Austen's Technique of Narration." Ph.D. dissertation, Syracuse University, 1981.

For an abstract see *Dissertation Abstracts International* 43 (1982–83), 173–74.

*Kronenberger, Louis. "Jane Austen: *Lady Susan* and *Pride and Prejudice," The Polished Surface: Essays in the Literature of Worldliness.* New York: Alfred A. Knopf, 1969, pp. 127–50.

*Lascelles, Mary. *Jane Austen and Her Art.* Oxford: Clarendon Press, 1939.

*Laski, Marganita. *Jane Austen and Her World.* London: Thames and Hudson, 1969.

Le Faye, Deirdre. "Jane Austen and Her Hancock Relatives," *Review of English Studies* NS 30 (1979), 12–27.

Their personal history's influence on the juvenilia and later novels.

*_____ . "Jane Austen's Verses and Lord Stanhope's Disappointment," *The Book Collector* 37:1 (Spring 1988).

Leavis, Queenie Dorothy. "A Critical Theory of Jane Austen's Writings," *Scrutiny* 10 (1941–42), 61–87, 114–42, 272–94; 12 (1944–45), 104–19.

   The second installment (in two parts) is subtitled: "'Lady Susan' into 'Mansfield Park'." Several times reprinted, most recently in the writer's *Collected Essays, Vol. 1: The Englishness of the English Novel,* edited by G. Singh, Cambridge: Cambridge University Press, 1983, pp. 86–130. See also *Notes and Queries* 182 (1942), 155 (editorial comment) and 212–13 (by Madeleine Hope Dodds).

_____ . Sense and Sensibility *with* Lady Susan *and* The Watsons, with an introduction by Q.D. Leavis. London: Macdonald, 1958.

   The introduction (pp. vii–xxiv) is reprinted in the writer's *Collected Essays,* vol. 1 (see above), pp. 147–60.

Lenta, Margaret. "Form and Content: A Study of the Epistolary Novel," *University of Cape Town Studies in English* 10 (1980), 14–30.

   Includes "Love and Freindship."

*Levine, George. "Translating the Monstrous: *Northanger Abbey,*" *Nineteenth-Century Fiction. Jane Austen, 1775–1975* 30:3 (December 1975), 335–50.

*Levine, Jay Arnold. *"Lady Susan:* Jane Austen's Character of the Merry Widow," *Studies in English Literature 1500–1900* 1:4 (1961), 23–34.

Liddell, Robert. *The Novels of Jane Austen.* London: Longmans, 1963.

   See pp. 57–60 for Q.D. Leavis's theory of *Lady Susan* as prototype of *Mansfield Park.*

Link, Frederick Martin. "The Reputation of Jane Austen in the Twentieth Century with an Annotated Enumerative Bibliography of Austen Criticism from 1811 to June 1957." Ph.D. dissertation, Boston University, 1958.

*Litz, Arthur Walton. *"The Loiterer:* A Reflection on Jane Austen's Early Environment," *Review of English Studies* NS 12 (1961), 251–61.

*_____ . *Jane Austen: A Study of Her Artistic Development.* London: Chatto and Windus; New York: Oxford University Press, 1965.

   Chapter 1, pp. 3–57: "The Land of Fiction: Juvenilia and *Lady Susan.*"

Lock, F.P. "A Jane Austen Quotation Identified," *Notes and Queries* 218 (1973), 289.

   The quotation "The more free, the more Wellcome" in "The Visit," unidentified by R.W.

Chapman, now traced to James Townley's *High Life below Stairs,* 1759 (a play performed at Steventon in 1789).

*McKillop, Alan Dugald. "Allusions to Prose Fiction in Jane Austen's *Volume the Third," Notes and Queries* 196 (1951), 428–29.

     Especially Richardson's *Sir Charles Grandison* and the novels of Charlotte Smith.

_____ . "Critical Realism in *Northanger Abbey,"* in *From Jane Austen to Joseph Conrad: Essays Collected in Memory of James T. Hillhouse,* edited by Robert C. Rathburn and Martin Steinmann, Jr., Minneapolis: University of Minnesota Press, 1958, pp. 35–45.

     Catherine Morland "emerges" in "Catharine, or The Bower."

*McMaster, Juliet. "The Continuity of Jane Austen's Novels," *SEL* 10 (1970), 723–39.

Malden, S.F. (Mrs. Charles). *Jane Austen.* "Eminent Women" Series. London: W H. Allen & Co., 1889.

     Chapter 2: "Girlhood and First Attempts at Writing" includes a reprint of "The Mystery," pp. 20–22, and discusses *Lady Susan,* pp. 23–26.

Mansell, Darrel, Jr. "Another Source of Jane Austen's 'The History of England,'" *Notes and Queries* 212 (1967), 305.

     The source being John Whitaker's *Mary Queen of Scots Vindicated,* 1787.

_____ . *The Novels of Jane Austen: An Interpretation.* London: The Macmillan Press Ltd., 1973.

     Many mentions of the juvenilia and *Lady Susan* throughout.

Miller, D.A. *Narrative and Its Discontents: Problems of Closure in the Traditional Novel.* Princeton, N.J.: Princeton University Press, 1981.

     Scene the 2nd from "The Mystery" is reprinted and discussed, pp. 47–48.

Moler, Kenneth Lloyd. "Fanny Burney's *Cecilia* and Jane Austen's "Jack & Alice," *English Language Notes* 3 (1965–66), 40–42.

     A parallel in *Cecilia* for the masquerade scene in "Jack & Alice."

*Mudrick, Marvin. *Jane Austen: Irony as Defense and Discovery.* Princeton, N.J.: Princeton University Press, 1952.

     Discusses the juvenilia in chapter 1, pp. 1–36, and *Lady Susan* in chapter 5, pp. 127–54.

_____ . "None but Eagles" (pp. 158–59) and "They Took Him for a Cucumber" (pp. 160–61), in *Nobody Here but Us Chickens: A Book about People in Books.* New Haven and New York: Ticknor & Fields, 1981.

The first allusion is to "Jack & Alice"; the second, to "Love and Freindship."

Page, Norman. *The Language of Jane Austen.* Oxford: Basil Blackwell, 1972.

See chapter 5: "The Epistolary Art," pp. 169–86.

Paris, Bernard J. *Character and Conflict in Jane Austen's Novels: A Psychological Approach.* Detroit: Wayne State University Press, 1978.

A large segment of chapter 6: "Jane Austen: The Authorial Personality," pp. 168–201, is devoted to the juvenilia and *Lady Susan.*

*Perry, Ruth. "Interrupted Friendships in Jane Austen's *Emma," Tulsa Studies in Women's Literature* 5 (Fall 1986), 185–202.

Person, Leland S., Jr. "Playing House: Jane Austen's Fabulous Space," *Philological Quarterly* 59 (1980), 62–75.

*Pinion, Francis Bertram. *A Jane Austen Companion: A Critical Survey and Reference Book.* London: Macmillan, 1973.

The two chapters entitled "Early Writing" and "More Mature Fiction," pp. 52–75, cover the juvenilia and *Lady Susan.*

———. "A Sterne Echo in 'Love and Freindship,'" *Notes and Queries* 222 (1977), 320–21.

On the passage beginning "A grove of full-grown Elms sheltered us from the East." R.W. Chapman had identified this as a parody of Johnson (from *A Journey to the Western Islands*); Pinion finds a more exact parallel in Sterne's *Tristram Shandy.*

*Polhemus, Robert M. *Comic Faith: The Great Tradition from Austen to Joyce.* Chicago and London: The University of Chicago Press, 1980.

Pollock, Walter Herries. *Jane Austen: Her Contemporaries and Herself.* London: Longmans, Green, and Co., 1899.

The last chapter, 14, concerns itself with *Lady Susan,* pp. 121–25.

*Poovey, Mary. *The Proper Lady and the Woman Writer: Ideology as Style in the Works of Mary Wollstonecraft, Mary Shelley, and Jane Austen.* Chicago: The University of Chicago Press, 1984.

See chapter 6: "Ideological Contradictions and the Consolations of Form: The Case of Jane Austen," especially "*Lady Susan,*" pp. 173–83.

Rawlence, Guy. *Jane Austen.* London: Duckworth, 1934.

Discusses the juvenilia, pp. 29–33, and *Lady Susan,* pp. 44–46.

*Rees, Joan. *Jane Austen: Woman and Writer.* London: Robert Hale & Company; New York: St. Martin's Press, 1976.

See "Juvenile Works" section, pp. 33–45.

Rhydderch, David. "Jane Austen's Reading," *Times Literary Supplement,* 17 April 1930, 336.

Suggests that Jane Austen took the phrase "Love and Freindship" from Garrick's play *Bon Ton* (acted by the Austen Family in 1787).

*———— . *Jane Austen: Her Life and Art*. London: Jonathan Cape, 1932.

Lady Susan is discussed on pp. 46–48.

*Roberts, Warren. *Jane Austen and the French Revolution*. London: Macmillan, 1979.

Rogers, Winfield H. "The Reaction against Melodramatic Sensibility in the English Novel, 1796–1830," *PMLA* 49 (1934), 98–122.

"Love and Freindship" is discussed, pp. 111–13.

Rosenbaum, Barbara, and White, Pamela. *Index of Literary Manuscripts*. Vol. 4: *1800–1900*. Part 1, *Arnold-Gissing*. London: Mansell, 1982.

Jane Austen: pp. 21–31, by Pamela White (including the manuscripts of the juvenilia and *Lady Susan*).

Saagpakk, Paul F. "A Survey of Psychopathology in British Literature from Shakespeare to Hardy." *Literature and Psychology* 18 (1968), 150.

Mr. Woodhouse and Lady Susan.

Schorer, Mark. *Persuasion and Lady Susan,* with an "Introduction" by Mark Schorer. New York: Dell, 1960.

Scott, Peter J.M. *Jane Austen: A Reassessment*. London: Vision Press; Totowa, New Jersey: Barnes & Noble, 1982.

On *Lady Susan:* pp. 9–23.

Shaw, Patricia. "Las novelas cortas de Jane Austen." *Fililogia moderna* 17 (1976–77), 125–47.

"Love and Freindship" foreshadows the later fiction; *Lady Susan* is unique.

Shipps, Anthony W. "Jane Austen's Minor Works," *Notes and Queries* 222 (1977), 48.

On the motto of "Love and Freindship." Partial response to B.W.C. (1950) and Chapman (1952).

Singer, Godfrey Frank. *The Epistolary Novel: Its Origin, Development, Decline and Residuary Influence*. Philadelphia: University of Pennsylvania Press, 1933.

Discusses *Lady Susan,* "Love and Freindship," and "Lesley Castle," pp. 158–60.

Smith, Goldwin. *Life of Jane Austen.* London: Walter Scott, 1890.

   Lady Susan is discussed, pp. 181–83 (the plot said to be "worthy a Parisian novelist"). A review of the book by John Mackinnon Robinson is reprinted in his *Criticisms,* vol. 1 (London: A. and H. Bradlaugh Bonner, 1902), pp. 21–27 (with a comment that *Lady Susan* seems to have inspired the plot of Ouida's *Moths*).

Smith, Leroy W. *Jane Austen and the Drama of Woman.* London: Macmillan, 1983.

   On the juvenilia, pp. 46–49, and *Lady Susan,* pp. 49–56.

Southam, Brian Charles. "Lady Susan's Husband," *Notes and Queries* 203 (1958), 307–8.

   Suggests that the Christian name of Lady Susan's husband was "Frederic."

_____ . "Interpolations to Jane Austen's *Volume the Third,*" *Notes and Queries* 207 (1962), 185–87.

   Suggests that some parts not in Jane Austen's hand were not composed by her.

*_____ . "The Manuscript of Jane Austen's *Volume the First,*" *The Library,* 5th series, 17 (1962), 231–37.

_____ . "A Note on Jane Austen's *Volume the First,*" *Notes and Queries* 207 (1962), 422.

   Corrections to the 1933 text.

_____ . "Preface" to *Volume the Second: by Jane Austen.* Oxford: Clarendon Press, 1963, pp. v–xii.

_____ . "Jane Austen's Juvenilia: The Question of Completeness," *Notes and Queries* 209 (1964), 180–81.

   Indicates what may be references to other juvenile compositions now lost.

*_____ . *Jane Austen's Literary Manuscripts: A Study of the Novelist's Development through the Surviving Papers.* London: Oxford University Press, 1964.

   Chapter 1, "The Writing of the Juvenilia"; chapter 2, "A Critical Study of the Juvenilia"; chapter 3, *"Lady Susan* and the lost originals, 1795–1800."

*Spacks, Patricia Meyer. "Sisters," in *Fettr'd or Free? British Women Novelists 1670–1815,* Mary Anne Schofield and Cecilia Macheski, eds. Athens, Ohio: Ohio University Press, 1986, pp. 136–51.

Stern, Gladys Bronwen. *A Name to Conjure With.* New York: The Macmillan Company, 1953, pp. 156–66.

Tallmadge, Abby Louise. "Jane Austen: Resemblances," *Times Literary Supplement,* 4 January 1934, 12.

The second of four parallels is between *Lady Susan* and Maria Edgeworth's *Leonora* (1806).

_____ . "Sense and Sensibility: Austenian Gleanings." Ph.D. dissertation, Northwestern University, 1935.

See chapter 2, pp. 15–57: "The Juvenilia."

Ten Harmsell, Henrietta. *Jane Austen: A Study in Fictional Conventions.* The Hague: Mouton, 1964.

See pp. 38–42: parallels between "Love and Freindship" and *Sense and Sensibility.*

*Thomson, Clara Linklater. *Jane Austen: A Survey.* London: Horace Marshall, 1929.

See chapter 2, "The Beginnings," pp. 55–73, discusses the juvenilia and *Lady Susan.*

_____ . "Jane Austen's Reading," *Times Literary Supplement,* 27 March 1930, 274.

Suggests that the description of Laura and Sophia, in "Love and Freindship," fainting alternately on the sofa, may be borrowed from a stage direction in Sheridan's *The Critic.*

Tiller, Terence. "Love and Freindship," dramatized and produced by Terence Tiller, BBC Third Program, 4 November 1953.

*Todd, Janet. *Women's Friendship in Literature.* New York: Columbia University Press, 1980.

_____ . ed. *Jane Austen: New Perspectives.* London, 1983.

Tucker, George Holbert. *A Goodly Heritage: A History of Jane Austen's Family.* Manchester: Carcanet New Press, 1983.

Juvenilia mentioned throughout mostly in connection with the pieces' dedications.

Villard, Léonie. *Jane Austen: Sa vie et son oeuvre, 1775–1817.* Saint Etienne: Société Anonyme de l'Imprimerie Mulcey, 1915.

Lady Susan is discussed, pp. 32–36.

_____ . "Les Juvenilia de Jane Austen," *Revue anglo-américaine* 12 (1934–35), 206–18.

On *Volume the First* and *Volume the Second.*

Vipoint, Elfrida. *A Little Bit of Ivory: A Life of Jane Austen.* London: Hamish Hamilton, 1977.

Chapters 3 and 4, pp. 27–52, allude to the juvenilia and *Lady Susan.*

*Watt, Ian. *Jane Austen: A Collection of Critical Essays.* Englewood Cliffs, N.J.: Prentice-Hall, Inc., 1963.

*Weinsheimer, Joel, ed. *Jane Austen Today.* Athens, Georgia: The University of Georgia Press, 1975.

White, Edward Michael. "Jane Austen and the Art of Parody." Ph.D. dissertation, Harvard University, 1960.

Wigginton, May Wood. "Love and Freindship . . . Dramatized from the Novel of Jane Austen." New York: French, 1925.

*Woolf, Virginia. *The Common Reader.* London: The Hogarth Press, 1925.

See "Jane Austen," pp. 168–83.

Wright, Andrew. "Jane Austen Adapted." *Nineteenth-Century Fiction* 30:3 (December 1975), 421–53.

Many of the dramatizations included here were noted in this valuable article. For "Love and Freindship" and *Lady Susan,* cf. 451.

Translations

Danish

Lady Susan. Kjøbenhavn: Carit Andersen, 1945, 157 pp. Translated by Jens Kruuse.

French

Lady Susan, Les Watson, Sanditon. Paris: Christian Bourgois, 1980, 227 pp.

Translated by Josette Salesse-Lavergne. *Lady Susan* occupies pp. 9–88 and is preceded by an editorial note and a descriptive list of characters. The translation is based on the 1974 Penguin English Library edition.

Juvenilia et autres textes. Paris: Christian Bourgois, 1984, 303 pp.

Translated by Josette Salesse-Lavergne. Includes all of the juvenilia, translated from R.W. Chapman's *Minor Works* volume (the only complete translation into any language).

German

Lady Susan. Zurich: Manesse-Verlag, 1964, 121–234 [of a volume entitled *Englische Erzähler,* vol. 1: *Von Daniel Defoe bis Oscar Wilde,* ed. by Richard Kraushaar], trans. by Ilse Leisi.

Italian

Amore & amicizia e altri romanzi. Milano: Edizioni La Tartaruga, 1979, 166 pp. Trans. by Letizia Ciotti Miller.

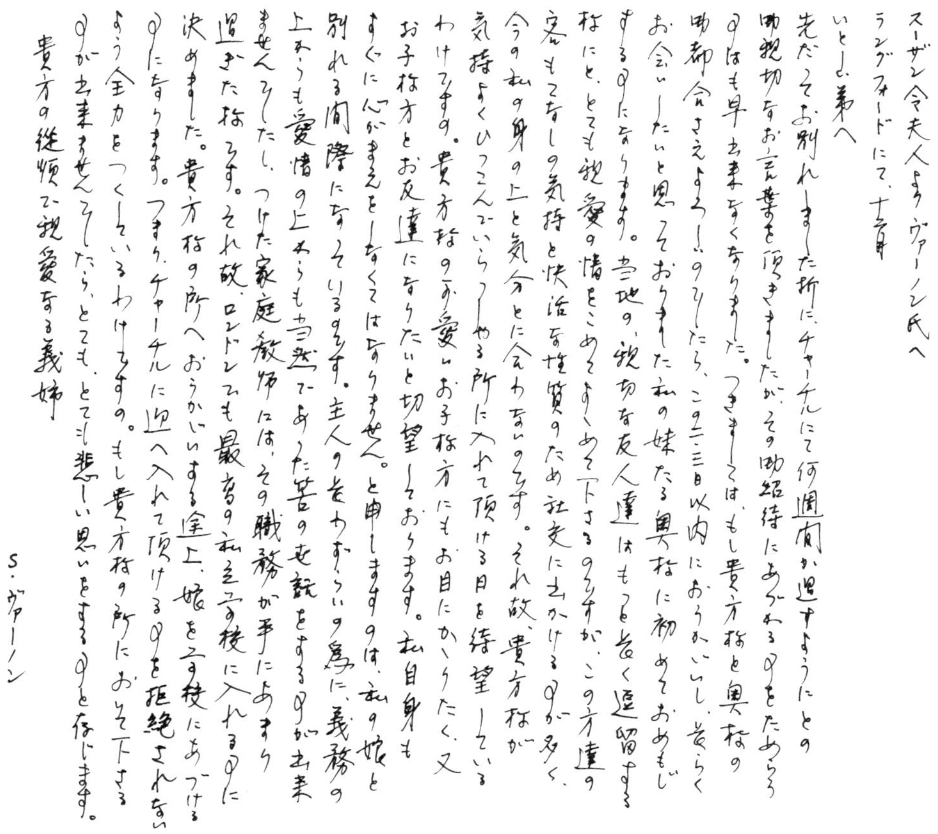

スーザン令夫人よりヴァーノン氏へ
ラングフォードにて、十二月
いとしい弟へ
先だってお別れしました折に、チャーチルにて何週間か過すようにとの御親切なお言葉を頂きましたが、その御招待にあずかるのをためらうのはも早出来なくなりました。つきましては、もし貴方様と奥様の御都合さえよろしかったら、この二、三日以内におうかがいし、長らくお会いしたいと思っておりました私の妹たる奥様に初めておめもじするのになります。当地の親切な友人達はもっと長く逗留するようにと、とても親愛の情をこめてすすめて下さるのですが、この方達の客もてなしの気持と快活な性質のため社交に出かけるのが多く、今の私の身の上と気分とに合わないのです。それ故、貴方様が気持よくひっこんでいらっしゃる所に入れて頂ける日を待望しているわけです。貴方様のお可愛いお子様方にもお目にかかりたく、又お子様方とお友達になりたいと切望しております。私自身もすぐに心がまえをしなくてはなりません。と申しますのは、私の娘と別れる間際になっているのです。主人の長わずらいの為に、義務の上からも愛情の上からも当然であった筈の世話をする事が出来ませんでしたし、つけた家庭教師には、その職務が手にあまり過ぎた様です。それ故、ロンドンでも最高の私立学校に入れるのに決めました。貴方様の所へおうかがいする途上、娘をその学校にあずけるのになります。つまり、チャーチルに迎へ入れて頂けるのを拒絶されないよう全力をつくしているわけです。もし貴方様の所においで下さるのが出来ませんでしたら、とてもとても悲しい思いをするのと存じます。
貴方の従順で親愛なる義姉
S・ヴァーノン

Figure 23. "Letter 1 " of *Lady Susan,* Japanese Translation by Keiko Parker
(Courtesy Keiko Parker)

Comprises "Frederic & Elfrida," "Jack & Alice," "Love and Freindship," and *Lady Susan.*

Russian

"Tri sestri," *Inostrannaya literatura* 1981, no. 7, pp. 237–41, trans. by Evgeniy Shvarts. A version of "The three Sisters."

Spanish

Lady Susan. Barcelona: Editorial Icaria, 1984, 118 pp. Trans. by Marcelo Cohen.

Contributors

BEATRICE ANDERSON is a graduate student at California State University, where she also teaches freshman composition. In 1986 she received an award for a Children's Literature paper. She is a member of the National English Honor Society and the Golden Key National Honor Society and is included in the 1987 edition of *Who's Who among Students in American Colleges and Universities.* She is a married suburbanite and has three children.

JOAN AUSTEN-LEIGH is a collateral descendant of Jane Austen and a founder of JASNA. She has written two novels, the later being *Stephanie at War* (A Room of One's Own Press, 1987). Under the name Joan Mason Hurley, she is the author of over 20 plays (including *Our Own Particular Jane*). These have been produced all over North America, in England, and in Australia and have received many awards including First Prize in the Canadian Playwriting Competition. Articles and stories have appeared in numerous journals in Canada and England. Ms. Austen-Leigh served as editor of JASNA's journal, *Persuasions,* for the first eight years of its publication.

REGINA BARRECA taught at Queens College of the City University of New York and has recently been appointed assistant professor of English at the University of Connecticut at Storrs. She edited and contributed several essays to *Last Laugh: Women and Comedy,* which has just been published.

RACHEL BROWNSTEIN teaches at Brooklyn College and the Graduate Center of the City University of New York. Her essays and reviews have appeared in *The Yale Review, The New York Times Book Review,* and *Modern Language Quarterly.* A large portion of her *Becoming a Heroine: Reading about Women in Novels* (1982) is devoted to Jane Austen. She obtained her doctorate at Yale University.

EDWARD COPELAND received his Ph.D. from Harvard and is professor of English at Pomona College, where he regularly teaches courses on Jane Austen and the eighteenth-century novel. He has published articles on Richardson, Smollett, Fanny Burney, Cleland, and, of course, Jane Austen. Primarily concerned with economics in fiction, his recent projects include the changing concept of London in eighteenth-century fiction and the role money plays in the works of Austen and her contemporary women novelists.

MARGARET DRABBLE is a British novelist and critic, educated at Newnham College, Cambridge. She is the author of ten novels, the most recent of which, *The Radiant Way,* appeared in 1987, and she edited the fifth edition of *The Oxford Companion to English Literature* (1985). She also introduced and edited *Lady Susan/The Watsons/Sanditon* (1974) for the Penguin English Library, and is currently working on introductions to Jane Austen's novels for Virago.

JAN FERGUS is associate professor of English at Lehigh University and previously taught at Brooklyn College. She has contributed to a collection of essays about Jane Austen and is the author of *Jane Austen and the Didactic Novel.* She is in the process of researching, on both sides of the Atlantic, her next book, *Jane Austen: The Literary Career,* to be published in 1989.

DAVID J. GILSON is an assistant librarian at the Taylorian Institute in Oxford. After 15 years of research he published *A Bibliography of Jane Austen* in 1982, definitive and a *sine qua non* for all research on Austen. Annually, an update appears in *The Jane Austen Society Report.* Mr. Gilson has published numerous scholarly articles and is currently coediting a new edition of the *Letters,* which will appear in the early nineties. Since 1975 he has been a member of the Jane Austen Society Committee.

J. DAVID GREY received his degrees from Fordham and Hunter. From 1978 to 1979 he cofounded JASNA with Joan Austen-Leigh and Henry Burke and served as its president for the first three years. He is the author of several articles and reviews concerning Jane Austen and edited *The Jane Austen Companion.* For over 25 years he has been at J.H.S.45 in East Harlem, as assistant principal for half that time.

JOHN HALPERIN is the author of *The Life of Jane Austen, C.P. Snow: An Oral Biography, Gissing: A Life in Books, Trollope and Politics,* and two books on the Victorian novel. *Jane Austen's Lovers,* a volume of his selected essays, was published in 1988. He has edited three collections of essays (one on Jane Austen) and a number of primary works in paperback. He has twice been a Guggenheim fellow. In 1985 he became one of the few Americans elected a fellow of the Royal Society of Literature. Currently he is centennial professor of English at Vanderbilt University.

BARBARA HORWITZ received her Ph.D. from S.U.N.Y. at Stony Brook. She has taught at the University of Tennessee and Hofstra College and is now at the C.W. Post Campus of Long Island University. She has written on the Romantics, Fanny Burney, contemporary and popular fiction, and Jane Austen. Her contribution to this collection is based on a paper delivered at the JASNA conference, October 1987, and a shortened version of it was published in the society's annual publication, *Persuasions* 9 (1987), 84–88.

CLAUDIA L. JOHNSON received her Ph.D. from Princeton in 1981 and is on the faculty of Marquette University. She has published articles and reviews in *Philological Quarterly, Eighteenth-Century Studies, Modern Language Quarterly,* and *Nineteenth-Century Literature.* She is currently working on sensibility and eighteenth-century fiction and her book, *Jane Austen: Women, Politics, and the Novel* was published by the University of Chicago Press in 1988.

LAURIE KAPLAN is assistant professor of English at Goucher College in Towson, Maryland. In 1988 she spent her sabbatical at Newnham College, Cambridge, investigating the metafiction of *Northanger Abbey.* She has published essays, reviews, and short stories. The essay in this volume is an expansion of a paper delivered at the JASNA conference, October 1987, and a version of it was published in the society's annual publication, *Persuasions* 9 (1987), pp. 71–75.

CHRISTOPHER KENT received his D. Phil. from the University of Sussex. He has been on the faculty of the University of Saskatchewan since 1970, professor since 1978. He is a fellow of the Royal Historical Society, edited the *Canadian Journal of History* for several years, and is presently a member of the advisory board of *Victorian Studies.* He has contributed many articles to publications in the fields of history, drama, music, and art. He is a patron of JASNA.

DEBORAH J. KNUTH is associate professor of University Studies at Colgate University and teaches English and women's studies there. She has published articles and reviews on Alexander Pope and Jane Austen. The article included here is based on a talk delivered at the JASNA conference, October 1987, and a version of it was published in the society's annual publication, *Persuasions* 9 (1987), 64, 66–71.

A. WALTON LITZ is Holmes Professor of English Literature at Princeton University. He is the author of *Jane Austen: A Study of Her Artistic Development, The Art of James Joyce,* and *Introspective Voyager: The Poetic Development of*

Wallace Stevens. Mr. Litz has also edited *Modern American Fiction: Essays in Criticism;* a volume of essays on T.S. Eliot; a collection of *Major American Short Stories;* and, with Robert Scholes, Joyce's *Dubliners.* He is a patron of JASNA and serves on its board of directors. His contribution to this volume was delivered as the keynote address to the October 1987 JASNA conference.

JOHN MCALEER's biography of Jane Austen will be published in 1992. He earned his Ph.D. at Harvard and, since 1965, he has been a professor of English at Boston College. He has published 15 books, including two novels (one, *Coign of Vantage,* in 1988) and widely respected biographies of Ralph Waldo Emerson, Rex Stout, and Theodore Dreiser. He is the former president of the Thoreau Society and is the president, now, of the Boston Authors Club, America's oldest literary society. His article in this collection is an expansion on a paper delivered at the JASNA conference in October 1987.

HUGH MCKELLAR holds degrees from the University of Western Ontario in English and French and from the University of Toronto in music, library science, and religious studies. He served the Toronto Board of Education's secondary school library system from 1958 to 1983, meanwhile editing three volumes for school use, traveling through 40 countries, and acquiring a villa in Barbados. In recent years he has contributed over 100 articles on sacred music to church-connected periodicals, prepared most of the Canadian material for The Hymn Society of America's *Dictionary of American Hymnology,* and reviewed books regularly for Canada's largest-circulation newspaper, the *Toronto Star.*

JULIET MCMASTER, a fellow of the Royal Society of Canada, took her degrees from Oxford and the University of Alberta. She is the author of *Thackeray's Major Novels* (1971), *Jane Austen on Love* (1978), *Trollope's Palliser Novels* (1978), and *Dickens the Designer* (1988), and of many articles on the eighteenth- and nineteenth-century novel. She is also coauthor (with R.D. McMaster) of *The Novel from Sterne to James* (1981), and editor of *Jane Austen's Achievement* (1976). She was a founding member of JASNA, serves on its board of directors, delivered two keynote addresses at its conferences, and participated in the last. She is now University Professor of English at the University of Alberta.

MARY GAITHER MARSHALL edited Anna Lefroy's completion of *Sanditon* (1983). She is on the board of directors of JASNA and is the chairman of its annual literary contest committee. As one of the country's most ardent Jane Austen bibliophiles, she has spoken on her interest at regional meetings and, on the subject of the article included here, at the 1987 conference in New York. She contributed to *The Jane Austen Companion* (1986). Ms. Marshall teaches composition and is the technical editor for the *Illinois Chess Bulletin*.

ELLEN E. MARTIN is assistant professor of English at Vassar College. She is finishing a book on Chaucer's dream poetry, and beginning a study of psychoanalytic readings of medieval literature. The article included here is based on a talk delivered at the JASNA conference, October 1987, and a version of it was published in the society's annual publication, *Persuasions* 9 (1987), 76, 78–84.

SUSAN PEPPER ROBBINS received her Ph.D. from the University of Virginia in 1976 and is a lecturer in the English Department at Virginia Commonwealth University. Between 1983 and 1986 she had 16 short stories accepted for publication in literary journals and four manuscripts (a short story collection and three novels) are in the hands of publishers under consideration. She has also written on James Joyce and James Baldwin. A version of this paper was read at the JASNA conference, October 1987.

SUSAN SCHWARTZ holds degrees from Bryn Mawr and Rutgers. She is the vice-president for Finance in one of the two largest geriatric medical centers in the U.S. She served as treasurer of JASNA 1981–1985 and coordinated the Annual General Meeting of the society in New York in 1987.

PATRICIA MEYER SPACKS is professor of English literature at Yale University. She holds degrees from Rollins College, Yale, and the University of California at Berkeley. She is the author of *Argument of Images,* a study of Alexander Pope; *The Poetry of Vision,* a critical study of eighteenth-century poets; *The Insistence of Horror: Aspects of the Supernatural in 18th-Century Poetry; The Adolescent Idea: Myths of Youth and the Adult Imagination; The Female Imagination.* Her most recent book is *Gossip* and she is completing a study of plot in the eighteenth-century novel.

DONALD STONE is professor of English at Queens College, the City University of New York. He is a member of the advisory boards of "Nineteenth-Century Literature" and "Dickens Studies" and is the author of *The Romantic Impulse in Victorian Fiction* and *Novelists in a Changing World* as well as many articles on topics ranging from Austen to Bennett. His proudest achievement is having introduced *Pride and Prejudice* to his students in Beijing.

Index